MW01156240

# GIVE MY POOR HEART EASE

## VOICES OF THE MISSISSIPPI BLUES

### WILLIAM FERRIS

THE UNIVERSITY OF NORTH CAROLINA PRESS  CHAPEL HILL

*This book was published with the assistance of the H. Eugene and Lillian Youngs Lehman Fund of the University of North Carolina Press. A complete list of books published in the Lehman Series appears after the index. The production of the CD and DVD that accompany this book was supported by grants from the Center for the Study of the American South and the University of North Carolina at Chapel Hill's University Research Council.*

© 2009 William Ferris
All rights reserved
Manufactured in Canada

Photographs by William Ferris

Designed by Richard Hendel
Set in Hawksmoor and Miller types
by Tseng Information Systems, Inc.

The paper in this book meets the
guidelines for permanence and
durability of the Committee on
Production Guidelines for Book
Longevity of the Council on Library
Resources.

The University of North Carolina Press
has been a member of the Green Press
Initiative since 2003.

Library of Congress
Cataloging-in-Publication Data
Give my poor heart ease : voices of
the Mississippi blues / [interviews by]
William Ferris.
    p. cm.
"This book was published with the
assistance of the H. Eugene and Lillian
Youngs Lehman Fund of the University
of North Carolina Press."
Includes bibliographical references and
index.
ISBN 978-0-8078-3325-4 (cloth : alk.
paper)
1. Blues musicians—Mississippi—
Interviews. 2. Blues (Music)—
Mississippi—History and criticism.
3. African Americans—Mississippi—
Music—History and criticism. I. Ferris,
William R.
ML3521.G58 2009
781.64309762—dc22    2009016647

13 12 11 10 09    5 4 3 2 1

For Grey Ferris, 1946–2008

*My beloved brother,*
*You taught me photography,*
*And so many other things.*

*Wherever rain falls on parched soil,*
*Wherever schoolchildren are excited and learn,*
*Wherever the poor find justice,*
*You will be there with your blessing.*

*Go in peace and know that*
*Your love, your vision, your kindness,*
*Will never be forgotten.*
*They will enrich all who follow.*

*I walked Highway 61 till I give down in my knees.*

*I walked Highway 61 till I give down in my knees.*

*You know, I ain't found nobody to give my poor heart ease.*

*—James "Son Ford" Thomas, Leland, Mississippi*

# CONTENTS

# ACKNOWLEDGMENTS

This work has been a long time coming, and I am indebted to many for their support along the way. First and foremost are the friends whom I recorded, photographed, and filmed. Their stories are the heart of the book that follows, and for their kindness and generous hospitality I am forever grateful.

B. B. King, my dear friend, understood the importance of building an academic home for the blues and blessed my work in so many ways over the years. From our first visits at Yale in the seventies, to the donation of his blues collection to help create the Blues Archive at the University of Mississippi in the eighties, to his visit to the National Endowment for the Humanities during my tenure as chairman in the nineties, B has been incredibly supportive of my work. His life and his music are an inspiration for all that I do. I am indebted to B's former manager Sid Seidenberg, his current manager Floyd Lieberman, and his dedicated assistant Tina France for their support over the years.

In their distinctive ways, Patti Black, Charlotte Capers, Alice Walker, and Eudora Welty inspired my work with folklore and the spoken word. As directors of the Old Capitol Museum of Mississippi History and the Mississippi Department of Archives and History, respectively, Patti and Charlotte organized exhibits and concerts that featured Fannie Bell Chapman, James "Son Ford" Thomas, and Otha Turner as performers and Bruce Payne as host. And through their friendship and their craft as writers, Alice Walker and Eudora Welty

helped me see the spoken word as a distinctive literary form. Their integration of music with literature in works like *The Color Purple* and "Powerhouse" is especially exciting to me.

Wendy Weil, my literary agent, has patiently waited for this book. Her support and belief in my work for many years has been unswerving. Wendy's husband, Michael Trossman, deeply loves blues, paints portraits of its performers, and always greets me with, "I got the blues. You got 'em too!"

Elaine Maisner, my editor at the University of North Carolina Press, encouraged and supported me throughout the writing of this book. She nurtured its creation and suggested important changes as I wrestled with the work.

Bruce Jackson and Tom Rankin, folklore colleagues and dear friends, read my manuscript and offered invaluable suggestions for its revision. I have admired their work for many years and am indebted to them for their support.

The Guggenheim Foundation, the University of North Carolina Institute for the Arts and Humanities, and UNC's Research Council provided generous support that allowed me to spend a year writing this book. Colleagues at IAH offered helpful suggestions as the work evolved.

My early fieldwork in the sixties and seventies was supported by friends at the Ford Foundation (Sheila Biddle), Mississippi Arts Commission (Lida Rogers), Mississippi Humanities Council (Cora Norman), National Endowment for the Arts (Bess Lomax Hawes and Alan Jabbour),

National Endowment for the Humanities (Joe Duffey), Rockefeller Foundation (Joel Colton and Peter Wood), Wenner-Gren Foundation (Lita Osmundson), and Yale University (Joseph Warner). I was blessed to receive generous support from each of these friends and their institutions in the sixties and seventies.

A key part of my fieldwork was done when I was a graduate student in folklore at the University of Pennsylvania from 1967 to 1969. My faculty advisers Dan Ben Amos, Kenneth Goldstein, and John Szwed (then at Temple University) supported and encouraged my research throughout those years.

During the seventies, I worked with Judy Peiser at the Center for Southern Folklore in Memphis. We made films and developed folklore projects that celebrated artists like Fannie Bell Chapman and Louis Dotson. At the center, Brenda McCallum did beautiful work editing interviews with musicians and artists—including Louis Dotson, James Thomas, and Otha Turner—that appeared in *Local Color: A Sense of Place in Folk Art*.

David Evans has provided counsel on this work since we first met in the sixties. His pioneering research on the blues is unparalleled. As a scholar, teacher, and performer, David raised the bar high for study of these worlds.

Over the years my friendship with Robert Palmer and Dick Waterman has been special to me. I arranged for Bob to teach at Yale, then later at the University of Mississippi, and we shared memorable times together in New York and Mississippi before his untimely death in 1997. Dick Waterman has helped me understand the blues from our first meeting in the sixties to the present.

Dick's important support of blues artists and his powerful photographs of their worlds make him a national treasure.

At Yale University, I was honored to work with Philip Garvan and Howard Weaver at the Media Design Center on the production of four films—*Give My Poor Heart Ease*, *I Ain't Lyin'*, *Made in Mississippi*, and *Two Black Churches*—included on the DVD that accompanies this book. Dale Lindquist, Trudier Miller, and Bob Slattery worked tirelessly on both filming and editing these productions.

At the University of Mississippi Center for the Study of Southern Culture, Ann Abadie, Peter Aschoff, Brenda Eagles, Sue Hart, Lisa Howorth, Mary Hartwell Howorth, Ted Ownby, and Charles Wilson encouraged my work in significant ways. Successive editors of *Living Blues*, Jim O'Neal, Amy van Singel, Peter Lee, David Nelson, and Brett Bonner, were important mentors. Directors of the University of Mississippi Blues Archive Suzanne Flandreau and Edward Komara also provided invaluable support.

At the University of North Carolina, my colleagues have helped me in more ways than I can count. Robin Chen and Steve Weiss worked tirelessly to locate and copy materials in the Southern Folklife Collection where my archive is housed. Ayse Erginer, Lisa Eveleigh, Larry Griffin, Dave Shaw, and Harry Watson worked on the publication of my B. B. King interview in *Southern Cultures*. Barb Call and Reid Johnson encouraged and helped me on a daily basis. My wonderful assistant, Dana Di Maio, provided constant, invaluable support as he edited and typed corrections in the many drafts of my manuscript. Tom

O'Keefe did amazing work transcribing tapes and editing field recordings. Katherine Smith helped organize my field recordings as a graduate student in the Curriculum in Folklore. And composer T. J. Anderson offered helpful suggestions about the overall work.

Rich Hendel brought his keen eye for design to the pages in this book and worked his magic, seamlessly laying out photographs and text. Gail Goers digitized negatives and worked with UNC Press staff to assure that they could reproduce the highest-quality images in the book. Josh Guthman selected and digitized performances from original analog field recordings and from recordings issued on long-playing vinyl records that are included on the CD. Brian Graves reedited three black-and-white Super 8 films and digitized all of the films that are included on the DVD. Aaron Smithers gathered references for the annotated bibliography, discography, filmography, and websites. And Rebecca Dobbs designed a Mississippi map that shows the places where speakers lived.

At the University of North Carolina Press, Paula Wald gave the entire manuscript a close read and made it a far tighter, better-edited text. The Press's talented marketing staff—Dino Battista, Michael Donatelli, Chris Egan, Gina Mahalek, Ellen Bush, Laura Gribbin, Ivis Bohlen, Rose Florence, and Joanne Thomas—worked closely with me to plan the release and promotion of the book. And Heidi Perov and Kim Bryant did a superb job of overseeing its production and design, respectively.

Since its founding in 1922, the UNC Press has pioneered in the publication of books on African American music and history. Howard Odum and Guy Johnson launched the scholarly study of blues when the Press published their *The Negro and His Songs* (1925) and *Negro Workaday Songs* (1926). The Press also published John Hope Franklin's first book, *The Free Negro in North Carolina, 1790–1860*, in 1943. This important work continues today under the able leadership of the Press's director, Kate Torrey, and its editor-in-chief, David Perry.

At the University of North Carolina, I have been blessed to work with Glenn Hinson, Joy Kasson, and Lloyd Kramer, who chair, respectively, the Curriculum in Folklore, American Studies Department, and Department of History. I am especially grateful to John Powell, who deeply loves the blues, generously endowed my professorship, and made it possible for me to teach at UNC.

Finally, I want to thank three women who helped me see this work through to the end—my mother, Shelby Ferris; my daughter, Virginia Ferris; and my wife, Marcie Ferris. Now in her ninetieth year, Mother always believed in my work as a writer and is an inspiration for all that I do. Virginia loves all music and offered invaluable editorial suggestions after reading my manuscript. And my beloved Marcie held my hand and encouraged me each day as I struggled to make sense of my field recordings and to frame them in a meaningful way. Marcie's counsel, her friendship, and her love are beyond measure and are reflected in every line of this work.

The interviews with Louis Dotson, Otha Turner, and James Thomas are revised from narratives originally published in *Local Color: A Sense of Place in Folk Art*, edited by Brenda McCallum

(New York: McGraw-Hill, 1982). The interview with Fannie Bell Chapman is adapted from the film *Fannie Bell Chapman, Gospel Singer* (Memphis: Center for Southern Folklore, 1975). The interview with Johnny Lee Thomas appeared in a different form in "Have Mercy," *New Journal* 6, no. 3 (January 1973): 8–10. Quotes from the sections on James Thomas, Shelby Brown, WOKJ Radio, and Beale Street and an earlier version of the Clarksdale house party appeared in *Blues from the Delta* (New York: Da Capo Press, 1988). The B. B. King interview has been reprinted in revised form from "'Everything Leads Me Back to the Feeling of the Blues': B. B. King, 1974," *Southern Cultures* 12, no. 4 (Winter 2006): 5–28. The Rose Hill Church service originally appeared in "Rose Hill Service," *Mississippi Folklore Register* 6, no. 1 (Summer 1972): 37–56.

# GIVE MY POOR HEART EASE

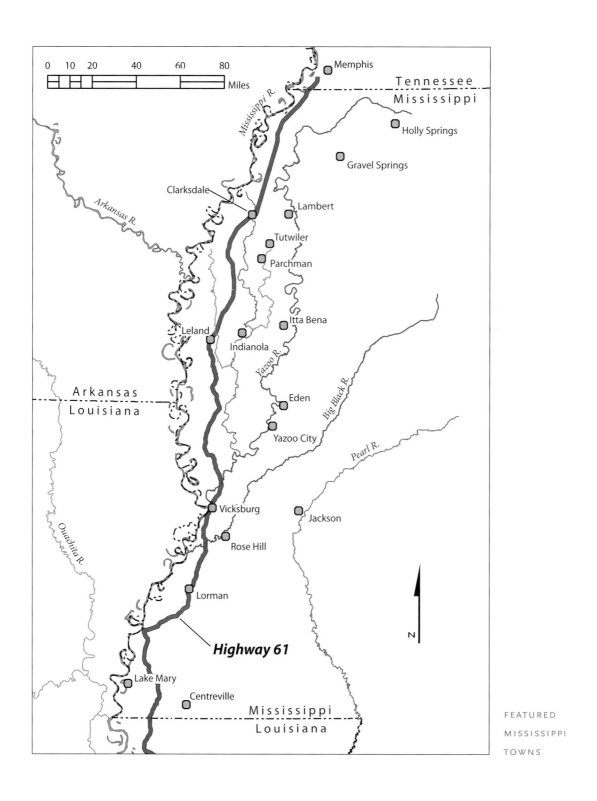

Miles

Mississippi R.

Memphis

Tennessee
Mississippi

Holly Springs

Gravel Springs

Arkansas R.

Clarksdale

Lambert

Tutwiler

Parchman

Itta Bena

Leland

Indianola

Yazoo R.

Arkansas
Louisiana

Big Black R.

Eden

Yazoo City

Pearl R.

Vicksburg

Jackson

Rose Hill

Ouachita R.

*Highway 61*

Lorman

N

Lake Mary

Centreville

Mississippi
Louisiana

FEATURED
MISSISSIPPI
TOWNS

# INTRODUCTION

When I, a white Mississippian, worked as a folklorist in my home state in the sixties and seventies, I set out to study African American music, but the people I met opened my eyes to much more than music. Each of the musicians I was privileged to record—through interviews, sound recordings, still photography, and film—revealed the fabric of life in their families and communities in powerful ways. By featuring their voices firsthand in this book, I attempt to give the reader the opportunity to hear, from the inside as much as possible, voices, stories, and music that are the roots of the blues. By trying to capture the faces and surroundings of these musicians through photographs and films that complement and deepen their recorded voices in important ways, I hope to make portraits of the speakers that respect their entire lives and their culture.

These African American musicians speak about and perform musical traditions that are the authentic roots of black music. Hailing from the Delta, as well as from northeastern, central, and southern Mississippi, these musicians represent a wide range of musical traditions that include one-strand instruments, bottle-blowing, fife and drum, hymns, spirituals, the banjo, the fiddle, and prison work chants, all of which helped define the blues.

In this volume, richly varied musical worlds are presented through the voices of the artists themselves. Their narratives are edited from field recordings I made in each artist's home and community. The artistically and emotionally rich profiles of musicians that emerge illuminate both the African American experience and the history and culture of America itself.

But here, in the introduction, I will tell you something about my own background and why seeking out the voices of the blues was so important to me. I grew up during the forties and fifties on my family's farm, located fifteen miles southeast of Vicksburg in Warren County. While my father owned the farm and black families lived and worked for him on the land, both my family and these black families had ancestral roots in the state that dated back to the nineteenth century.

Before telephones and television arrived in the fifties, members of the community either walked or drove to Vicksburg on a gravel road. Today, local residents still orient their lives in relation to Fisher Ferry Road, which passes through the farm and connects it to the outside world. Travelers either head "up the road" to Vicksburg or "down the road" to the Big Black River. Residents often study travelers on the road and speculate aloud on where they are headed. Drivers, in turn, blow their horns and wave at friends who sit on porches that face the road.

On the farm, my family had daily, if not hourly, interactions with black families in our home and in the fields. Their lives and ours were intimately linked. The farm was in fact inhabited by many more black people than white people, and in important ways, I always felt that it was a black community. Our nearest white neighbors—George and Clara Rummage, whom we called Uncle George and Aunt Clara—lived three miles up the road.

When my parents drove to a party in Vicksburg on a Saturday night, a black woman named Virgil Simpson babysat us. My four siblings and I were quite young, and I remember my parents returned one night around midnight to find us all dancing with Virgil with the radio turned up full blast. They sent us straight to bed, but I never forgot the association of music and dance with freedom.

Some days Virgil walked with us through pastures where we looked for guinea eggs that we found in nests along fencerows. She carefully took the eggs out of the nests with a spoon so as not to leave the scent of her hands. In the summer, we went out with Virgil, Mother, and others to gather blackberries in large briar patches. At the end of an afternoon, we had filled a large washtub with berries that we later ate in pies and jam.

My mother and my father taught us that we should always respect others regardless of their race. My family differed from many white families, southern or otherwise, in their views about race.

I remember that Jessie Cooper, a young man who worked for my father, contracted polio while visiting a family near our farm. When my father learned of Jessie's condition, he drove to Jessie's home with "Little" Isaiah Brown and Lou Vell Vickers, and together they carried Jessie out to the car and drove him to the Vicksburg hospital.

Jessie recalls that his medical bills were forgiven by the hospital because his disease was polio.

My first sense of the existence of racism came at the age of five, when I entered Jefferson Davis Academy, an all-white public school in Warren County where three teachers—Clara Stevens, Lucille Hilderbrand, and Gladys Barfield—taught all six grades. My friends Amos Griffin and William Appleton, who were children of black families living on the farm, stayed on the farm and attended Rose Hill School, where one teacher—Lou Roan—taught all six grades.

While traveling home on the school bus one afternoon, we passed a black child riding a mule on the side of the road. Several children leaned out the window and yelled racist epithets at the rider, scaring him and his mule terribly. I can only imagine how he felt, and I know that the scene frightened me and still haunts me today.

Another time, one of my classmates visited me on the farm, and when he saw the Rose Hill schoolteacher's new car, he remarked, "That's an awful nice car for a nigger." And when my father improved the homes of families who worked for him on the farm, my barber in Vicksburg casually remarked while cutting my hair, "I hear your daddy is fixing up those nigger houses on his farm." My parents made it clear to me and my siblings that we were never to use that word. Its use always reminded me that my family and I were different.

While the ugliness of racism lingered nearby, my siblings and I, as children, shared a world that was filled with natural beauty, mystery, and wonder. Mother took us on walks in the woods and showed us green moss beneath trees where, she explained, fairies came out at night and danced. At picnics on the farm, she read us stories that stirred our imagination. She took us swimming in Hamer Bayou on hot summer days. Once each week she insisted we remain quiet while she listened to classical music on the radio on the *Firestone Hour*.

A childhood friend named Tommy Curtis and I created an imaginary world we called Wolf Town that was located in a badly eroded part of a pasture. It was a secret place where we imagined adventures that we later described to our parents and siblings.

During the summer my younger brother Grey and I worked with the men on the farm to bale hay, loaded the bales on a truck, and stacked them in the barn to feed cattle and horses in the winter. Those were long, hot days broken up by noon dinners of fried chicken cooked by our black housekeeper Mary Gordon and washed down with glasses of her sweet iced tea. Those days were our father's way of teaching us the value of hard work.

Grey and I both raised 4-H Club calves that we proudly exhibited at the Miss-Lou Fair, an agricultural show held each year at the Vicksburg fairgrounds. We had bought two registered Angus calves and, for a year, had groomed and taught them to stand to impress the judges. Growing up on the farm, I benefited from a rich web of friendships with carpenters, cowboys, doctors, electricians, farmers, hunters, lawyers, loggers, mechanics, painters, politicians, and teachers.

Grey taught me to use a camera, and together we set up a small darkroom where he showed me how to develop black-and-white negatives and to process prints. In that room I watched the images in this book appear on sheets of print paper as they steeped in the tray of processing fluid. While Grey encouraged me in my career as a folklorist, he also loved to tease me about how I was paid to collect stories and songs, saying, "I never knew anyone who went further on less than my brother."

Though we rarely think about it, every member of my family loves to tell stories. Storytelling runs in our blood, and when we gather for holidays, the stories begin. They start over breakfast and do not stop until we retire to sleep. We push back sleep, not wanting to miss the end of a story.

For many years, each morning I have spoken by phone with members of my family to get their latest stories. As early morning light fell across fields on the farm, I would speak with my mother, Shelby Ferris, as she drank her first cup of coffee. After getting her news, I would then call my brother Grey in his truck as he and "the men"— William Appleton, Dickie Thomas, Joe Thomas, and John Henry Wright—headed into the fields. Those conversations tug at my heart and remind me that while I may live and work in other places, my real home is the farm. It is my spiritual compass.

So it is not surprising that the first stories I recorded in the late fifties were from families on the farm. These recordings led me up the road to Vicksburg and from there into the Mississippi Delta in the sixties. My Mississippi Delta recordings were the subject of my doctoral dissertation in folklore at the University of Pennsylvania and later were the focus of my teaching. In effect, I did what I loved, and—to the amazement of my parents and their friends—I found employment.

Throughout my life, I have traveled with a camera and tape recorder and tried to capture the spoken word in all its mystery and beauty through tales such as the ones presented in this book, tales that are both moving and chilling. As a teenager, I began to photograph speakers and record their stories to preserve the precious and already fleeting world of the black community on the farm around me. As a college student, I was drawn into the civil rights movement and saw my photographs and recordings as a way to honor a proud culture that stood outside the academy. I saw my work as both a political and a cultural statement. Whites often asked why I spent so much time with blacks. The implication of their question was that black lives were not worthy of serious study. In the sixties black civil rights activists faced down murderous powers, and my work as a folklorist, while it did not begin to compare in terms of the danger those activists faced, sometimes also took place in threatening circumstances. I often saw Ku Klux Klan signs and graffiti along the roads that I traveled. For a white southerner, the work I did was considered taboo.

The worlds of the Mississippi Delta blues musicians whom I recorded and filmed as a graduate student in folklore in the late sixties was dramatically different from those I had known on the farm where I grew up. With angry voices, speakers described the conditions they had endured in Delta towns like Clarksdale and Leland.

In these towns, I recorded musicians and their friends who gathered like a family each Saturday night at blues house parties.

I was drawn to the voices and stories of these families. My recordings, photographs, and films captured their faces, their homes, and their communities in ways that were unplanned. One speaker led me to others, and together they introduced me to a world that was foreign to my own. I entered their homes as a guest and promised that I would attempt to tell their stories faithfully and fully. They understood my purpose and generously shared their stories and songs with me. The trust these families bestowed on me was both surprising and understandable.

Over the past forty years, their stories have been an important influence on my work as a folklorist. While teaching at Jackson State University, Yale University, the University of Mississippi, and the University of North Carolina and while chairing the National Endowment for the Humanities, I continued to hear their voices. This book brings these stories together to create a portrait of a people, their time, and their place in history. Their tales seem timeless because the struggles, hopes, and suffering of black families are familiar themes in our culture. From slavery to Reconstruction, from the Jim Crow era to the civil rights movement, from the 1927 Mississippi River flood to Hurricane Katrina, tales endure in black families and resonate with the power of oral tradition. Throughout black history, these stories persist, and their telling becomes a means of survival. Today, as Barack Obama assumes the mantle of our nation's first black president, this history takes a dramatic turn that will inspire stories and music in exciting new ways. It is a moment many have dreamed of.

My parents, William and Shelby Ferris, and my siblings, Shelby, Hester, Grey, and Martha, understood the journey that led me to this book, and their support set us apart from other white families in our community. While an undergraduate student at Davidson College from 1960 to 1964, I helped organize civil rights marches in Charlotte, North Carolina. Other Davidson students and I met on campus with Allard Lowenstein and James Farmer and tried to desegregate both the college and local churches. During this time, my parents received an anonymous postcard telling them that I was "dating niggers."

My siblings and several other local white students met with Robert Moses in Vicksburg during the Mississippi Freedom Summer in 1964. My father was the only white adult who joined us. He was genuinely curious and questioned Moses about the civil rights movement and his work. Moses told my father that the meeting was the first time he had sat across the table from and had a conversation with a white Mississippian. After that evening, Ku Klux Klan flyers were thrown on the ground near our mailbox.

In Vicksburg, there were several places where we could speak openly about the movement. One was the COFO house, an old home in a black neighborhood rented by the Council of Federated Organizations, where we visited with Paul Cowan and others during the Mississippi Freedom Summer. We also attended services at the Anshe Chesed Temple, where, after the deaths of James Chaney, Andrew Goodman, and Michael Schwerner, Rabbi Alvin Blinder declared, "When they kill three civil rights workers, and the Jews outnumber the blacks, it is time we speak out."

When I was discharged from the army as a conscientious objector during the Vietnam War in 1969, my family again understood and supported me. After dismissal from the military, I taught at Jackson State University and lived in Jackson on Guynes Street, two doors from the home where Medgar Evers was assassinated. My parents and siblings visited my home, met my black friends, and respected and blessed my journey. They understood that I inherited my commitment to education from generations of teachers in our family. I found that the natural focus for my study and teaching was the people and places I knew as I was growing up.

The farm has always been the center of my life, and the families who lived there shaped me in enduring ways. My roots on the farm were grounded at the dinner table, where Mary Gordon cared for our family throughout her lifetime. I remember her voice and the rich language of her stories and hymns that I heard each day from childhood. Our last visit was in a nursing home in Vicksburg shortly before her death. Her family sat with her, and when I rose to leave, she hugged me and said, "You know, you are my white child." I answered, "I know." Looking back, I realize that our worlds were so very different, but we connected in a special way during that final visit in the nursing home.

The farm is where I first heard the voices of my own family and of the black community in which we lived. I have long wrestled with how to connect myself to these stories. How can I animate the voices of the storytellers? How can I explain the motivation that led me to record their worlds? These recordings were my lifeline, and I made myself promise that I would never forget the speakers who taught me in such deeply moving, sometimes frightening ways.

The power of place was embedded in me as I grew up on our family farm through the beauty of its changing seasons and its deep ties to history. Local legend claimed that treasure stolen by the nineteenth-century robbers Samuel Mason and Wiley "Little" Harpe from travelers on the nearby Natchez Trace was buried on the farm. As a child, I saw a deep hole that had been dug the night before in the yard of a home on the farm by someone looking for that treasure. Years later, beginning in high school, I dug for a different kind of treasure in that same community using my tape recorder and camera. This work captures a journey that began with my birth in 1942 on the farm to which I continue to return several times a year. Those childhood roots led me to record, photograph, and film worlds that I continue to study today. As a child, teenager, and adult, I saw music as a bridge that allowed me to connect to the black community.

Looking back on the speakers in this work, I want to frame them in terms of both my own life and their own. In the process of making my recordings in the Mississippi Delta in the sixties, I returned periodically to the family farm to develop film and transcribe interviews. The fieldwork was emotionally exhausting, so I took breaks to gather my thoughts and strength before returning to the Delta to continue the journey. Some of the worlds described by the speakers were intimately familiar to me, and others I entered as

a total stranger. When I knocked at the speakers' doors, they welcomed me and encouraged me to learn from elders whose voices are the heart of this book. As Reverend Isaac Thomas said to me, "The door here swings on the hinge of good welcome at all time."

I found a narrative that served as the door through which I discovered the cultures of the American South. I erected my own brush-arbor shelter through which I wandered into the region's history and culture and explored its art, folklore, history, music, and religion. I connected to an oral tradition of many thousands gone whose spirits inspired my work.

As I tried to find my voice as a writer—first of fiction, then of folklore—the voices I heard as a child always remained in my ear. They were like teachers who led me as a white person to embrace black culture. These voices were the beacon that led me into a territory that was forbidden, sometimes dangerous, yet intimately interwoven with my own life. Barred by segregation from entering these worlds, I went against the grain as I embraced the rich stories that follow.

As I worked within the black community in the sixties, I realized that I could not rely on introductions by local whites. During one painful introduction, a white farmer agreed to let me record a black musician who worked for him. He told me to meet him at the musician's home that evening. I arrived at the home and found the farmer and several other whites there. Rifles hung from rear-window racks in their pickup trucks, and they were standing together admiring a gun when I arrived.

After greeting me, the farmer called the musician. When he did not come to the door, the farmer threw rocks on his tin roof. The singer emerged and sang several songs on his front porch while the whites watched him from their trucks. Then he complained that his finger was cramped, and he refused to play anymore. The white men went home, and I made an appointment to meet the musician at the home of another black singer the following night.

The next night he played at length, and toward the end of the session, he began drinking whiskey, cursed his white boss, and told me that he owned the farm where he worked. He told me that the next time I came to town, I could come to his home and eat and sleep there if I wished. He swore he would see that I was safe when I entered his home. I recorded his conversation and was moved by his courage in defying his boss:

> Next time you come, come on to my house and walk right on in. If I eat a piece of bread, you eat too. I'm the boss of that whole place over there. I don't know how many acres it is. You ain't got to ask none of these white folks about coming to my house. Any time you come to my house, and I ain't there, stay right there until I come. Don't leave. I'm coming back, because I've gone to get some pussy, and I'll be back in a minute. Any time you want to come down here, you drive to my damn house. Ain't a damn soul gonner fuck with you, white or black.

After that experience, I entered the black community without contacting local whites. In doing so, I exposed myself to the possibility of arrest, and my black friends were well aware of this. By entering black homes and sharing meals with black families, I broke racial taboos that were ingrained in the lives of white and black southerners from childhood. When blacks saw that I was willing to break traditional taboos to be a part of their lives, they accepted the integrity of my work and did everything possible to assist me. I felt I became a friend rather than a "white man" and was often called "soul brother" or "brother" by teenagers in the black communities where I worked.

During the telling of a racial joke directed against whites, the eyes of the audience followed my reaction to the joke. My laughter indicated sympathy with the black protagonist in the joke and bonded us. Once this rapport was established, recording sessions became much more spontaneous, and I could enter blues juke joints and record in an optimum context.

I explained my work and asked speakers if they would like to be part of a project to record their music and stories. They were surprised that a book might be written about their daily lives, which they assumed held little interest outside their own community.

I bought groceries for families in exchange for the hospitality they showed me, and when I attended religious services, I made offerings to the congregation. I also sent my photographs to the speakers with a note of thanks for their support, and they displayed them in their homes. When I returned to their homes again, I was touched by the effect my letters and photographs had on families.

I did my fieldwork with a Sony half-track reel-to-reel tape recorder, two Electrovoice directional microphones with stands, a Pentax 35mm camera, a Sony Super 8 movie camera, and two snap-on 200 watt lightbulbs for interior filming, all of which I viewed as essential. I operated all of the equipment myself during each recording session. I first set up the recorder and then made still and motion pictures of events, while talking with friends in the room.

I traveled in an old Chevrolet Nova and kept my equipment in the trunk. A long metal tool chest with a removable top drawer contained my microphones, cables, electrical extension cords, and blank recording tape and film. I learned to quickly set up my equipment and begin recording and filming.

Later in the evening, after the recording session had ended, I took out pen and paper to write my thoughts about the day's work. This was the most tiring part of the day, but this documentation while the events were still fresh in my mind was essential to my fieldwork. There were always dramatic moments that I felt sure I would never forget, but without these notes, I realize that many details would have slipped from my memory.

In taking photographs I shot Tri-X black-and-white film. I did my own developing and was able to make prints to my own taste at a considerable financial savings. I always took portraits of the speaker's face. If he or she sang or danced, I took wider shots, and I used a strobe flash unit for interior pictures. Inside homes, I photographed furniture, pictures on walls, medical supplies, and food to record the household inventory. Outside the home, I photographed streets and fields to give a feeling for the community and the countryside in which the speakers lived.

I began using black-and-white Super 8 motion picture film in June 1968. The drama of a blues singer performing in a juke joint on a Saturday night for local dancers could not be adequately captured by sound recordings, still photography, and verbal descriptions. Equally dramatic were the religious services with the preachers' chanted sermons and the women who "fall out" in ecstasy and have to be carried outside to cool down.

After working in both juke joints and churches, I saw how they were interrelated and central to the black community. Film was the best way to make a permanent record of their drama and beauty. I used sound recordings, still photography, and film to create the broadest portrait of speakers and their families in these worlds.

This book first explores the musical roots of the blues, starting with the stories and hymns of Mary Gordon and Reverend Isaac Thomas in the Rose Hill community. The voices of Scott Dunbar (traditional songster), Louis Dotson (one-strand guitar player), Fannie Bell Chapman (gospel singer and faith healer), Otha Turner (fife player), Johnny Lee "Have Mercy" Thomas (former Parchman Penitentiary inmate), Tom Dumas (fiddle and banjo player), and Lee Kizart (blues pianist), among others, come next. Each speaker describes musical traditions that shaped the blues in significant ways.

The book's second section is set in black neighborhoods like Kent's Alley in Leland and the Brickyard in Clarksdale where the blues developed in dramatic ways. In Leland, we meet James "Son Ford" Thomas, Gussie Tobe, and Shelby "Poppa Jazz" Brown; in Clarksdale, Jasper Love and Wade Walton; in Jackson, WOKJ radio announcer Bruce Payne; and in Memphis, clothing salesman Robert Shaw.

The third section looks back on the blues through two of the most significant figures in blues history: composer and performer Willie Dixon and performer B. B. King.

The fourth and final section joins sacred and secular worlds by presenting a Rose Hill church service and a Clarksdale blues house party, each of which celebrates and affirms the spirit in distinctive ways.

Each speaker's narrative is transcribed from my field recordings. In some cases I worked with many hours of recordings, and in other cases, very few. Some names mentioned in the narratives have been changed. As in the films and sound recordings that accompany this book, my voice is not included in the published text. Instead, I try to present an authentic, flowing, dramatic monologue, a narrative that has both literary and documentary value.

Together, speakers in each of these four sec-

tions offer a portrait of the blues and of the worlds that shaped the music. The book closes with a selected bibliography, discography, filmography, and list of websites that helps frame the lives of these musicians and their music. As a teacher and scholar, I know the importance that publications, sound recordings, films, and websites have for both classroom teaching and scholarly research.

This book also includes a CD and a DVD with field recordings and documentary films that feature many of the speakers. The films range from early black-and-white Super 8 film without synchronized sound to 16mm color film with synchronized sound. Through the book and the accompanying CD and DVD, the reader will encounter performers and speakers whose lives shaped the roots of American music. While most of the speakers are no longer alive, their voices bear intimate witness to a world of beauty, pain, and sadness that defined the blues.

# BLUES
# ROOTS

*Blues and sacred music are joined at the hip. Most blues musicians grow up in the church where as children they learn to sing hymns and spirituals. One blues musician told me that if a singer wants to cross over from sacred music to the blues, he simply replaces "my God" with "my baby" and continues singing the same song. Our journey through blues roots begins with the stories and hymns of Mary Gordon and her minister in the Rose Hill community, Reverend Isaac Thomas.*

*We then visit musicians who perform with instruments that shaped the blues. The sounds of the one-strand-on-the-wall, fife and drum, piano, fiddle, and banjo; gospel songs; and prison work chants all echo the blues in special ways. Together, the voices in this section make up a chorus that describes the roots of the blues in rural Mississippi. Both the music and the lives of these speakers help us understand the complex, rich story of blues roots.*

# ROSE HILL

Mary "Monk" Gordon and Reverend Isaac Thomas were two of the most important leaders in the Rose Hill community, fifteen miles southeast of Vicksburg. Gordon told me that her grandmother was a slave who walked from Natchez to the Rose Hill community. She and many of Gordon's other ancestors are buried on the hillside around Rose Hill Church.

Mary Gordon often sang church hymns while working in her garden or doing housework and was deeply attached to the history of Rose Hill Church. As a young woman, she had religious visions that she interpreted as signs that she should join the church. One of these visions foretold the birth of her daughter. She also sang a parody of preachers entitled "You Shall Be Free." When she sang it for me, she asked that I not let Reverend Thomas hear it.

Reverend Isaac Thomas lived in Vicksburg and preached at Rose Hill Church on the first Sunday of every month. He served four churches by preaching in one each Sunday of the month. During his childhood he preached funerals for animals that died, so it was only natural that as an adult he entered the ministry. He was the last in a line of preachers who served Rose Hill Church for over 150 years. After his death, the church was used primarily for funerals of deceased members who are buried in its cemetery.

These interviews were recorded in 1974 during the filming of *Two Black Churches*. Mary Gordon spoke on the porch of the home of her stepmother, Amanda Gordon, and Reverend Thomas spoke from his chair behind the pulpit in Rose Hill Church.

# MARY GORDON

That church was there many years before I was born. My grandfathers and great-grandfathers helped build it. They say they first started the church up there on that hill when they made a little brush arbor, and they started singing and praying. So many people started coming in and joining the church, until they got enough members to fill a little small church. And when they built the little small church on the hill, they got more and more members. Then they made it a larger and larger church. There was so many people that come in, that they would sit out among the roses up there on the hill. Big beautiful roses, everybody had roses up on the hill. So that's where Rose Hill Church got its name from. There were so many roses up there. That was before I was born, and I've been going there ever since I was born.

When people die in the North and they belong to this church here, if the relatives is able, they will send them back here, and they will be buried up there. There isn't any place you can walk up on that hill that you aren't walking over somebody that is buried. I know so many, and there was so many before I was born—my father and his family, my mother and her family. I got a brother too. I got lots of relatives up on that hill. My mother and father, brother, and lots of uncles and aunts and others all up on the hill there.

People who live in Chicago want to be buried here because this is their home. They were born and raised here, and when they joined the church, they joined this church. All their relatives are buried up there. When people go away from here and they die, they want their bodies to come back here where their mother, father, and all their relatives are. That's why they brings them back. Some of them make a request that they want to go back home, you know, when they die. So their families will bring them back and bury them up on Rose Hill.

When I die, heaven will be my home. It will be my home. All you have to do is believe and be baptized. Just believe that Jesus will save you. He will save you if you believe that and if you die with that belief.

I sing the hymns anywhere—out in the field or in the house. When you have a real service, you sing them in the church. But anytime I feel like singing, I just sing. It makes me feel good, singing. I always did love to be around the house singing. When I'm singing, I'm feeling jolly and happy, and it makes me feel good.

When people are in church and get the spirit, they get full up. Some of them jumps up and makes a loud noise. I never do that. I never make a lot of hollering and jump up. When I feel the spirit, it brings tears to my eyes. You feel sorry for yourself, I guess. I don't know what it is. It just hits you somewhere and makes you feel sorry for yourself.

I know what to sing, and it's always something about the Lord. Whether I'm home, in the

MARY GORDON, ROSE HILL, 1978

church, anywhere, I believe in Jesus, and I believe that when the Lord call me home, I'll see
Him when I leave here. I'm looking to see Jesus
in my whole heart and eyes. I've seen Him in a
dream, but I have never seen Him in person.

I dreamed I saw Him come in the church
down here. When I looked out the side door,
I saw four men on a round chair like a couch
coming right across the paths. I was standing in
the door at the church. That couch didn't have
wheels on it. It was just coming on in. It come
on in the side door and angled right across the
pulpit up there where the preacher was stand-

ing. There was four mens in there, and Dad and
I were sitting in the rear of the church. He said
to me, "Do you know any of us here?"

I got up and walked up close to Him, and I
said, "I don't know their names, but this is Jesus
here."

He looked at me, and He smiled. He said,
"This is Abraham, Isaac, and Jacob."

He asked where the Sunday school books
were, and I told Him, "Well we don't have no
books, but we have Bibles when we come to
Sunday school."

Four white men, I don't know how they ever

got in there. It looked just like a couch. Big enough for the four mens to get into. And He told me the others were Abraham, Isaac, and Jacob, and He was Jesus. They were sitting right down there in that church. That was a dream. That's been many years ago, and I don't never forget about it. I will never forget it.

I dreamed that a house was up on the hill when I was a little girl. There was nothing else but bushes all before I was born. I dreamed there was a house on that hill, and I was up there in it. We was walking through the hall. We was walking side by side. She had one of those high-posted beds in the front room with the white cotton spread. Those white spreads with the fringes all around it. When me and her was walking up the hall, she looked at me and said, "This is your house."

But there was no house up there at all at that time. As I was walking up the hall, she said, "This is your house."

That's been a long time ago. There wasn't a house up there. We used to go there picking berries and sour grass. Going to school, we used to go there and play all the time. I dreamed about that house up on the hill, but it was a good many years ago.

I dreamed I saw Jesus. Looked like He was walking in clouds. He was way up in the sky. He had on a long white coat, and He was barefeeted. I could see His bare feets, but I couldn't see nothing under them. He was just walking, walking along in the air with a white coat touching down along His feet. One of my cousins come out, and she say, "Look a'yonder. Who is that?"

I said, "That's Jesus."
I say, "Don't you know Him?"
I say, "That's Jesus."

And He just walked on in the cloud. Walked on until He vanished away. He had long hair with a long white coat on. He was a white man with a long white robe. He didn't say anything. He was just standing in the air walking.

And I dreamed I saw Jesus's mother too. I prayed and asked the Lord to show me His mother. And I saw her. She was riding way yonder in the east, in the sky, and she was on something like a train. When she passed, the window opened, and I saw her from her head to her waist. She just looked out. She looked like a large stout woman. Mary, the mother of Jesus, I saw her.

That was in a dream now. Nobody ever seen Jesus with the natural eye. Least I ain't never heard nobody said they did. If you ask the Lord to show you something in a dream and He show it, then you got to get up and tell the church about it. Then you just believe on that, and you will be baptized and you will still believe on that until you die. That's what you call a Baptist believer. And that's what we are, Baptists. You believe on the Lord, Jesus Christ, with all your soul and heart and don't ever get off of it. You can't never turn back off of that. Just stay on it. And I always will believe in Jesus.

One day I was standing in the kitchen, in the back door, looking at the sun when it come up in the morning. I always get up early in the morning and watch the sun turn different colors. I was standing there, and all at once the sun got strong to my eyes, and I closed my eyes. And when I closed my eyes, I saw Jesus in the sun just hanging on the cross, both arms stretched. He was nailed to the cross, and His head was laying with the locks on His shoulders and the crown of thorns on His head just as plain as I'm looking at you now. But I wasn't asleep. I was standing in the door, looking at the sun. And every time I would close my eyes, I could see it again. When I opened my eyes wide, I couldn't see it. If I closed my eyes just about like halfway, I saw Him again. I saw Him three times hanging there, and I got nervous. I walked out the back door, went on around the side of the house, and I stood around the side of the house. I shut my eyes again, and I saw the same thing.

So I stood there a few minutes. Then I went on around to the front door, walked on inside the house, and I sat down on the little stool. I closed my eyes. I saw Him again. I sat there with my eyes closed until He got out of my sight. Then I opened my eyes, closed them again, and I ain't seen Him no more from that day to this. I been getting up on Sunday mornings and watching the sun to see if I could see Him again. But I can't see Him no more. Now I didn't dream that. I saw that, just like me and you sitting here talking.

I dreamed of a vision when I was trying to pray. It seemed to me like I left home wandering, and I got in a little roadway. And this little road led me to a crossroads. I used to love to dance. And when I got to the crossroads, I heard guitar picking. It seemed to me like it was a house on a hill, and they was picking guitars up there. They was out on the porch trying to tempt me in. It was a real fat lady come out there. She

was just dancing and twisting, you know. It's strange, but that's the truth.

So I got back onto that road. And when I got to the crossroads, I didn't know which way to go. I looked back at the house, and I knew I couldn't go that way, didn't want to go that way. So I got in the crossroads. There was a gate in the middle of this crossroads. One road was going this way. One road was going that way. And a tall gate was there. I had to choose the road I wanted to take. So on the other side of the gate, it was three great big black bulls, and the road I wanted to take was the one those bulls were standing in. I didn't know what to do, I wanted to get in that road. So I said, "Lord, I don't know what to do."

I was scared of those bulls on the other side, but I had to go that way. I put my hand on the gate, and I climbed up one panel. Then I got onto the top. I got to sit astraddle of the gate. I was on one side looking this way, and I looked the other way where the music was. Something told me I got to go this way, got to go down between them bulls. I put one foot on the middle of the panel, and I looked back at the bulls. I got down there, and I was trembling. I was so scared, and I put my feet on the ground between those bulls. When I put my feet on the ground, it looked like the bulls just got congealed. They didn't move. I walked on through them. I got a little piece down the road, and I looked back. It was nearly about night, and I had to make it to where I was going. I got on a little narrow road, looked like it just about that wide. On the east side of that road there was something growing like wheat, and I had to go through it. When I got in there, every time I'd make a step, it was a big snake would rise up on this side. I had a stick, and I'd hit it. I'd take another step, and one would rise on this side. I hit it. I was fighting and fighting and fighting until I saw George Carter, a man I had asked to pray for me. I saw him coming through this wheat. He was coming, and he had a big stick. He started helping me to fight, and I was fighting and fighting and fighting.

After a while I looked, and I saw a man come out of the sun when the sun rose. He was riding a white horse, and his horse was just leaping. That horse was leaping. The man on the white horse had long pretty hair, and his horse had a pretty mane. When he come up to me, he reached his hand out. I handed him my hand, and he took me up on that horse. When he was taking me up on that horse, the snakes was rearing up at my feet. He just lifted me up and carried me to a great big building. He put me off in that building, and I walked to the door. It looked like a big church. I knocked on the door, and when the door opened, my mother opened the door. When she opened the door, I walked in. I said, "Howdy."

The whole building was full of people in there. They said, "Howdy, Mother. Howdy. Howdy, Mother. Howdy. Howdy, Mother."

That's all they was saying, "Howdy, Mother. Howdy."

And by the time they quit speaking, everybody in the building looked just alike. Wasn't nobody in there different. Everybody looked just alike. When I got to the end of that dream, my eyes flew open, and I found I was still at home

in the bed. That was in 1920. That's when that happened, nineteen and twenty. And I ain't forgot it yet. Never will, I don't think. Never will forget that.

Everybody just looked like one solid color, white people with hair just wavy. Everybody had it. Everybody looked just alike. It was so many people that you just couldn't get through them. I just got to the door. When I said, "Howdy, Mother," they all went to singing real low, "Howdy, Mother. Howdy, howdy, Mother."

It had a little motion to it, saying, "Howdy, Mother. Howdy, Mother, howdy."

Since I waked up, I hadn't seen that vision no more. But it always stays in my mind. I won't ever get it out. I think I'll go home to God with that same vision. It makes you feel funny when you start to talking about it. But I tell you, I know that happened when I was praying, trying to get religion. That was when I saw that vision, and it never has left me. I hope I'm going to keep the faith so I can meet the man on the horse when I leave here. I want him to meet me on that same horse and take me on home.

I was walking down the road one day, and I was thinking I didn't have no children at all. So I said to myself, "I ain't got nobody."

I said, "Lord, I wonder why I don't have a child."

I said, "Lord, would you just give me one child?"

I said, "I'd be satisfied with just one."

That night I dreamed I had a little baby. I found the baby sitting in a stump. A lot of green vines was growed all around that stump. I went and looked over in there, and there was a little baby, pretty little old baby. I went down and said, "This is my baby."

I picked the baby up, and I carried the baby home with me. I was standing right there when he cried.

When I waked up that morning, I thought sure I had the baby in the bed with me. I was laying there, and it looked like a lady came, and she told me I couldn't eat anything but rice. It looked like somebody was in the kitchen fixing me some rice, and I was in the bed. I waked up real good, and I said, "I ain't got no baby. Let me get up from here."

I got up and went and put my clothes on. I set around thinking about the baby. It was the next year before the baby was born. I think that must have been the same baby. I reckon it must have been. I saw her before she was born, and it looked like they said, "That's your baby."

I just couldn't believe that I was going to have a baby. I never did have in mind that I ever would have a child. But I wanted one. And so when I first came pregnant with the child, I kinda got worried. I didn't know. I said, "Now what is it I'm gonna do with this baby? I can't do nothing with this child."

I was telling another lady about it, and she say, "Aaww, you oughtn't to have no baby. You oughta do away with it."

I walked on away from her. I said, "If I have it, I'll be glad of it."

So I went to the doctor, and the doctor told me I was pregnant. He said, "If you don't believe me, you come back here in about nine months time."

I laughed about it, and I went on. And sure enough, I had a little girl. That's all I had, just that one. It seems like I saw some more children, but they was in a house. I was up in a building, and they was down on the ground reaching they hands up to me. And every time I'd come down a step, the little baby would be so low he couldn't get up. I'd reach down a hand to try to get him up. I had to step, step, step, until I come to the bottom. And there at the bottom, I got this other little girl. And looked like when I went on up in that building, all those little children was outside playing. I said, "No, all them wasn't my children, but I guess they grandchildren."

That's what I got. I got one child and a bunch of grandchildren. I dreamed about that. So I say, "That's the way it worked out. It worked out just fine."

Sometimes the women used to be together quilting at night. We used to quilt before we got electric lights. We used tin lights, those small tin lights. They would have them sitting all over the quilt. Maybe one of the lamps would be sitting on the shelf or down on the table, somewhere close around where everybody could see. Then when they couldn't see to thread the needle, they had to get the children. The young children would thread needles. Maybe some of the old ones would get up and get them a cup of coffee to drink at night. Then the ladies would invite one another around during the daytime to help, you know, on the quilt.

Blue is my favorite color. If you want to have a lively quilt, you put red, like these here. Sometimes you make it out of just two colors, red and white or red and blue, and make a quilt out of it. Most the time you make the quilt from scraps. You put the pieces together, and they make a nice big quilt. It takes time—about two weeks—to get them together. I've tried to get one together. It takes me a long time. I don't like quilting on red or quilting on blue because it shows your stitches too much. If you have a flower pattern, it won't show so many stitches. But if you just use solid red or blue color, it will show up all the white stitches.

With this here print, you make a little block like that and sew them on and on. Then you have the quilt. We call it a scrap wheel. We go around picking up pieces from almost any place. When you cut your dress out, you have some pieces left. You put them all together and make a long row. You put little bits of pieces between those, and you make a full quilt out of it. It's very tedious. But it seems like it's nothing but a smile to her [Amanda Gordon] because she loves to do it.

Before you join the church, you got to believe that Jesus died for you. You got to believe it deep from your heart. And then you got to get on your knees and go to the Lord and ask Him to forgive you for everything that you have did wrong. You ask Him to forgive you for it, and you ask Him until the tears come outta your eyes. Just like if I go down there and do something wrong to you, and then I get sorry for it. Then I come down there and beg your pardon for it.

Well that's the way I believe in it. I ask the

Lord to forgive me, but I got to get saintly sorry for what I done. When you first join the church, you ask the Lord to forgive you for your sins.

When we sing in the church, somebody have to bass, and somebody have to alto, and somebody have to lead. See, if you lead, somebody have to come along behind you and catch these songs. You just can't sing them all—lead and alto and bass—all together. It usually takes three voices to make it sound right.

They would teach you how to do it. You would get a musicianer to come in, and they would teach you the song. A musicianer is somebody would come in who already know how to play a piano and already know all the notes about a song. They come and teach you the words and how to put the tune and the sound to the words you sing in the song. That's what we did. We had a lady by the name of Miss Cora used to come in and sing for us. But Miss Cora dead now. She lived at Waterville. All the teachers what I used to know passed. All of them dead now. But they was good teachers at the time.

A Dr. Watts hymn is a good hymn to sing. It makes you feel happy. When the people didn't know how to sing, there was a man, I think he must have been named Watts, and he would lead these songs like, "I'm gonna tell my Lord when I go home."

All the congregation would join in and sing the same thing that he would sing. Everybody sings those songs, and they call them Dr. Watts hymns because Dr. Watts must have been the first one started the music. When I got here, that's the way people were singing. They called them Dr. Watts hymns before I was born.

When you're baptized, you get up and confess that you believe in the Lord Jesus Christ, who saves you in your dying hour. You tell that to the public. You let everybody know that you believe that Jesus will save you in your dying hour. Then you get up, and the preacher comes around and asks you who you believe in. You tell him you believe in Jesus, and then you actually become a Christian, and they take you in the church. Then on Sunday, the believer gets ready to go down to the water. They tell everybody that they believe that Jesus died for their sins and that they want to be baptized. Then they baptize you in the name of the Lord, the Father, and the Son and the Holy Ghost. That's the way we baptize.

If I sing this song, don't you let my pastor hear it. Oh Jesus, it's an old one.

> Our Father, who art in Heaven.
> Preacher owed me ten dollars,
> He paid me seven.
> Kingdom come, your will be done.
> If I hadn't took the seven,
> I wouldn't have got none.

> I had a fight about my money,
> What he owed me,
> You shall be free.

> Some people tell me that a preacher won't
>     steal.
> Caught about seven in my watermelon field,
> Just a'crushing and a'slicing,
> Tearing up my vines.

> They was talking over my melons,
> You shall be free.
> Save my rind, brother,
> You shall be free.
> Save my vines,
> You shall be free.
> Oh, when the Good Lord sets you free.

> See that preacher laying behind the log,
> Finger on the trigger, got his eye on the hog.
> The gun says boom, the hog says bop.
> He jumped on the hog with all his grip.
> He had pork chops,
> You shall be free.
> He had back bones, he had chitterlings,
> You shall be free.
> Oh, when the Good Lord sets you free.

> The rooster and the preacher had a falling
>     out.
> The rooster kicked the preacher clean out of
>     sight.
> The preacher told the rooster, say,
> "That's alright.
> "I'll meet you at the hen house tomorrow
>     night
> "With a croker sack.
> "I'll have chicken pie,"
> You shall be free.
> Oh, when the Good Lord sets you free.

> When I first moved to Memphis, Tennessee,
> I was crazy about the preacher as I could be.
> I went out on my front porch walking around.
> I invite the preacher over to my house,
> Washed his face, combed his head.

Next thing he wanted to do was slip in my
   bed.
I caught him by the head, man, and kicked
   him out the door.
I don't allow no preachers around my house
   no more.

Don't allow . . .
Oh, when the Good Lord sets you free.

I don't want Reverend Thomas to hear me singing that. [Laughs.]

# REVEREND ISAAC THOMAS

My calling was something like Moses when he was called to go down into the land of Egypt to bring his people out. When I heard this calling from God, I didn't think this job was for me. But at the end, I heard the voice just like I hear your voice. And when I asked Him, I said, "Now Lord, I feel my insufficiency. Would you have me preach your word?"

Then I saw Him in a vision as I am looking at you. He spoke to me the Christian way, as a revelation.

Sometimes you have a prepared sermon, and that's how you train yourself. Sometimes I use a prepared sermon. But most generally, according to the scripture, He say, "Open your mouth and I'll speak through you."

Then if you study God's word, then it will become a part of you, and you don't need no paper to get it on.

There is a difference between preachers of the book and preachers of the spirit. The preacher of the book is a preacher that goes off to school and prepares himself. He gets well versed and well qualified, so he can come back and compile a sermon. But that's not the spirit of God. The Book says many are called, but few chosen. But very few are chosen preachers. You can find plenty of them out there, prepared preachers who think they can go to school and get their master's and doctor's and come back to preach. But that's not true. You may not know A from B. If God call you to preach, you can preach. I know several preachers who hardly know

their name, but they were profound preachers because God gave them the calling from their hearts. Those that went to school, you could make a rag doll out of them because they just don't have the calling. It takes spirit to indulge the sermon. A sermon is a spoken communication with divine persuasion. That moves people from doing wrong to doing right.

Now, anytime that the blood as we talked about today has been applied to you, you are truly saved. You know, not everybody is saved. Some people just say they are saved. But I mean, when you have been truly saved by grace, then you have a wireless phone. There's no wire hanging like you see on these here. It's something you can communicate with, between you and God. You can talk with Him. You can lay up in your bed any hour, midnight, before day in the morning, and you can talk to God. That's the wireless telephone working. His line never gets busy. He always has time to see what you want. He hears the groan from the church. He loves the church. He died for the church, and therefore he loves it.

Several times I have seen Him with the eye of faith. You know, anybody that stays close to God, and walks with God, and stays meek and humble in prayer, He will carry them away. Sometimes He will carry them away into a vision land, and He will show many things that are pertaining to the spiritual life. I saw Jesus standing in the air. I saw that. He was standing with a long white robe, a circle around His head, standing in the air. He wasn't standing on noth-

ing, just standing in the air. That's revelation, you know. I seen that with the natural eye.

Another revelation I saw was a ball of fire. I used to read often about the consummation of the world. What I mean by that is, the end of the world. I used to read often about that. And reading about these things, the more likely you are to dream about them. Anything you read about and boil down to a real hard sincere study, well, quite naturally you gonna have a dream. You'll have a dream about what you're doing.

I had a zeal in me when I was five or six years old to preach, but I really didn't think it would lead up to the position which I hold now. I didn't have no idea of that at the time. Everything that would die that our parents was raising—animals or chickens—almost anything that would die, I'd have church over. I'd have a funeral, and I would always be the preacher to preach those animals' funerals.

It rocked on from there. I was very interested in church back in that day and time. We wasn't enlightened like we are today about the Bible. We teach according to the Bible now. He that believe and is baptized shall be saved.

During that time, they were preaching and praying on the ground and on down through the woods and different places, trying to find the Lord. And I went down there several times trying to find Him, but I never did run up on Him down there in those woods. I didn't have the knowledge to know that I was carrying Him along with me, because the tenth chapter of Romans says, "The word is denied thee even in your mouth and in your heart."

That is the word of faith that we preach. I didn't know that I was carrying the word with me all the time I was looking for it.

At baptism, it's almost something like conversion. If you would allow me to go back a little bit on that baptism, you know during that time, I think fifty-six of us went down in the water that Sunday. And the minister, he told us to pray again. He said, "Now you all gonna join church, and I want you to pray again and ask the Lord is you worthy to be baptized."

So I prayed. That's what made me so happy that morning when I was going to the water. The Lord showed me in a dream that we would be marching in white and would be paired off two by two. The Lord showed me that. That give me more confidence to step further out on His word. And when I was baptized that Sunday morning, I felt brand-new again. I felt good. I felt like shouting, as they say.

What happens in a sermon would be hard to explain when you have never felt the visitation of the spirit. It would be a little hard because it's a feeling that you never felt before. When you get happy, you feel different from the way you felt before. It's a different feeling, this spiritual feeling for a conversion. I think Isaac Watts caught a glimpse of that when he said, "How precious did that grace appear, the hour I first believed."

That's a precious moment, when you believe God's word. It changes things. Everything changes. Everything looks new when you believe on God's word. That's the way that works.

The minister is the least careful person there is on earth. He's the least careful man among all nations on the earth. There are some that will say, "I don't want a preacher at my house," and all that kind of stuff, when it's a mighty fine thing for a minister to come to your house. It's a blessed thing when he come there in the right spirit. It's a blessed thing for him to come there.

I remember a lady once, she didn't have no bread, no meal, nothing, and her son was getting ready to eat the last cake and die. A preacher by the name of Elijah came along. He asked the lady for a little morsel of bread, and she told him, "I'm just picking up two sticks to cook this. This is all we have to subsist upon. We gonna eat this, and then we gonna die."

What he said to her was, "Fix me a little feast first."

So she did it. She obeyed God's man and went on and fixed him a little cake. And when she went back in the kitchen, her meal there was running over. Oh, it was running out the door. God had opened up the windows of heaven and poured a blessing on her for taking care of His preacher. It's a fine thing to take care of God's ambassador, because he's the only man that God is depending on to bring the word home.

If it wasn't for the preacher, all our faith and all our hopes and all our running will be in vain. See, preaching is a spoken communication to sway folks to come to the Lord, to sway Christian people to do the right thing. Two-thirds of the world is civilized under the preaching of the gospel. It makes many people do the right thing. If you just turn all these people loose and throw the preaching away, this wouldn't be a safe place to live, which it ain't too much of a safe place now. But it wouldn't be safe at all then. If the preacher would quit preaching and turn the

people loose to do as they wish, it wouldn't be a safe place to live. So preaching is of great importance.

And singing is an important part of the worship. We get glory out of singing, and we sing to the glory of God. It feel good sometimes, singing. Just like, "I love the Lord, He heard my cry."

That means the individual loves the Lord because He returned them favors. He answered their prayers that have been going up before Him. "I love the Lord, He heard my cry."

He pitied every groan. He had compassion on my groans. After He pitied my groan, as long as I live, while trouble rises, I will be in a hurry to get to His throne. I'll try to make it there and do everything I can for the humanity, that I might obtain a crown of life. All this striving that we are doing, and all the singing, and all the good lives that we are living, the crown is the one thing that is promised to the Christian that overcomes. In our Bible, He says, "It hasn't been told, nor has it been revealed what the Lord have in store for those who overcome you."

The only thing that we know about is a crown of life, but there is many other things that our ears haven't heard. Now it hasn't been revealed nor has it been told what the Lord have in store for us. It's like a song where Paul prayed to the Lord, and the Lord answered his prayer immediately. "What did I do? What did I say when the jailer cried out what must I do to be saved?"

The Lord said, "Lean on the Lord Jesus, and thy shalt be saved."

The song doesn't mean that he just actually heard God's voice, but that God reduced His voice to the preaching of the Gospels. You see, when God talks, trees move about. Mountains skip like lambs when God speaks. It makes man tremble when God speaks. Therefore, He had to reduce His voice through preaching of the word. And when you hear the preaching of God's word, then you heard God's voice. You heard God's voice.

That's the way He talks. He talks today through man because if God had to talk Himself, we couldn't stand it. The earth would move at the sound of His voice. One day He talked on Mt. Sinai, and lightning started to do skip jacks on the bosom of the clouds. Dark clouds started to roll like sheets. Thunder began to beat like drums, like a funeral march, and began to blow around the sides of the mountain. People call for God to stop. They don't want to hear no more. See, God had to reduce His voice in order to get it over to the people. And when I preach, "He that believes and is baptized is saved."

That's God's voice then. Then the song says, "I heard the voice of Jesus saying, Come unto me and rest."

That's the preaching. The preaching is preaching that he that believes and is baptized shall be saved. There shall be rest for the weary. When the minister is there, that's God's voice, and the church cries out, "I heard the voice of Jesus saying, Come unto me and rest."

Then it says, "Lay down your weary worn head where I put my head, on Jesus."

I don't think blues should be in a church or nowhere else. But that is a part of the world. Christ told the church that "ye are part in the world but not of the world."

I don't think the church should take part in no devil work, and the blues and all that stuff ain't nothing but the devil's work. I don't think it should mix with God's work.

I read a story once about a parrot—you know one of those talking birds—that was in a church. The church was next door to a juke house, and that bird would sit up there and talk and carry on with them. So eventually they thought they would move the church and carry it on down the road about a mile away from that juke house. When the minister got out there for the last service, the parrot was still there. The preacher came out there and said, "Parrot, we left your place down at that juke house and come way up here so we wouldn't hear all that noise."

The parrot said, "Yes, but you have the same gang up here. The same gang that go to the juke house is going to the church."

That's what he had reference to. So I think the church people should draw themselves out from the world and be separated from the world of people.

# LAKE MARY

Martha and Scott Dunbar lived on the bank of Lake Mary, an oxbow lake twenty miles west of Woodville in Wilkinson County. The lake formed when the Mississippi River changed its course, and the abandoned riverbed became a lake. Lake Mary is famed for its fishing, and Scott Dunbar worked most of his life as a fishing guide and as a musician who performed at parties in the area.

Dunbar was a songster who composed and sang a wide range of blues. One of his most unusual songs is a cante-fable—a sung story—about a young man who courts his sweetheart. He brings corn whiskey to her parents to make them fall asleep, and then he courts their daughter through the night.

Dunbar was also a gifted storyteller whose tales vividly describe the worlds of black religion, white fishermen, and the military at Camp Shelby, Mississippi. He used his wit to survive in these worlds, and his stories are filled with both humor and pathos, as are those of his wife, Martha Dunbar.

These interviews were recorded during the summer of 1968 at the Dunbars' home.

# MARTHA DUNBAR

My mother's name was Martha Patrick, from birth until she died. She never married. And my mother and grandmother raised Sister and I by theyself. When we got grown, we had nobody to plow. You know people had to farm in those days. My sister went to New Orleans, and I hitched up two mares and went to plowing. I plowed four years and made my own crop.

And Scott, when I met Scott, Scott was wagging with two girls. He and his wife had separated. He married my stepbrother's daughter. I wanted to take the children. I asked him to let me take the children and raise them, and he wouldn't. I said, "Well let them stay with me about two or three weeks or a month."

He did. And when he came for them, they started crying and me too because I didn't want to give them up. I came down here and I stayed about one week with the children. I know my peoples and everybody else, they talked. I said, "What you gonner do? You won't give me the children, and I ain't gonner stay in no house with no man I ain't married to."

We went to Woodville on the eighteenth of September 1944 and was married. I didn't love Scott. I liked him, you know. Just liked him. I married him to be with those children. But I couldn't have got a better husband no kind of way. That's the truth. He's good and he been good all the way. I could of got a better-looking man and a better-educated man, and he'd of been beating me and throwed me in the river cause I'm kind of fussy sometime.

I was fifty and Scott was thirty-seven when we got married. Scott would go around here saying, "Old woman this and old woman that."

I would say, "Man, look in the mirror and see your gray head, please."

I know Scott's sixty-five. But you know Scott can't get his Social Security, and that's shameful. And the people that don't deserve it, they getting it. People lie and get it, and he tell the truth and can't get it. That's the way it goes.

Oh, I had hard times plowing, you know. I have plowed all week and on Saturday rode from Woodstock to Woodville to get my rations for the next week. I'd leave Saturday before daybreak, get my rations, come back, feed my horse, catch another, and go plow till sundown on Saturday. I did that. I got witnesses—white and black—to tell you that. I drove cattle up and down the Gin Place hill there, and men wouldn't do that.

I'm scared of a horse now. I look at a horse and wonder what I was thinking about, getting up on it. I wouldn't dare get on one now. People living today will tell you I could ride, rope, and do everything. The boys was mean to me, you know. I was so mannish, they couldn't do nothing with me. When the boss man ordered them to fix fence or drive cattle, they'd make me go. I didn't give a kick. I'd get my horse and go fix the fence. I oughta hate them for it, but I don't care. I'm glad I learned how to do stuff like that. It made me independent. I don't back down for nothing. The only thing stop me now is my knees. I got along with them because they didn't dish out a bit more than I could. I never had a fight or nothing in my life. Never been in court-house for nothing but to pay taxes and get mar-ried. I had friends go to jail, and they would say, "Come to see me."

I told them I wouldn't go in the jail unless I go for myself and I was trying to keep out. None of my people never went to jail. And Scott, I don't think he ever been. I had a good life cause I didn't mind working. And when I started working, what you think I was getting a day? Thirty cents. When I got fifty cents, I was rich.

I was hoeing and packing water to the hands. I remember one day Sister and Aunt Nettie was gonner have something at the church, and I wanted to go. They went and got new dresses. I said, "Momma, how's Sister getting a new dress like that?"

She said, "Well your sister working."

I had my cousin, Cap'n Jones. He was a big farmer, white man. I called him cousin. I caught the mare and had her tied out and said, "I'm going to the store, Momma."

"What you going to the store for?"

"I'll be back to reckon. Don't matter."

I caught Cap'n Jones. I said, "Cap'n Jones, Sister and Nettie getting dresses. I don't have no money, and I want a silk dress too."

He said, "Go in there and tell them to give you whatever money you need to get the dress."

I went in there and got the dress. Momma say, "Where you been?"

"I went to Cap'n Jones to get me some money to get me a dress. I'll work it out."

I could get anything I wanted. To get that money, I'd go and pick cotton. I could pick two hundred pounds of cotton in a day. I have worked, and I'm glad of it. I wish these young people had to do what I did.

# SCOTT DUNBAR

I worked for four bits a day back there. When I got big enough to saw them old big trees down, I got a dollar and a quarter a day. That's all they give you, a dollar and a quarter a day. Then I went to grafting them trees, sawing them limbs off to make them great big pecans. That was my job. They was paying good money for that. I started driving a tractor and bulldozing. I couldn't stand all that noise and stuff, and I quit that job. I came here to Lake Mary and went to fishing for a living.

A man from Gloucester come over here, and he wanted me to tend to a tent. I stayed over here and tended to his tent. He told me, "You stay here every month, and every two weeks I'll give you fifty dollars."

I tended to his tent and paddled him out in the boat. He kept coming down here till he died. He died yonder in Crosby. That's where he had a place. And I played the guitar for parties and things. Oh man, we had a time then. I was a little old boy then.

My momma and poppa didn't never let me go to school. They made me work. All my sisters and brothers, they went to school. Now I know more than them that went to school.

If I had went to school, oh Lord, no telling what I'd have been. But that's all saved me out of the army. I couldn't write. I went over to Camp Shelby, and they carried me in that office and put me at a little desk and said, "Now write what you think of the army, Scott."

All that was before my eyes was trees and girls, but I couldn't map that out right. I couldn't put it down straight. I ain't never went to school, you see. That man come and looked at the paper and say, "Boy, you ain't done nothing."

I said, "I told you I can't write. Anything else I'll do it but write. I can't write."

"You putting on, boy. You fooling me."

I say, "I shore ain't, Cap'n."

He say, "Look in this book."

He got one of them big old books that gave records where you went to school, and he flipped that book, and he couldn't find my record.

I say, "Flip it a little more, cause you ain't gonner find my record in there. Keep a'flipping that book."

That man kept flipping. "Boy, I believe you telling the truth."

I said, "I'm is. I ain't went to school. Come on down on Lake Mary. I'll carry you to them old folk, and you can ask them did they send me to school."

He says, "It's a shame they didn't let you go to school. They done wrong with you."

I say, "That's what I know."

He say, "Well come here. Let me show you how to write."

He was gonner show me. His hand was going like this and mine was shaking too, you see. Both of us hands shaking, and he supposed to be still. And know one thing? Me and him both had the rubber part down and the lead part sticking up. Gonner show me how to write. He

say, "Boy, you get out of here. I don't know what ails me."

I said, "Well you gonner show me. I'm just taking your word. I'm way over here. I'm a long way from home, and I'm doing what you say. Now you got to show me."

He say, "I can't do it. Ever time I fool with you, I get a nervous breakdown."

That grass was tall out there in Camp Shelby, and he told me to go out there and catch some air. I made two steps, and I was out there in my brand-new blue serge suit, laying flat on my back, looking up in the sky. The sun come up this way. That's the way it come up. It didn't come up the way it does here. They was so far back, it come from yonder way. And that made me lost. I was lost out there cause it come up that a'way. I'd wake up in the morning and see the sun coming up that a'way, and I'd know I was lost. That man asked me, "What you looking at?"

"I'm looking at the sun yonder, Cap'n. Where I stay down yonder on Lake Mary, it come from this way."

Them was the littlest trees I ever seen in my life. Even the womens was little. Like that little girl there, that's a grown woman down there. I said, "Say, girl, will you show me where to go around here. It's hot now. I want something to drink."

I say, "Are you a woman? Where I come from you would be a little old child. I'm lost now. I know I'm is. Say, woman. Will you show me where to go down here to get me a drink, beer or something? I'm just as thirsty as I can be."

I had done got hot in that room naked. All us boys was in that room—a row on this side and a row on that side—in the wintertime. Everybody had the chills. They teeth was knocking. It was cold, and I was just sweating up a breeze in the winter. Sweat was running from my ears to my toes. I was so worried till I was sweating up a breeze in the wintertime. The Cap'n was looking at me, and he say, "What you sweating for?"

"Man, I wanta know what you gonner do with me."

He say, "I tell you this. Ain't nothing for me to do with you but send you home."

That scared me. I ain't thought I could get back to Lake Mary from out there. I say, "Yes sir. I got to go. But you ain't through with me yet. You gotta carry me through them rooms and exanimate me and test me out. I don't know how to read and write. I'm liable to get over there and go in the wrong place."

Oh, I put it on some kind of way, and he said, "Go in yonder. Go in number 3 yonder."

That's what he told me. I say, "Yes sir. I don't know number 3."

"See all them signs on that door. You just walk up there and read."

"That's what I'm talking about. I can't read. You gotta show me which is number 2 or number 3 or what."

I knowed it alright cause I went in there. I just said that to try to get back to Lake Mary. Cap'n, he say, "Go in number 2."

When I went up yonder, he hollered, "Come back here. Don't you see them signs yonder?"

He was pointing me to it, and I'd get mostly

to it and go in the wrong door every time. He say, "I can't do nothing with him. He better go back home and rest a little bit more."

That made me feel good then. And all of them there, them was the tallest peoples I ever seen. They couldn't come in this house. They too tall. I was six foot tall, but they was too tall. He said, "They tell me it's a boy from Lake Mary can play a guitar."

I had a old white handkerchief and helt it up. Couldn't see myself for so many people. He say, "You come here and play."

I say, "Yes sir. What I'm gonner play, though? What you want?"

"I want that 'Pistol-Packing Momma.'"

"Yes sir. I don't know nothing about the 'Pistol-Packing Momma.'"

He said, "If I whistle it, you better play it, or you won't ever see home no more."

Oh, I got up on that guitar, and I went to doing something. Oh, I made that guitar come on in there to the "Pistol-Packing Momma." Just as far as you could see, they was clapping their hands. And the man announced it. He say, "Well I don't think he ever see home no more."

And Lord, when that man told me that, Cap'n, I tore up every string on that guitar. Every time I hit a tune, I'd pull up on them strings, and they'd break and holler, "Bang. Bang."

And I say, "Ain't but one string left."

He say, "Play on one."

I say, "I can't play on one. It takes six to play on. I can't play on one."

"Do something."

"I can't without I get drunk. Go get me some

beer. If I get drunk, I can hit on that one string, Cap'n. But I can't do nothing else."

That man looked at me, and he say, "You the worse one that ever been over here to Camp Shelby. You better go back home and rest, and I'll send for you later."

I say, "Yes sir."

He said, "Reckon you'll find Lake Mary."

"I sure couldn't find it without I was in a airplane."

He say, "Which a'way do you start home?"

I say, "I don't know. I don't know, sir. You got to show me."

He say, "If I give you a airplane, will you go home?"

I say, "That's the only way I'll find it. I'll fly over there till I see the lake, and I'll come down."

My partner, they had him in the room, and he couldn't squat. That's what tickled the whole thing, Cap'n. He couldn't squat. I never knowed nobody couldn't squat. My partner would get this far down, and that's as far as he could squat. He grunted, "Oh, I'm hurting all over, Cap'n. I can't squat."

The man say, "Squat down there, boy. Squat."

He'd get so far down, and he couldn't squat. It was in the wintertime. I was just falling out laughing. I said, "Man, squat. You know you can squat."

That man say, "Well how do you shit then?"

Oh boy. I got on my face and rolled. That man say, "You wait a minute."

That man went back there and got one of the long needles. I said, "I know if he give you a shot with that penicillin shot, you'll squat then."

That man seed that needle. Cap'n, he seed

that big needle, and he got down there good as I could. He could squat and do everything cause he didn't want that needle in him. That tickled me. And that man say, "I better let you go out of here, fellow. You the worst young fellow I ever see. I could keep you here."

I said, "Please don't keep me. Don't keep me here. Please."

They didn't allow you to have nothing on. I didn't know my clothes from nobody else's in them rooms. It was so many clothes. I reached up and put my clothes high, and some man come in there that was taller than me and put his clothes on top of mine. He said, "You got something on your wrist. You got to take it off."

I said, "If I take that off my wrist, I'll die. That ain't got anything to do with you. It got to do with me. Just let that white handkerchief stay around my wrist."

He say, "What ails your hand? I got something here to cure it."

I say, "Yes sir. I'd like for you to cure it, but that got to stay around there."

That was that money I had tied around there so nobody would take it. That man looked at me, and he say, "I believe you got something in that handkerchief."

I say, "I don't know if there's something in it. That's my luck if it is. It may be luck in that handkerchief, but I doubt if I'll take it off. You can do anything you want to me. Shoot me."

And them X-ray pictures that pick you up on your tiptoes, he sent me up to that. Oh, I was used to that. Pick you right up on your tiptoes. They raise up on it, and that thing just tick, tick, tick. Carry you right on up till you get on your tiptoes. And then you got to stand there. Oh, I could do that. He just kept a looking at my hand. He wanted me to take that handkerchief off. I say, "I can't. I told you I can't. I'm naked and don't know where my clothes are. You gotta find them. All these clothes. I had a navy blue serge suit, and outta all these clothes, how I'm gonner know mine?"

Another boy come in there, and he say, "Them my pants there, that navy blue serge suit."

I say, "Mind how you put your hand on it, son. That ain't none of your'n. Them old black pants up there are your'n. You know that suit ain't none of your'n. You see that handkerchief and that black hat up on top of it? You know them my clothes. Now, man, mind out. I'll fight you anyhow. Us naked people fight. You better put my clothes down."

He say, "It ain't so."

And he took them down and aimed to put them on. A little bitty old fellow, and he must have had some balls as big as my fist. I never seen so many different balls in my life. That's what made us feel good. I seen something I hadn't never seen. Everywhere I cast my eye, little fellows no bigger'n that one had balls look like a stag. I'm excited right now thinking about it. I backed over here to this wall, and he backed over to that one, and we was looking right at one another. I say, "Say, podner. Wheew, has you got something that big?"

He looked down and said, "Man, shut up. That man ought to be shamed to let us be naked in here."

I said, "But boy, you take the something.

Looka yonder. You be so little and got them things. Them's the biggest balls I seen in my life."

That man had one of them things what pick you up on the head, and he come through there, and he pick me up on the head. He said, "Now, Scott, what you doing over here?"

I say, "You got me over here with that little old piece of paper. What that little old piece of paper gonner tell you to do with me?"

"You gonner stay. Ain't nothing ails you. You might as well to stay."

I said, "Yes sir. I don't think so."

He say, "Yeah, you got to stay. You got to stay. You just go on out yonder and get your clothes right now cause me and you got to have a talk."

See, that man knowed me, and he done me a favor when he said put my clothes on. Them other people said, "How bout me, Cap'n. I'm chilly here, and even my balls cold."

He say, "I ain't got nothing to do with that."

I say, "Boy, mine is sweating up a breeze. I need to get in a bathtub the way I'm sweating. I don't know what ails y'all."

Some of them was crying, "Hee. Hee. Hee. I want to go back home and see my wife and baby. I left my wife at home. She about to have a baby, and I'm dying."

That man say, "You better shut up."

I said, "Man, y'all quit crying in here. It's more than sad news cause us don't know which way us gwine yet. Y'all better quit that crying. I left my baby and wife home too, but now what can I do bout it? Y'all quit crying."

That man say, "Wait. I got something here to make all them what cry quit crying."

That man come through there with that needle what put you to sleep. Them colored people didn't want that needle. I know I didn't. Ever now and then that man sends me a letter from over there saying I oughta come back. I told him I'd never come without he come and get me. I said, "I done got too old now. Please don't tell me that."

I enjoyed that. I had a good time over there. And that dime beer, I couldn't get enough of that. It wadn't but a dime, and it was in them little old short bottles. As fast as you drink one, look like that woman couldn't reach it to me fast enough. I told them, "That's the best beer I ever drunk."

The whole while I was there, I had to run from here to way up yonder and turn in. You got to run. I was the leader, and I was running in the lead. Hear the foots going like cows and mules. I never heard that in my whole life till I got over there. Clap, te clap, te clap, running one into the other'n just like a drove of cows. And get up there and turn and double back, and then you bop down on that table. Oh, that beat all I ever seen, Cap'n. When I got to that table, I couldn't eat a thing. Oh, them scrambled eggs and milk. They had me so I couldn't eat a thing. I just filled up on that beer. That beer kept me living, Cap'n, till I got back to Mississippi. I got back to Woodville.

It was the cleanest place you ever see. I didn't never pick up a matchstick till I got over there. They had all of us in a row like cows to go along and pick up matchsticks. And I hadn't ever picked up a matchstick. I don't smoke. They had us in all them bushes over there picking up matchsticks. They say, "Everybody here gotta pick up matchsticks."

Before we started, I went and filled my shirt pockets up with matchsticks. I filled them up. Every time you passed the can, you had to throw something in that can. Every fellow passed in a row from here to yonder. I dropped my matches in and just kept a'strutting. That man watched me. I'd bow, but I'd never get down. I'd keep going till I got to the next trash can. Some men was eating pinders [peanuts]—just like a hog eat corn—and dropping them hulls down on the ground. They made us come back and pick up the pinder hulls. That got me. I say, "Man, you oughta be shamed eating them pinders, and us got to pick them up. You oughta pick them up yourself."

That man come with that little "toot, toot," blowing that whistle. He asked who dropped the pinder hulls. "Who dropped them? They gonner pick them up."

I say, "Yes sir. I know. I ain't eat no pinder. I ain't had none. Yon' the man dropped them. See yonder. See his mouth full of hulls and everything."

He told that man, "Come here. Pick up them hulls."

He say, "Cap, I'm so hungry. I'm eating the hulls and everything, and I can't help it."

"Well you pick them up. If you don't, I'm going back and get something, and when I get through with you, you'll pick them up."

I said, "Man, you better get them hulls up. I'm gonner get over here so I can scat out the way."

Cap'n got the whip. I seed that, and I got over there in the corner. When he seen that, the man took his hands and brushed them pinder hulls up.

I was a little child when me and three or four boys put a bell on that buzzard. In them days, when I was little, everything that roar, them old folks would say, "That's the Lord coming. The Lord is coming."

And you had to get on your knees and pray. If you didn't pray, they'd hit you on the head with a stick. They was right across Lake Mary. I said, "Y'all old folks got too much religion. Y'all know that's a boat or airplane or something. Y'all old folks got too much religion for me."

Me and a bunch of boys found a buzzard down in a stump hole. We went there and caught that buzzard, put a string around his neck, and pulled him up out the stump where he was laying on his nest. Another fellow brought a bell, and he held the buzzard while I tied the bell to the string around his neck. We turned that old buzzard loose, and he went up in the air with that old bell hollering, "Jing a'ling. Jing a'ling."

Them old people went to hollering, "Oh boy. I told you the world coming to a end. Don't you hear the Lord calling you? The world coming to a end."

Every time that buzzard flapped his wings, that bell would "jing a'ling, jing a'ling."

It did sound stressful, and that made that old buzzard like to run hisself to death, that bell round his neck. He would get up higher and higher and higher. He would get up so high till you couldn't hardly glimpse that buzzard. You just could hear that racket up in the air hollering, "Jing a'ling. Jing a'ling."

Them old folks would peep out the door. "Oh Lord, have mercy. You told me You coming. You told me You coming. Ain't nobody like Jesus."

And the sun just hot as it is today. I say, "Y'all folks sweating now, but y'all ain't sweat yet. Y'all quit that hollering bout that's the Lord. Y'all hush."

"You don't know what you talking bout, boy. Shut up."

They'd hit you right in the mouth. I had to get down on my knees and sit there and laugh under my little knee pants. Just sit there and laugh. They better not hear you laugh. I said, "That's a shame these folks got so much religion here. A buzzard in the air hollering, 'Jing a'ling. Jing a'ling,' and they hollering, 'Oh, here come the Lord.'"

"Shut up. I hear the Lord coming. Be still, chillun."

If you was biting on a piece of bread, you had to keep your mouth still. They was just that scared. Here come a preacher with a Bible. Everybody was sweating and hot, and here he come. He wanted that money that night. He was gonner preach that sermon about the Lord going through the air hollering, "Jing a'ling."

Everybody got on the gallery and said, "How do you do?"

Oh, they "mister" that preacher. "How you do, Mister Preacher? What you gonner preach on tonight?"

"Let me tell all y'all sisters. Come here."

The people was hot and hungry, and he rared back on that porch with his coat and necktie on. "You hear that something flying through the air?"

"Yes sir, Preacher. Yes sir, Preacher."

"I been up there, and I talked to the Man. The Man say, 'All them ain't got religion, I'll send something down there and make them kill theyself.'"

I say, "Yeah, and you bout to kill yourself. You know you ain't been up yonder. How you get up there if you ain't had no wings to fly? How you get up there?"

"Boy, shut up. That's the preacher."

I say, "Momma, you don't know if he a preacher or what. Go kill that chicken and give him some thighs, and he'll preach alright. He's talking about that thing up in the air going 'jing a'ling, jing a'ling.'"

Oh man. Sundown couldn't come fast enough. Everybody went to church that night. That preacher started off with "Amen. I went up there in a chariot. I went up yonder, and I told Him to make something go through the sky to make the people get right. They ain't right."

When he say that, them old sisters, they say, "Woooo. Woooo. Woooo."

I mean some fainted so till their dresses come up over their heads. Up over their heads, and us just laying back laughing. "Say, woman, pull your dress down. You ain't got that much religion. Keep it down. Something else coming off direckly to shame you with your dresses up there."

I said, "That's a shame. Y'all better keep them dresses down fore something happen here."

That preacher, he looked at that woman with that dress up and said, "Amen."

Everybody was setting there saying, "Yeah, Preacher. You know what you talking about."

After a while, when it got sort of quiet, that buzzard come down low over the church, and that old bell was hollering, "Jing a'ling. Jing a'ling."

"Don't you hear him? Don't you hear him out there? Let's get outdoors and see what that is."

"That's the Lord."

And that old buzzard just "jing a'ling," and them people just hollering and carrying on. And us kids just sitting there laughing. They had some ice water there in a bucket, and one woman fainted so till she couldn't hardly move. A great big woman. I knowed the onlest thing to get her cured was to get a bucket of ice water, throw it up under her dress, and let it run over her. When that ice water hit her, that woman jumped straight up in the air and hollered, "Weeoo. That ain't the Lord, is it? Let me get up from here."

I said, "Y'all cut this sermon off cause I'm gonner talk now. Y'all people hush your mouth and let us talk. Y'all don't know what that is going through the sky? Say, Preacher, you the main one. You say you went up there?"

"Yeah, boy."

I say, "I ain't no boy now. You ain't went nowhere. How did you get up there, Preacher?"

"Boy, I went up there with a Indian."

"A Indian ain't never went up there. No kind of Indian went up yonder with God. That ain't it yet. You got all these people here crazy by you preaching a sermon for what us boys done. Us boys done this here for to fool y'all. What y'all gonner do now? Us put that bell on that buzzard and sent him through the sky. Y'all wadn't doing right. Y'all had too much religion. Everything

you hear roaring, you get out there and holler, 'Here come the Lord.' Airplane, 'Here come the Lord.' Everything. Couldn't a motor or nothing run without 'That's the Lord coming.' All y'all sisters and brothers here now, y'all just go back home and study about something else."

"Boy, us oughta kill y'all. Us like to killed us fool selves here listening at the preacher."

I said, "That's what I wanted y'all to do cause y'all like to killed us. Everything come along, y'all hit us in the head. My head sore now from y'all knocking me in the head and talking about the Lord coming."

Nowadays with all the cars coming, I reckon they would have killed us.

It was a man betted me once I couldn't swim cross Lake Mary. When I was little, I could swim cross to this side and back over there to the other'n. That was a mile swim from here over yonder and back. That man told me, "Now I got fifty dollars. You swim from over yonder and back, and you can have it."

I said, "Yes sir. That's a'plenty money, ain't it? I believe I'll try it."

I jumped in that river, and I went on cross there. I got out there, and something eased right tween these legs. That thing got tween my legs, and I hugged it. You know that thing just carried me on cross that river. I don't know if it was a alligator or what, but I thought I was dead. When I got over to the other side, I said, "Thank God for whatever that was. He shore done helped me on my journey. I shore am glad he didn't bite me."

That man hollered on this side, "What you swimming so fast for?"

"Man, something was behind me. I had to move up."

"I never seen nobody move that fast."

"Well that thing helped me on my journey. You just have the fifty dollars when I get back there."

I got up in a tree and rested a little bit. After I rested, I took a little piece of board and put between my legs to come back. That helped hold me up to come back cross that long journey. I got almost to the bank, and then I kicked the board out from under me, and I come onto the bank. I got to the bank, and this man said, "You didn't win that fifty dollars right. Here's fifty more that says I'll swim it."

I said, "You'll never make it, Cap'n."

He said, "Let's take a drink."

He had a gallon of that old moonshine liquor down there. I was ready to drink cause I had made my journey. I knowed he wadn't gonner make his journey without no boat following him. I was laughing and drinking, and he got in that river. His wife was up on the hill and said, "Earl, don't go in there. Please, Earl, don't go in there. Don't go in there."

Earl went in the water there. She said, "God damn you. You drown then. If he drown, Scott, don't get him."

I say, "I ain't gonner let him drown cause I'm gonner follow him in the boat."

I got in the boat. He didn't know I was going along behind him paddling, but I know he wadn't gonner make it. He got about ten steps out in the river, this white man, and his hair got to standing up on his head. I know if he go under three time, he gonner drown. I said to myself, "That's a hundred dollars I done won off that man. He bet it, and it ain't none of my money."

I just pulled him into the boat. That man lay there and wadn't breathing, and I say, "Mr. Earl?"

He ain't said nothing. "I'm gonner give you your money back."

"What you say?"

"I want you to come to life cause you ain't gonner get that money back. You playing dead."

His wife hollered out and say, "Scott, throw him overboard. Let that son of a gun drown. I don't want him nohow."

"I don't want him to drown in Lake Mary while I'm here, miss. You just carry him home and throw him in a pond."

"I'll kill him if he come back here."

I say, "Don't pull that pistol on me. Just wait till us get up on the hill, and then you can shoot him."

His wife, she the one had the money, and she told me, "I'm gonner give the money to you, but let him drown."

"No ma'am. I ain't gonner drown your husband out here. I got him in the boat."

"Throw him out of there. Throw him out of there. If he comes up that hill, I'm gonner kill him cause I told him not to go out there swimming. He done lost all his money, and that's us last hundred dollars."

I say, "Oh, his daddy got a'plenty of it. I ain't worried."

His daddy come down here the next day and

asked me, "What you done to my boy and his wife?"

"I ain't done nothing. He bet me fifty dollars I couldn't swim cross Lake Mary, and I went cross there and made that fifty. And I bet fifty more he couldn't swim. The best thing for you to do is go back home. You got a'plenty of money. Go there to his wife, and tell her I sent the hundred dollars back to her."

He had a'plenty of money, and I told him what to do with the boy's wife. He went back there and give her a hundred and said I sent it. That next day him and her was down here. She come down here and say, "Scott, that's nice of you to send us money back. I had left the son of a gun and felt like killing him, but that solved the problem."

"Thank God. Don't let him bet no more. That gonner kill him."

Another white man asked me to paddle him in a skiff from here to way up there in Lake Mary. In them days they had a pair of oars in a skiff. You had to have wind to pull. I pulled from right here to up there at Homochitto, four miles up there. Got up there to Homochitto and come back, and he had left the car in the hot sun with a bucket of syrup in it. We come back and got almost to the bank, and he was telling me about the bucket of syrup. He say, "That syrup too good to give you cause you ain't worth a bucket of syrup. Them syrup the best syrup I ever seed in my life. If you was worth them syrup, fellow, you'll be a good one. But today, you ain't worth a bucket of syrup."

I say, "Yes sir. That is all I'm worth? When I get up to that car, them syrup gonner fly all up in the air. They gonner shoot sky-high cause they hear what you telling me. I know I'm worth more than a bucket of syrup. Man, don't tell me that."

He had left the car in the hot sun. I was so tired and mad too cause he told me I wadn't worth a bucket of syrup. He got up there and opened the top of that syrup, and that syrup shot sky-high and went all over his car. He said, "I'll declare. I said you ain't worth a bucket of syrup. Come up here. Don't you want to pick 'em up?"

"Man, I don't lick up no syrup. You told me that I ain't worth a bucket of syrup."

"Go down there and get some water, and let's wash it out."

I say, "I declare if that's so. You gonner carry that car back to where you got it from and let the hose pipe wipe it out. I ain't gonner tote no water up the hill."

And the flies about to take the car. I say, "I'm gonner see if you worth a bucket of syrup to get down there and tote that water up that hill."

That water was way down that hill. He got down there and got to panting. "Well I be doggone. This is the hottest job I ever had in my life."

"You sweat a little bit. I sweated on them paddles, and I'm gonner lay right up here under this shade tree."

"You ain't gonner help me?"

"No. I can't help a fellow if I ain't worth a bucket of syrup. Them syrup gotta go back where the people can see your car."

Everybody come down here told me it took concentrate lye to get them syrups out of that man's car. And they asked what did I do that for. I said, "God done that. God done that for him cause he said I wadn't worth a bucket of syrup."

He calls me Lightning. Every time I see that man, he say, "Aw, Lightning."

I call him Slim.

"Alright, Slim."

He told me, "You know that car ruined till today. I told you bout the bucket of syrup, and I'll never tell nobody that no more. When I come out here again, I'll set my syrup outdoors. I'll set them under a tree. Won't get in my car no more."

"Well don't bring me none. I ain't worth a bucket of syrup, and I don't want a bucket of them syrups. I don't like them nohow."

He come up after the syrup flew and say, "Well I gotta give you a little money. The syrup gone."

I say, "Yes sir. The money liable to fly out your hand too if you say I ain't worth it. You better not say that. If you do, it'll fly out your hand."

You know that man aimed to get the money out his pocket. His pocketbook dropped, and he didn't know where it was. I was standing right over the top of it. I said, "I told you that money gonner fly."

"Lightning, I believe you's a durn hoodoo. You a hoodoo, Lightning. You go away from here. Please help me find my pocketbook so I can pay you and go home cause I'm nervy. I don't know what ails me."

"I told you that in that boat. I told you that if you said I wadn't worth a bucket of syrup, something was gonner happen to you. You can't even pick up your pocketbook. There it is on the ground. Pick it up. Pick it up."

Oh that man was crying. I said, "I'm glad I didn't come up there cause that syrup would have got on my old black hat. I didn't want it on there, and flies coming on me."

That was the ticklest thing I ever seen.

I wish I was a jaybird in the air.
I'd build my nest up in some big house.

*In those days the momma didn't allow you to speak to the daughter. The daughter be here and the momma in the back. You go to the house and the momma ask you, "Son, you come to see me? You ain't come to see my daughter, son."*

*I shore didn't come to see her. I come to see the daughter, I didn't come to see the momma. I said, "Alright. Set down, Momma."*

I wish I was a jaybird in the air.

*"How you like that, Momma? How you like that, Momma?"*

I'd build my nest up in some big house.

*"What you say now, Momma. How about it, Momma?" Oh, she setting up there with her head down. "Wake up, Momma. Wake up."*

I wish I was a jaybird in the air.

*See, Momma can't hear what I tell her now. "What that you told my daughter, son? I was looking at you. You can't fool this old woman. You told her something."*

I say, "I ain't told her nothing. Nothing but 'hello.' That's all I told her, 'hello.'"

"You told her something else."

"Oh Momma. Be shamed."

I wish I was a jaybird in the air.
My momma told me, my poppa told me too.
I wish I was a jaybird in the air.

*Alright, the old momma fixing to go to sleep now. I had a quart of that old moonshine liquor too. I'm gonner put her to sleep now, where I can talk to the daughter. I reach down here and get this old quart of liquor. "Help yourself, Momma."*

*Momma turned it up to her mouth. Droop. Droop. Droop. I know she'll go to sleep now alright.*

I wish I was a jaybird in the air.

*She going to sleep now. Setting up there with her mouth wide open. Oh, I got her now.*

My momma told me I never would die.

*Oh, Momma gone. Bout to break her neck. I got you, Momma. I got to get with the girl now. I'll tell her something now. Me and her got to get the talk out now.*

*"If I was you, Momma, I'd shore lay down."*

*Old Momma asleep now, and me and her get her up and carry her way over there in the bed. Lay her on the bed and put a white sheet around her neck, and me and her coming over here and set down. Here we go.*

I wish I was a jaybird in the air.
I wish I was a jaybird in the air.
My momma told me I'd never die.

*By the time we got that, here come the old poppa. "Oh son. Twelve o'clock now. Time for you to go home now."*

*I say, "Let me look at my watch. The night just a baby."*

*I pulled my watch out, and it was twelve o'clock alright. I wadn't ready to go then, you see. "Son, I been working hard, and I got to take some sleep. Where the old lady?"*

*"She over yonder. I done put her to sleep. You set down here, old man. I know you tired. Don't you want you a drink?"*

*"Yes indeed. I want me a drink. That'll do me all the good."*

*"Help yourself. Help yourself."*

*That old man turned that bottle up and glook, glook, glook. After a while he sat it down.*

I wish I was a jaybird in the air.

*He setting, and I could hear him snoring. That's the old man. I got him now. "Wake up, old man."*

*I got him. I get him and walk over and lay him in the bed side his wife. Him and his wife with her mouth wide open talking about "Coook."*

*Just look at the old lady. Just look at the old lady.*

I wish I was a jaybird in air, the air.

*She sitting here just laughing to herself. I say, "You know it twelve o'clock now and it ain't gonner be long fore daylight. I had two little old fried chickens out in the car. "I'm hungry now. You go out in the kitchen and I'm gonner still play the guitar. Them old folks may wake up."*

*If that chicken wadn't gonner wake them up, I know they wadn't gonner wake up cause that moonshine had them dead to the world. I look over there at that old man, and I hear that old man snoring. Hooo.*

I wish I was a jaybird in the air.

*I look at her and she come over with the fried chicken. I ain't never quit playing now. She brought the fried chicken in there. Me and her ate up one and left the other one for the old folks. I sat there at the table and ain't never quit playing. Eating chicken and playing just like I'm doing now. I'd bite off a piece, and she'd put it in my mouth like that. Time come, and it was broad open daylight, and I say, "I better quit. I better get out of this house."*

*Well them old T-model cars, if you go out there and crank them up, they go like they got a cutout on them. I went out there to crank that old T-model, and she went off, "Brrrrr." I had it running, and I come on back in the house, and I called the old folks. "Y'all wake up, old folks. Daylight. Time to go to the fields."*

*"Oh son. I'm shore glad to see you."*

*And I ain't went nowhere. I ain't never left the house. "I'm shore glad to see you. Come on in. What your car running out there for?"*

*"Well it getting hot, and I want to let it bile up a little bit."*

*I was just getting it cranked up to take off, you see. I say, "Here y'all some fried chicken I brought y'all."*

*"Yeah, Poppa. He brought the chicken and cooked it for y'all's breakfast."*

*"Thank God. Let's eat and go to the field. Alright, son. Us got to go to the field."*

*"I got to go home now, Poppa."*

*I got out there in that old T-model, and I cocked them two levers down, and she come off towards the river then.*

I wish I was a jaybird in the air.

I made that one up. That's the jaybird in the air. I made that one about how you cut out the momma and the poppa so you can talk to the daughter.

# LORMAN

I met Louis and Addie Mae Dotson in the late sixties while doing field recordings near Lorman. The Dotsons lived on a hill at the end of a dirt road a mile to the east of Highway 61. A vegetable garden and peach trees provided much of their food. They bought staples like coffee, sugar, salt, and pepper at the Brassfield country store a mile south of their home. The store was also a place to socialize with neighbors as they sat on benches in the front, watching passing traffic and exchanging news.

Louis Dotson introduced me to the one-strand guitar that he learned to play as a child. He showed me how he unwound the wire from a broom handle and attached it to the front wall of his home. He plucked the wire with a metal object while he slid a small bottle up and down to change its pitch.

Dotson's one-strand guitar is related to African one-strand instruments and is an important reminder of how African musical roots survive in the American South. Because it was easily accessible and cost nothing, many blues artists—including B. B. King—played the one-strand guitar as a child. The instrument influenced the bottleneck guitar style popularized by blues performers Elmore James and "Mississippi" Fred McDowell. Today, the bottleneck style is used by musicians like Eric Clapton, Bonnie Raitt, and Keith Richards. The one-strand instrument was sometimes called the diddley bow.

Louis Dotson also showed me how he "blew the bottle." Using either a small Dr. Tichenor's Antiseptic bottle or a larger Coca-Cola bottle, he changed his pitch by adding water to the bottle. Sometimes called "whooping the bottle," the tradition inspired jug bands that were popular in Memphis and other parts of the South in the early twentieth century. When Dotson blew the bottle, he used the bottle as an echo chamber for his voice, and the sound bore a strong resemblance to the Ba Benzele pygmie yodel in Africa.

When I first met the Dotsons in 1968, I recorded and filmed Louis playing his one-strand-on-the-wall with my Super 8 camera. Later in 1973, Judy Peiser and I made a film *Bottle Up and Go* on the lives of the Dotsons.

This interview is compiled from interviews done in the Dotsons' home in 1968 and 1973.

# LOUIS DOTSON

You know, I never did like the city. I always liked to be in the sticks. I just don't like to be in no town. I've been to Jackson, Natchez, Vicksburg, and Tallulah. When I go there, I'll just get what I'm going after, then come right on back out. I won't stay there. I head right for home. I like Tallulah best, but I wouldn't stay over there. It's too low there for me. When that water gets up out of the river, it takes all of that town with it.

I'd rather be in the country than be in town. A person could go into a town and ask for some- body, and if they ain't got the house number, the street number, they'd never know where they were. You'd just be blundering around all over that town. But in the country, people know other people.

In town, you can't even find your own kin- folks. My wife Addie Mae went to Jackson once to see her cousin. He lives on Pascagoula Street. That's all she knew. So she went there and asked them if they knew her cousin, Arthur Menefee. Everybody told her they didn't know nothing about that name. She didn't know his house number. So she just fooled around there on his street, and finally he come out. That's the way she finally found him, just by passing him on the street. In town, they ain't going to tell you nothing about nobody. Not even about your own people. That was in Jackson. And I imagine it's the same in any other big city.

I like it in the country. I don't get lonesome here. There always be some company around. See, right here in this community, it's all family

people—my sister, my brother-in-law, my auntie, and my sister's oldest daughter. And the kids would rather be in the country where they can run over the hills and holler and play. I haven't ever been nowhere I'd like to live but right around here in Lorman.

I was born on April 25, 1917, in Franklin County, Mississippi. My mama and my daddy was born here too. And that's where I was raised. My people moved up here to Lorman, and they brought me with them. I was just a kid, and I had to follow. I had seven sisters and eight brothers. There were sixteen of us children. My father, he farmed and he logged. He raised cot- ton, corn, sweet potatoes, peas, and peanuts. He had good gardens. My father wasn't no lazy man. He always liked to be doing something. My mama was the same way.

I got through the first and second grades in school. I had to walk about four miles. It was on gravel too, and my feet would be so sore that I could hardly stand on them. It was just too far. When I was twelve or thirteen year old, I started picking cotton. I made me some knee pads and put them on, and I went to picking cotton on my knees. I picked 250 pounds some days.

I remember I used to get up and make coffee for my daddy when he had to go to work. He would get up around four o'clock in the morning and say, "Get up, son, and make me some coffee and fix my lunch for me. Mama's sick. She ain't able to get up. So you get up and fix my lunch. I got to go to work and try to make it for you all."

So I'd get up and wash my face, go into the kitchen, put the pot on the stove for coffee, and fix his lunch. We'd get that ground coffee, you know. You'd put a little cornmeal in it after you'd ground it, and you'd put it in the pot and put the cup under the bottom of it to catch it when it ran out down there. I'd fix me a little cup of coffee too and put it on the side, out of the way. Then I'd bring him a cup, and he'd say, "Well I'll save you a little swallow from my cup, son." He didn't know that I'd had me a cup already.

I can cook most anything I want to, and I can clean house. I can do all of that.

Ever since I was a little bit of a boy, I used to blow the bottle. Me and another boy, name of Richard Coleman, used to blow them Coca-Cola bottles. He was a little older than I was. We was raised up together. We'd be down there at Brass-field's Store all the time. Richard used to live on one hill, and I lived on another one. We'd blow them bottles to call one another. See, when I'd blow in the bottle and whoop in it, he'd know what I meant. If he'd blow in his and whoop in it, I'd hear him, and I'd go to him. We'd meet up then, see. We'd always carry a bottle around with us so we'd be able to get to one another. We called that "talking the bottle." See, you have to fill that Coke bottle a little over half full of water. You can blow and whoop in it then. If you don't have the water in it, it takes up too much air, and you can't do no whooping.

Sometimes we'd leave home, and Mama'd tell us what to do for our work. She'd say, "You'd better not go nowhere until you get your work done, you hear? If you do, I'm going to skin you!"

But we'd slip off anyhow. I'd go to blowing my bottle. Richard, he'd go to blowing his, and we'd meet up. But when I got back there to the house, Mama'd sure put it on me. She'd have that switch in the corner, waiting. And she'd go to working on me with that switch. My mother would always tell me, "You all better not let sun-down catch you away from here."

So when that sun started to fall over that west corner yonder, we'd get back for the night. If we were a great distance away, we'd have to run so we could be home when that sun got hid.

I used to work down at Harrison County cutting logs, burning logs, loading logs. That was for pulpwood. I worked at the box factory in Port Gibson too. You know, when I was logging, I could take an ax and just stand off from a tree and throw that ax, and it would stick in that tree with the handle down. We sawed with them old crosscut saws then. I would hang my saw up on that ax, and it'd stay there until the next morning. Those saws used to be called "old thousand legs." You see them now sometimes. People got them hanging up in their houses. We'd take them things and cut logs all day long. They had a handle on each end. But now they cut logs with them power saws.

When I moved over here, there wasn't a fruit tree on this hill. Not no kind. Now I got thirteen peach trees, apricot trees, and one little apple tree. I planted all that. I bought peaches from different people off these trucks. I just throwed them seeds on the ground, and they started coming up. That's how I come to having them peach trees. They bear pretty good. We don't never sell none. We just give people peaches when they come to the house. And I set them chinaberry trees out too. They're for shade trees. I put them trees out there, and they just growed up and spreaded out. So now it's cool on the porch. Anytime you go there, it's cool.

Addie Mae, she's the one that works the garden. She always plants three days before or three days after the full moon. If you want okra to start blooming right from the ground on up, you got to let a little chap plant it. He's got to squat down as low as he can get to the ground when he plants it. If you let a young child plant it, it'll start fruiting from the ground. See, if you just take it and stand straight up and plant it, the okra is going to get just as tall as you are before it starts to bloom. My grandbaby planted that okra back there for me.

I enjoy making different little things. I make fish boxes, them little old cages you tote in your hand when you go fishing. You use them to put your fish inside, down in the water. You make them out of a piece of wire. You take you a little piece of screen, and you make it so you can open it and shut it up again. You put a little bit of chain on it, fasten it onto the cage, and just drop it down in the water. When you catch a fish, you put him in that box and set your top down on it. Can't no snake get in there. Your fish stay fresh, and when you carry him home he'll still be alive. I make me dip nets to catch minnows too. They're made out of screen wire. You spread the net open and lay it down in the water. When the minnows come up there, you can just pick them right up. I catch minnows in that ditch down there by the big pond. If you want to catch catfish, you fish on the dark moon. An old fellow told me, "Catfish bite on the dark moon."

Sometimes you can throw your hook out there, and by the time you get it out, a fish already took your hook. There be some in there big as a buffalo [fish]. At night you can see them jump up out of the water, then just turn bottom-up-ards right in the middle of that pond. We got bass and catfish in that pond over there. But the secret to good fishing is patience. They'll bite minnows and earthworms and crickets, and they'll bite these artificial baits too. I had a reel I used to use, but I ain't got no reel now. It got burned up in the house fire. Using a plain old cane fishing pole is alright. But I haven't been fishing in about a month. Been so dry, we couldn't find nothing to fish with. They say it's good luck to spit on your bait when you put it on your hook. Sometimes it don't help none. It just takes patience.

I like to make little feed cups for the chickens. I made me a good henhouse with nests for them. I put plenty of dry grass in the nests so they can lay.

I've been living in this house twenty-one years. Charlie Patten, he put this house up. His wife is my sister. I was sick at the time, and I wasn't able to do nothing. If I had built it my-self, it would of been built better than this. I'd call this a little bungalow. If you'd like, you could add two more rooms on this one. We lived right down the road for seven years before we moved here.

I been playing the harmonica a long time. I used to keep it in my pocket when I was going

to the woods working. I used to play a Jew's harp too. And I could play piano pretty good. I used to play a guitar. But one instrument I never could play was a fiddle. I never could do nothing with a fiddle. I used to be a pretty good tap dancer. That was in my younger days. I had some plates on the toes and heels of my shoes. I could get out there on that floor, and I could get right with that music, right there with it. That'd be at a juke, at them old country balls. I'd go a lot to them juke joints. There'd always be tap dancing going on there, and I'd step right in there with them. They paid me too. I'd say, "I ain't going to tap dance for nothing. It takes something to tap dance. It's hard to do."

So they would pay me. Carl and Felix Williams was brothers, and they had a juke house back behind that brick church over there. I remember they'd have records that people would play. They'd have them old blues, them old hard blues. They'd have them breakdown blues too. And they'd play them old tap dance pieces. There'd be a lot of us out there dancing— womens and mens. You could catch them by the hands and set them spinning around and not miss a lick. You'd keep right up with it.

My daddy used to play music. He used to play all the time. That's how I learned to play the guitar. After he died, the other boys, they took the guitar. I couldn't get another one. So I decided to put me up a wire. I just call it "part of a guitar." It's a one-string guitar, but it sounds like it's got six strings on it.

It's been a long time ago when I made the first one. I didn't have no radio then. I had to have some music. So I put me a one-strand up,

and I made my own music. I started making one-strands when I was young. I was about twenty-some years old then. I never did see nobody do that. I just took it up my own self. Nobody else around here can play it but me. People, they come and listen to me. They say they don't see how I can do it.

I used to be sitting up here at the house, and they all would be out working. I'd be lonesome here by myself. I got to sitting down and thinking, and I said, "Well I'm going to put one up there and try it. Let's see what I can make out of it."

I put it up there up on the side of the house, and it sounded pretty good. At first I tried it on that tree out there, but it wouldn't give no kind of sound. So I put it on the wall of the house. It's got to be upside of the house, else it ain't going to play. You put it upside of this wall, and it'll play. I'd say the house must give a sound to it. Like with a guitar, you hear the sound of that box. I say the house must have the sound in it.

Me and another boy used to put us up a one-strand side by side and play blues. He'd have his and I'd have mine, and we'd be playing together. A lot of the youngsters would come and dance. They had some sort of dance they called the snake hip. That was just a little old light two-step. We'd make a good tune up there, and they'd be dancing right along. We used to have plenty of fun.

You get your wire off a broom handle. Just unwind it from around the handle and cut it off. Broom wire is the only wire that plays. Any other kind of wire won't work. I tried every other kind of wire, but it won't work. I've tried wire off a fence. I tried hay wire. It just wouldn't play. It's funny the way that you can take an ordinary broom wire, and it sounds like it's near six strings.

First you put a staple up yonder, wrap your wire around it, and put you a brick up there. Then you put you a nail or a little bolt on that brick so your wire don't touch that brick. You pull that wire real tight. You get your tightening from the bottom. You've got to knock it down until you get the wire real tight. That keeps it from growling on you. It'll sound louder the tighter it is. You got to pull it just as tight as you can get it. The tighter it is, the better it plays. If it's real slack, it ain't going to do nothing. If you have it real tight, it's going to play. If you get it tight enough, it'll talk. I use a castor oil bottle to note it. It has a little higher ridge on the corners, and that makes that wire sound louder. It works better on the one-string. It'll play most anything you want. I learned different pieces. I play "Sitting on Top of the World," "Bottle Up and Go," "Vicksburg on a High Hill and Louisiana Just Below," "Forty-four Blues," "Going Down to New Orleans and Get Me a Mojo Hand," "Monday Morning Blues," and "When the Saints Go Marching In."

Some of them I heard on the radio. As for TV, I watch just the news on it. When the news is over, I be through with it. I really likes the radio. I listen from four o'clock in the morning until daylight. I like radio because I can catch good spirituals on the radio. But I'll tell you, one thing I never got is religion. I say when you die, your soul dies too. That's right. That preacher can't preach to you up there in heaven, so he can't preach to you down here. There's no need of me walking up behind the preacher and telling him what I got and what I ain't got. I just don't have no religion. But I decided I'd get just as far as the next fellow. All you have to do is treat everybody right.

# CENTREVILLE

Fannie Bell Chapman was a charismatic faith healer who composed gospel music that she sang at religious ceremonies she conducted in Centreville. Centreville was also the home of Anne Moody, whose book *Coming of Age in Mississippi* chronicled her struggles during the civil rights movement.

Chapman was part of a long, important tradition of black women who sang and healed outside the male-dominated church. Denied access to the pulpit, these women became spiritual healers who performed their own religious ceremonies. They took their healing into the streets and back roads of their community and had a significant impact on their followers.

Chapman described her healing ceremony as "a hallelujah time." During the ceremony, the spirit descended and people were possessed, some spoke in tongues, and Chapman healed the sick. During one memorable ceremony in her living room, the floor began to shake as worshippers danced. Chapman continued to sing as she waved her hand and summoned dancers out of the house and into her backyard, where she continued the ceremony.

I first met Fannie Bell Chapman when I was recording blues singers around Centreville in the late sixties. I recorded her gospel music and interviewed Chapman and her family. Impressed by the quality of her music, I returned in 1972 with Judy Peiser and made a documentary film on Chapman and her family entitled *Fannie Bell Chapman, Gospel Singer* that was produced by the Center for Southern Folklore.

As a folklorist, I was deeply influenced by Chapman. She told me I had "power eyes" and that with help from her I could have the power to heal with my eyes. She said, "I know because I have that same power."

Chapman told me that she also had the power to control weather and could summon a thunderstorm. While she could do more than heal if she wished, she chose to only use her healing powers. We had a very special relationship for which I am grateful.

Chapman kept her large backyard swept clean. The yard was an extension of her house, an outdoor room shaded by trees. Here she taught her grandchildren games, served them food, visited with friends and family, and held healing ceremonies. The space provided a cool, natural environment for both daytime and nighttime activities.

A gospel-singing band drawn from a single family is common in the South. Family groups who perform sacred music range from the nationally known Staple Singers, who moved from Drew, Mississippi, to Chicago, to those who are locally celebrated like the Chapman family. Family is clearly an important link through which music is passed from generation to generation.

During the summer Chapman often fed her grandchildren in the backyard. She offered them Coca-Cola and crackers spread with peanut butter and jelly. The five daughters of Fannie Bell and Fred Chapman—Elnora Chapman, Velma Singleton, Rose Marie "Doll" Moody, Shirley Mae Cotton, and Betty Franklin—lived with their husbands and children in a compound of homes near their parents.

The Chapman family performed in the Centreville area and conducted healing ceremonies at the invitation of local families. When someone was ill either in the hospital or at home, Chapman went to them and conducted a healing service. As a traveling band, she and her family reached out to sick people wherever they were located.

This interview is drawn from my visits with Fannie Bell Chapman in 1968 and 1972. Our conversations took place in her home, often with her husband, children, and grandchildren listening.

# FANNIE BELL CHAPMAN

I was born in Wilkinson County to a place that you call Capleville, Mississippi. I was there until I got married. After that, I moved to Centreville and to Amite County. I can say that I am truly a Christian and a church worker and a missionary of the praying brand here in Centreville, Mississippi. I prays for the sick people and go into homes and hospitals. I have so much missionary work to do until I can hardly get around to it.

We just a family, you know. A family that prays together stays together as a hallelujah. You know what I mean by hallelujah? We be singing and having a jolly time, loving one another. When it gets to where the music be sounding good, we reach back and get our guitars and our drums. You talking about a hallelujah time. We have it then. Yes, we have it together, oh my Lord.

All my songs come in an inspiration. My mouth fly open just like a mockingbird and I sing, though I ain't never heard that song in my life. I cried when God spoke in His holiness and said to me, "You must be born again." I just cried and said, "Oh Lord."

"Y'all," I say, "come here. Oh my goodness. I got something."

One early morning at the rising of the sun, I called my baby girl and said, "Get on your piano and play this for me."

The background and everything was all together, and my mouth just opened up and sang:

God spoke, yes He did,
He spoke in His holiness.
God spoke.
He spoke in His holiness.
God spoke.
He spoke in His holiness.
He said that you must be born again.
Oh, God spoke, yes He did,
To Daniel in the lion's den.
God spoke
To Daniel in the lion's den.
He said that you must be born again.

I cried. "Oh," I said, "that's the most wonderful thing, Lord, I ever heard in my life. It's so beautiful, Master."

I just wrang my hands and walked through the house and cried. I couldn't help it. My mouth would fly open and I sang:

Oh! God spoke, yes he did.
I recognized His voice.
God spoke. God spoke.
Then I done made my choice.
God spoke. God spoke.
He said that you must be born again.

And I been carrying it ever since. Everywhere I went—at my churches—they say it's one of the beautifulest songs they ever heard in their life. And I told them, "The Spirit of God moved upon me, and I had to sing it. I'm just hoping one day that my song will go all over the world."

FANNIE BELL CHAPMAN, CENTREVILLE, 1972

I came up in singing school, Sunday school, and whatnot. My daddy, he always used to read the Bible to us. My mother, she couldn't read nothing but an almanac. Daddy would get that Bible and read it to her. I would lay there and listen to him, and I would take every word in. Oh Lord, I'd take in every word, and I'm glad now, today, that I did.

There's no more beautiful thing in the world, you know, than a family that loves one another like my children love me. And I love my children. And my grandchildren, I just love them. If I didn't love them, I wouldn't have so many around me. I'd brush them away. Sometimes I have to get them back, you know. They just huddle around. They huddle until they see me point my finger. That means go! That means go!

I had just about forgot all these singing games until they got to playing and singing. Then they come back to my remembrance. They sing,

Little Sally Walker,
Setting in a saucer,
Weeping and a'crying for a cool drink of
     water.

Rise, Sally, rise.
Wipe your weeping eyes.
Put your hand on your hip.
Let your backbone slip.
Gonna shake it to the east.

They just be shaking it out there, and they be playing and having a good time. I say, "We used to play that way when we used to go to school."

They say, "Oh Big Momma, they used to sing that then?"

I told them, "Yeah, they used to sing that. That's way back stuff."

When I was a little tiny thing, my daddy and my mother would fix my dinner. And every time they would feed me, I would leave the house. They didn't pay too much attention to me as a little thing. I left so many times from the dinner table, you know. I would crawl on out, hoddle out some way. I was big enough to hold my plate and get out to where I was going.

My daddy say, "You know that gal."

That was the way my daddy talked. He said, "Every day that baby gets out and goes somewhere. Every time we finish eating, she not in the house. She outside somewhere. Tomorrow I'm gonna watch and see where is she going."

So that next day, my daddy and my mother watched me when I got down with my little pan and went on outside. They didn't feed me on a plate. It was a little pan. When I went out the door, they watched me, my daddy and my mother. And as a little old thing, I hoddled on up to a bushy place, where my daddy say there used to be an old well. I went on up there.

Daddy said, "Oh Lord, I wonder, where is my baby going?"

I hoddled on, went on up to the well, and I sat down there, you know. And when I hoddled up there, a great big snake came up out of that old well. That well was filled in with lots of trash and bricks and things. The snake come wobbling on out to my plate, and I taken and give him some of my food. He opened his little mouth and licked the food, and I took what was left and ate it myself. My daddy said he liked to fainted when he seen that. He didn't know what to do when he seen that. He got him a stick, but the snake went back down in the hole before he could get there to kill it. So he burnt it up instead.

And every evening at that time I would go back out there with my plate and just cry. Just cry. I wasn't big enough to speak, and I would just cry and cry and cry. They said they hated to kill him, but they had to get rid of him. I don't know how long I had been doing it. They had been noticing for quite a while that I was feeding the snake. It looked like I had done made the rest of my life with that snake.

When we were in school, one day my husband was running one way and I was running another way. I ran into him and nearly killed him dead as a nit. Ooo, the blood gushed, and there was no water. They had to run to get water to throw on him. They did that to bring him to. His nose was bleeding. You could just hear his nose popping. That just knocked all the love that was in the world into us. We come to love a little bit out of school, and then we just loved a while and kept on loving until I got to be big enough to

FANNIE BELL CHAPMAN, CENTREVILLE, 1972

take company. Then he would come to my house to see me. And from that, me and him have come to be husband and wife.

I hear people say, "Oh my Lord, the world is in a fix."

You know, that hurts me. We got a beautiful world. We got the most beautiful world, more beautiful now than it was when it first began. The trees and the flowers, the butterflies and the bees, and the human nation of people. I can't say nothing but "World, you is a beautiful dress."

If I didn't have nothing but a chair to sit out in the yard, I wouldn't say, "Ain't this world in a fix."

Uh unh. I don't like that kind of conversation. I likes a conversation that say, "World, you is a beautiful dress."

Ain't it beautiful? The sun is so beautiful. It never has changed, or the moon. I couldn't say nothing but, "The Lord did it. That's His way. He grew the trees."

I couldn't say nothing but, "Lord, this is a beautiful world."

Oh yeah. We should give our King that praise, you see.

It was a pillar of cloud rose. I knew it had appeared there for something. I was praying to God, looking at that beautiful pillar of cloud. It was just floating in the air. And all of a sudden, I say, "Father, if You want me to go out in the world and tell the people that You is the savior of the world, You flash lightning through that pillar of cloud, and I will go ahead. And if You don't flash it, Lord, I know You won't be with me. I wants to know if You will be with me and if You want me to do Your handiwork because I am willing to go on and do my Master's will."

And all of a sudden, an airplane passed. It passed close to that pillar of cloud. I knew He had tried to fool me. If I had took my belief from that airplane, I wouldn't have been up under the understandings of God. And I said, "No Lord. That's not the handiwork of You. That's the handiwork of man. I want You to flash that pillar of cloud with lightning. And if You flash that pillar of cloud with lightning, I know man can't do it, Heavenly Father. And I will go out in the world amongst the people and tell them that You are the savior of the world."

And you know what happened? When the cloud got to be just smoke—where you could see through it—He flashed it. That lightning was so bright and beautiful until I could pick up anything in the world I wanted to. I could see the trees. They was so pretty, you know. There wasn't nothing in the element but that lightning. It was a ball of lightning. It was just like you take an eggplant whip and throw it out and bring it back. Well when He did that, now I've got to go. I've just got to go and tend to my Master's business because I know He have a job for me. And when I be out on my missionary work, I'm not worried. He is there. And if He hadn't been there, He wouldn't have flashed that lightning to say, "Go ahead."

Nails and different cuts will cause the lockjaw. And it comes from all that old blood, you see. That blood is going to infect back up in you. That's going to bring swelling and will poison your blood, you know, from the draw of suction of that blood. All the time, it's working in you like that. It'll get snatched up in there and go on without you knowing until it form a good doctor's scrape. But if I can get to it, it won't cause no more trouble.

A little old girl got cut, and they brought her here. Oh Lordy. I said, "Bring the child here. Lord, have mercy. Be quiet now."

She had done stabbed herself with glass real deep. That blood was bleeding just like milking a cow. I got there and went to popping. You know, you got to pop above that cut. You really got to pop it, you understand. You got to beat the cut first, and then you go around it, hitting those veins. When you hit those veins, the blood runs out of there. I hit those veins, and it run right out of there. Then the blood is drained all over, you know. And that main vein, I had popped it. I beat up above it, way up above it, and I went all the way down the foot. I just kept a'beating it like that, and it stopped bleeding in just a second. I didn't want to give her the lockjaw. All that causes the lockjaw. I beat it and mashed it and did everything I could until no blood would come. Then I took it and I hit it again, and it was gone.

I have a way to find your disease. I take your temperature with my hand. I just put it over your mouth and take your temperature with my fingers. Then my hand just be hitting and find that place in you wherever the disease is at. I find the disease like that because, you know, my hand is gonna stay there. You can't move my hand. It's gonna stay there, and you better believe that's where the misery is at.

I start at the top of your head, like I'm untying the disease. Well all the flesh, even the blood that runs and circulates through your body, it has a defect to do with your whole body when you are sick. He give that to me to work the sick peoples over, from the top of their heads out into the end of their feets. I be twisting it and undoing it from them and getting all that old disease and throwing it on out into the atmosphere. They say, "Yea, I come therefore in the name of the Lord."

That's the way I works them over now. I get all that mingling and twists all over. You're sick somewhere. You gotta throw it out. You gotta get it out. And I touch you and say, "Come ye therefore, from that pillar of cloud. In the name of the Lord, the Spirit, and the Holy Ghost, go! Go!"

I tell them to get up now and go. And they're gone, if it's the Lord's will. Prayer is the key to heaven. You pray and beg and plead and ask God to help you when you are sick. It's some groaning and needful people is in their homes now. Some of them is not able enough to get out and go to church. So peoples can go around and talk to them about the Bible and God and the church work, you see.

When you're praying, your prayer goes to the Son, and the Son delivers the message to God. Then, if it's okay with God, He come back to the Son, and He'll send a message back to you as an answer. But when you come to be a Christian, then He will send that message straight all the way through to you.

When I get my holy reaction, I speaks in tongues. I have been speaking in tongues for many years. My mouth would be popping open, just like it was in the wintertime. And I just be speaking in tongues. Christ is talking to me, and I'm not understanding the meaning of it, you see. I've spoke many times in tongues with my family, and they have too. To find Jesus, that was the onliest way.

I have more than one job. The Lord give you more than one job. Amen. He gives me singing and praying. I'm not a great singer. But when I do sing, you know, they told me I open my mouth too big for it. I told them that the Bible tell me there in Psalms to sing and make a joyful noise. So that's what I does. I don't care how ugly I get on a job like that. I don't mind doing nothing for the Lord. When I'm doing my Master's will—what was promised on the pillar of cloud—I'm satisfied.

Ohhh! I know, that it was the blood.
I know,
I know it was the blood,

It was the blood.
Yeah!
I know,
I know it was the blood, saved me.

Oh! One day!
One day when I was lost,
One day when I was lost.
Oh.
He died upon the cross,
He died upon the cross.
And I know,
Oh, the blood come streaming down,
I say the blood comes streaming out.
I know it was the blood, saved me.
Oh . . . me!

Oh!
One day when I was lost,
When I was lost.

Oh! I know,
It was the blood,
It was the blood.
Lord, I know,
It was the blood,
It was the blood.
I know,
It was the blood,
It was the blood, Lord, saved me.

Oh! One day,
One day when I was lost,
When I was lost.
Oh, he died,
He died upon the cross,
Died upon the cross.
And I know,
I know it was the blood, saved me.
It was the blood, saved me.

# GRAVEL SPRINGS

Otha Turner lived in the Gravel Springs community, in the hill country of northeast Mississippi, the world that William Faulkner chronicled in his fictional Yoknapatawpha County. Although the Delta has been the primary focus for the study of the blues in Mississippi, there is a growing recognition of black music in this area of the state. Important recordings made by folksong collectors David Evans, Alan Lomax, and George Mitchell document music that has existed in the Gravel Springs community for generations. Recent commercial recordings of R. L. Burnside and Junior Kimbrough on Fat Possum Records have drawn national attention to musicians near Holly Springs. Their musical style and that of Otha Turner strongly influenced the sound of the North Mississippi Allstars.

In the late sixties I visited the Gravel Springs community in search of blues artists. During that trip I recorded "Mississippi" Fred McDowell and spent a memorable night in his home. I vividly remember awakening to a breakfast of hot biscuits, coffee, and cane syrup. In 1970 I returned to the community with David Evans to film Otha Turner during a Labor Day picnic at L. P. Buford's store where Turner played fife and drum music with his band. This interview is drawn from David's field recordings, as well as my own.

Otha Turner was a strong, forceful person who spoke with authority about his life and music. Turner was respected as a leader in his community, and the picnic he launched on the fourth weekend of August each year at his home in Gravel Springs is now attended by visitors from throughout the world. Other annual festivals like the Delta Blues Festival in Greenville opened each year with a performance by Otha Turner and his band to acknowledge their importance in the history of black music.

Many black families in the Gravel Springs area own their farms, and they are proud of their community and of their musical heritage. Because drums were banned throughout much of the American South during slavery, very few drumming traditions survived in the region. The Gravel Springs tradition is a rare example of black drumming that has both African and European musical roots.

My last visit with Otha Turner was in Oxford in the fall of 2002, when his Rising Star Fife and Drum Band performed one evening at the Southern Foodways Alliance. We stood together and watched Turner's twelve-year-old granddaughter, Sharde Thomas, play the fife and lead her band as they played the same fife and drum tunes that Turner had performed when we first met in 1970. The sweet smell of barbecue and the sound of fife and drum music filled the air as Turner and I reminisced about our visits over the years. He died four months later at the age of ninety-four.

# OTHA TURNER

Gonner get up in the morning,
Gonner wash my face in a brand-new pan.
Oh Captain, it won't be long.
Gonner get up in the morning,
With the rising sun.
Oh, how can I drive it, how can I drive it,
Done broke my line.
Well my wheel mule crippled,
And my lead mule blind.

I used to snake logs with just a pair of mules. You had a mule in the back and one in the front. That was the lead mule. That song, "Levee Camp Blues," I used to sing that all through the woods.

I was born the second day of June in 1908, in Canton, Mississippi. That's where I was born at. I was brought here in my mother's arms, a little-bitty suckling baby. Free Springs is where I was raised at. As a running kid on the ground, that's where I was, right there. And I been around here for all my days, right in this community. I been right around from Free Springs Church, Water Valley, Oxford, Holly Springs, Chulahoma, Looxahoma, Senatobia, Thyatira, Como, and Sardis.

I can dance. I can sing, ride horses, chop cotton and plow, whoop and holler, cut somersets, do all that stuff. I been on a farm all of my days. Right in this vicinity here, it's all a colored settlement. I got two acres and two-tenths of land. I bought it. Scurrying hard, my labor paid for it. I paid one thousand for the land and 150

dollars for the house. Paid three hundred dollars to move the house. And I rent twelve acres and a half of cotton land.

I always did farming. Plowing a mule, chopping cotton, driving two mules with the lines. I raise my own hogs, cows, chickens, corn, peas, sweet potatoes, tomatoes, okra, beans, turnip salad, and watermelons. And I kill my own meat. Sugar, flour, coffee, snuff, tobacco, and salt, that's what I have to buy from the store.

I have four head of stock—an iron-gray mare and a colt, a bay horse with white feet and a blaze on the face, and a red sow. And I have three head of cattle—one black-and-white-faced motley cow, a solid black cow, and a bull calf with a white tip in his tail and a star on his face. And I got one goat, two head of geese, about fifteen hens, and one rooster. I've got eight dogs and one cat too. That cat don't allow a mouse to walk across the floor. And when I'm out hunting, you know, I just blow my horn for the dogs. I hit that horn a note, and they hear me and come on back to me. There's no special call or tune. I just blow for them.

I shoe all my own horses myself. Practically all the work on the farm, I do it myself. I reckon it's just bred into me. My father could do it, and my granddaddy could do it, and now I do it. There's certain things you can do. That's the way it goes.

When dinnertime comes, Ada will blow the horn to call me. I'll be down there plowing and maybe singing. When they get that horn

and blow it, I'll stop and come back in. I'll say, "Whoa, time done come now. I'm going to feed my face."

When I get back home, the first thing I do is take my mules out and water them. Turn them loose and put the feed out. Then I come on into the house, wash my face and hands, sit down and eat my supper. I sit there and relax and talk a while. And then I go to bed.

In my band, there's four pieces—two kettle drums, a bass drum, and the fife. You've got a lead kettle, and you've got a bass kettle. Now the bass kettle, it plays a little heavier, grosser. But the lead kettle is real light, it's smaller. It's got a different head in it. It don't play as loudly. The bass drum is right behind the kettle, and the fife is in the front. That's the four. You play them all standing up. Drums like we got, you play them standing up, and you play them in a march.

When the dew falls, the drums get slack. You've got to keep a good tight head on the drum to put out the right sound so you can hear the music. You make a little blast of fire to tighten the heads, just like when the sun shines. You build your fire and hold your drum to the fire, rub them heads good, and tap them. You can hear that drum popping, tightening all the time. When it gets tight, it changes the tune of the drum. You can play on it all day, and you'll never bust it. But if you got a slack head, you're not going to hear it too good, and you just might bust it. That's right.

I can play anything I want on a drum. But the whole group's got to know it too. That makes a difference. I can play all of it—cane blowing, kettle playing, bass, all of it. My real boys—who

we generally play with—they can play all the parts too, from the kettle to the bass and back from the bass to the kettle.

When we have a picnic, we put it out from three to four weeks ahead. That's the broadcasting: "I'm giving a picnic—Otha Turner's place. Everybody come. It'll be an enjoyment. Everybody's welcome."

Then I go ahead and get ready. I kill my hog. Scald him. Cook my meat. Barbecue it and take it to my stand. We sells it by the sandwich. And we'll have pork meat, fish, and drinks.

Then I start the drums to playing and the cane fifes to blowing. We play "Shimmy She Wobble," "My Baby Don't Stand No Cheating on Her," "Granny, Will Your Dog Bite?," "Rolling and Tumbling," "Glory Hallelujah," and "When the Saints Go Marching In."

We go out there and go to playing the drums, go to hollering and playing and making monkeyshine with the drums, just cutting up. That's what will draw your crowd. That's the drawment, and all the people start to come from that. That's what draws the people from further and nearer. The people come from everywhere.

People are laughing and talking, associating with one another. Little kids go out there and dance behind the drums. We have all of that. It's really what you call a good time. That's what it is. Just for enjoyment, to keep from being at home and lonesome.

We all meet there—white people come there just like the colored, and we sit down and laugh and talk. White peoples, they stand around and pay us to play. They don't ever try to learn. They'd just rather hear us play. They get more

OTHA TURNER, GRAVEL SPRINGS, 1970

enjoyment out of just standing and looking. They be dancing, laughing, talking, enjoying, smoking cigarettes, looking, listening to the music.

And we has the law [the sheriff]. All the picnics we give, we have the law to come there. That's for to keep down the stabbings, to keep people from getting killed. Keep people from wrecking cars. Keep people from shooting one another. That's for peace. You have that for peace. No clowning, no cursing and hooting and hollering. No guns. No cutting and shooting. That's what that's for. No trouble, we don't have

any trouble. Everybody be loving and peaceful. We all are one then. That's the way we have it.

So that's the picnic. Everybody's welcome that wants to come. You barbecue Friday night. The picnic starts at one o'clock on Saturday and goes until twelve that night. That's the end. When twelve rolls up, then Sunday takes over. That's the closeout, see. We don't have drum playing on Sunday.

I learned myself to make a cane fife. I was thirteen years old, and there were these old drum players around here, Bill and Will. I would stand there and look at them. They had

OTHA TURNER AND SHARDE TURNER, GRAVEL SPRINGS, 1976

a player that blew a cane too. I said, "I wished I could do that."

See, I'd already taken up learning how to beat the drum. I asked him let me see his fife. I figured I could do it too. So he revealed something to me. He said, "Now look. What you see somebody else doing, there's no way to make a failure but to try. If you think that you can do it, and you believe that you can do it, try."

So I just kept a'tuning and tuning and blowing and tuning. The more you do a thing, the more perfect it comes to you. The more I tried, the better it come to me. I tried and tried, and I learned it. That's my make. Ain't nobody trained me. I took that for myself.

And I made canes for other people. I don't know how many I done made for them. I made the first cane Napoleon Strickland [neighbor] ever blowed in his life. I made it and gave it to him. That's right. As soon as he learned to blow one piece, he learned him another. So I made Napoleon his cane, and he tried to blow like me. He took it up hisself after he heard me blow a piece. And now Napoleon can really blow a cane.

I make my own fifes. The cane grows right

OTHA TURNER, GRAVEL SPRINGS, 1976

down there in the bottom. First you go out there and cut you a piece of cane. You judge the length you want your cane. A two-foot cane is really too long to blow. It's best a foot or so. And your cane should be a medium size around. Too large a cane, and you can't tune it. The cane grows from the earth so high, see, and it's jointed. You pick you out so many joints and cut it off. Then you take your knife and dress it down.

You get you a iron rod, put it in the fire, and get it red hot to make a hole in your cane. If you don't get your hole large enough, that fife won't blow good. You got to twist that hot rod around in there so it starts smoking and steaming. You put all them holes in the cane that way.

You space your fingers on the cane to see what distance apart to make the holes. I always measure mine with my fingers. Then I take me a pencil, and I mark right there where my finger's at. Then when I go to burn the holes in the cane, I get right at the center of that place where that black mark is. You got to line your holes up — straight up and down that piece of cane. I put five holes in my cane. I never use but five holes in a cane to blow it. Of course, the hole what you blow through with your mouth makes six holes.

OTHA TURNER, GRAVEL SPRINGS, 1976 ▶

It depends on how hard you blow. It's different in blowing a church song than in blowing a blues or a reel on a cane. You got to tune it with your finger. That's your tuner. I blow a cane from the left. Some people blows from the right. You can blow it either from the right or the left.

I used to be a real blues singer before I married. I'd sing through the night when I was out riding my horse. Folks would get up, light a lamp, and come out into the yard to hear me singing the blues. I used to ride my horse at night, just hollering the blues, just riding along singing.

Now I can be out there working in the fields, and something will come to me. I can sing the blues so well then that it'll do you good to stop and listen. It's true. The blues is a kind of thing that if you're driving along, plowing in the field, and something comes to you, you just start to sing. You make that up yourself. You can put anything in a blues.

Sitting here wondering,
With my matchbox open and closed.
I ain't got so many matches,
But I got so far to go.

Now that just naturally comes to you. You make up your own blues. I can't play someone else's songs and their tune. I have to play mine, or I can't play at all. The words come from me. They're just thoughts that come to me when I'm out working. It do me good to be out there plowing a mule and hollering on high. I like that. Singing, that's my pedigree.

My mother taught me from a baby to treat everybody right. Treat people like you wish to be treated. I want friends and good left behind me when I'm dead and gone. I want people to speak well of me. I work for that. I meet everybody with a smiling face. That's the way I live, and that's the way I hope I'll go.

# PARCHMAN PENITENTIARY

Parchman Penitentiary is an 18,000-acre penal farm located in the heart of the Delta. For many years, Parchman was farmed with mules driven by white and black convicts. Inmates were segregated, and one of the largest black camps was Camp B, which was located near the community of Lambert.

During the summer of 1968 I visited Camp B and recorded and filmed black inmates chopping wood to the rhythm of work chants, a musical tradition that originated in West Africa. From five to fifteen men lifted their axes in unison and chopped wood to the beat of a work chant called by a leader who faced them. Verses in the chant described inmates who escaped from Parchman by swimming the Sunflower River to confuse the trailing bloodhounds, prisoners who returned their hoes to the "Captain" and refused to work, and a beautiful woman named Rosie who waited outside the camp for her man.

Prisoners at Parchman were known by nicknames they received after they entered the prison. These nicknames reflected either personality traits or physical characteristics. Johnny Lee Thomas, a former Parchman inmate, received the nickname "Have Mercy" when he protested the brutal beating of another prisoner.

Thomas was at Parchman when inmates served as "trustees" and carried weapons with live ammunition to guard other inmates. Thomas told me about "Old Timer" or "Timer," a prison trustee who was ninety-six. He described Parchman Penitentiary as a world of fear in which only the strong and intelligent survive. Like the trickster rabbit, the black prisoner had to move quickly and think faster than his white boss. Because he was a "high roller" who hoed weeds and "chopped" cotton as fast as most men could walk, Thomas gained favor with prison guards and escaped the beatings that others received.

I returned to Parchman's Camp B in 1974 to film and record work chants and interviews with inmates. During that visit James "Blood" Shelby, Ben Gooch, and Roosevelt Stewart Jr. spoke about their lives in moving ways. I also interviewed Sergeant Webb, the camp overseer who recalled his many years at Parchman and how times had changed since he first arrived.

For all of these inmates, music was a means to survive within the prison's grim world.

# JOHNNY LEE "HAVE MERCY" THOMAS

Chopping cotton, picking cotton, pulling stalks, ditching, cutting down trees in the woods, lifting up and toting logs, we did all that kind of stuff. We would have a log about eight feet long. Be as long as from here to the door there. We would have six mens with hand sticks. Just like me and James are here, he'd tote right-hand, and I'd tote left. And then the man is up there walking, up on the log. He weighed 250 now. He'd say, "Better not drop this log and hurt me. Better not drop me."

We would get up at three o'clock in the morning. Eat breakfast at the long table, and at three-thirty we'd be setting on the end of the cotton row in the field, waiting till it got light enough to see and work. Cold, ooo wee! That's what be the matter with my foots. My hands, sometimes they just ache all across there, you know, from cold. I can't straighten my hand out no straighter than that.

We pulled up the cotton stalks ahead of the folks that was breaking up ground. Every man pulled up cotton stalks and piled them in his own middle from end to end. And the half trustees come along behind us and burn them up out of the plowhand's way. The plowhand would be breaking up ground with four mules and a great big old plow. They called it a road plow, a sand buster, and they had four mules hitched to it. They would get right up in the top of that row and split the middle of that row with four mules pulling. We didn't go in from the field until it was night—summer, winter, and fall and spring.

I was up at Parchman for seven years. My crime was following bad company. A gang of us was gambling in an old juke house, you know. We'd meet to gamble every Saturday night. We'd meet there and get to shooting dice.

The gang I was with, they shot about three or four games. If you followed a gang of people, it makes no difference about whether you did something or no. If they do something and you with them, why you in the blame too. Somebody got killed, and three got wounded. I couldn't get out of there. I was in it, but I hadn't did nary a shot. So they sent me up to Parchman.

At Parchman, they had "high rollers" that get up through the field, and I was one of them. I could chop cotton as fast as I could trot along the road. I didn't care about the grass. I chopped that grass, left that stand of cotton, and didn't stop walking.

They had a lot of them up there was supposed to have been higher rollers than me. But when they got in that grass and I was at the other end, they said, "Now what kind of lick is that nigger got? Ooo wee, he gone. Great goodness alive."

I'd be trying to stay out the way of that white man. I said, "White folks, when you get to throwing that leather, my foots get as light under the bottom as a piece of paper. I wonder when is my time?"

He say, "I ain't gonner bother you. You's a high roller."

I be knowing that, but I still clown, you know. If I see his shoes unlaced, I run there and jump on my knees and lace 'em up. If I see them nasty on the toe, I get my old rag out of my pocket and wipe them off for him. All that's to make it. You got to do all that. Act the fool. You got to act the fool to make it easy on you. They'll look at you and say, "Now you know he want to make it. He's a good worker, and then he clowns too. We ain't gonner bother him."

And it was another thing I could do. They had about three or four handmade guitars. I could play them. And I'd get somebody else to play it, and I'd dance by it. I can do the buck dance if you play the music. I'd rather buck dance than eat a ball of onions.

They was beating a man to death one day, and this very man had been chopping cotton. He told them, "Spare my life. Here's the grass, and here's the cotton. You can beat me to death, but that's all I can do. I can't do no more."

The sun was beating down, and I say, "Looka here. Don't you hear the man say, "'Spare life,' and he doing all he can? There's more workdays than one. Have mercy on that man and let him up from there. Don't hit him another lick."

They started to calling me Have Mercy. I went there in '29. I left in '37. I got the name there, and it followed me on out here. "Have Mercy." My real name is Johnny Lee Thomas, and my home is Arcola, Mississippi.

They might beat you half to death, but they give you plenty to eat. They give you a'plenty, but it was half cooked. They fed us good when folks come on the Fourth of July and Thanksgiving and Christmas. And after that they fed us like a gang of dogs.

It was two drivers at every camp and a sergeant and a night watchman. They tell me now that don't nobody whip you but the sergeant, and you have to do a mighty bad crime for him to whip you.

When I was there, they'd hit you just as long as they felt like raising up their arm. I never did get marked up or scarred up cause I could chop cotton as fast as you could walk along the road. If you caught the cage—you know what I mean—the cage is where you would stay in the camp during the day if you didn't work. If you take what they give you, why you was welcome to stay in there. Course me, myself, I never was sick. If you took a quart of castor oil and a pint of Epsom salts, you could stay in there. Now who wanted all that? You didn't need all of it. I'm glad I never was sick. They kept me straight up a line in the field.

After they beat them, they had some kind of grease there they'd grease them up with and make them go to work the next day like they ain't hit you nary a lick. They pull your breetches down. And that strap was that wide, that thick, and that long with the handle. And that leather is loaded. The leather, you see, is loaded. They have something in there that cut your flesh up. It mark you up. They didn't have to hit you all that hard with it. It's a certain way they hit you. They have a man on your head, and they have you flat on your stomach, and a man on each arm, and a man on each leg. You can't do nothing but lay there. He gonner hit you seventy-five or eighty licks. And some of them, when they let them up, the clothes would stick to their flesh. I knowed a'many a man had to wear padding between his clothes to set down. All back there was just raw. In other words, it was like that when I was there.

But I wasn't marked up cause I could get on out of the way. But there's a whole lot of them that's out here today that is marked up. But you gonner work right on. I don't care if you is marked.

And them guards. At that time they guarded you with their hand on the trigger. Just like, "Over here is my catch, and over there is yours."

If a man jump and come this way, I supposed to stop him. But if you see I can't get him, why ain't no harm for you to take a couple of cracks at him. But that guard worked as hard as me because he's all the time looking. His eyes is in a strain all day. He don't know who gonner try to get away. It was a old man up there. He was ninety-six years old, a old timer. He'd been there since 1900. I had done picked him out and said, "If that old man can't shoot, I'm shore gonner run over him."

I thought that, but I wanted somebody else to try it. If they'd get away, then it'd be my time. Well a good friend of mine—I loved that boy— his wife wrote him a letter and said, "Well, John Thomas, I done all I could for you. But I didn't know you had "'natural life.'"

See "natural life" is longer than a lifetime sentence. A lifetime is just a hundred years. But natural life mean that if you live two or three hundred years, you still ain't served your time. And the governor, he don't give no pardon for natural life. Well he had that kind of time, and she didn't know it. So after she found that he had natural life, she wrote him and say, "I'm sorry, but I can't do you no good. You know I been single now for four years. I done married and started a new family."

Johnny had a nice learning, and he sat out in the sun and read the letter. He shook his head and said, "No, I don't like it. If she was married, she had no business writing me. I'll tell you what I'm gonner do. I'm going out there and kill her. I ain't gonner bother the man. Then I'll come back."

I said, "Aw naw. You wouldn't come back."

"Yeah I would. I swear, cause I wouldn't of wrote her no such a letter as this."

I saw him again, and I said, "Wait a minute."

He said, "Wait what?"

"Wait till we get in the woods."

He say, "Aw naw. That'll be a little too long. We won't get in the woods until this winter."

We was chopping cotton and had got across the field. I said, "Johnny, I like you. I don't want you to try and jump."

He say, "I'm gonner jump. I'm going over Old Timer cause he's ninety-six years old, and near about a hundred, and can't see good."

I said to myself, "I shore hope you get away, and that will be my go. That way, the next day will be my day."

But that old man, let me tell you. You know he wore his straw hat with the screen wore out in the front in the summertime. Johnny say, "Tomorrow evening at three o'clock, when we go out on the end, I'm gonner take this hat off and throw it as far up in the air as I can get it. And I'm going right on behind that hat. You just look out for that hat."

And so, sure enough, one of the guards, "Black Gal," he said, "It's three o'clock."

About the time us all got us rows started, Johnny throwed that hat up in the air and lit out. He runned over Old Timer. The captain, he said, "Look out, Old Timer. That's one you just as well to let go."

Old Timer said, "Oh no."

Captain said, "I bet you twenty-five dollars."

Old Timer said, "Wait a minute."

I said to myself, "Run, Johnny, run. Run, Johnny, run."

He was aping too, getting cross that field. They was still standing up talking. Old Timer told him, "Captain Tom," he said. "What this gun sight on here for? There he is right there on the end of the gun barrel."

I said, "Run, Johnny, run."

Captain Tom say, "I bet you twenty-five dollars."

Old Timer say, "I bet you twenty-five."

So Captain Tom throwed down his twenty-five and Black Gal, the guard, throwed down his twenty-five too. Old, old man. Head white as snow. He say, "I been here ever since 1900. I ain't shot at a man and missed him yet. I'm gonner cut his jumper collar behind and leave it hanging three inches."

I said, "That old man's a mess. If Johnny get away, he's a liar. I'm gonner run if Johnny get away."

But he didn't get away. Old Timer squatted and throwed that cap good on the side to shade his eyes. He said, "Wait a minute."

You know the woods had a wire fence around it. And right at the edge of the woods was a great big oak tree. I can't measure with my arms how large it was. "Wait a minute. He crossing the wire fence. Let me make him think he gone."

He was fixing to go around that great big oak tree. Old Timer say, "There he is right there."

"Yoow!"

He say, "There he is. I saw him when he fell. Send somebody with the dead wagon to get him."

I said to myself, "Don't you run over that old man. You better stay here. He'll get you."

But if he had of missed Johnny, I would of run the next day. Old, old man. He was ninety-six.

I said, "That old man. Good God Almighty. He been here ever since 1900. I wadn't even in the world in 1900."

So I didn't mess with Old Timer. If you want to get away from the penitentiary, don't mess with Timer. If you do, why he got you. So I wadn't glad for Johnny to have got killed, but I'd rather for it to have been him than me. If he had got away, the next day was my day. But you see he didn't get away. He was on his way out to kill his wife. He said he was coming back. I told him, "Ain't no need of you doing that, Johnny. She had to have somebody."

"I don't care. She didn't have no business writing me such a letter as that over here."

It was the letter more than it was getting another husband. Johnny said, "If I knowed you was all hemmed up and couldn't get out, I wouldn't write you nothing like that."

So he started crying, and I knowed then he was gonner try to get away. That was more than something. I hated that boy got killed. I'm the man went down there and got him with the dead wagon. It broke his neck. If you trying to get away, that's where they gonner shoot you, in the neck or in the head. That old man, I didn't think he could shoot good by being that old.

# CAMP B WORK CHANT[1]

Peaches I love don't grow on trees,
Little hard navel, just above her knees.
That's the thing you call her stingaree.
Little before day, she puts that thing on me.
Oh Lordy, Berta, Berta. Oh Lord, gal.

Be my woman, gal, I'll be your man.
Every day Sunday, dollar in your hand.
Cut your wood, I'll make your fire.
Tote your water from the boggy bayou.
Would do your cooking if I just knowed how.

# JAMES "BLOOD" SHELBY

I got my nickname "Blood" when my mother was sick. I was working, and I couldn't make enough money to support her doctor bill. So I went out gambling. And every time I would win, the fellows would ask me to let them have a piece of my money. I'd tell them, say, "No, I gotta go buy Momma some blood."

They'd say, "That's the blood-buyingest nigger we ever seen."

So everybody just started calling me Blood. Now these work songs, when you working and you singing, it makes you get your mind off everything else and get it on your work. You just feel good, and you do a good day's work. I learned these songs from an older fellow who was here before I got here. I heard him sing them, so I just started helping him sing them.

I came here in 1942. I was twenty-two years old. I been here five times since then. They talk about this place as the inside world. That mean we be doing different things from the people in the outside world. In here, we don't know what's going on out there, and they don't know what's going on in here. When I first come to Parchman, you would leave this camp in the morning when you just can see and come back in at night when you can't see. We would work from can to can't see. And sometimes we didn't come in for dinner. We'd eat dinner in the field.

The work they doing now, ain't nothing to it. It's like a summer resort compared to the time when I come here. We were sure nuff working. You had to work or get beat half to death. I worked so hard, look like I was going to fall dead every minute. If I hadn't been a good man, I couldn't have stood it.

# BEN GOOCH

I first came here in 1934, November the fifth. Parchman was pretty rough then. Whatever they had you doing, you had to run with it. I imagine I was around twenty-six or twenty-seven when I came here.

Now those works songs, that just something just come to you out there on the job when you're working. At the time when I come here, you couldn't talk on the job. You just had to sing. They didn't allow you to talk in the field. Only time you could talk was in the cage. They didn't allow you to talk at all when you was working in line.

I was rode so hard that when we'd go eat dinner, I couldn't eat with a spoon. The food would shake off because I was so nervous, you know. I'd be so hot I couldn't eat. I'd just lick some of the food. But I made it. I made it through alright.

# SERGEANT WEBB

I started to work here the fifteenth of January in '42. I worked down at Camp 2. Then on the twenty-eighth of December in '42, I moved here to Camp B. And I been here ever since. I worked convicts on the long line and on the road crew. I been overseeing the farm here since the third day of April in '53. We was farming with mules at that time. Back from 1943 to about '45, we hauled logs out of the woods with oxen.

They sing those work songs to get the trouble off their mind, I guess. They used to sing, and you could hear them for miles, just all of them singing. But they don't do that much now. I'd be here in the afternoon, and I'd hear them singing and hollering plumb over a mile and a half, over around the railroad. I don't know, but it seems like they was happier then than they are now. Wasn't as much griping. Obeyed better. Worked better. Back then you could holler for one, and he'd come on to you. He wouldn't just stand around and look.

We used to cut all the wood with crosscut saws and axes. Couldn't get the mules in the woods down there to tote posts up. Prisoners would tote posts from the woods out half a mile to where they loaded them on a truck and carried them to Parchman.

We used to have a baseball team here. We won the trophy for about five years straight here playing down on the big farm at Parchman. And we used to have a good gospel quartet up here. When they was plowing, you could hear them sing, and the quartet sang while they was plowing mules. From the time I come here until about 1960, we worked mules all the time. We had about seventy-five mules here. That was my best time, when we was farming with mules. When they worked those seventy-five mules, all the prisoners would be hollering and singing. It was a thrill to be down there with them.

We grow practically everything we eat at Camp B. When garden time is in, we have everything in the way of vegetables.

# ROOSEVELT STEWART JR.

My name is Roosevelt Stewart Jr. I been working mules off and on for thirty-five years. You got to train the mules to help you and not to help nobody else. You got to train them to do what you tell them to do. You have to know how to work them right. See, this is a young team here. The people they was working for before I got them, they couldn't handle them. The mules would run away every day. Every time they hook them up, they would run away. Since I had them, they been doing alright.

I turn them loose in the lot. Then, when I go out there and call them, they come to me. I got them tamed down where I can handle them. I put ribbons on them and call myself decorating them to make them look nice.

When you teach the mule, you teach him with one line, just like you will a person going to school. Put one line on him. If you want him to go to the right, you tell him, "Gee. Go to the right."

You got to pull the line, so that make him go to the right. You teach him that for about two or three weeks. Then you teach him to "haw." When you tell him to "haw," he goes to the left. You have to handle a mule like you do yourself. You want to be treated nice, and that's the way you got to treat the mule. If you do, he'll mind and do whatever you tell him. I can ride him, do anything I want with him.

I got this license tag off an old raggledy truck and put it on that box there. That's what I call my toolbox, where I carry my wrenches and things. That basket up there, that's for my watercooler. When I'm going to a different field, I put the watercooler in the basket and take it along with me.

# TUTWILER

W. C. Handy first heard the blues in 1903 while waiting for a train in Tutwiler. A traveling musician playing slide guitar near the train tracks sang that he was "goin' where the Southern cross the Dog." Handy later recalled that it was "the weirdest music I had ever heard."

The small town—1,364 people in the 2000 census—has changed little since Handy visited it over a century ago. In 1968 I approached Tutwiler as a sacred place because of its association with Handy and the blues.

In Tutwiler, I visited with Lee Kizart, a gifted blues pianist and storyteller who recalled the Delta worlds of his youth and their vital blues scene. We found an old piano in the local high school where he played and talked about his career.

I also spent an afternoon with Kizart's friend Tom Dumas, who played old-time country tunes on the fiddle and banjo. Dumas grew up in the Mississippi hills, and he and his music were clearly out of step with the Delta blues worlds in which he lived.

# TOM DUMAS

This fiddle been in my family for three generations. It come from Italy. My daddy's great-great-granddaddy lived in Baltimore, Maryland, and he bought this fiddle from Andrew Jackson, the seventh president. My daddy's granddaddy learned on it and played, and my daddy learned on it and played. In 1897, I took it up and learned on it.

I throwed this fiddle away in 1904. I forgot all about fiddling. When I come down from the hills to the Delta forty-five years ago, they began to come out with the talking machines, the radio. I would listen in to the *Grand Ole Opry* and hear the old-timey fiddle tunes, and I thought about my old fiddle. I hadn't played this fiddle in forty-five years. So I went back home and got this old fiddle and brought it back to the Delta. The rats had bored a hole there, and the neck was broke off. A white fellow fixed it up for me about twelve years ago.

MR. AND MRS. TOM DUMAS, TUTWILER, 1968

◀ TOM DUMAS, TUTWILER, 1968

I used to play for dances when I was a boy, fifteen or sixteen years old. We used to give dances about five nights out of every week for colored folks. That was in Walthall, Webster County, Mississippi. I played from 1897 until 1904. We had a band with a fiddle and a banjo and a guitar and a mandolin.

We would call sets. We would have thirty-two people in a house, sixteen men and sixteen girls. One man sat down at the fiddle, and he called and told everybody what to do. Like, if you wanted the partners to swing, why that man would call it. He was just like a preacher. Four of them would be together, you know, two men and two women. He would tell them to promenade, and one man would get his partner, and they'd go all the way around. Then he would tell them, "Back to the wall."

And the men would circle around. All sixteen women would turn, and the men would go all the way around. They would swing corners until they got all the way around, and then he would holler, "Swing partners," and they would carry them to the table to treat them.

I have sat in a corner many a night and played all night long. I used to pick a banjo, and my daddy, he'd play the fiddle. We used to play "Cotton-Eyed Joe" and "Old Hen Cackle." One of my daddy's uncles, Sylvester McGee, lived at Vicksburg and was 126 years old when he died. He was born in 1841.

# LEE KIZART

My home is Glendora, Mississippi. That's where I was raised at. I used to tune pianos, overhaul them, build them. I did everything there is to do to a piano. I'm thinking of going to Dallas, Texas, and I'll start playing the piano when I get there.

I play in the swing style. Course I don't read no music. I can't read or write, as far as that's concerned. But I know this piano. I can play some old blues I used to play back along in '25. I been playing piano a long time.

One time I had a piano, and rats got in it and cut all the felts out. Strings was all broke up in there. I decided I was gonner fix it. After I done that, I understood how to work on pianos.

A blind man can play the "St. Louis Blues." Look at Ray Charles. He don't know where he putting his hands, but he get up there and know his keys.

I'm sixty-five years old. I have thirteen children. I had one got killed in July in St. Louis. I had fourteen. He was killed in an incident of some kind in a café. They stabbed him up there.

I had a boy got burnt before Christmas. He worked in a steel plant in East St. Louis. I sent my wife up there to take care of him. He couldn't feed himself. He was burnt from his neck down. They grafted skin off his arm onto the other places to get him fixed up. He got his insurance. I sent my baby boy to help him. My baby boy, he tall as that boy there, but he ain't as heavy as him. He stayed with his brother till he got him in pretty good position with his insurance.

I can play spirituals on the piano, but I don't like it. I won't do like a lot of folks and mix the blues with the spirituals. Disc jockeys, they want you to play that mix-up rhythm, but I won't do it. I won't cross up. I've had church singers come to me and want to play with me, but I wouldn't hire them. They say, "I can sing that stuff."

I say, "Yeah, but I don't do business that way."

I may be punished for doing it—not by you, but by the Good Lord above—but I won't play church music. I used to play all night long on Saturday nights back in '25. I would play the "Forty-four Blues." I played in a honky-tonk right in Glendora. I played by myself with nothing but a good piano. That was when Ida Cox was on a passenger train that run through here. They called it the Teddy, with all them steel cars. I left Glendora in the fall of '26 and went over to Aberdeen.

Along in them times, this country was in her bloom. She tore up bad now. But she was in her bloom then. I seen a'many a fellow got killed at night and drug up under the skin table. I've had this door on the piano to get busted right in front of me. A woman was singing and had her hand on this door, and a guy shot her here. He shot her with his pistol and shot this door and busted it too. I was looking at her when she fell. I don't know who shot. You couldn't see who shot, as many folks as it was.

I seen a woman get shot one night when I was playing at a juke joint way out in the country. She had just come in from St. Louis, and her head fell just about that far from the end of the porch. Just broke her neck. It was a forty-five bullet alright enough. It broke her neck, and she fell with her head just about that far from the edge of the porch.

Well my car was setting right up next to the edge of the porch. I was setting down inside the joint playing. I jumped out the back door and run around the side of the house. I got in my car. And when I cranked up, I liked to drove over I don't know how many folks that was up under my old racer. I had a racer then.

They was getting out of the way. Just like I'd of been doing. It wadn't none of me did it. I was just playing for that twenty dollars. I didn't live there. I lived in Glendora and had a café there. Twenty dollars a night is what they paid me. That's what I would get. It didn't bother me about the woman getting killed. Ever since it's been a world, somebody's been getting killed, as far as that's concerned. I wadn't too scared.

When I had my band, there were four of us. We played all the big clubs, down at Tchula—the Midnight Club—and at Goodman, Winona, Jackson, Canton, all back down through there. I'd get five, six, or seven hundred dollars on a good night.

I lost my wife because she was sanctified. I done a trick when I married her. I pretended I was sanctified to get her, you understand. I got her, and after I stayed so long, I went back to playing. I come home one Sunday morning, and

she told me that if I wanted to play the blues, I could get my clothes and go on home. I said, "Thank you."

I just packed my clothes in my suitcase. I didn't have far to go to my mother's house. It was about as far as from here across the railroad. My wife and her people was sanctified, and they called theyselves right.

Then she come and told me that the sanctified people had got on her. They said she was wrong for telling me to leave like that, the words that she said to me. She called me to the house and said she didn't want me to go nowhere. She told me to come on back home. But my clothes was down at my mother's. I said, "No. I won't go get them. You told me to take them out of here. You will be the one to go get them. I won't go get them. But I will come back if you beg me apology."

Didn't bother me. I didn't get hurt. Fact of the business is, it's no more harm for me to play the blues than for Louis Jordan and all them other big stars up there. But in my day in this community, they'd say, "You know that old man toting that guitar yonder, he oughta be going to church."

That's what everybody said about me, you know. But now, you take up the road, maybe. Ain't no maybe in it. I know what's happening. In Chicago, down in the basement there in the churches, they got a saloon down there and every kind of hamburger and steak you want to cook, down in the basement. But upstairs, they in church. No doubt, it's some big reverend's place of business. He go down and shoot hisself

good with some alcohol, and then he go back up and serve.

But now, I don't do that. I just serve one way. I won't cross up church stuff with my stuff cause you can't do everything and be saved. I was play-ing with a boy that wanted to fit my stuff in with church songs. Course you can fit that in with church songs if you want and know how to do it. But now, I don't like that.

◄ WALL IN LEE KIZART'S HOME, TUTWILER, 1968

# A DELTA ROAD IN COAHOMA COUNTY

Highway 61 and many smaller roads connect Mississippi Delta worlds and carry colorful travelers along their journeys by day and night. While driving through the Delta in 1968, I met C. L. Redwine, a local fruit and vegetable salesman, with one of his clients, Corine Gardner. I was struck by the hand-painted signs asking, "Are you prepared to die?," on Redwine's truck and stopped to speak with them.

Redwine and Gardner gave me a glimpse into their worlds. They had known each other for many years, and Gardner told me how grateful she and her family were for the fresh produce they purchased from Redwine. The dramatic religious signage on Redwine's truck suggested that he was on a mission. His produce was only a part of what led him on his journey through the Delta. We spoke on a road in Coahoma County.

# C. L. REDWINE

I was at Myrtle, Mississippi, at Camp Zion, about three years ago. There was an old man came there. I don't remember his name, but he said the Lord told him to carry signs. He had signs on his suitcase and on the front and back of his body, hanging on him, all he could carry. He refused to take any ride with anybody. He said the Lord told him to walk up and down the highway and carry the gospel—preach the gospel—with those signs.

After he had got up and give his testimony, our pastor, Jimmy Jones, asked us not to be talking or making slight remarks about him or saying anything that we might be sorry for cause he believed he was a man of God. He wanted to know how many of us would be willing to carry them signs like that man was doing if we knew the Lord had laid it on our heart to do it.

It was some three or four of us agreed that we would do that. It wasn't but a few minutes until

C. L. REDWINE, COAHOMA COUNTY, 1968

I felt like the Lord had told me that if I would hang these signs on my truck, I wouldn't have to carry them. If I didn't, I might have to carry them. I sell produce for a living. So I been carrying them almost three years on my truck. I been criticized many times by many people.

Every once in a while, maybe one out of a hundred will come along and compliment me for my signs. But very seldom do I hear anything about it myself. I hear about it after I have gone. I hear slight remarks being made about it. People have made slight remarks before my family until they're ashamed of me. My wife is gone from me now, and my children won't associate with me very much. I moved my membership to Myrtle Baptist Church, which is a Missionary Baptist of the very deepest that I know about in the United States. I believe it has the deepest Christian people that I know of.

I been told that if I would move my membership and take these signs off my truck, my family would be back together. I can't do it. I love my family as much as anybody, but I love God more. So I want everybody to pray for me that I'll hold out and be faithful and do what the Lord said regardless of whether I'll ever have a home.

We have a camp meeting there at Myrtle three times a year. Anybody that likes fish and food can come free of charge. It costs a dollar and a half to stay there four days. We have one in July and August and January.

That man I first met with those signs had a beard and was walking down the road. He was walking down the road unshaven and hadn't had his hair cut in a long time. He was sunburned until you couldn't tell if he was a white man or a colored man. He refused to ride with anybody. He said the Lord didn't want him to ride. He wanted him to walk. He told us he'd been doing that about two years, and he hadn't never missed a night of having a bed to sleep in or a meal of having something to eat. Somebody always taken care of him.

I don't know if my signs have helped along the way. I hear very little about them. I hope they have. That's the intention that I've got anyway. There's lots of good people misunderstood me though, and they think I'm just being fanatic, trying to get a pat on the back. But the Lord knows better. I'm not.

# CORINE GARDNER

I've known Mr. Redwine ever since my first twins were born. He sweet. I'm gonner give him that credit. My first twins is fourteen, James and John Edward. That man would come along if I were hungry, and if he had anything on that truck out there that I wanted, he would bring it to me.

When we were hungry, he hauled food up and down the road to feed the people. Didn't I just tell you? I know him. See, I'm a witness to him.

And he left it up to me to pay him. There he is. I'm just a witness for him. That's him. I lost my house, and he didn't know what I was at. But since we moved here, he found me. He's still the same. He's a nice white man, see. He always helps, regardless to the color. There he is. There he is.

I had two sets of twins straight, and my little children would go out there and tell him, "Please bring some food in here."

C. L. REDWINE AND CORINE GARDNER, COAHOMA COUNTY, 1968

He brought it just like he doing now. That sign he got up now, he didn't have that then. He just helped me along the way. And I thank the Lord for him today. He was sick once and was on crutches. He said, "Look. I'm going back home. But if I get over this sickness, I will be back." I was glad to meet the man. See, there he is. As much food as that man put in my house, what I'm against him for? Regardless to us color. I ain't lying. That's true. There he is. That's right. He helped me with all these kids of mine.

# BLUES TOWNS AND CITIES

*The blues developed in Mississippi towns and cities in significant ways. Within urban worlds, musicians lived in black neighborhoods where blues clubs and house parties thrived. These neighborhoods provided greater protection and economic opportunities for performers who moved there from surrounding rural areas. Musicians polished their blues styles and became celebrities in Delta towns like Leland and Clarksdale, in Mississippi's capital city of Jackson, and in Memphis, Tennessee. Within these urban worlds, the blues were heard on the radio and in barbershops and clothing stores, as well as in clubs. They became a familiar part of the fabric of daily life.*

# LELAND

I first encountered the Delta blues in Leland. During the summer of 1968, I met James "Son Ford" Thomas, a gifted musician, storyteller, and sculptor. We became friends, and our lives remained closely tied together for over twenty-six years until his death in 1993. Allen Ginsberg told me that Thomas was my "guru," a description that clearly fit the relationship I shared with him over the years. Thomas performed regularly in my classes at Jackson State University, Yale University, and the University of Mississippi. We also traveled together to the Smithsonian Festival on the Mall and to the White House, where President Ronald Reagan's press secretary Larry Speakes— who was also from Leland—had Thomas open his daily press conference by singing a blues song.

When I first entered the black community in Leland, I asked if there were any blues singers in the area and was quickly directed to the home of James Thomas. I found his house in the section of Leland known as "Black Dog" and asked his wife Christine if he was at home. She said there was no one named James Thomas living there and asked why I wanted him. When I explained that I was writing a book on the blues and wanted to include him in it, she admitted that she was his wife and told me where I could find him. I understood and respected her suspicion of whites.

I soon found Thomas and began a friendship that deepened throughout the summer. I measured the depth of our friendship through the reactions of his children toward me. They were much more direct than their parents in showing feelings of caution toward me as a white outsider. When I first entered their home, the Thomas children avoided me and spoke little in my presence. Once I had established a relationship with their father and spent many hours in their home, when I arrived, the children ran to the door, held my hands, and led me into the house, telling me jokes and stories they wanted me to record. They often held my hands while I spoke with their father about his work.

Their expression of affection through physical touch was characteristic of all age groups in the black community. When I was introduced to Thomas's friend Shelby Brown, who was known as "Poppa Jazz" because he had run a blues joint in Leland for over thirty years, we shook hands. Afterward a friend of Shelby's asked me, "Do you know what you just shook?"

"No. What?"

"A handful of love."

An extension of this warmth was the verbal banter that occurred whenever Shelby met his friend Gussie Tobe. Tobe turned to me once and said, "I want you to whip his ass for me. If you don't, I'm gonner go home for my shotgun and shoot the son of a bitch dead."

Shelby looked at me and said, "I'm waiting for him. I'm waiting for him."

Shelby then walked around shirtless with his chest pushed forward. Tobe whispered loudly to me, "You wouldn't think that man's eighty and can walk around sometime without his cane."

When James Thomas mentioned that the white funeral home where he worked had asked him to dig a grave the next day, Shelby replied, "Another rich one gone. Boy, you gonner have plenty of money. Lend me a dollar."

Just as the neighborhood children showed their trust through physical touch, my deepening friendship with James Thomas, Gussie Tobe, and Shelby Brown was measured by the lore that I collected. My acceptance was reflected in the increased level of protest and obscenity contained in the stories they shared with me. As I became closer to Thomas, he sang songs with which he identified as a black man, such as "Smoky Mountain Blues," which contains the verse:

God forgive a black man most anything he do.

God forgive a black man most anything he do.

Now I'm dark-complexioned, looks like he'd forgive me too.


I was sometimes confronted with both the humorous and the tragic as my relations deepened with the community. When I first met Shelby Brown, a man in his sixties, he lived with a woman he had married over thirty years before who had just returned to live with him after a twenty-year separation. While I was in their home, a local woman who had "stayed with" Shelby for seven years dropped in and appeared surprised to see Mrs. Brown there. Since the visitor had never met Mrs. Brown before, she was curious about her relationship with Shelby and asked a number of questions. After she left, Mrs. Brown turned to me and said, "I told her quick who was running this house. She must have thought I was just a whore he had picked up."

Mrs. Brown later told me of her experiences in the civil rights movement and how she had risked her life to organize voter registration in Leland. Because of her bravery in the face of white intimidation, she was selected to participate in the 1963 March on Washington. She was very proud of her work and described her experiences in detail.

When Shelby saw that I listened sympathetically to his wife's civil rights experiences, he told me about the injustices he had known as a young man in Leland. He said local whites considered blacks "crazy" when they retaliated against white violence. Shelby left Leland as a young man and lived in Chicago because he refused to accept white intimidation. He felt he would have been killed if he had remained. He recalled one incident during his youth when he bought peanuts from a white man in Leland who was known for his hatred of blacks.

Shelby had been warned that the peanut vendor often tried to trip young blacks and was ready for him. When the white man tried to trip him, Shelby threw the man on his back and ran. The white man called some of his friends, and when they found Shelby near his home, they whipped him. When Shelby recovered, he took his father's shotgun and walked to town looking for the whites who had whipped him. News of his coming reached town before him, and when he arrived, he said, "there wadn't a dog on the streets."

Shelby recalled a black man who killed two sheriffs in retaliation for their violent acts in the black community. When the black man was captured, he was placed in a wooden box, and railroad cross ties were piled on top. Gasoline was then thrown on the box and lit. The black man managed to open the lid of the box and escape the fire, but he was caught again and hung from a bridge over the local railroad tracks. He was still hanging when a passenger train passed, and the railroad company sued the town for the act.

Stories like these helped me understand the Delta saying, "In those days, it was 'Kill a mule, buy another. Kill a nigger, hire another.' They had to have a license to kill everything but a nigger. We was always in season."

Through my friendship with James Thomas, I discovered the "blues family" in Leland. This group of older men and women gathered each Saturday night in Kent's Alley at the home of Poppa Jazz Brown, the blues patriarch of Leland. Brown served sandwiches and corn liquor to musicians and dancers in the back room of his home. He knew everyone who walked through his door, and his jokes and stories always enlivened the evening.

Gussie Tobe was a regular at these Saturday night gatherings. Tobe worked hard during the week for the railroad and sometimes sang at Poppa Jazz's home. Tobe's stories capture both his hope for the future and his anger at the racism he endured throughout his life. When we spoke, he was drinking from a fifth of Jack Daniels, and his speech sometimes was affected by the whiskey he continued to drink during the interview.

James Thomas, Gussie Tobe, and Shelby Brown were intimate friends whose shared love for the blues drew them together. Their voices capture Mississippi Delta blues worlds with painful clarity.

# JAMES "SON FORD" THOMAS

I was born in Yazoo County, Mississippi, in 1926. When I was small, I went to Memphis once. All I can remember is, I saw a streetcar. That's all I can remember about Memphis. I was real small.

I had two brothers and a sister, but we wasn't raised up together. My grandmother and granddaddy raised me. I never did live with my mother. My mother gave me to my grandmother, and I stayed with her until I got grown. We lived in the hills over at Eden, south of Yazoo City. Eden is a tough place, toughest I've ever lived in.

When I was a boy, me and my granddaddy made his crop together. We didn't get but about six dollars a month apiece. That was to buy groceries. We didn't have rent to pay. He'd wind up with some change every month, and every month I'd come out a dollar or two behind. He'd ask me, "How much money you got?"

I'd say, "I ain't got nothing. I owe the store two dollars." So he'd give me the couple of dollars he had left.

When work time started, the boss man would come around in the morning about eight o'clock. We'd all be out there in the field hoeing. And when he'd leave and go into town, we'd slip off and go fishing.

I could sort of have my way with my grandmother. With my grandmother, if I didn't want to go to school, she wouldn't make me. I could go fishing or hunting or do like I wanted to. I didn't like to go to school too well, and with her I could play sick. She'd put her hand up there on my head and say, "That boy got hot fever. I ain't going to let him go to that school and fall down."

I'd get back in the bed, and I'd grunt around there till schooltime was over with. Then granddaddy'd get his fishing pole and get ready to go fishing. I'd jump up out of bed and say, "I feel a whole lot better now."

Most of the time when I was young, I never did fool with no boys. I mostly played by myself. I never did play with too many children. I had one friend that I played with. We'd go out and shoot BB guns or go swimming or hunting or fishing over on the Yazoo River. Things like that. But I never did fool with too many boys because I was always busy. Just anything would run across my mind, I'd do it. I was always around the house making fish nets or molding clay or something.

I used to listen to the *Grand Ole Opry* before television come out. We tuned the radio in every Saturday night, me and my granddaddy would. We'd just sit there and listen at the *Grand Ole Opry*. I believe we tuned in to Cincinnati too.

A long time ago, all we had to play records on was those graphophones because we didn't have no electricity. Friends would come by to listen to our graphophone, and we'd stay up all night long listening to that thing. My granddaddy, he was kind of scared of it when it first come out. He was scared to play it. He'd say, "If you play that thing in the house, it'll tell the boss man what's going on."

◄ JAMES "SON FORD" THOMAS, LELAND, 1968

JAMES "SON FORD" THOMAS AND CLAY SKULL, LELAND, 1971

He'd holler to me, "Cut that damn thing off, or the boss man will come!"

My granddaddy, Eddie Collins, was a musician. He played guitar, and my grandmother, she could play piano. I remember my granddaddy used to play that song "Little Red Shoes" for white people at dances. He's dead now. He died in 1957. He played them old-time blues. He used to keep a gang around the house all the time. He'd play guitar and tell funny jokes, and it'd be just like we was selling whiskey, there'd be so many people there.

My uncle learned me how to play guitar when I was eight or nine. He put marks on there, and that started me off. After I learned how to make a couple of chords, I could beat him. He started charging me fifty cents or a dollar to play his guitar. He wouldn't let me play his guitar unless I paid him. When he'd go to work, his wife would let me play his guitar, and I'd play until noon. Then when he'd come in, I'd quit. And I'd start back playing again when he went back to work at one o'clock. I learned to play real good that way. Then I got able enough to buy me one.

The first guitar I owned was in 1942. I picked enough cotton to pay for that. I ordered me a guitar out of Sears and Roebuck, a Gene Autry guitar. It cost eight dollars and fifty cents. After I got my guitar, I wouldn't pick no more cotton. That was it. That's how I learned to play the guitar. My uncle played, and my granddaddy played too.

The blues has been out so long, you can't hardly tell where it started. My granddaddy was about seventy-five years old when he died, and I used to hear him talk about the blues. There must have been blues before his time because there was blues when he was a boy. I think there always was the blues. They come from the country. You take a long time ago, you'd catch fellows out in the field plowing a mule. You'd hear them way down in the field late in the evening singing the blues. That's why I say blues come from the country.

I heard them old songs when I was a young boy. I'd slip around to dances, and I'd hear them old-time blues. There would be house parties back in the hills, out in the country at what you call juke houses. Those are them old raggedy houses way back out in the country. We didn't have but one night to have a good time. We'd stay up all Saturday night and try to get some rest on Sunday. All in the late hours of the night, you could hear those guitars. You could hear them for three miles either way. And if you be quiet, you could hear them singing.

We danced the slow drag. You know, that's the old style. They used to do the cakewalk. But now, if you come to a Saturday night dance, they just want the slow drag. And every time a man turns his back to his girlfriend or wife, he's whistling at another woman.

I'm going to ask you this now. Just like you eat eggs and bacon in the morning for breakfast. Would you want that every morning and every night? Nothing else but eggs and bacon every morning, and dinnertime come around, serve the same thing? Well that's the way this love goes. You get tired of the same woman all the time. You want to change up. You'll be walking down the street and say, "She sure look good."

There you go. Everybody can get that on their mind. You can marry and love your wife, but you're going to see somebody out there on that street and go, "Ooo wee!" That's the way it goes down in Mississippi.

The blues is nothing but the devil. You couldn't go to church and sing a blues song. You wouldn't do that. But a spiritual song, well, you wouldn't mind playing that in church. I don't belong to no church because I haven't made up my mind to join a church. It's just like if you went to that store over there, and they said, "You want a Coca-Cola?"

You say, "No, I don't believe I want any."

See, you ain't ready for that Coca-Cola. You ain't thirsty. You just ain't ready. When you make up your mind to do something, then you go ahead and do it. But if you ain't got your mind made up, nobody can force you into it. I always say that when I decide to join a church, I'll lay all them blues aside. I'd probably quit playing the guitar, period. I always say that if I ever join the church, I'm going to let all that go.

You can't carry both of them on. You can't go over to Greenville Saturday night and play the blues at a nightclub over there, then come Sunday morning, you call yourself a church member. I'd be afraid to do that because something bad can happen to you. If you play spirituals and you used to play the blues, the next thing you know, the devil gets in you, and you're going to start right back playing the blues. That's what you call "going too far wrong." You can't serve the Lord and the devil too. You can only serve one at a time.

And you can't always go by what them preachers say because right now some of them drink more whiskey than me. Some of them preachers ain't living for nothing but money and some chicken and a nice-looking woman. That's all they're living for. So you can't go by them. You have to go by what you believe. You have a feeling, you know, when you're right.

Women is what give me the blues. A woman tell you, "I love you." Then you go and find out she in love with somebody else. Well you can't have nothing but the blues.

I get a feeling out of the blues. That may be because I been worried a lot. After my first wife quit me, I had the blues. I was working in the field, and I come in one evening. I had bought her a pack of cigarettes. I never will forget that. A little boy told me, "Your wife gone."

And I got sick all at once. I said, "I know she gone."

"She carried all her clothes."

I said, "Get on away from here, boy."

But that hurts you. After that, anytime you get lonesome, you gonner want to hear some blues. Like that record come out, "Baby, Please Don't Go." That's just like you got a wife, and she packed up and getting ready to go. That's how blues started. It ain't very many blues that ain't made up about a woman. There's a few, but most of them is "My baby this" or "My baby that." Something like "Little Honey Bee." You ever heard that record?

Sail on, sail on, my little honey bee, sail on.
You going to keep on sailing till you lose your
    happy home.

That's one of Muddy Waters's recordings. In other words, he wasn't actually talking about a bee. He was talking about a woman, but he called her "my little honey bee." Mighty near every record where they sing the blues is made up about a woman. Your mind is on your woman. She's giving you the blues. You get worried over something, what you call a "deep study." That's the blues. You'll be thinking way back about how some woman left you. You want her, and she don't want you. That's what the blues is about.

Some of my songs are just made-up tunes. I couldn't necessarily go back over them again because they're make-ups. Just like if somebody mistreats you, you can make up a song about them. You might sing,

You mistreat me now,
But you can't when I go home.

That's the starting of a song. From there on, you can put in anything else you want. You just think up a verse and go from there. You get you some more verses and put them together. I can make you one up right now.

Beefsteak when I'm hungry, whiskey when
    I'm dry,

JAMES "SON FORD" THOMAS, YALE UNIVERSITY, 1976

Beefsteak when I'm hungry, whiskey when
    I'm dry,
Good-looking woman while I'm living,
    heaven when I die.

See, that has never been recorded. I just
made that up myself out of my head. But being
there's so many records out, I don't care what
verse you pick out, it will be something out of
somebody's record. They've just about done run
out of verses. So you get all your verses together.
You just sit down, and they'll come to you.
Sometimes I try to make new songs up because
you got to try to get some of these new verses
going or you can't get to play at these clubs. Just
like you hear a record on the radio, you try to
learn some of the verses in that. Nobody's going
to get it just like another man plays it. But you
can play close enough for them to know who
you're playing after. You get some of their style
mixed up with some of yours.

Back when I lived in Yazoo County, they
wouldn't hardly know who you was talking
about if you would go over there and ask for
James Henry Thomas. But if you say, "Son
Ford," they would know because they give me

that name when I was going to school. I used to make little Ford tractors out of clay. I'd put me some sticks through there as axles and made me some wheels and let it dry. Then I'd have something to roll across the floor. That was back in 1937, when they first started calling me Thirty-seven Ford. Then they started calling me just regular Ford. So I said, if I ever record records, I'd have them put my name in as "Sonny Ford." That's so all my friends back in Yazoo County would know who I was.

This sculpture is all done by head, not by no book or no picture. I never went to school to do this. No teacher has ever taught me nothing about it. My Uncle Joe Cooper started me off molding. He never did make nothing but little mules and stuff like that. If my uncle had kept on, he probably could do as good as me. But now, I doubt whether he could make anything. He didn't know what there was to it. After he quit, then I taken that trade up. I tried the same thing that he tried, and I done pretty good on it. So I took it over. It wasn't too hard to me to catch on. I just kept on trying until I got perfect on it.

A lot of days I'd walk two or three miles to get me some clay. I'd come back home and sit up by the fireplace at night and make things until I got sleepy. I got where I could make mules and rabbits and squirrels and things like that. From that, I went to making birds. See, this is a quail I made here. In Mississippi, the white people didn't want the colored people to eat no quail. Quail had more meat than other birds, better meat. I don't care if he had a license for hunt-

ing, a colored man couldn't kill no quail and let it be known. You could kill blackbirds. But if you killed a quail, it was just like you done shot somebody.

When I was a little-bitty boy going to school—I'd say about six years old—my sculpture was how I got my school money. I did this sculpturing to buy me crayons, pencils, paper, and all like that. My grandmother and granddaddy would work a whole week for two dollars, so they wasn't able to buy none of that stuff for me. I'd sell the things that looked good enough around the neighborhood where we lived at. After I got grown, I liked to be doing it, and I just kept going.

When I was small, I sold some horses, and I got three dollars for them. A fellow from Vicksburg was over at Eden, and I had them horses in a box. He said, "Where'd you get them little horses?"

I told him, "I made them."

He said, "I'll give you three dollars for them."

Well that sounded big then, and I just handed him the whole box. I would wind up making more than my grandmother and granddaddy, and I was just sitting at the house sculpturing.

The first time I made a skull, I was living with my grandpapa in Yazoo County. I made a great big skeleton head, and I had corn in his mouth for teeth. I brought it in the house and set it up on the shelf. We didn't have no electric lights then. My granddaddy was scared of dead folks, and one night he stayed up late. He came in and struck a match to light the lamp. And first thing, he looked in the skeleton's face. Instead of pulling the globe off the lamp, he jumped, dropped the globe, and run into my room. He told me, said, "Boy, you get this thing out of my house and don't bring another one in here. I already can't rest at night for spooks now."

You don't never hear nobody talking about being scared of spirits now. They ain't got no time to think of it. But a long time ago, there was a whole lot of people would talk of spooks. White people would use the word "ghosts." They say "ghosts," and not "spooks." I don't know why there's the separation in that. But right now, the average person in Leland, if you go and talk with them, they'll say, "Oh, there ain't no such thing as a ghost."

Some don't believe in them. But I believe in ghosts. I dig graves for a funeral home. But I don't never let night catch me out in the cemetery. I always get through before night or either wait and finish the next day.

A lot of colored people believe in what they call the hoodoo. Most of the white people, they don't believe in hoodoo. But it is something. It's got to be. You can get sick—you don't have to be real sick—but your blood can get wrong, and you get where you'll lay down and see things. People like that are "low sick," and they'll see things. When my stepdaddy died, he used to say, "Look at them dogs. Get them dogs out of here."

Well that's low sick. I got that way once. I was small, and my grandmother made me sleep on this cot that we had got from some white people. I just couldn't rest on that cot. I'd see all kinds of men and little boys and everything coming up around that cot and hitting at me. And I heard my grandmother and them whispering and saying they believed I was going to die, the way I was carrying on. So they finally got rid of that cot. And I didn't feel that way no more. I don't know what it was.

I moved to Leland from Eden in 1961, and I've been here ever since. I started working at the funeral home—working in the yard, mowing grass, and digging graves. I been opening and closing graves ever since 1961. I always say that I got a cemetery of my own, I done dug so many graves. I used to help my stepdaddy dig graves, and I got to where I liked to do it. My stepdaddy didn't have but one arm, and he used a three-foot shovel. I used to come out and help him. He'd tell me, "Son, I believe I can beat you digging."

Even though I had two hands, it didn't make no difference. He always beat me. So he learned me how to do it. And after he died, I taken over the job. I never did do no easy work. I thought digging graves was alright for me.

Today, I make deer, rabbits, quails, fishes, skeleton heads, and solid heads. I make them out of gumbo clay. Some of it comes from the hills on the other side of Greenville. It holds together just like the regular molding clay. I get some clay south of Leland, down at Black Bottom too. It really is black gumbo, but some people call it buckshot because it's so sticky that it takes a buck to run through it. It is sticky. I've known places where people raised chickens. Come a rain, those little baby chickens, they would get stuck in that clay. It would be all balled up under their feet.

When it rains, I let the clay soak up the water. Sometimes I mix a little wax with it to help hold it together. Then I put hair grease on there to smooth it down and get the wrinkles out of it.

When I do my sculpturing work, things just roll across my mind. If I see a picture in a magazine or on television, that's what I'll go by. I look at the picture to get the future of it better. The futures come in dreams. I lay down and dream about the sculpture, about how to fix one of the heads. I'm liable to dream anything. That gives you in your head what to do. Then you wake up and try it. If you can't hold it in your head, you can't do it in your hand.

I make a face first. I shape it up like a regular man's head. Then I cut it down to a skeleton head. That's the onliest way you can get a shape. The cause of me taking the top out of the head, that's to make an ashtray. That's about the best ashtray you can have because you can put a whole lot of stuff in there if you make it big enough. I take both thumbs at the same time and squeeze the clay in to make the eyes. I put marbles in there for eyes. You have to draw your eyes in there before you can get them lined up. Your eyes are on a level with your ears. They can't be a bit higher than your ears, and they can't be no lower. They got to be the same level your ears is, and that's why you don't have no trouble making glasses. If some people's eyes was down below their nose, they couldn't get no glasses to fit them.

Then I go back to where I done mashed up there to make the eyes, and that's automatic the nose. Then I cut the nose off to get the holes in the direct place. I use corn for teeth because I couldn't think of nothing else. You know the reason I started cutting that corn off? Because the first one I made, I noticed the teeths would move. That corn was sprouting in there. That's when I decided that the next one I made, I would cut that corn off to where it wouldn't sprout.

A skull has got to be ugly because it's nothing but bones and teeth. People are more likely to be interested in something like that than they would be in a bird. They'd rather see a skull. A lot of people have never seen a real skull, and they're probably wondering how it will be when they die. They say, "Will I be in the same shape that skull there is in?"

When I get it worked out, I stand back and look at it to see if I have it in shape. You have to get off from it and look and see what shape you got it in. You have to see if you got it too large on one side or not large enough. Then you level it up. You stand off from it to tell what you've done. It's got to be even on each side, see.

I don't like to do my sculpturing all the time. It just hits me by spells. A spell will hit me, and sometimes I can make them for half a day. Then I'll get tired of that and be wanting to go somewhere or do something else. In the wintertime, I'll be sitting up and not doing nothing, so I'll just sculpture a while and then quit. I don't know what I'd make if I'd just go steady at it all the time. To do this, you got to have patience. You got to feel like doing it. You can do a whole lot better when you don't try to make too many skulls. You just have to take your time.

If I could get to a mountain where they have this clay like I use, I believe I could do me a whole man. I believe I could put a whole statue of a man standing up in that mountain. If the clay worked right, I could start at the head and come right down to the feets. I believe I could work a statue as big as a man. I believe I could make him just as tall as me or you, if I could get the right height dirt. That's six foot high. I haven't ever did it, but I believe I could.

# GUSSIE TOBE

I was born in 1916, the seventh day of September. I had two sisters to raise me because I never did know my mother. But I think they did just as good a job as Mother could have done. I think I'm going on about fifty-two years old. I was born in Spratt Junction, Alabama.

This is my wife. Make yourself acquainted with this boy. He's just like anybody else. He ain't nasty. He ain't smutty and all that bunch of shit. She's half crazy, but you are welcome here. Now what did you want me to talk about? Some of those blues about who, where, when, and what happened? Oh yes!

> Oh, you got a gal and you want to treat her
> right.
> You got a gal and you want her to treat you
> right.
> Give her your loving, baby, don't you fuss and
> fight.
> You got a gal and you want her to treat you
> right.
> Give her all your loving, baby, don't you try to
> fuss and fight.

You hear all types of blues like "Rock Me, Momma, Like You Roll Your Wagon Wheel" and "Love Me, Baby, All Night Long" and "Short Fat Woman." You may hear some band playing an old waltz. But now this here young-time stuff, we really has that here. Just like "Short-Dressed Woman" and "My Little-Bitty Baby." Now when you hear that stuff, it makes you lush. In other words, when it goes like that, you want to get into it too.

When you get down here in Mississippi, man, you got a whole lot of stuff here. It's no better place in Mississippi on one hand. We got some of the prettiest women here you ever laid eyes on, and they not white either.

Okay, look here. I see some pretty white girls too. A bunch of us do, but we love ours. That's the way we go. When you get to Chicago, there's blues there. And when you leave out of Chicago, there's blues. And when you get over into Pittsburgh, that is a pretty place. Pittsburgh is the prettiest town that you gonna light in. You see, Pittsburgh, it's not close like Chicago.

They don't have no blues in Pittsburgh, like they do here. They have bowling, golfs, and they have beer rooms and joints. The reason why blues is here is that a bunch of us likes the blues. We studies that. That's all we can do. We don't have no money. What else we gonna study but something to have a good time with? So that's why these blues come from us. We never had no place to go and have a nice time. We work all the time and got no money, so we get us an old guitar. Gimme a bucket and let me knock it here and show him how it go. We have a good time. Take a washboard. Take a comb with paper. Sometime we have a guitar. Sometime we have a broom. We play them all.

That was our music back yonder. What we got now? Count Basie and the *Joey Bishop*

*LEFT TO RIGHT*: "LITTLE SON" JEFFERSON, "MOON SHINE"
(FRONT), JAMES "SON FORD" THOMAS, AND GUSSIE TOBE, LELAND, 1968

*Show*. Them gals come there with all that mini-stuff on. Boy, you know they jump up and holler about, "Whiskey, whiskey!"

We ain't never had no whiskey. You know the reason why? We never had no money to buy none with. That's the way we is now. We ain't never had no money to spend on our lady folks to make them look good. A man like me, I don't make no money. But you know what? I got a child out there. I wants that boy to look good when he walks out there with his schoolbooks.

My wife will get her bag and say, "I'm going to get him fixed up. I want so and so."

I say, "Go right over there to the store, baby. You know I done got so I can make some money now."

I drink me a few bottles of beer, but I don't get outlaw. When you get outlaw, that makes it bad getting along in each other's homes. I can live next door to you—you white and I'm colored. I can live here, and if I'm outlaw, you say, "Oh well, my neighbor's carrying on over there."

You gonna tell that down there to Mr. The Mayor. But if I'm a good neighbor and act right, I can walk over and knock on your door, and you say, "Who is that?"

I say, "It's Tobe."

"Alright, Mr. Tobe. What is it?"

"So and so."

"Alright, Mr. Tobe."

I say, "Alright, Mr. So and So. Let's jump in my pickup and go."

That's the way it oughta go down here. Mississippi's a good country. It's a rich country. It's plenty of money in this country. It's lovely. But the problem is, it's the old peoples. The old peoples, they don't want no regulations because they have it like they want it, and they'll die before they let it change. What it is, the young generation is coming. That means my childrens and your childrens and everybody's childrens, they wants to be like all the rest of the childrens.

Through all that we want a bunch of jazz to tell the whole world how the state's doing. Sonny Boy Williams used to say back in his time, he say, "Now look, I declare you pretty, and the whole state know you fine."

When you say, "I declare you pretty, and the whole state know you fine," that go for white and for black. And you know what that do when he say that? That brings eyesight back to the blind.

I think we all have good hearts. We love one another, and that is what we are supposed to do. We all wants to be wonderful.

It was a white man came through here riding one of those locomotives. He got off. He had two little boys, and he had two big sacks. If I make no mistake, he had come from Texas, but he had lost his children's mother. He come here, and it was warm like it is right now. He asked me could he rest out there, and I said, "Sure, you can rest out there."

He said, "Can I cook me and my two sons some food?"

I said, "Oh, you most certainly can."

I had a daybed out there, my drunk bed. I says, "Bertha, look here. We got company."

That bed right there, my bed what I lays in and sleep in every night, them two little boys after they had done gone in the house and washed up, I say, "Lay 'em in that bed there. And don't you fix a box of your food. Don't do it. Berta, come in here and prepare dinner for these people. We gonna rustle them up some money and give it to them."

He says, "I don't want no money. When I get to St. Louis, I'm gonna get me a job. I just want a place to put my kids."

Okay, here's my goddamned, low-down foreman. The son of a bitch, his name is Mr. Jones. Goddamn him and broadcast this motherfucker all cross the United States. Here's what he done. He sent the police here. The chief of police come right there, and I said, "Oh, what you want, Chief?"

"I'm looking for them white folks."

"Who sent you over here?"

"Mr. Jones."

"What he sent you for?"

"His stuff."

"Mr. Jones told you a goddamned lie. That man is poor. He had money. He bought me half pint of whiskey after I fed him. He didn't want to take no charity. But he did want to keep his money until he got where he going to so he could get a job and take care of his two boys."

He say, "Well I tell you what you do. Can you find them?"

I say, "I don't know whether I can or not, Chief. But I'll try."

I walked through the yard. I called. I called. He hid from me because he seed that car come up. He hadn't done nothing to nobody. The chief told me, "If you can catch them and bring them here, I'll give them the fare where they wanna go and give them food."

I went right back to my boss man, Mr. Jones, about 260 yards from my house. I walked right up to him, and I said, "You the dirtiest goddamned white man I ever seed in my life because goddamnit that was your color and not mine. Don't you fuck with them like that. Goddamnit, who you think you are? Because you working peoples, and I'm your labor, what the hell you do that for? They wasn't none of my color. Goddamnit, they was your goddamn color. Don't fuck with me no more if you don't mean right."

And Mrs. Jones walked out there and said, "Mr. Jones, you oughta be ashamed of yourself."

I said, "Goddamn your goddamn husband."

One time he walked up to me and he fucked with me, and I told him, "Look, I'll take you up to the supervisor, and you write my time out, mister."

I had me a gallon of good corn whiskey. We love that here in Mississippi. And if you drink that goddamn corn whiskey, you ain't gonna get no goddamn work done. Your goddamn work gonna fall and fall. I said to him, "Take me over there and gimme my time cause I don't like the way you fuck with me."

The little old office was right up on the hill, just up the hill from my house. I said, "Come over here and gimme my time. That's one goddamned thing about you. You too goddamned chicken cause I won't have but one motherfucking time to die. I wants my money or get your foot outta my ass. That's what I want."

Supervisor say, "What's the matter? What's the matter?"

I say, "I want you to tell Mr. Jones to get his foot outta my ass. I been working for y'all twenty-five or twenty-six years, and I do what you tell me to do. But I want his foots outta my ass."

"Go on home, Tobe. I'll take care of Jones."

Hadn't had a minute's trouble since. We gotta stand up for our rights here. If I'm working for you, whatever you tell me to do, I'll go do that. You the boss, and I'm supposed to do that. But now you ain't got to make no goddamned prisoner out of me. Just think about how you would feel if you was picking up them goddamned log and blocks with a shovel like that all day. Think about how you would make it like that. We all got to live. This here dollar with the eagle on it, I made that with the greatest of care, with this Lord's care. He enabled me to make this, and that's what we all working for. Ain't no use of us killing one another about this.

If I work and if you on the same job, if I get twenty-five dollars a day, you probably make thirty. If I can command your job, goddamnit, I'm supposed to have just as much money as you have. I think that's civil rights.

The civil rights is fine, but I don't give a damn about the integration. The civil rights is what I want. This dollar is what I live off of. Ever since way back yonder when, who is that? George Washington, ain't it? And what the other president's name? Hell, every damn good one you had got killed ever since Lincoln's times. When the slaves was working, you know how it was? It was like: "Here I come on my big horse. I'm gonna beat your ass and make you tote logs. You gonna clean up the goddamned grounds over here. I'm gonna raise meat and stuff to feed you. I ain't gonna give you no goddamned clothes. And you gonna work. When you raise up a daughter big as that teenaged girl there, she got to come over here where I'm at, and I'm gonna send you over in the new ground. She's gonna be here with me."

Okay. Here we come. We got a white and brown baby. So that's the way it all transpires. So here come the black boy around. Now he done something too. Don't you never think that through all them times them white women never loved them colored boys too. But they was too damn scared to tell about it. Here come John clipping them flowers. John got him some too. You understand that?

But now, what don't kill you don't kill me. What's good for you is good for me. But these old heads, shit, they got about five guns in the back of their pickup right now. They say, "Ain't no bears in this country." They say, "Goddamn nigger son of a bitch. I'm gonna find that son of a bitch, and we gonna kill him."

They called colored folks bears. Because his flesh wasn't the color of theirs, they called him a bear. They say, "Yon come a goddamned bear. Let's skin him."

His white blood is the same as my blood right now. He could get shot or cut, and my blood would save him. But he say, "There come a bear. Let's get the goddamned bear. Let's get him."

See what I mean? Well God don't love that. Look in your books. Jesus wants everybody to live in equality. He told you already that it's gonna be wars and rumors of wars. Did he tell you when the end gonna be? No. Never spoke of when the end gonna be. The wars and rumors of wars is here. And then he said through that time sons would be against daddies. Mothers would be against daughters. And it's here now. It's here, right here on hand now.

Look what they done for my boy. I call him my boy, this Robert Kennedy and also Martin Luther King. What did they do that for? In other words the whole world and United States know it's gotta be something done. It may be me gets killed over it and you too, but some killing's got to be done cause this thing gonna come out. These old heads what's older than me and you, eighty years old some of 'em, if you just look at their daughter, they say, "Hang that son of a bitch! He looked at my daughter. Goddamn, hang him. He looked at her."

I say, "No, boss, I ain't done it."

"Get him. Let's take him and hang him up to this tree here. We'll hang you up there and put smoke under you. And take them guns. Boom! Boom!"

Ain't no sheriff coming. Other words, this is why I want you to take this to Congress. If they come and kill me, I don't give a goddamn.

Ain't no use to carry a thing to Congress cause Congress ain't worth a good goddamn. It take powerful mens out here to go up there and get the work done. Congress ain't shit. Cause if Congress was worth a good goddamn, they would go and do something about them men that got killed over here at Ole Miss [the University of Mississippi] and get something done about killing Dr. Martin and them two presidents—one was president and one was running for president. Now what you think gonna happen? If mens what got the money and got power don't go and do this, well goddamn Congress. Another man said that over the news, and I think he was right. Goddamn Congress! Get up and get your goddamned money and force it through. Money is what rules the world. They say, "Oh, I got my money here. I'll give you about twenty thousand dollars. Go over there and kill that son of a bitch."

Okay. Here I come. You've got twenty thousand. He got twenty thousand. Here's another one over here, he say, "Hell, I got forty thousand. Grease your hand with that."

Well don't you know that's bribing? It's not the man shooting the gun. The man shooting the gun ain't worth a goddamn. He don't have as much as you and me. It's the other one behind him, the one putting the money up.

The United States of America is a good country, providing if the people in America could treat each other right. They put us outta jobs. They won't give us no food. And they just do us any kind of way. And they taking the money out the states and send it way over yonder to Czechoslovakia and anybody else over there.

Okay. Look at Dwight D. Eisenhower. He was a Republican, see. He had two faces—Republican and Democrat too. They asked him, "We want so many Caterpillars over here to push rocks and mountains down. And we want so much money. We want so many fine Cadillacs to ride in."

Well goddamnit, he took this out of our internal taxes—what I'm paying today and you too if you were working here—and sent it over there to them. Now is that right? Hell no. That's not right. We wants right. I'm too goddamned old to vote, but the rightness will be for you and then your childrens to see.

You seen more light babies in our race, but now, who done that? Old boss. You know in those days they had to do that or get hung or burnt. The Lord fixed it so that we don't have to live that way no more.

These childrens of mine and yours now got a silver spoon. Here come the school bus to pick my son up. It'll pick him up and carry him to the schoolhouse. In my day you didn't know what a pair of nice school shoes was. These children now, white or colored, they go to the store and get them some socks and slippers. And if I'd had a pair like they got, they'd have to last me a whole year. One pair of socks, and if I didn't keep up with them and wash them every time I wore them, I didn't have no more.

They done got to the place now where they got the colored people stirred up. They got the colored stirred up, and they don't even want to go to church. One-third of the peoples would rather stand on the corner and say, "Man, you know I bought me a pistol last night."

You know what the president gone and done?

He done made it so we can't get no guns now. But that old piece of a son of a bitch I've got, I'm gonna keep it. Gonna go down there and get me a bucket full of shells. And if something start, I'm gonna fire them off.

On the average, what do the common farm labor make? Eight dollars a day. Well you know what eight dollars do? Just make him mad and make him and his family want to eat. That man is working and driving one of them great big farm tractors—that son of a bitch is heavy now. Don't think it ain't. He go down there and gets paid off, gets his wife a dress costs eight dollars. She wants some new slippers, and she may want her a goddamned wig. These women is wearing a bunch of wigs. Old Berthie Mae here, she got three, and they cost eighty dollars apiece.

She get ready to cook in the morning time, and I say, "What the hell you cook so darn much for? It ain't but two of us."

I go down there and pay the grocery sometimes, and it's fifty and sixty and sometimes ninety dollars. I say I don't give a goddamn cause I ain't never had nothing nohow. Ain't used to nothing. Them white folks out there, hell they be used to getting all they want all the time, and the reason I'm a damn fool is I ain't used to having nothing.

I remember the time I was plowing for fifty cents a day. Shit. What could you buy with it? And when you plow for that fifty cents a day, you know what they'd do? They'd say, "Come down to the commissary there, Gussie."

He'd pay you half in money and the other half they'd pay you off in their money. But you couldn't spend it a damn place but at that store.

Have a pocketful of money, but where could you spend it? You couldn't go out there and buy you a beer or maybe go get you a girl and go out to a good old restful place and enjoy your life some. You had to spend it right down there at that goddamned robbissary—not a commissary—a robbissary.

They had this country sewed up bad. A shirt like you've got on now, I've seen the time when if you come in this country with a shirt on like that, and we'd eat your ass up, man. We'd strip you of them clothes and set you out there naked if we would have had the guts. We had it in our minds, but we didn't have the guts to do that. So all we ever done was drink us plenty of white whiskey.

Oh, it's some of our people will always do something. You look in the papers and read, "A Negro done so and so."

Well you made him mad. If you hadn't made him mad, he wouldn't have done it. In other words, all through those times, it was hard. I remember in nineteen and twenty-seven we were hungry. We had some home-ground meal and no meat and had some of that old fatback, you know.

It rained in '27, and the levee broke up here at Scott. I got me a little fishing pole and put me a little old hook on it. It rained so you could pick up bait just like you picking up stones off the ground. I went down there and had to drag 'em in. My sister told me, "Son, today's Sunday."

I said, "I know it, sister, but we're hungry. Don't whip me for getting something to eat for us."

What do you pay for shoes now? Twelve dollars? Jesus Christ. In those days, do you know what twelve dollars could bring you if you had got it? You'd of had to have a transport to bring the stuff in here. You wadn't getting but fifty cents a day. You ever pick cotton for thirty-five cents a hundred? You ever work for fifty cents a day from sun to sun? Well I done it. Back in slavery times, those peoples whipped my daddy's ass and my mammy's ass and made my mamma's daughter have them, and that's where the white children come from. But yet and still, the black man was around there, and he got some too. When Ole Master get on that damn horse, she called John and learnt John. In other words, when Ole Miss get ready for it, she got that too.

I know a place in Pascagoula, Arkansas, where they had to pull the blinds down for you to be on the train. If you were colored and showed up there, they would take you off the train and hang your ass. And wasn't nobody coming in there after them. You hear what I say? It was slavery then. But now the slave is no more. You hear me? That's what us wants. That's what us wants.

Then too I will say this. I will always say this. We do have some good white peoples, and they are hard to get to. A good Samaritan white man, you can hardly get to him. If he's good, he will help a colored man. But a Samaritan, you can't hardly get to a Samaritan.

I'll tell you about a good Samaritan. It was snowing in December way back years and years. He was walking along way up north. He had on his snowsuit and snow boots and everything to stand in the climate. He walked through there and seed a rattlesnake down on the ground. That snake was so cold, wasn't nothing living but his head. The Samaritan walked there and looked down at the snake and say, "Where you wanna go?"

The snake say, "I wanna go down into Virginia."

He wrapped him up and put him in his bosom, zipped him up. When snake woke up and got good and warm, he say, "[rattles matchbox]." You know what that was? That was them rattlers, mad rattlers! And the snake had promised him before the Samaritan picked him up, say, "I won't bite you if you carry me."

When he went to rattling, the Samaritan said, "What's the matter?"

Snake say, "I'm gonna bite you."

He say, "Don't do that. You told me when I picked you up that you wouldn't bite me. You said if I could get you to Virginia, you'd help me."

The snake said, "Yes, but goddamnit, you knowed I was a goddamn snake. You knowed I was a goddamned snake when you picked me up."

He said, "I know that, but I didn't thought your word would fail on me."

Today, if you go to a white man, he'll say, "I'm your friend. You can have what you want. Come over here and get it."

You know what that mean? That mean you can get my dollar if you give me thirty cents on my dollar. So you have borrowed about seventy cents from him. You got no dollar cause you gotta pay thirty cents on the dollar. All these loan companies here in the state of Mississippi, you can walk up there and say, "I wants me eight hundred dollars."

You know what they gonna have to have? They need your recommendations and how long you been working and what do you own and who do you owe over yonder. What store you buy your food at? They gonna call them. And if you owe a furniture company, they gonna call them. Other words, they gonna keep you about two hours to sit there to see will you pass through. If you borrow two hundred dollars and pay thirty cents on the dollar, how much money have you borrowed? That is what got this state messed up now.

You go to the furniture company, and you can't never get through paying them. The Household Loan Associations, they sound so easy. But when you get the loan, you can't hardly meet the notes on it. Then when you miss the payment, they got the whole house back. This is true.

We work, and we pay. If we buy a new automobile, we won't never get through paying for that car. You know what happens to that car? We have to take that car and trade it in for another, and we still ain't through paying for the old car. You know what pays our bills? I can tell you if you don't know. Death! Death pays us bills off. That comes from way back yonder when they paid you off, and if you said something, they'd say, "What did you say?"

"I didn't say nothing, sir."

That the way it used to be. We got some colored folks out here now got money. But us colored folks won't do near as good with our money as you white folks with yours. Now, you got some good white peoples. Don't get me wrong. You got some good white peoples on your side, but here's what they'll do. If you show yourself right, they'll help you. But you got to first show that you wanna do right. But if you gonna be a destruction, they're not gonna give you nothing. But could you blame them for that? Naw. But now, here come one along and say, "Come over here, John. Goddamnit, drive my goddamn tractor. Hell, I got everything you want over here. Come over here goddamnit. I got a house over here for you. How much money you want, John?"

"Oh, Captain John, I wants four hundred dollars."

"Here."

You'll never get through paying him that loan back. Better yet, a policeman come up there and say, "Come here, John. You're under arrest."

"What I done?"

"Goddamnit, you was speeding."

You go down there and buy you a bottle of whiskey, and he down there and see you when you buy it. Come right out behind you and lock you up. Here come the state troopers. If you live in this state, it ain't but one way you can live and get by. You gotta be eating out of the garbage can. If you live and work and make much money, they know you are making money. If you ride around in a nice car or something like that, they gonna be messing with you. In other words, they don't like the colored. But that's what they oughta love because here's one thing we always have done. There's my wife there, and there's my mother and sisters. They come and says, "I want you to babysit for me. Come on and take care of my house and clean for me."

When the whole thing wind up, they say, "Oh shit. Sally wasn't worth a goddamn."

Sally done took care of Little Junior, and he a big bookkeeper now. And we got to call him Mister So and So. Well goddamn him. He ain't no more than Jesus Christ, and we don't "mister" him, do we?

We ain't never had a schoolhouse. You know what they had for us? They had school in that little church over yonder. My daddy and my uncles had to go out in the woods and saw wood and send a nickel or dime for coal. That was the school we had. And then when our color try to get a job, the first thing they ask is what grade you made. And they know goddamn well you ain't made no grade. But the white man come on up there, and he done made it. Course sometimes he had patches on his knees, and his shoes had holes in them. But he had on some shoes. Goddamn, the school bus picked him up, and he learnt.

You know what happened? They'd say, "Looka here, Old Man Tobe. Gotta have these stalks cut."

They'd make me get out there and knock stalks with a damn ax. Cut bushes and clean up new ground. And if it didn't rain, I didn't go to school. I only went to school on rainy days. How far can I be behind? How far can we be behind? I wants a good education done for my color and for your color too.

Look here. Do you know one thing? We love white peoples. We does not hate the white folks. We love them. Do you know what white peoples is good to us? The merchants. Do you know why? Do you know why the merchants is good to us? Like I trade with this merchant here, and I pay him up. He gonna tell the other man over there. The other man'll get in his car and ride over here. You know what for? The money.

That's what we're fighting for, just like Dr. Martin. What had he done? Nothing. And that president and the one intending to be a president, they wasn't fighting to hurt nobody. The mens what killed them was money mens. Don't you forget that. Who pulled the trigger? Who pulled the trigger? You know who done that? That was the man behind him. The man what shot don't know his way out, but the man got the money knowed his way out. America is a good country. Course now, Mr. Johnson, goddamn him, sent all our boys and girls over there. They just booming and booming and killing. One man gonna have to stop that. One man started it, didn't he? One man gonna have to stop it.

This year's 1968. How many years is it before 1970? Two. Well I want this to go on record tomorrow. I'll take me a great big drink of whiskey before I tell this lie. I guess I wants to be in history. In 1970 it's gonna be a colored man gonna be a president of the United States. 1970. I don't know where he coming from, but he's gonna be there.

Up North, it's just as bad as it is here. The reason why I say so is if my boy go for a job and a white boy go for a job, they'll hire the white boy. They won't hire mine. That's the trouble. They not treating us right. They won't give us a fair decision. I go up there, and I been to school as much as you has. My face won't get it but yours will, whether you better or not. That's the whole shit. So that's the reason Chicago, New York, and everywhere else gonna get tore up. They gonna get burnt down. But the boys is wrong. You know why I say they's wrong? Because they doing things to innocent peoples. They not going to the right place.

They should go where they report to ask for a job. And if they don't get a job, then people that give jobs, they should give them some actions. They say, "Don't blame me. I'm a individual."

The first thing they oughta do is tear the goddamn employment office down. Burn that son of a bitch and whoever working there and go to the goddamn White House and start in there.

We all looking for jobs, and they looking over us. Don't put no bridge over my face for yours. I know that ain't right, see. They may go downtown and walk up to a nightclub, and a white girl in there. She's just a white girl, and you's a colored boy. She sit down and talk with you, and you talk with her. You not allowed to have a beer with her or drink liquor with her. You can't eat her up, and she can't eat you up.

Alright, Old Boss, goddamnit, he's riding his motherfucking horse and send me over behind that tree. And he here with my wife and daughter too. But now there ain't no more damn trees, is there? Ain't nothing to get behind now. Just ride on the train or on the bus or whatnot. The integration, I don't give a goddamn. What I want is civil rights. That civil rights keeps me

living and you too. These young people could get nervous, I don't know. But me, for my part, I wants more money for to buy more bread and to have a decent place to sleep. And they don't want you to have that.

I'll tell you where I'd rather live. Course I don't know if they got any good corn whiskey there. If I could get there and hadn't got so old, I'll tell you where I would settle down at. I would want to settle down between Pittsburgh and New Cassidy, Pennsylvania. That's oil country, and it's rich. You don't see but a few peoples up there. But them few peoples is good. Course you have to go maybe forty or fifty miles to a town.

The reason why I'd wanna go up there is I wouldn't be amongst no whole lot of this, that, and the other. I could be up there and be on my job all the time. If I had to come to town for something, I'd come and get it and go back home. I believe in these times here if you could get off and settle down to yourself and live right, you could live a good life, and that would be to your advantage.

You know how come? They pay good money. They treat you like you are colored folks. They don't treat you like you's a dog. If you was to go out there, you probably wouldn't wanna come back here no more.

I carried my wife to Chicago a couple of times, and I told her then, "If I ever get you over in Pennsylvania, goddamn this railroad. I'm gonna leave this son of a bitch."

The next thing should be done, somebody should look over this Illinois Central Railroad. They need to look over it. It's alright, but the jobs ain't done right. On the Illinois Central Railroad, the jobs ain't done like they should be done. You ask me why? A white machine operator, he gets about thirty dollars a day, and I gets about twenty-one. He gets that kind of pay, and on top of that, you know what happens? They pays his expenses. Pays his room rent and pays him for every mile he got to come. And by George, goddamnit, the black man can't get a goddamned thing but a cross tie and a mother-fucking tie plate. They transfer and run us from one place to another, just like they do the whites, but we don't get no difficult pay. So how much take-home money can we bring? He can live off his expenses and then take his paycheck home. You know what I have to do every morning? See my car there? I have to go to Greenville to work every day. I pay my own expenses. Now when white peoples out there working, they pays the expenses and room rent and everything. Now I can't get a good goddamned thing. I hope this goddamned record go to New York and someone look over this Illinois Central Railroad cause they ain't treating the colored people right. The white folks is fine, but we ain't. If you say any-thing about it, they say, "Aw hell, I'll run you off."

I don't give a damn about being run off. I'll go on and work cause I ain't got too many years to live no way. You know how come? When you get my age, you'll say the same thing. You done worked and worked and done all you could. You supposed to have your rights, and you gonna stay in the place where you're supposed to have your rights. That's the way I feel about it. I feel that way about everybody on the damn railroad. Plenty of days I go to work. I get up and go out there and do my share and do my job. I don't argue with nobody. Don't say nothing to no-body. I just go ahead on and work cause I done it for twenty-six years. So I just as well to go and keep on.

My wife got a plantation out there in the hills. Her son live on it, and she got a bunch of cows and whatnot. I say, "Well I wish sometime we could just give up and go."

We stayed through all these hard times. People don't know who ain't been here. It's a lot of boys and girls now is born with a silver spoon in their mouth. You know what that is? You got what clothes you want to wear, wristwatches, bicycles to ride, and motor scooters. Your daddy buy you a car. Goddamn, when I was a boy, my daddy couldn't buy me one skate to skate on just one foot. You know what? He made the money, and Old Boss taken it and then give him just so much at the commissary. We had to sleep in our clothes at night cause we didn't have no bed cover to cover with. We slept in our clothes. What we had, we wore until it wore out, and then we'd get some more. That's what Old Boss done in the state of Mississippi. But now, when old Old Boss finish up and let Old Boss grand-son come along, he gonna let us live.

And then they'll say, "A colored man this and a colored man that."

Down through old times they'd say, "Come up here, John. Here, get you a drink of whiskey."

Just like this. [Drinks a long drink of corn whiskey.]. Ahhhhhh. Good whiskey, white folks. And then they say, "Goddamnit. Go do so and so."

After all that, you know what he'd make you

do? He'd say, "Go over and bring me a bale of cotton over here tonight off of Dr. Swain's place. Go over and steal it. Steal it!"

You'd bring it back to him and help put it in his gin house. Then he'd turn around and say, "John ain't worth a goddamn. We oughta hang that son of a bitch."

After all that, I wanna make this statement. After all that, we still love the white man. We never hates the white man. But what he hates us for, we don't know. We never had no power to do him no harm. He always done what he wanted to do, and we never could do nothing but what he said to do. Just like me, I'm an employee now. A man tells me, say, "Go down yonder and get such and such a thing."

Just like the other night, I was down at Rolling Fork. I got off at eight o'clock at night. I come in, and I had to walk nearly a quarter of a mile to pull the darn flag down on the damn railroad. Boss say, "Go yonder and pull that flag down and put it in the truck."

It was right next to his goddamned house. I said, "You know that's something. These peoples down here ain't worth a good goddamn."

You know, I was speaking to myself alone. But now if they gets me funky, brother, I really would tell them what funky, funky Broadway means. It means you gonna get your ass whipped if you fuck with me too much. That's what it means, cause I ain't scared.

But now the state of Mississippi is a good state. I never cut it down. It's the people in the state of Mississippi what makes the state so bad. In the state of Mississippi, the taxes is too rough. On that damn old piece of car I got, it run seventeen or eighteen dollars. And if you get you a new car, you gotta pay eighty or hundred dollars. After the money we pay for taxes, the highways of Mississippi should ride just like a rubberized mattress. If you have one light out, the highway patrol will stop you. He ain't gonna talk to you when he stop you. You gonna pay that money.

And out of all that money they got, why shouldn't they come up and make improvements with the highway? Every time we hit a rough bump on that road, you know what it do? Knock one of your lights off balance. Well when you get a inspection, that's when it all counts up. That's when you have to pay.

If a black boy see a white gal and he wanna talk to her, don't you talk to her in Mississippi. If she want to talk to you that bad, take her right on cross the line over there. If she wanna talk to you, she'll talk to you. But now don't try to sleep with her here cause if they catch you sleeping with her here, the first thing you know, she gonna say, "Oh, he ravishing me."

You say, "What the hell they talking about?"

But that's the way they all go. Ain't you always reading papers about, "Oh, he ravished Mrs. So and So."

That's a goddamned lie. They just caught him getting it. She squealed to keep them from saying what she was doing. Can't you understand? Alright. Now these times is coming. These times is coming around. Today or tomorrow, if I makes up my mind that I want me a white girl, I ain't gonna talk to nobody. Shit, I'll get my damn ass outta here and go to a place where we can mix with one another. There's been a place ever since it's been a world where we can mix with one another. But now, here's what it is. You got to pick your people to mix with, I don't care what you say. She can be white as you. She can be pretty as she is. I think a Italian woman is the prettiest woman in the world. What I mean, she makes a pretty picture, a pretty figure. I don't mean the prettiest woman in the world, but she right next to my color in the world. My color in the world is one of the prettiest womens, and the Italian is just as pretty.

Now an American woman is pretty too, but she's not built up. A real American woman, look at her real good. Shit, she look like one of them old horses that win the races. She look just like one of them goddamned racehorses. But now, the colored woman and a Italian woman, if you size 'em down, is about the prettiest women in the world. Oh, you see a lot of different mixes alright enough, but a colored woman, when you get her fixed up, and a Italian woman, put some stuff on her, she damn sure looks good.

You don't find no American folks ain't got money. You don't find no American white folks ain't got sense enough to have it. All the Italians, all the goddamned Chinamen, all the Jews come right over here and take the money right from under our noses.

Jews loves colored peoples, and they treat us good. If you want something, they'll give it to you. My wife works for the Jack Cookie peoples. They just bring me cookies and stack 'em all around my head in the bed there. That's the reason I tell you all the time there is some good white peoples, and there is some white peoples

that ain't fit for a dog to bark at. It's the same way with my color.

Integration is real fine, but I don't make no pronouncements on that. You know who I'm gonna let do that? The ones coming. I'm nearly about going home now. I'm too old to participate in that integration part.

Old Bilbo, he was a guy. In 1932, that was just before President Roosevelt come in. Let me tell you what statement he made. Wait just a minute. I'm gonna have to drink whiskey to talk about hard fellows like that. He made a statement about "I'm gonna castrate all the black mens."

That's in the record. He made that statement. Bilbo said, "I'm gonna castrate all the black mens."

Okay, President Roosevelt he was running for president then. He says, "Okay, Mr. Bilbo. You do that. But I tell you what I'm gonna do. Before that happen, I'm gonna arm every black man in the United States. Then you castrate them, but not before."

Then what happened? When he found out Mr. Roosevelt was gonna win the election, the old son of a bitch got all the money and started across the damn river with it. They had to catch him and bring the money back to the United States. If you don't believe me, get your history book, the history of the United States.

You could see the folks coming from the hills with great big sacks of money bringing it up to the bank. After Bilbo got it in the bank, he took the money out the bank and had a whole ship going across the Atlantic Ocean to the South

Pacific. They had to catch him and bring him back here. That was in 1932. You hear me?

It's one thing I can say. We needs us a president. We needs a president of the United States. There's my people here. They needs help. They're getting some, but it's not enough. We gonna be here. I live here, and I done got too old to go somewhere now. Bertha Mae say she gonna quit me. But it'll be alright. If she do, I will reach back and get my washwoman, and we can live together. So I'm gonna sign off now.

# SHELBY "POPPA JAZZ" BROWN

They got the blues because of how they made the folks here plow and hoe and chop cotton at daylight in the morning. They would get out there and work so hard they would sing, "Hurry, hurry, sundown. Let tomorrow shine." They wanted the sun to go down so they could stop work. They worked too hard, and they learned the blues from that.

Once there was two brothers. One was named Heaven and the other was named Hell. One boy would pray all the time and preach, and the other boy what had hell in him would say, "Man, what you gonner do now? You gonner always pray and ain't never gonner try to get hold of none?"

Heaven said, "That's right, brother. I'm on the Lord's side. I'm gonner pray. You pray for what you want, and I'm gonner pray for what I want."

So this old boy named Hell said, "Let me tell you something. Now we brothers. The first one die, that's gonner be me. Now when I die, I know the devil ain't gonner let me come up from where I'm at, but the Lord will let you loose. When you die and get to heaven, I want you to come and see me."

So sure enough, the old boy died. And in a few months the other brother died too and went to heaven. He was up there drinking that wine and eating that good bread. They had milk and honey and everything. So he finally thought, "You know, my brother told me to come and see him when I die. He's in hell, and I wonder if the Lord'll let me go down to hell and see him."

So one of the Lord's prophets was there. He was standing listening, and he say, "What you want?"

He say, "Reckon the Lord'll let me off and let me go down to hell to see my brother?"

He say, "You ain't got nothing to do but go ask him."

So he went up there and say, "Lord. Lord, come here. Would you mind letting me off for a few hours to go down to hell to see my brother?"

The Lord told him, "Yeah. But if you go down to hell, I got to give you a length of time to stay before you come back here."

He say, "Well alright. I'll take that chance."

The Lord say, "Well I'll give you until nine o'clock."

It was twelve that day. He wouldn't eat dinner. The Lord went down, and he saw Jonah. Jonah was standing at the gate. He said, "Jonah, give that preacher there a pair of wings and let him fly on down to see his brother. If he don't be back here by nine o'clock, don't let him in the gate."

Preacher say, "That's alright. That's a bet, Lord."

They give him his wings, and he stretched them out and flew on down to hell. When he got to hell, he knocked on the door. "Who is that?" One of the devil's imps opened the door.

He said, "This is Preacher."

"What do you want?"

"You got a boy down here named Willie. This is Preacher. This is his brother."

The imp opened the door and said, "Hey! Come on in."

The little imp started dancing around him. He come on in there. His brother saw him and said, "Lord, have mercy. When did you die?"

"A few months ago."

He said, "Well come on in."

He first walked in and looked over there at a nice table where they were playing cards. Then he looked over there, and they was shooting dice. He said, "They allow you to do that here?"

He said, "Yeah, man. We pitches a bitch here. We pitches a bitch."

Walked up there to the bar. They had whiskey, wine, everything. He said, "Wait a minute, man. Here's where I want to stop, right here."

He grabbed him some whiskey and started drinking. He turned his wings to the bar. When he turned his wings to the bar, he looked over and seed them pretty gals with hair all down here and said, "Wait a minute. Come on and let's go over here."

He went over there. (He's forgetting the time! He's forgetting the time! He had to be back in heaven at nine!) He went on over there where them gals was, and when the gal looked at him, she got up and give him a seat. He set down, and she set in his lap and put her arm around him. With all that hair, he knowed he was in heaven. She put that hair and them legs around him, and he said, "Huh! Lord, have mercy. I ain't never had this good treatment up in heaven."

He called his brother. "Come here, brother. Ain't nowhere I can go?"

He said, "Yeah. Just tell her."

So he whispered to her. They got up, and she had her arm around him and went up to the room where they go. He got them wings unbuckled and set them up 'side the bed where he could get in them quick. They laid there, you know, playing with one another and everything. And way along about 8:45, he said, "Huh! You know one thing, this here's a nice place."

He dozed off to sleep, and when he woke up, it was ten o'clock. He said, "Oh, baby. Wait here. Look, what time is it?"

She said, "It's after ten o'clock."

He said, "Lord, I'm supposed to have been back in heaven. I'm supposed to been back up there at nine. Wonder if they'd let me in?"

He grabbed his wings and stretched them out and flew on back to heaven. And when he got there, he had to ring the bell. "Booo!" [Imitates bell.] Wouldn't nobody say nothing. He shook the bars. He said, "Ain't nobody in this son of a gun. They may not let me back up in heaven."

He kept up so much noise that Jonah walked up there and said, "Who is that?"

He said, "You know who I is. I'm the man you sent to hell on wings."

"Who do you want to see?"

"I want to see the Lord."

"The Lord's asleep. You can't see him this time of night. He's asleep. What you want with the Lord?"

"Let me talk to the Lord. I want to talk to the Lord."

"Well you keeping up so much noise and waking everybody up so, I'm going to get the Lord. But you can't come in."

JOHNNY BROWN AND SHELBY "POPPA JAZZ" BROWN, LELAND, 1968

"Just let me talk to the Lord."

So he kept worrying Jonah till Jonah went on and got the Lord and brought him up there. The Lord opened the door and said, "Preacher, what do you want?"

"Lord, I just want to let you know one thing. I brought these damn wings back to you, and I'm going back down to hell where I belong. You can take these sons of bitches. Here they is."

So he went on back to hell. No bullshit. I ain't lying either. I ain't lying.

They play the blues in Mississippi because the folks here chop cotton and start work early in the morning. They be looking at the sun, and they learn the blues from that. Then you can get the blues from a woman. You can be kissing her, then you won't see her for three or four nights. You can get the blues from that. You understand me now? Most anything like that will give you the blues. Mississippi got more of that than anywhere. All the blues people come up here singing the blues. They couldn't sing nothing else around here but the blues. What you gonna do? You working every day. You gotta sing the blues. You can't go nowhere except on the white man's place. Other than that, what are you gonna do?

They take you out of school, made us quit going to school to work the land. That's why so much blues come out of Mississippi.

People like the blues. Good times. You couldn't have nothing but a good time. When you're all by yourself, what you gonna do? You can't be with nobody else. White folks on that side, and the Negroes on this side. You couldn't go to the white side of Leland. You couldn't go over there. They better not catch you on their side of the tracks. They would put you in jail, like you was trying to steal something.

We made our syrup out of sugar and watermelon rind. All we could get to eat was corn bread. We had to grow the corn and grind it to make corn bread, and we made syrup out of sugar and watermelon rind. You hear me? You tell these folks that, and they laugh.

You know what I can do right now? I can go in there and cook neck bones. You know, my boy said, "I won't eat no neck bones."

That made me mad, and I told him the truth. I said, "Son, you will eat shit. You will eat shit if you get hungry."

You don't believe that? I don't want it to come to that. He would never do that now. But if he come up like I come up, he would eat shit. He tells me he won't eat it.

"Don't give me no beans," he says. "I don't want that."

What you talking about, man? I would be glad to get anything. I went one time and got cow shit and made a meal of it. And he won't eat neck bones. I ain't lying. I said, "Eat eggs."

He said, "I don't want eggs."

What the hell you talking about? You be glad you got it. If you don't like it, why don't you get out there and get it yourself? If you don't like a thing, you get out and get something for yourself, right? I used to want pork chops. I'd smell them when the folks eat them, but I couldn't eat them. But something told me, said, "Shelby, why don't you go to work and save your money?"

And I did. Every time I worked, I ate anything I wanted to. I can get anything I want right now today. But these youngsters now, they don't believe that. They don't believe it. If I tell them right now about how I got twenty-five cents a day for picking cotton, they won't believe it. They say, "He's lying."

But that's the truth. When I got my fingers cut off, I was working at the sawmill for a dollar and a half a day. Look at that. What did I get for it? Nothing. Look at my hand. See that. I made a living for all of them with this hand. The Lord blessed me, didn't he? This boy right here don't want to listen to me.

Everybody you see goes to Chicago. When I grew up, everybody wanted to go there. I went and stayed there thirteen years. When I got ready to go there, people told me that money was growing on trees. I went there, and I thought money would be growing on a tree. So I got me two sacks and carried them with me to get money off that money tree in Chicago. I took two sacks with me. I stayed with my brother. I got his picture right over there. I went there, and he saw me with them two sacks.

He said, "What you carrying them sacks for?"

"Man, I'm looking for that money tree that's here in Chicago. They told me about the money tree, and I was looking at every tree. But I didn't see no money."

He said, "Look, man, there ain't no money growing on a tree in Chicago."

He grabbed the sacks, threw them in the garbage can, and said, "Don't do that. You let folks make a fool out of you, telling you that money is growing on trees in Chicago. Chicago is a free place. Everybody is free. But, man, don't come and look for money on the tree. You ain't nothing but a fool."

He was right. I come looking for money on a tree. So I woke up. I stayed thirteen years too long up there. It ain't no lie. Shit. I got too tough. They sent me back to Mississippi. I got too rough in Chicago. They sent me away, and I was glad to get away. We'd go out in the streets all night long, and nobody bothered us. If you do that now, you're a dead man. You can't walk in Chicago at night right now.

You know, this boy, he was a real good piano player, and this woman, she had a husband who was a railroad man. He'd go to work on the railroad every morning. He'd get up, and this boy knew exactly when he going, and his old lady knew exactly when this boy would come. Every time the railroad man would go to work, this boy would go over there and play the piano. She had this one number she wanted him to play. "I want you to play this till the longest day you live."

He would sing,

I've been sitting here, a thousand miles away.
I've been sitting here, looking a thousand
    miles away.
Come here, baby.

Goddamn! She'd come and sit on his knee. Every morning they would do this. They would hug and kiss. The old man is gone to work.

So one time someone told the man, said, "You know, you's a fool. You go to work every morning, and that girl drops the bucket down, and that boy goes there and plays the piano, and they have a time."

He didn't want to believe nothing. "Don't tell me about my wife. She's not that kind. Don't tell me about what my wife did."

He turned around and said, "Goddamn! I'm going home. I don't feel good."

So he went on home and went on to his room. He heard the piano. "Dum, dum, dum . . . a thousand miles away."

He said, "I'm going to go back to work."

So he turned around and went on back to the job. He's going to get that boy the next morning. He worked all day, wouldn't say nothing to his boss, wouldn't tell nobody nothing. When he got home that evening, the wife had supper ready. He ate and told his wife, "We got a whole lot of work to do in the morning, so you got to get up early and fix my breakfast."

She got up and fixed his breakfast and had it ready quick. He grabbed his bucket that morning and said, "Baby, we got to go about seven or eight miles today from here, and I won't be back until late tonight. You know how the railroad is."

She said, "Alright, darling. I understand."

She wanted the boy to come in and play the piano. The man went out the front door and came back in the side door and got over behind the piano with his lunch bucket and all. Long about seven or eight o'clock that morning, there come a knock. She said, "Come on in, daddy. I know it's you."

The man stayed there behind the piano. "Come on, baby. Give me the blues. I'm glad that old guy went on to work. Shit, I got the blues so bad, I couldn't go back to bed after he left. I had to sit here until you come. Come on."

The man sits there behind the piano with his bucket. "Dum, dum, dum."

"Come on, baby, play that piano. Play that son of a bitch. I can sit right here and look a thousand miles away. Look here, I got nothing but this gown on, baby. Play that number for me. I'm gonna sit right down and dum, dum, dum, and look a thousand miles away."

The husband got up and said, "You say you can look a thousand miles away. Goddamn! But you can't see me behind the piano."

Man, all hell broke loose then. I ain't lying. I'm telling the truth.

Let me tell you one about the woman. If I had a dick like a ten-foot pole and a woman had a pussy like a mule's asshole, I would drive it up to her soul, and I'd play doodle de do on her black asshole. It's short, but it's funny.

Now, do you want to hear one about the squirrel? Of all the beasts that's in the woods, I'd rather be a squirrel. I would climb up in the tallest tree in the woods, and I'd piss all over the motherfucking world. That's a short one.

Look here.
Up to my lips and down to my toes,
I don't care what nobody says.
You can hit me in my nose and dig my soul,
But this good nice cool whiskey here,
Away this son of a bitch goes.
Ah. Ahh. Ahhh.
Kiss my grandmomma's preserves.

Who's gonna talk about Mississippi if they can get out of it? I love it myself. I'm scared to go to Chicago. They kill you up there, and they used to kill you here. But now they alright. Kiss my grandmother for that. That's good hospitality.

Just keep on living, and you'll be just like me. You gonna get like me one of these days. I thank you all for everything you ever did for me. But there's one thing I thank you for, one thing. Looka here.

Lord, have mercy on my soul.
How many chickens did I ever stole?
Four last night and five before.
I'm going back now to get some more.
I ain't lying.
Put the jug up there in my hand.
Where's the jug?
Here I am,
And I'm forty-five years old.

# CLARKSDALE

If there is a musical navel or crossroads for Mississippi Delta blues, it must be on the streets of Clarksdale, a city that lies in the heart of the region known for the blues. Generations of young black musicians fled surrounding plantations and moved to Clarksdale, where department stores, restaurants, barbershops, and WROX radio station were beacons of hope and excitement.

Celebrated musicians like Muddy Waters, Ike Turner, Reverend C. L. Franklin (father of Aretha Franklin), and Sam Cooke grew up in and around Clarksdale. Artists like B. B. King regularly visited and performed at clubs in the city, and Bessie Smith tragically died in Clarksdale from injuries she received in an automobile accident. The city's beloved disc jockey Early Wright played the blues and announced that "nighttime is the right time, the Early Wright time," for over forty years at WROX radio station.

In 1968, I recorded many hours of Jasper Love's stories in his home at 420 McKinley Street. Love told me that his grandparents were brought to the Clarksdale area as slaves, and he vividly recalled the experiences they described when he was a child. He also remembered being "scared to death" to meet British blues scholar Paul Oliver and California music producer Chris Strachwitz. Love's tales are set in and around the city and frame the musical worlds of which he was an important part.

Jasper Love's friend Wade Walton also grew up near Clarksdale, and musicians and friends gathered for conversation and drinks each week in the back of his barbershop. Known for his "barbershop boogie-woogie," Walton recalled Ike Turner's early days, Sonny Boy Williamson's funeral, and Howling Wolf's reunion with his mother.

Within these worlds, blues house parties were common, and I was privileged to join Jasper Love, Wallace "Pine Top" Johnson, Maudie Shirley, and Floyd Thomas at a house party that I filmed with Super 8 black-and-white film that is included in the fourth section of this book. During the party people of all ages danced to the blues and exchanged stories in a dramatic display of blues and storytelling, both of which were anchored in Clarksdale.

# JASPER LOVE

My grandmother told me about things she remembered when she was twelve years old. These white peoples would take two hundred dollars, and they would buy them black people like you would a mule or a car. They brought her and my grandfather up here from Decatur, Alabama. My grandmother said they brought her up here on a boat called the *Choctaw* in the Tallahatchie River. When I was a child, my grandmother would be setting down sewing quilts, and I would stay with her to keep her company.

She said the white man would feed them and give them clothes, and they would live in a house on his place. Her and her husband, they would go out there and work side by side cleaning up his land. After slavery, they finally got to where the white man would pay them so much an acre for their work. He called himself paying them, you know. The white man would say, "If you clean up ten acres today, I'll give you a couple of dollars."

But the land wasn't none of theirs. If they cleaned off the land, it would still belong to the white man. In the wintertime, they worked when the ground would be froze. She would put her gloves on and get out there and break cotton stalks. She actually got alongside of her husband, and they would go along with a stick and knock them stalks down. When the stalks froze, they broke better.

When they was farming, my grandfather would go to the lot and catch the mule. Then he'd come back to the house, and she'd have breakfast ready for him. Three times, they'd ring that bell. First time, wake up. Second time, be at the lot. If you wadn't at that lot when that second bell ring, why no doubt about it, you and that man was gonner have trouble. In other words, he was gonner whip you. In those days, he'd just whip you.

My grandmother used to tell me about it. She told me so plain about it, till I never will forget it. It was like I lived that life. She said she have taken my granddaddy's plow and mule and plowed a'many a day for him. I asked her, "Was that actually true?"

She said, "That was actually true."

They couldn't do no other way. The white man would ride a horse. And if he wanted your wife to work, he wouldn't ask you. He would tell you, "What your wife doing today? I want her to work for me."

He would go on and put you to work and then tell her, "Come on. I want you to go to work."

There wadn't nothing you could do about it. If you said anything about it, three or four or five or six of them would get together, and they would whip you. Maybe kill you, if you try to resist. She used to tell me about it.

My grandmother died in '25, and she was about ninety years old. She lived through the Civil War. She used to sing those old hymns. In slavery, they would get to talking about leaving and going to another place. Those hymns was

signaturing about what they was gonner do, you know. Just like you sing, "I'm going to meet Jesus down at the river."

Well it wouldn't actually be Jesus you were going to meet. It would be some man down there. That day or maybe that night, when they sang that song, it would let the others know that this particular man was at the river. When they would give out that hymn, the man was supposed to answer back and sing something like, "It's no dangers in the water."

That meant for them to come on to where he was. When they got there, they would camp by a fire. My grandmother told me sometimes they would be too scared to make a fire, and they would just sit there in the cold. The man would sing, "My child, it's alright. My child, it's alright."

When he would sing that song, they would know that the road was clear. You see, the white man didn't allow them to leave. He would buy them, and when the black man got ready to leave, he had to run off. That was before the Civil War. That was way back. My grandmother's mother and father used to sing those hymns.

In my days of coming up, I remember my mother and other ladies, they would go from house to house singing and praying. They would put the children to sleep, and they would sing them old songs. They was just treated so bad. They would sit up all night singing them old songs and talking about "Wonder what's gonner happen and how it's gonner happen."

They was just hurt at the way they was working. They'd sing those old songs, kind of like "If the Lord don't help me, I can't make it through."

They had to have some kind of music, you know. Mother would get in the church and sing, "I know I am a child of God."

I remember my daddy, he would call hisself singing on the blues side. He'd be plowing the mule and get hot, and you'd hear him out there in the field hollering, "I'm going up the bayou, baby, and I can't carry you."

The blues came from them old peoples. I knowed a old player called Old Poppa Stovepipe. He was older than I was. He would get a washtub, and he would play it like the piano. He would sing some kind of old something there about "She used to be your woman, but look who got her now."

In fact, he played a organ, one of those you pump. He played that and a piano. Those blues come from way back when they had to study something to try to give them some consolation. The man was doing them so bad—taking all they had and working them to death—that they just had to do something.

The way I see it, the difference between the blues and the spirituals is they think that if you singing the blues that you sinning. And when a guy is singing a church song, he's automatically doing something for the Lord.

My mother and father always taught me that the blues was sin and spirituals were serving the Lord. I remember a preacher said that if the blues hit him, he would go off by himself, and he would sing the blues. That was to get it off his conscience. And then he would ask the Lord to forgive him.

It's like, if you was singing the blues right now and you die, well, they say you going to hell because you was singing the blues. But if you was singing a church song, you would go to heaven. That's the difference they always told me. I never was a Bible reader. I remember church songs that I used to hear my mother sing like "Oh, when the saints go marching in."

They would get happy off of that, and they would cry and shout. But if I was singing blues like James Brown and sang, "Good God, can't stand myself," I'd get me a drink of whiskey and want to dance. A lot of people sing the blues, and they can't be all bad. The people that sing the blues, they not as bad as some people that I see going to church. Aretha Franklin, she sings both blues and church songs.

When my grandparents was coming along, the white people was so hard on them until the first thing they sang was "Lord, have mercy."

It hit their hearts, you know. They was thinking about how they was treated. Well here comes a guy that is maybe a little evil. He say, "The onliest way I can get relief from the way Boss is doing me is to sing me a blues."

It's what you call a worry song. I know I gets worried right here at the house. I used to do a lot of blues singing, but I drunk so much of that good whiskey—and that bad whiskey before I got the good—until it got to my voice. Now I play me a couple of records, and it give me ease.

It was some old man or some old lady thought of that song, "Lord, have mercy," trying to save they soul, trying to get free, trying to raise their children, to bring them up and keep the man from taking them. And they figured that if a man sung the blues, that he wadn't praising the Lord. I've heard them say when I

was a little boy, "You so and so, you picking that guitar when you should be praying."

I heard a guy speaking about how prayer unlocks everything. Paul and Silas was bound in jail, and prayer unlocked the door. The fellow said, "Yeah, in those days, prayer unlocked the door. But they got some new locks now. Prayer won't unlock these doors now."

My grandmother said she worked on that boat they called the *Choctaw*. She used to roll a barrel of molasses up the gangplank right alongside of her husband. Them old ladies would have aprons on, and my father, he'd have on the overalls called Big Smith. Everything you get now will have a crease in it that run straight down the front and back of the leg. In them old times, they would iron the overalls, and the crease would be standing on the side. If my wife was to iron my pants with that crease like that now, me and her would get to knocking. It was real funny, you know, with the crease on the inside and outside.

I remember my mother, she had a pair of these shoes you call booties. They lace up with these leather laces like you see in men's boots now. They come about half up your leg. And those old big socks they called knits, she would put them on and wear them to church. There wasn't no such thing as these hairy-legged women that you see now. These women now are wearing stockings, and you can see the hair on their legs. You couldn't see Momma's leg. You could just see the shape with them big socks.

I can reach back as far as nineteen hundred and twenty-two. I came up in the country on a farm with my daddy and mother. When I went to school, I had to walk maybe four or five miles. We had an old wood heater. After we'd get to school, the bigger boys, they'd go out and cut the wood to keep us warm.

We would study arithmetic, geometry. We had a primer book with A, B, C's. We had fifty students in school. But we didn't go to school like they do now. When it got time to chop cotton, that school door closed. Those children had to get out there and help their mothers and fathers chop cotton.

My daddy was what you call a day hand man. He didn't make no crop. That give me a little relief. I didn't have to go out there and chop cotton. My mother would be doing "day work." In other words, he worked, and she worked, and they didn't make no crop. I would be there at the house, running around there snotty-nosed, barefeeted, and raggedy.

They would work all day long. Daddy quit work when it got where you couldn't see. He would come on in, and he'd get out there with his ax, cut his wood, and make his fire. Momma, she'd cook by the lamp light.

We were short of cover, and we'd take cotton sacks and put them on the bed to keep warm. There was no such thing as a screen on the windows. In the summer, my mother got out in the yard and made a fire. Then she'd get a bucket and bring the fire inside the house to smoke those mosquitoes out. She would burn old rags, then get sulfur and put in there. That run the mosquitoes away. Then later they got what you call a mosquito bar, a little thin knit thing that we would put over us.

My daddy, he made a couple of crops there, and we'd be picking cotton way over in March the next year. We would settle up. And out of fifteen or twenty bales of cotton, we'd be lucky to get any money at all. The man would show my daddy the place where the crop done ate it up. Then he'd turn around, and he'd lend Daddy some money. They'd loan you eight or ten or twelve hundred dollars if you had a family. But you had to work for him another year.

After I growed up and got to be a young man, around about fourteen or fifteen years old, I married my wife over there. She was twelve, and I was fourteen. We was married right at her auntie's house. We had a preacher and paid three dollars for a license. We had cake and a nice service. After her and me married, I decided I'd make me a crop. After I made my first crop, I was in debt. The man loaned me thirty dollars. I lived with that thirty dollars all through the winter. The second crop, I was still in debt. I owed it all to the man.

They had a thing they called "Roosevelt's padded check." That's to give you about thirty or forty dollars in the next year. But if you owed the white man, you didn't get that check. When that check come, it come to you. But that white man knowed just the day that check was coming, and he made you sign that check and give it to him. Then he went and cashed it.

Back in '30 and '31, it was rough. We lived down on Swan Lake at a little place called Glendora. It's about six miles south of Swan Lake. We were with a man that had plenty of money. You know what that man was paying my father a day? One dollar. The hog was so poor till we had to tote him up to the slop trough to feed him.

Times was so tough, we couldn't cut them with a knife. In '29, we had that bad freeze, and I was up big enough to work. I was plowing four mules that was pulling one of those "true blue" or "yellow jacket" middle busters. You would hit them stumps, and that plow would kick you in the stomach.

I had to get up around three in the morning when the bell rang. The bell rang two times. First time, you get up. The second time, be at the barn. Not on your way, at the barn. A guy that was called the hostler, he walked around with a lantern. A lot of guys, they'd wear that cloth called gingham. They'd tie a rag on the mule's tail where I wouldn't get yours, and you wouldn't get mine. The boss man would be standing at the lot gate with an arm of bridles. If you was late, he'd take that bridle and whip you all around the yard.

You had to work those mules all day. They was big fat mules, and it seemed like them mules would carry you near about twenty miles an hour. And you was scared to hit them. I worked for a guy once, and he had some young mules. Them mules kept us running, and if you cussed one of them mules, that guy would absolutely fight you. Don't cuss that mule and don't hit him. If that mule come in and that man see a scar on him, he gonner take that leather line and put a scar on you. When the mules played out, I drove a tractor for a guy. He paid me five dollars a day. At the end of the week, my money come up short, and I asked him, "What's the trouble?"

"Well you riding my tractor and riding over my land like that. Don't you know that every time you turn around on the end and knock down a stalk of my cotton, it costs me?"

I told him, "Yes sir."

He say, "Well now, if you can drive that tractor out there right and don't tear down that cotton, I'll give you back your money."

He took out about three dollars from my pay one week like that. He wanted me to go out there on the end and do what you call "airplane" them plows around over that cotton. If you didn't, he'd make you pay for it.

They never did whip me or my daddy because my daddy was kind of like these youngsters now. You draw back to hit him, and he'd draw back too. I've been lucky. I always tried to do my best, and I made it up to now. I lived to be fifty years old before I got in jail right here in Clarksdale, Mississippi. A man looked at me one day, Brickyard Jones. He say, "Don't I know you?"

I say, "Yeah. You shore do."

"Ain't you kin to Old Man Jack Love?"

"I'm his son."

"The next time you come down the street like that, I'm gonner arrest you."

I said, "I'm not drunk."

"You say you're not drunk, and I know you is."

So about that time, a man they call Milk Man, one Tom Harris, come. I had been doing some work for him over at Girrard. He said, "Well what's the trouble?"

"This so and so nigger's drunk."

"Well he's a good boy. I know him. Are you drunk, son?"

"No sir."

The policeman said, "You just gonner call me a liar anyhow?"

Well Tom Harris told him to let me go, which he did. About a week after that, that same fellow met me. It was a Saturday night around ten o'clock. Me and three more was walking together. He drove up and said, "Alright. All four of you are drunk."

"Naw. We're not drunk."

"I had that argument when I seen you once before."

He let the other three go. Him and me goes on over to the jail and walks up to the desk sergeant, a bad man. "What you got this nigger for?"

"Drunk."

"Get in there, nigger."

"Yes sir."

That desk sergeant, you know what I've seen him do? You know how these guys go around with the shirt open. I've seen him take his hand and catch and pull the hair on them boys' bellies. I've seen the time he would meet you with a pair of wire pliers and pull out your whiskers.

Back in my father's day, we could say, "Boss," and they would let us go. We had to say, "Mr. Two-Time Boss." You know what I mean. Mister Two-Time Boss and Miss Two-Time Ole Miss. When Boss used to get mad at us, we'd say, "I'm gonner tell Ole Miss and make you leave me alone."

You would go up there with your hat off and one hand scratching your head and the other one scratching you in the side, talking to Ole Miss. She would say, "What's the matter with you now, nigger? Ole Master done something to you?"

"Yas'm."

"I'm gonner talk to him when he come in for supper."

If you was a good-working nigger, you could get by like that. But if you go up there and wake Ole Miss up, Boss gonner whip you for going up there. And when you went to see that white lady, you'd go up to the back door and pull your hat off. I don't care how cold it was. Take your hat off, and she'd tell you to come, and you'd stop on the back porch.

If you done worked two weeks and ready to get paid off, just about the time you get ready to go up to the commissary for your money, Boss, he'd walk out and tell you he was going home and go to sleep. Well you're scared to wake him up. His cook was a colored lady. You'd go there and touch the back door light. You couldn't hit it hard. She'd stick her head out the door and say, "Well he sleep right now."

He'd sleep till maybe around nine or ten o'clock. Then he'd get up and come out there to pay you off. You maybe done borrowed about five dollars, and you ain't got but about four dollars worth of work a week. "You want to be paid now, Old Nigger? You work pretty good. I reckon I'll let you have some money."

"Yes sir."

"Go home and get you a half pint of whiskey and go on that all-night juke. If one of them niggers over there do anything to you, kill him and come on back home and tell them you live with Uncle Tom."

All that happened. You know what I mean. Kill a nigger, hire another. Kill a mule, buy another. I lived through them days.

I married in '34. My daddy was a big gambler,

and he kept things going pretty well. I could duck Old Boss. But I seen what he'd do to the boys what was coming up with me. He had them out there plowing. They had to do it. They'd get about twelve dollars a month, and they had about fifteen children in the family. Hook your wagon up soon Saturday morning, and Saturday night when you got off work, you'd drive it to the store and buy you twelve dollars worth of groceries. That had to last you that month. That was what they called "furnishing your own and making your crop."

When you get through in this field, you go to that next one. They'd give you about thirty-five acres of land. And once a year—I think it was in July—they would issue you groceries, overalls, and big-nosed shoes. You'd get your wife some cloth, and she'd make a couple of dresses. And just before cotton-picking time, you'd go up and get you another issue—a barrel of flour, a lot of sardines, and a pint jar of smoking tobacco. And if you a good worker, the boss might loan you five dollars.

Then you start picking cotton. At settling time, you done picked twenty-five bales of cotton. So you go in to settle up, and the boss pop his finger on you when you walk in. "Joe, I sat up all night trying to figure things out. Here you done made twenty-five bales of cotton. I just don't want to tell you, Joe, hard as you worked. I don't want to tell you. Here, smoke a cigarette."

He's setting up at the table and ain't nothing on the table but money. You think you gonner get any? Out of the question. He'd set there, and he'd figure, and he'd figure. And when he get through, he'd pop his finger again. "Looka here.

If you'd have made one more bale of cotton, this is what you'd of had as your part. But by the time I get all of mine and add in your eating and everything, Joe, I just ain't got the heart to tell you. How much you want to borrow?"

"I want to borrow twelve hundred dollars."

He'd loan you twelve or thirteen hundred dollars. You think you could make out with twelve or thirteen hundred? Them people had big families. This thirteen hundred dollars what he loaning you, you done made that already. But he done popped his finger on it. "If you'd have made one more bale of cotton, this would have been your stack of dollars. I tell you what I'm gonner do, Joe. I'm gonner loan you this money."

The first time I come here to Clarksdale, it was just like New York City to me. We used to walk from Swan Lake to Clarksdale. Me and a bunch of boys would hit that Delta road barefeeted and have us belts off popping each other. We would come on up here to Clarksdale, and the streets was narrow. We'd have about a quarter in us pocket, and we'd have about fifteen cents of that left when we got back.

My cousin bought a radio. His mother bought it for him, you know. It was a radio that had the ear muffs over it. They told him, "Don't be talking while you listening at that radio because the white man will hear you if you say something."

In other words, you've heard of people getting together in the fall, and they might say, "I'm gonner move off this place. Let's move over yonder with Mr. So and So."

If that radio would be playing, they wouldn't talk like that. I remember I had an old record

player with a bulldog on it, one of them an-
tiques that you wind up. That dog would sit
up there while that record was playing Bessie
Smith or Blind Lemon Jefferson, and those old
folks wouldn't say nothing. They might just say,
"That's a good record."

The man had them fooled that he could hear
what they said through that dog. Those people
really believed that.

They had guys that would hang around
people's houses all night in the fall of the year.
If he heard you mention you were moving, he
would go tell the white man. The white man
would send for you and get you in the gear
house and hit you with an ax handle. "I heard
you was gonner move, Joe."

"Well, Boss, Mr. So and So was talking to me."

"Well I know what I'm gonner do. I'm gonner
hit you and swell your head up."

Joe would go back home, and he'd be scared
to move. Now if you run up on another white
man and this man was bad as your boss was,
he'd tell you to move over there on his plantation. He wouldn't let you come back to your old
house. He'd send his wagon and mule over there
to get your family. You would be scared to go
back to your old house for four or five years.

We had a white guy here that was going with
a colored fellow's wife. The white man told the
colored fellow, "You go out there and chop cotton."

"Well my crop is already in fair shape."

"I seen some weeds on the end. You don't
need to take your wife out there with what little
you've got to do."

That particular day, he wanted to see the

nigger woman, you know. In other words, the
nigger woman then was what we call the colored
lady now. You get the message on what I'm trying to hand you, you know. The colored guy said,
"I'm not going nowhere."

"You wait till I go home and get my gun."

"Don't you come back."

"I'll be back."

The white fellow went home to get his pistol, thinking he would run the nigger out. The
nigger got his old gun. He sat there in the door
and said, "This is one morning I'm not gonner
let this man whip me or run me off."

The white man was hot to see this nigger
woman. He goes back to the woman's home with
his pistol and pushed the door open. When he
pushed that door open, the colored guy cut him
half in two. He shot him with a shotgun. You
ever went hunting and shot a rabbit with a shotgun and tore him all to pieces? Well that's what
happened to that white man. He was gonner
take this colored man's wife. He was already
doing with her what he wanted. That particular
day, he wanted to see her bad.

The fellow that shot him got away. Some
say he was a big Mason, and some say the laws
helped get him away. Fact is, I don't know what
happened to him. But I do know what happened
to that white man. They put him in a box.

That particular white man wadn't the onliest one doing that, you know. You'd be walking
along the road with your wife, and a white man
would drive up behind you and say, "Where you
going, Joe? You going to town?"

"Yes sir."

"Let's see here. I don't know, Joe. I got a low

tire back there. Your wife can ride, and you walk."

He'd leave you walking. He'd take off, and automatic he going through them woods. But you scared to say anything. I've known that to actually happen. So you'd get to town walking. "Well, Joe, you finally made it?"

"Yes sir."

"Here's you a half a pint."

But when you see the white man's wife, you got to scratch under your arm and in your head. That's the way we had to scratch. When a nigger talked to a white person, he's always had one hand in his head. We used to have to do that. Like if you have your hat on, and you walk up to a white man, you'd pull that hat off. You didn't walk up to him like the youngsters do now and keep that hat on. You'd walk up to him and take the itch. You was so scared of the white man. Just take the itch. You had to be scratching when you was talking to him. The man had them scared to death.

If a guy got hungry and stole a hog, they'd send him down to Parchman for twenty years. He'd stay down there and work. They used to whip them buck naked. Whip all the blood out of them. Things are a little better now. I don't think they whip you there now.

It was a white lady made them cut out that whipping. They had a guy working in a crew on the side of the road, and they did what they call "throwed him" on the side of the road when this white lady was passing by. They stripped him and bent him over the barrel, they called it. And the white man was throwing that leather. I'm telling you, you put that leather on that naked

meat, and you gonner have some action. The white lady reported them, and they cut it out. That's been quite a while back. She reported it.

After that, they'd have to carry them into the camp and whip them there. Somehow, this Red Cross and all, they put a stop to it. I don't know how. I have known many mens went there well, and they brought them back in a box.

I have known many men to just walk around, and these white people kill them out on their place. That's a fact. They ain't never had to have no license to kill a nigger. It's a license for everything else. You got to buy a license to kill everything but a nigger. We was always in season. But if we keep on, you'll have to have a license to kill a nigger. Then it won't be so many of them doing it. They used to kill them whenever they wanted to. Beat them to death.

It's a little place down below here where white mens got half drunk on a Saturday night and made a Negro jump in the river and drown. I'm telling you the truth. We was out on the street and seen them carrying a Negro around back. After a while, they come back, but he didn't come back no more. You didn't see him no more. They threw him in the river and killed him.

I know you heard tell of this boy Emmett Till, how they did him. They say he wolf-whistled at a white lady. [Whistles.] They call that a wolf whistle. I hadn't never heard tell of that before. They claim he actually didn't even see the lady. But Boss said it, and that's the way it had to be. Whatever Boss says, that's got to be.

I remember I was in Chicago when some of these same things we got here went on there. I got a job out in Cicero at the time this colored boy was out looking for a job, and those white boys taken a baseball bat and killed him. They beat him to death.

It seemed like every colored guy up there was from Mississippi. Most of them we worked with was Italians, not white men. You hardly catch a white man working in Chicago. They most was Italians. They was good guys.

It's a lot of things I just don't understand. I guess it's because the white man has had us like he wanted all the time, and it wadn't never anything you could do about it. You know these places they call gear houses where they keep gear for the mules. I've known them to actually whip niggers in there. Say, "Nigger, I told you to do so and so."

"Yes sir."

"You failed to do it, and we gonner see about that."

I remember the time my daddy was telling my mother a story. I used to be a bad eavesdropper, you know. A white man told the nigger to do something, and he was working him so hard, he forgot to do it. The nigger would milk the cow, and when he got through, he carried the milk in to the family. The white man said, "John, did you do what I told you to do?"

"Boss, I swear I forgot about it."

The white man went to cussing and went out in the backyard where the nigger had the milk. He said, "I told you to do something, and you didn't do it. If I had my pistol."

The nigger was scared, you know. He said, "Sir?"

"You heard what I said. If I had my pistol."

"Boss, I know you got it."

"No. I ain't."

"Well, Boss, if you ain't got your pistol, it's too damn bad for you."

And that nigger like to damn near killed that white man for what he had said.

In the sixties, a nice fellow came in here from California named Chris Strachwitz. He met me, and I was scared to death. A white man meeting a nigger, you know, and he met me with a smile. We talked, and he tried to get me to make some music for him. He told me that a white man named Paul Oliver and a white lady was coming from England. So they came up, and they made me acquainted with them, and they shook my hand. Man, I had the jitters standing up and shaking a white lady's hand on the streets. They didn't allow no niggers to shake no white lady's hand regardless to what. Finally I kind of got on to it.

Now after Kennedy come here, he put everybody free. We had a young colored boy running mail routes here. He would go deliver mail down Oakhurst Road in the white section. They used not to allow them colored boys over there.

So there was a young white girl had an old maid, an old nigger woman back there. She had her bonnet on and everything. This colored boy run the mail route that day. Well quite naturally this young white girl, she would run out there and meet the postman and get the mail. She run out there, and she seen that colored guy. She was glad to talk to him, and she told him, "Come on in. Bring the mail in. Bring the mail in."

He carried it in there, and this young white girl must have been just getting up and straightening around the house. She had on what you call a housecoat, and it flopped open in front. She just hauled off and set right down on the bed, and this nigger woman was peeping through in there with her bonnet on.

The white girl kept making passes at this colored mail boy, and so he grabbed her and hauled off and dived down there with his head. You know what I mean. Boy, that white girl had her legs up and had that Negro's head down there scratching him in the head. And this nigger woman, she commenced alarming. Called all these bad policemen what we got here. She got them alarmed up, and everybody run out. The nigger heard it, and he broke out the window and run. The police come up and said, "What did he do?"

"Aw, it was just a sight. You just oughta been see how he was doing Ole Miss's daughter. Why that nigger had his big black head down there, and he was going to town."

"Going to town doing what?"

"He was down there just licking her little cat, and she was just snorting and carrying on."

The policeman said, "Aw well. Since they got that damn John F. Kennedy in the White House, you're free to eat anywhere you want to now. We can't arrest this nigger for eating a little bit cause it's free now."

They didn't charge him for eating. But they did make him pay six dollars for breaking the window.

Speaking of ugly, I got a friend up at Tunica named Bobby Parker. He's so ugly that you could sue God for making him and get all of hell and half of heaven. That cat know he's ugly. He's so ugly till when he was born, they had to slap him and make him cry so they could tell where his mouth was.

You know what's giving heart attacks now? I'm gonner tell you what giving heart attacks now, because it's getting onto me. I near about have them sometime. You walk out in the streets and see one of those fifteen-year-olds, big knees, built shapely, zoops up like a Coca-Cola bottle, and got on one of them dresses touching her way up above possible. An old man get to looking at her, and that's when he have the heart attack and fall dead. These young girls are causing these heart attacks.

# WADE WALTON

I like the blues. I learned the blues from my brother and from playing them out on the farm. There wasn't anything else much that we could do but go fishing, pick cotton, and play blues. I came out of a family of seventeen, and we sharecropped. I was born at Lombardy, Mississippi. We left there when we were small kids and went to Goldfield, Mississippi, where we lived on a plantation. That's about five miles from Plattsville, Mississippi. The state penitentiary was just about four or five miles north of there.

We lived there for quite some time and went to a church school. Had the old wood heaters, and people that had kids that went to that school had to cut wood and pile it up. We burned the wood in the stove, you know.

There was seventeen children in my family, and my mother couldn't afford to get our hair cut. So she bought a pair of clippers, and she said, "One of you is going to have to learn to cut the others' hair because I'm not able to pay for all of you to get haircuts."

So I took the trade up, giving haircuts. My brother would cut mine, and I'd cut his. Later on, I left and went to Memphis. That's where I went to Modern Barber College and took up the trade of barbering. I came here and started working with some professional barbers named Donny and Jake on the 17th of May, 1943. They both gone now. Both of them dead.

Then I started playing music around the barbershop. I met Ike Turner when he was a pianist—nothing but a pianist—and lived in Riverton. Ike would go up and act as a disc jockey. There was a place known as Bennett Furniture Company which would sponsor a program for Ike Turner playing his piano. Ike was a very much delightful boogie-woogie man on the piano.

He would come down to my barbershop and get his hair cut. He'd see me with my old guitar, and he would ask me how to tune it. I'd show him how to tune it. So Ike decided he would buy him a guitar. He went to Florida, and when he came back, he had a very nice guitar. I think it was a Fender. He had learned quite a bit about the guitar. He came in the barbershop and said, "Look what I've learned, man."

He played a boogie or something like that.

I knew B. B. King years back before he got popular. He used to be in town all the time in fact. I used to go down there quite a bit to the nightclub. This is years back. I knew Sonny Boy Williamson. I used to play with Sonny Boy. I knew him back then. About two weeks before Sonny Boy died, I played with him at the City Café where Ike Turner used to play, just across the street from the Big Six Barbershop. I used to go over and take my guitar, and he would tune it and show me what key he wanted to play in and how he wanted me to play so he could play his harp.

This was about two weeks before Sonny Boy Williamson died. They buried Sonny Boy in Tutwiler. I remember the color of the casket, and I remember how many harps he had. He had thirty-five to forty harps, and he traveled all over the country and even in England. He wore a two-tone suit, and it cost 250 dollars. He was a very cheery fellow, and he was a very wild fellow. His habit was to drink about a quart of whiskey a day. I know that to be a fact. He was a good friend of mine. I remember him playing in the café in Arkansas. When I was a cotton chopper, I would turn the radio to *King Biscuit Time*, and he would be advertising the King Biscuit meal and flour.

Howling Wolf's mother lives in Clarksdale. Howling Wolf came here five or six years ago, and he was playing over at the VFW. Howling Wolf's mother is very close to me. We sit down and drink coffee together. She's an elderly lady, and she's a nice lady. But she don't believe in the blues. She's more on the Christian side, you know. When Howling Wolf played at the VFW about four or five years ago, he hadn't seen his mother in about twenty or twenty-five years.

This fellow told Wolf, "Don't your mother live in Clarksdale?"

"I don't know."

"I'll take you to the fellow who knows. There's a barber that know where your mother live."

So they came to the Big Six Barbershop. They pulled around the backyard and parked. Wolf got out and asked me, "Where does my mother live?"

"She just passed along here a few minutes ago."

One fellow went around the front of the shop, and the other went around the back and they found her.

They called her, "Miss Wolf, your son is here. You want to see him?"

She said, "Oh, you boys. You all are kidding. I don't want you to fool me."

So they went and got Wolf and brought Wolf to his mother. She saw him and said, "Yes, that's my son."

And he grabbed his mother and picked her up like that. He wanted to give her some money, but she said, "I don't want that money. Boy, you been playing in those blues places."

He hadn't seen her for fifteen or twenty years, but he gave her some money anyways. She felt that the money wasn't good money because he was playing the blues. He cried and he cried. He was so glad to see his mother, but she felt that he was in another world from her.

Wolf played out at the VFW, and I went out there that night. He sat down in that chair, and he rocked that chair. He sang that little thing about, "Shake it, little baby. Oh, shake it for me."

The people were trying to get his mother to go out there, but she said, "No. I'm not going. I'm not going."

And she's here now. I have some pictures taken with her with my arm around her and all. She is very fond of me. She seems to think a lot of me, you know. I tell her I'm crazy about Wolf, but she doesn't seem to take with it too much, you know.

I've played with some very renowned fellows, you know. I followed Ike as far as Biloxi, Mississippi, and Itta Bena, Mississippi. But when he went further, he had to leave me because I had to get back to my business to cut hair every day. That's where he would lose me, you see, because I'm strictly in the haircutting business. We had a lot of fun. Sometimes he would come to the barbershop, spend an hour with me, and have a session. I always kept a guitar around the barbershop. Yes, this old guitar here. I leave it on the wall and look at it.

[To a customer:] You got tough whiskers. You want a quick shave, I know. If you want a dry shave, I'll give you a dry shave. I'll tell you what I'm gonna do. I'll just pull the fuzz off of you, and you won't need another one. Hold your chin up like that. You want to be whipped out. You want one of those scissor shaves. Oh, here you go. The whiskers are kind of tough, you know. You want to leave that Afro beard? How does that feel? I'll leave your mustache. I won't bother with that. These whiskers are not so tough, are they? What I'll do is cream you down. How does that feel?

Let me get you all slathered up here. So you want your Vandyke and whatever you got up there is alright. We got the style you know. Did they give you a beat on it like this?

[Customer:] "Now, I want to know how much you're gonna charge me for this haircut."

The idea of beating this razor on the strap came from listening to music and hearing the beat. That gave me the idea of keeping up a beat with the razor. I call it the barbershop boogie. A lot of people come by, and it just doesn't seem like Wade if I don't beat the razor out on the strap. Usually I go to the jukebox and play a record, and then I start my beat with this razor. Everybody seems to get tickled, you know. It's a lot of fun to them. I've had quite a few people to come by to see me with the razor.

Paul Oliver and his wife from Middlesex, England, came by, and they seemed to enjoy it quite a bit. He was able to record sounds of me. And when he left and went back to England, he gave the tape to the British Broadcasting Company and they broadcasted it to the British listeners. They sent me a small token from the broadcasting company. I still have the little slip. It's about ten dollars. That's a lot of money, I understand, in that part.

# WOKJ, JACKSON

WOKJ radio station has been the voice of the black community in Jackson and surrounding areas since it first went on the air in 1954. In addition to its rich fare of blues and gospel music, the station reports on local events. Its disc jockeys are considered heroes, and their verbal skills are legendary.

Bruce Payne grew up in Vicksburg and worked at WOKJ for twenty-seven of his fifty years as a radio announcer. Known as the "Dean" of gospel music, Payne produced a variety of programs over the years. He brought the Staple Singers to Jackson for a concert and helped launch the annual Jackson Music Awards in 1979.

Payne recalled the critical role that he and others at WOKJ played during the civil rights movement. On May 14, 1970, two Jackson State University students were killed and twelve others were wounded by police as WOKJ announcers watched from their window on Lynch Street, just a few blocks from the campus.

My teaching career began in the English Department at Jackson State in September 1970, three months after the shootings. Bruce Payne was a regular visitor in my black folklore course, and he spoke eloquently to my students about the history of the blues and gospel. He also moderated the Mississippi Folk Voices concert series that I organized at the Mississippi History Museum in Jackson.

The voices of Joe "Poppa Rock" Louis, Reverend Marcus Butler, and Bruce Payne anchored WOKJ's sound in the hearts and minds of their listeners. The station is deeply connected to the musical roots of the Jackson community. I recorded these radio programs and the interview with Payne during the summer of 1974 at WOKJ for the film *Give My Poor Heart Ease*.

Radio played a key role in introducing me to the blues as a white teenager.

During the late fifties, I listened faithfully each Saturday to a late-night blues program on WLAC radio. Spirited disc jockeys John R. Richbourg and Bill "Hoss" Allen hosted the program, which was sponsored by Randy's Record Shop in Gallatin, Tennessee.

When I return to the farm, I always tune my car radio to black radio in Jackson and listen to the colorful voice of the "Rag Man" as he introduces music and announces upcoming barbecues and musical events. The Rag Man's voice and the music he plays let me know that I have indeed come back home.

# JOE "POPPA ROCK" LOUIS
## *The Big Daddy Show*

We're in the capital city at six minutes before nine. Good morning, and welcome to the *Big Daddy Show*. Let's listen now to Tyrone Davis. This is Tyrone, doing it to the death. Sixty-eight degrees outside, and the wax is even hotter in here. You wrong do me, and I'm gonna wrong do you. We're gonna pay back when the big payback comes back.

That's the voice of Tyrone Davis, a Mississippian born right in the Greenville area. Doing it to the death. And when you think about blues, you got to think about Indianola, Mississippi. And now for the man who put it all together, as far as blues is concerned. The man who is not only a goodwill ambassador for the state of Mississippi, but for the entire world. I'm talking about Mr. B. B. King.

> The man says, why I sing the blues is because
>     I lived it.
> I know how it feels.
> When you're hurt
> You gotta tell somebody.
> Someone must understand
> How you feel.
> The only way to do it is to say it loud and
>     clear.
> Make sure that everyone will hear.
> It's the truth the way it is.
> That's why I sing the blues.
> This is B. B. King,
> Making a statement
> And a natural fact.
> All you got to do is sit back
> And dig where it's coming from,

> Not only with your ear, but with your heart.
> Everybody want to know
> Why I sing the blues.

How you feeling out there? Good. Thanks for calling here. We love you madly. Bye, bye.

And that was B. B. King. That's all of our time for this morning. I want to thank you for joining us.

> It's been a ball.
> It's been a pleasure,
> One that we'll treasure
> Until the next time we get together.
> Maybe we'll have a better time,
> But right now,
> That's all the time.
> So have a good day.
> And if you're driving,
> Remember to drive carefully.
> And if you're not driving,
> Walk on, baby.
> We dig that anyway.
> However and whatever.
> But just remember,
> What goes up
> Must come down.
> And what goes around
> Must come around.
> This is the Big Daddy.
> I'll see you tomorrow morning,
> The Good Lord willing
> And nothing happens until then.
> Bye.

# BRUCE PAYNE

*News*

This is WOKJ, 1550 on your radio dial, Jackson, Mississippi. And in the capital city, it's 9:02, and *ABC News* is next.

This is Bruce Payne with WOKJ News Notes. The Political Science Department at Jackson State University will conduct a two-day workshop on southern Africa. The workshop will feature outstanding national and local scholars in African history and culture.

Also in Mississippi news, Jackson State will host residents from all over the state of Mississippi for a community development and leadership conference. This is the second annual conference, and it is designed to bring together rural residents, community leaders, and representatives from public social agencies.

# REVEREND MARCUS BUTLER
*Gospel Music*

Well a pleasant good morning to you. Once again, it's time for the *Mid-Morning Gospel Hour*. Stay tuned from now to eleven for the best of gospel and spiritual music. This is your mid-morning host, Reverend Marcus Butler, reminding you that this morning we going to be playing gospel music for all the hospitals and convalescent homes and the rest homes, wherever you are. To all our senior citizens down around Piney Woods, Mississippi, this morning, let's open the program with one of our local groups right here in the city of Jackson, the Soul Southerners, with "I'm going home."

Alright. Alright. You got the Soul Southerners this morning at fourteen minutes past the hour of nine with "I'm going, I'm going home."

Yes, those of you just joining us, welcome. Welcome to the very best of gospel and spiritual music on the *Mid-Morning Gospel Hour*. "I will lift mine eyes to the hills from whence comes my health. My health cometh from the Lord, who made the heaven and the earth. Thou art called. Do not pass me by."

This is WOKJ, 1550 on your radio dial in Jackson, Mississippi. We feel this morning, somewhere there's someone that has problems. If so, don't worry about it because Eugene Williams and Ida Lee Brown say, "Give it to Jesus, and He will fix it for you."

Let Jesus fix it this morning. Let's listen to Eugene Williams and Sister Ida Lee Brown, "Give it to Jesus, and He will fix it for you."

We'll be back with more gospel music after this message. And my friends, just remember, those of you who go to church every Sunday, you must go straight because there is no side door in heaven. Sister Victoria Hawkins says, "No side door in heaven."

You got to come by Jesus. Yes, if you expect to get into heaven, you got to go in the front door, for there's no side door in heaven. Don't go away friends. We'll be back in just a moment with more music.

# GARY'S MEAT HOUSE AD

Say, friends, why not do something this year for the Fourth of July. No, I don't mean celebrate the Fourth with a fifth. No, I don't mean that at all. I mean go out to Gary's Meat House and get all the pork ribs, all the beef steaks, and all the pork chops that you can eat for the big cookout that you're going to have.

And the reason why you need to go to Gary's is you can find pork ribs for just eighty-nine cents per pound, a ten-pound box of baby T-bones for just $12.90, and a ten-pound box of sirloin for just $11.90. And you can get a whole goat—that's right, a whole goat—for just ninety-nine cents per pound. Limited supply.

Plus, they got the fifteen-pound meat special. You get three pounds of bacon, three pounds of pork chops, three pounds of ground beef, three pounds of steak chops, and three pounds of either beef or pork liver. And you can get it all for just $12.95. That's all at Gary's Meat House, right here in Jackson, where you can get ready for the Fourth of July.

# BRUCE PAYNE

Flash back eleven years ago in May of 1963. The late Medgar Evers appeared on Jackson television and was given equal time to respond to thoughts of then Jackson mayor, Allen Thompson, who had spoken out against the NAACP. Medgar Evers talked about the NAACP. He also talked briefly about himself. [Evers's speech is played on tape.]

There are only three recordings of this tape. This was the last speech Medgar Evers made. Less than ten days later, he was killed. Now when the community hears this speech, it's going to bring back 1963, and we will close like this: "The voice of Medgar Evers recorded eleven years ago just before his assassination."

Then we will go into other news, and when you come out of that, you play a record from '63, see. There are a lot of young blacks—not only young blacks but a lot of young people period—who never heard of Medgar Evers. So we're going to flash back, particularly during the music festival—the Medgar Evers Mississippi Homecoming—to what actually happened. It's increasing our role in the community to help the people who listen to the station learn about Medgar's life.

There was a time when the black community did not get news. They didn't know about the American Legion picnic or the VFW outing. They didn't know what this minister across town was doing. Now they have an opportunity to tune in to a radio station such as this and get news about rock concerts, gospel programs, Headstart meetings, maybe about the poor woman who has lost a purse with her spectacles in it. We give them all this information.

Something really strange happened this morning. A lady called me, and we were talking. She calls here often. She said that her son had been involved in an altercation with another gentleman, and a life had been lost. She was concerned that we as a radio station feel her loss.

People call for everything. We are here all the time. People reach out to us because we are in their homes all the time. They call about donations of blood, lost articles, clothing, food. For twenty years, the station has been doing that.

I remember back in 1970 when the National Guard rolled into Jackson to quiet the racial unrest. Right out the window of our control room, there they were. You could see them right out there on the street when Jackson, Mississippi, was in the throes of strife. And I mean strife. This is when B. B. was singing, "Worry, worry all the time."

You know, the blues then was so heavy that it was agony. Today, music has changed and is about peace and love and understanding. But then it was focused on that hard-core experience. The Staple Singers were singing about "Help me, Jesus."

Now they're singing about "Come go with me, I want to take you to a better place."

As times have changed, the music has changed. When I got in radio, if you could

BRUCE PAYNE, WOKJ, JACKSON, 1974

holler, you could be an announcer. But the black community will not accept that anymore. You got to be able to read. You need decent diction. And a high school education will not get you a job in radio. You need to have at least two, three years in college and preferably a full college education.

We used to play records all day long. Now black radio has evolved to where we go to the governor's office for press conferences. We're covering civil rights organizations. We're going to career education conferences. If there's an accident where a truck falls off the viaduct, we're there. We interrupt the music if it's important enough. We interrupt that record, even though it's enjoyable and the audience is enjoying it. We interrupt for important news.

I love to talk about black music. It goes back further than the sixties, further than the thirties, back further than the twenties. Throughout the black man's trouble, all he had to lean on was his music. When he thought about his relation with his woman and whether it was good or bad, he sang. And blues was his way of saying what he wanted her to know. Music was his way of saying that he was downtrodden, that his personal relationship with his woman was getting on his mind and on his nerves. He sang blues to express himself.

Black people also loved to sing gospel. It came from back in slavery days when the black man tried hard to get the message over to his master that he was sick and tired of being down-trodden. He might sing something like "I'm going to make it to the Kingdom one of these days" or "I'm gonna throw off these burdens."

Gospel was a means of communication. The white overseer would be out in the field, and this black guy would be chopping cotton. And a brother would be getting down through his music. He would sing, "Steal away, steal away to heaven."

The white man was not listening. If he was listening, he didn't understand. The black man was talking about stealing away, but he wasn't talking about stealing away to a heaven up there in the sky. He was talking about stealing away to the North. That was a message he used for the underground railroad. "Steal away," like "Swing low sweet chariot," meant that somebody from the underground railroad was coming that night.

And when you talk about how the bluesman sings about his woman all the time, that is the only thing the black man had to cling to. Now you go back to the thirties and forties, it was so dark in those days that no one ever thought about anything else except their love.

Now we're living for the city, the inner-city blues, or "What's going on," you know. I think it's a mixture of gospel and blues. Just like Al Green on every one of his albums expresses him-self with his love for a woman. And then he adds God into it. So I think music today is a mixture of blues and gospel.

Let me ask you a question. Have you ever been to a country church where there was no piano? All that foot stomping and clapping hands, that's black music—the untrained voice, the untrained foot stomping and clapping. If you really want to hear black music, if you really want to know what black music is all about, go to a country church.

# BEALE STREET

It is said that the two capitals of Mississippi are New Orleans and Memphis. When blacks moved north to escape the Delta, Memphis was their first destination. And in Memphis, Beale Street was the celebrated hub of music and nightlife.

As musicians aspired to successful careers, they bought stylish clothes for their stage performances. Lansky Brothers clothing store at 126 Beale Street provided suits for both B. B. King and Elvis Presley when they launched their careers. During the filming in 1974 for *Give My Poor Heart Ease*, Robert Shaw, a veteran salesman at Lansky's, told me how he sold B. B. King a pair of pants and showed how he greeted his customers with a pitch that was as colorful as his clothes.

# ROBERT SHAW

I sold B. B. King his first pair of tailor-made pants something like thirty years ago. I was the one sold him his first pair of tailor-made pants on Beale Street. That was when he first came to Memphis. He was working over at WDIA, and he really was a terrific fellow.

The reason Beale Street is so important is it's where the blues began. They say the start of the blues began right here, and that's why the street is so famous. Once upon a time Beale Street really jumped, and I think it will jump again.

Beale Street at that time was really going. It was something else. At this time of the year, it'd be crowded. There'd be about one hundred people down on the street every day—Monday through Saturday—especially during cotton time. It really was something here. There were nice parades, and people were doing good.

Rufus Thomas and B. B. King really started the blues. They had the medley down at the New Daisy Theatre every Friday night. That's where we used to go out and ramble every Friday night. That's where the blues really started. Down at the One Minute Café and Mitchell Hotel, they really was jumping on Beale Street.

B. B. King first came to Beale Street about thirty-five years ago. He come by the shop and asked me about making a suit. He said, "All I want is a black pair of pants to go with my coat. I already have a black coat."

And I said, "Come on in. Come on in. I'm gonna make you a pair of black gabardine pants

to go with your coat. How big do you want them in the bottom?"

He said, "I want them wide in the bottom."

I said, "We'll make them about 26–17 at the bottom."

We chatted for a good while, and then he gave me five dollars. Pants didn't cost but twelve dollars at the time. He said, "Well I'm gonna pay you five dollars down on them."

He came back that next week, and he didn't have all the money. He had about six dollars. He was lacking a dollar. He said, "Just charge that to me."

The next time he came in, he said, "I want a two-piece suit."

At that time, he was wearing what you call zoot suits. He said, "I want one with a long coat, two pleats in the side, two tone."

The coat was seventeen at the bottom and about thirty-four inches long. We made them real long at that time. We been here for about thirty years, and we started the high-style fashions from Elvis to all the entertainers. All the entertainers come here and get their stuff. Everybody is trying to get in on the act, but we're still leading the styles in Memphis. We set the pace, and everybody stays behind us.

One thing about it, the style just comes back to repeating every twenty-five years. We used to have a belt in the back of suits and bell-bottom trousers back about twenty-five years ago. The same thing is coming back today. Like this here vest, this three-piece suit. It was in style twenty-five years ago. They're just repeating right back. And the bell-bottoms, they have come right back in too. You had them back about twenty-five years ago, the same bell-bottoms.

[To customer:] What it's gonna be, you all? Tell me. I know you want it cause I see a dollar sign on your hat. There it is. You choose. There it is. I know you want it back cause I see a dollar sign on your hat. There it is. Choose a few, and you will be the chosen one. It all begins at 126 Beale.

There's a certain walk a black man has when he's really dressed up and moving right. That's what they call moving with the beat as they walk down the street. Like I'm walking down the street, and I feel real groovy. I feel like I'm really hip. I feel real confident about the day. I've really got something going for myself. I'm just basically being myself, happy-go-lucky, that's all. I'm just happy-go-lucky. People enjoy dancing. They enjoy going out, having a ball, and they don't want to think about their problems. They don't think about tomorrow. They say, "Who's promised tomorrow? Let's enjoy today."

Basically, the thing is, they enjoy themselves. They get together, listen to music, play their records, play their blues, play their sounds. They create a sound, create dances, and do their own thing. That's it.

This is where it all began, 126 Beale. This is where it all began. I know. Give me your hand now. Now give me a chance. Okay, you're the chosen one. There it is. What's it gonna be. You all tell me.

That style of talking? That's just facts of life. It's easy to make someone happy. It's easy to make a man smile, so why not make someone smile? You understand what I'm talking about. It's easy to make a man smile while he spends his money. And when he gets to Lansky Brothers, we make him smile. You understand what I'm talking about? That's what it's all about—making somebody smile. You understand. While they're dressing and resting, you making someone else smile. This talk is what you call "born with it." You must be born with it before you can get with it. And once you're born with it, you're already down to the beat, the beat in the street. Understand, it's down, hip, what they call hip. Understand? They're the chosen few or the chosen one if they come to Lansky Brothers because this is where it all began. You understand what I'm talking about? 126 Beale. Don't you forget that now.

This is the original created thing here. This is what they call a love house. When you come in here, you got a love house. You gonna smile before you walk out because we got all pros up in here. We got the best salesmen in the city of Memphis right here. You understand what I'm talking about. I'm telling you all what it is.

I never fooled with the dozens. Dozens is not a proper thing. We call it mackin, fackin, stackin, and rackin, down with it. Can't quit it. It's good for you. So stick with it. That's what we call it here. You know. We don't call it dozens. We call it facts and figures. Mackin and fackin, stackin and rackin. You understand. Chosen few with it, chosen few not with it. But if you come in here, you gonna be a chosen one. You understand. You understand what I'm saying. I know you understand.

It's nice having you all in here in Lansky Brothers. Now you all know what it's all about. Everything here is blues. You understand. Everybody has the blues sometime. You get the blues sometime when you feel bad. You feel sad, and you all in motion. You don't know which way to go.

Everybody have the blues. You don't have to be black to get the blues. We all get the blues sometime or another, you know. Blues goes back to feelings, how you feel today. You can wake up in the morning, and something is blue around your bed. You understand. Your old lady just quit you, and you're blue. So you understand what I'm talking about. Everybody have the blues sometime or another. You understand what I'm talking about. I know you had the blues. Have you ever had the blues? I'm sure you've had the blues sometime or other in your life. Like when your girlfriend quit you. You thought she was in love, and all at once you found out she's gone. And you go and say, "Man, I'm sad here, and I'm blue."

You understand. That's the way it is. Uh huh. Everybody get the blues. Huh? It's sure enough the blues. If you wake up in the morning, don't have no money in your pocket, and you can't get a loaf of bread, ain't you blue? And the baby crying too. Huh? I'm gonna tell you about life and the blues. Now this is the blues.

> Living ain't easy and times are tough.
> Money's scarce. We all can't get enough.
> Now my insurance is lapsed and my food is
>     low,
> And the landlord knocking at my door.
> Now last night I dreamed I died,
> And the undertaker came to take me for a
>     ride.
> I couldn't afford a casket and embalming was
>     so high.
> I got up from my sickbed because I was too
>     poor to die.

Now ain't that blue? You can imagine the man that made that blues up. He got the blues on top of the blues. You understand what I'm talking about. I know you understand what it is.

# LOOKING BACK

*Willie Dixon and B. B. King are two of the most important figures in the history of the blues, and their lives and music have deep roots in Mississippi. Still performing in his eighties, King is acknowledged as America's greatest blues artist, and Dixon composed many of the most beloved blues lyrics. The interviews that follow were both recorded at Yale University in 1975 when I taught as a joint professor in the American studies and Afro-American studies programs. During that time I invited James Thomas to perform and speak to my classes each academic year, and in the summers I returned to Mississippi to continue my field recordings, photography, and filming.*

*Though we met and spoke far from the Mississippi blues worlds, those worlds were clearly alive and well for both Willie Dixon and B. B. King. They acknowledged how their early musical experiences shaped their careers as blues artists in deep, enduring ways.*

# WILLIE DIXON

I met Willie Dixon in 1976 when I attended his concert at Toad's Place, a music club at 300 York Street in New Haven, just off the Yale campus. Toad's Place has hosted blues musicians for over thirty-three years and was a favorite venue for my students.

Dixon and I both grew up in Vicksburg, and I had long admired his career as a blues composer and performer. The morning after his concert, Dixon came to the apartment where I lived as a resident fellow in Calhoun College at Yale, and we spoke there about his life. It was especially moving to share our memories of Vicksburg as we spoke in New Haven.

Willie Dixon was born on July 1, 1915. He first discovered the blues in Vicksburg and composed songs such as "Sweet Louise" while he was in high school. After graduating from high school, he moved to Chicago in 1927, where he launched his prolific career as a blues performer and composer.

Compositions such as "Hoochie Koochie Man," "Spoonful," "Wang Dang Doodle," "Little Red Rooster," and "Evil" established Dixon as America's foremost blues composer. His education in Vicksburg and his early decision to compose blues songs underscore the importance of literary expression within the southern black community. Dixon's work also helps us understand the crucial link between the oral tradition of the blues and writers like Richard Wright, who captured these worlds through his fiction. Wright's literary career and Dixon's musical career reflect the power of black worlds that moved from Mississippi to Chicago during the first half of the twentieth century.

In folk tradition the blues performer and his music are associated with the devil. Delta bluesman Robert Johnson is reputed to have traded his soul to Satan for musical skills that gave him special power over women. Links between the blues and voodoo, the African religion whose chief god, Damballah, is a snake, strengthen the power of the bluesman.

Willie Dixon draws on the ties between the blues and voodoo in his "Hoochie Koochie Man" when he declares:

> I got a black cat bone, I got a mojo too.
> I got the John the Conqueror root. I'm gonner mess with you.
> I'm gonner make you girls lead me by the hand.
> Then the world will know, I'm the hoochie koochie man.

A large, powerful man, Dixon won the Illinois heavyweight Golden Gloves championship and actually sparred with Joe Louis. Foreshadowing the historic fight in which Joe "The Brown Bomber" Louis defeated Max Schmeling in record time at Yankee Stadium on June 22, 1938, Dixon defeated a German boxer known as "The White Bomber out of Germany" one year earlier.

Inspired by a popular toast called the signifying monkey that he first heard at his high school in Vicksburg, Dixon published a song that he composed with the same title and sold thirty to forty thousand copies on the streets of Chicago. Then Dixon and his Big Three Trio recorded the song on March 11, 1947. The record was an immediate hit on the national race records chart and launched Dixon's career as a blues composer and performer.

In this interview, Dixon recalled his youth in Vicksburg warmly and reflected on how blacks endured through the power of the blues. He reached out to his audience with the music he composed, and his songs are among the most beloved and widely recorded in blues history.

# WILLIE DIXON

Vicksburg, Mississippi, is my home. I was born in what they call Crawfish Creek Bottom, right over from Cray's Creek. My mother had a little restaurant up on Jackson Road for a long time. Then we moved up on Jackson and Locust Streets. Right around the corner was a fire engine house, and they had a big water trough out there where they used to water the horses. I remember all that.

I used to sing when I was in Vicksburg. We had a group called the Union Jubilee Singers. A fellow named Theodore Phelps talked me into singing harmony. We used to go up to his house and practice. Theodore Phelps was also a carpenter, and I used to do carpentry work with him. We used to build those little shotgun houses.

My mother and my sisters and brothers sang in the choir at Spring Hill Baptist Church up on Jackson Road. There was always blues around. Anybody that sung that wasn't singing spirituals was singing blues. And my mother would say, "You can't sing those kind of songs."

She called those old songs that wasn't spiritual songs reels. "Don't be singing the reels around the house," she would say.

Well you take the average person that would be doing any kind of work, they'd be singing blues songs. There used to be a fellow down there named Tom Jones. He played a mandolin and a guitar, and he used to play every Saturday night at somebody's house party. Every Satur-

day night somewhere he would be having a real rockhouse. We would stand on the outside. They had some of those windup gramophones. They had records of Victoria Spivey and "Black Snake Moan" and all that kind of stuff. My mother didn't like for us to sing them, but we would sing them anyway, you know.

I remember Tom Wince who ran the Blue Room. Tom Wince's auntie was named Miss Annie Short, and that was my godmother. His auntie was my godmother.

In my mind, I wanted to be a fighter, and I had one fight down in Vicksburg. I hadn't never had no training or anything, and then I left Vicksburg and came to Chicago. I won the Golden Gloves in 1937. At that time I was fighting under the name of James Dixon. My name is Willie James Dixon, but they always called me W. J. Dixon in Vicksburg. After I won Golden Gloves, I fought a couple of pro fights. Fighting was kind of slow.

A fellow used to hang around the gymnasium playing the guitar called Leonard Caston. They called him Baby Doo Caston. He used to tell me all the time that if I would sing bass with his group, they could make money. So I decided I'd go out with them a couple of times and sing. We got out there in the nightclubs and were having a good time playing and singing. What I used to do was imitate the bass fiddle with my mouth, like the Mills Brothers, and I got pretty good at that. Then a guy told me, said, "Man, if you

WILLIE DIXON, YALE UNIVERSITY, 1976

could learn to do the same thing on a bass fiddle that you do with your mouth, why, you'd have no trouble playing the bass."

We worked at several places around Chicago. Used to be an old place they called the Pink Poodle over there at 502 South State Street. All up and down there was an entertainment area with pinball machines. We worked there, and then I got a job at a place called Martin's Corner. Jim Martin was a Chicago politician, and he was pretty strong on the West Side of Chicago at that time. He had a club out there called Martin's Corner, and we got a job working there. Baby

Doo Caston made me a one-string bass on a tin can. I learned how to play pretty good, and I asked Mr. Jim Martin about getting me a real bass. He said he'd give me the money to buy a bass, a couple of hundred dollars. We worked out there about a month, and when I left, I could play the bass fiddle.

When I was in the South, I wrote a lot of poems. I was trying to sell them as poems in book form, and nobody wanted them. So I started adding popular lyrics to make popular songs out of them. I made songs called "The West Ain't Wild No More," "Sweet Louise," and

"Monday Man." I never got no pay for them. I'd just give them to the guys just to put my name on a record. They would give me a few dollars whenever they would see me. I was quite young then. I was in my early teens.

But in Chicago, I started playing with Baby Doo Caston and writing songs. We had a group called the Five Blazers and the Four Jumps of Jive. Then we had a group called the Big Three Trio. We recorded for Columbia at the time with the Big Three, and we also recorded for Bullet and Delta Recording Company with a fellow out of Nashville called Jim Bulleit who had a recording studio there. One of the things we done that got real popular was "Wee Wee Baby, You Sure Look Good to Me." At that time the title of it was "You Sure Look Good to Me." And I had done "The Signifying Monkey." I wrote it when I was going to school in Vicksburg. It used to be kind of a toast.

When I was in Vicksburg, there was a fellow named Eddie Cooper who was in my class. He was a born cartoonist. He would draw animals, and he would make pictures. So one day Eddie came up with this idea of the monkey and the elephant. He said because I was fat, I was the elephant. And another fellow named T. W. Grier, who was tall and lanky, he called him the monkey.

So I made up a song about the signifying monkey. We used to play the dozens with each other, talk about people's parents and like that, and I put a song together about the signifying monkey. We had a lot of pamphlets made of it. When I came to Chicago, I started selling those pamphlets, and I would get a dime for them. I

sold a gob, as many as I could make up. Then it got to be a popular toast called the signifying monkey. After it got to be such a popular toast, our Big Three Trio recorded it in 1946. And that's when I put the words to music. We recorded it for Lestor Melrose and put it on the Bullet label, and it was also on the Columbia label. Cab Calloway recorded it, and Count Basie recorded it too, "The Signifying Monkey."

After the Big Three Trio, I decided I'd go with a band of my own, and I got with Memphis Slim. I had been working with the Chess Company because they used to call me in to play bass on sessions with Muddy Waters. I got involved with Eddie Boyd, and I wrote a few things for him, along with Muddy Waters. After then is when me and Memphis Slim started at the Gate of Horn in downtown Chicago. We worked all over Israel, and when we came to France, Slim got a job at the Trois Mailletz in Paris. It was a place in the basement over there. We called it the Left Bank. There was a woman who owned the place called Madame Calvet, and I used to go down there and sit in with Memphis Slim. He would always give me part of his money, just to play with him. After a while, Madame Calvet would pay me a little bit too. Memphis Slim and I would go throughout Europe doing these concerts—just the two of us—and we'd get paid for them. Me and Slim played a lot of places over there together on the American Folk Blues Festival. We'd take our little show on the road and make all the smaller cities.

I began to take apart life and put it together in words. I would try to find the right tone to emphasize the facts of life. I found out that things from my past it fitted a lot of people in the present and also the hopes of the future. Building these things up in your mind and putting the various tones into them always interested people. It didn't always have to be a sad song. I noticed most people think that blues is a sad thing, but blues can be happy as well as sad. I remember one of the songs we used to sing when I was in the South was "I'm going up the country, and I won't be back no more."

We felt like there was a better salvation in the northern countries, better opportunities. It was a great idea for people to be leaving Mississippi. They used to say, "I'm going where the water drink like cherry wine. This Mississippi water taste like turpentine."

We used to sing these kind of things. We inherited them, one generation from the other. When I came to Chicago, I had more ambition to write. So I just kept on writing, and now I do it all the time. I keep writing about something all the time, one way or the other.

I don't have no set time to write. When I get the right idea, I start writing. I always have a book, and I think about it a lot. If I don't have a book and pencil with me, I keep it in my mind. Sometimes I'll stop to think it over. And after I think it over, when I get to the house, I write on it. In fact, I just wrote a thing the other day. It's called "The Wiggling Worm." I just wrote the melody to it. When I get back home tomorrow, I'll copyright it. I got the music and the words down.

I remember when I wrote "Sit and Cry and Sing the Blues." You know there are a lot of

people who feel like blues is sad. A lot of times people think of the shape they're in, and they feel like sitting and crying because of the blues. I used to do this song in Europe a lot, "Sit and Cry and Sing the Blues":

> No one to have fun with since my baby's love
>     has been done with.
> All I do is think of you and sit and cry and
>     sing the blues.

The song tells about

> The blues all in my bloodstream.
> The blues all in my home.
> Blues all in my soul.
> Blues all in my bones.

Those are the words to the song.

> Oh, there's no one to talk to,
> And my love is so true.
> Lord I don't know what to do.
> I just sit and cry and sing the blues.

You write songs of different qualities, different sounds, different angles. If they all sound alike, then you wouldn't have no contrast, and you wouldn't have nothing to change your mood or feelings.

After I got involved in the blues, I noticed that people always wanted something different. There used to be a time when the majority of the blues players and singers, if they heard something that was selling good, that's what they built their songs on. It got to the place where if you had heard one blues song, you had heard them all. The only thing different would be the

WILLIE DIXON, TOAD'S PLACE, NEW HAVEN, 1976

changes of verses. They used to have what they called a twelve-bar thing. Anything that was twelve bars was considered the blues.

Well I began trying to put some form to these things, giving it poetic style and putting in a middle and bridges to give the song a better balance of understanding. I started making these various changes in the pattern of the blues.

The blues has been around a long time, and I really think the conditions of the people is what created the blues. Being poverty-stricken gave them a feeling of insecurity. The blues was made to deliver a message and also to make the task easier for the people because they was involved in long hours of work. They had to make the time pass by singing these dreary songs.

I went to the sixth grade, but I think I have developed quite a bit since then. I always did like poetry. I always liked to hear people that speak good poetry. Every time I write a song, I feel like it will make somebody feel good. It will bring back memories, make high hopes.

There is no doubt about it, the blues came from work songs. Blues made the task easier so that people could work by these songs. People that's working hard and got a long task to do, if they get to thinking about working, it makes it hard on them. But if they get to singing a song and swinging axes or picks or shovels or sawing to a rhythm, then the day and the time pass easier, and it's not a hard job for them. When night comes, they're tired, and they wonder, "How did I get tired? It don't look like I was working that hard."

If you didn't have these various rhythms to carry on, it would make the task much harder. There are certain things about life that prepare an individual for whatever task there is to be done. If you sing the blues, you can do this task in the way that it couldn't be done otherwise. It won't look like it's harmful.

I feel like the blues has been a great help to the black man. The blues helped him to carry out his task. If he hadn't had the blues, he probably could of never made it. His hard job was just another easy thing because he could work and sing and be happy. A lot of people wondered, "Why does this guy work like hell, and he don't have nothing and ain't getting nothing and ain't making nothing? But yet and still he survives off of nothing. He don't have much hope, but he's always singing and happy."

The blues prepared him to feel good and undergo punishment when other people couldn't. The Indians were killed out because they couldn't undergo the punishment. But this fellow come along with nothing else but the blues, and he survives. These are the ways of the blues, and there are many ways of the blues. The blues inspire you. There's always a song to help inspire you, regardless of what condition you're in. Here's a guy talking about how he can make forty cents shining shoes and he feel like he's in good shape. The blues make him feel like that. If he didn't have the blues, he'd say it ain't worth it. He would rather die and forget it. But you take a guy like that, as long as he got hope, he'll survive a long time.

Just like my mother, she never had very much money, never had very much of nothing. And all the doctors predicted her to be dead years ago. Hell, she's still living, and all her doctors are dead. She's ninety-four years old, and she's in better shape than I am. I took her to the doctor not long ago, and she told him she hadn't never been to a doctor but a couple of times before in her life. And the doctor says that's the reason she's still living. This is what I'm talking about. She was poverty-stricken all her life, didn't ever have nothing. And people with millions, with all the conveniences, most of them are dead and gone that came along with her. So that proves one thing. It's not the amount of money you have. It's the condition that you're in.

The blues can give you a feeling that nothing else can give you. And once I get that feeling, I smile to myself. Somebody will say, "What are you so happy about?" Well there are a lot of things to be happy about, you know. You look at yourself, and you see where you came from and where you're going. And you feel like you got a beautiful chance, thanks to the blues.

# B. B. KING

B. B. King's name is synonymous with the blues. At the age of eighty-four in 2009, the blues patriarch follows a rigorous schedule of performances throughout the United States and overseas that would exhaust a much younger artist. King's performances and recordings have defined the blues for more than six decades as he has reached out to members of each new generation with music they understand and embrace.

As an artist, B. B. King defies definition. Born Riley B. King on September 16, 1925, on a plantation in the Mississippi Delta near the towns of Itta Bena and Indianola, he was influenced by gospel singers in the black church, as well as by blues artists like Blind Lemon Jefferson and Lonnie Johnson. In 1946 King hitched a ride to Memphis, where he lived with his cousin Bukka White, a noted blues artist. In Memphis he launched his career as the "Pep-ti-kon Boy," advertising Pep-ti-kon health tonic on radio station WDIA. King also performed with Bobby Bland, Johnny Ace, and Earl Forest in a group called the Beale Streeters. King adopted the nickname the Beale Street Blues Boy, which he shortened to Blues Boy, and then to B. B.

In 1950 King's "Three O'Clock Blues" topped the rhythm-and-blues charts for four months and launched his career as a professional musician. He organized his own band and went on the road, barely two years after he made his last cotton crop in the Delta. Thus began a career that has continued uninterrupted to the present and underscores the power of his line, "Nightlife is a good life, the only life I know."

For twenty years, King played over three hundred one-night stands a year in black-owned clubs on the "Chitlin Circuit." He also played weeklong engagements each year in large, urban black theaters such as the Howard in Washington, the Regal in Chicago, and the Apollo in New York.

As the civil rights movement developed in the early sixties, King's career fell into a slump. Young black audiences found his music uncomfortably close to the world of Jim Crow, and white fans of the folk music revival felt he was too commercial. Only when the Rolling Stones, the Paul Butterfield Blues Band, and British and American rock groups acknowledged King as their idol did his career revive. After his first European tour in 1968, King was embraced by white audiences in the United States, and their support has steadily grown since that time.

Unlike many other blues artists, King blends diverse styles in his music. As a child, he learned to play the blues on the one-strand-on-the-wall, a traditional instrument made by musicians like Louis Dotson by stretching a wire from a broom handle between two bricks across a metal bolt on each brick. Like Dotson, King plucked the string and moved a bottle up and down to change notes. King's guitar style is strongly influenced by blues guitarists Lonnie Johnson and T-Bone Walker and by jazz guitarists Django Reinhardt and Charlie Christian. He blends their styles with delicately "bent" notes and powerful vocals drawn from his musical roots in the Mississippi Delta.

B. B. King's recording and performing career is truly unique. He has issued over seven hundred recordings and has met presidents, heads of state, and the Pope. A familiar figure on television and in advertisements, he continues to tour and greets fans with warmth and humor.

I first heard King's music in the 1950s on Nashville radio station WLAC's late-night blues show sponsored by Randy's Record Shop, which was hosted by John R. Richbourg, Gene Nobles, and Bill "Hoss" Allen. As a teenager in Vicksburg, I danced to King's records, along with those of Elvis Presley. The blues and rock and roll were intimate parts of my life during those years.

Our personal friendship began in the 1970s when I taught at Yale University. King generously agreed to visit my class and spoke with my students.

In 1977 the Yale senior class selected King as its commencement speaker, and President Kingman Brewster awarded him an honorary doctorate of humane letters, stating, "In your rendition of the blues you have taken us beyond entertainment to the deeper message of suffering and endurance that gave rise to the form."

I did a series of interviews with B. B. King during his visits at Yale University and at his home in New York City. Portions of these interviews are also featured in the film *Give My Poor Heart Ease*.

Since those years at Yale, B. B. King's friendship has blessed my life in more ways than I can count. Our relationship grew in part because of King's strong belief that the blues should be an essential part of education at every level. At Yale he met with colleagues like historian John Blassingame and literary scholar Charles Davis, chair of the Afro-American studies program.

While at Yale, I joined King at concerts in Boston and in Germany. The excitement of his performances and his warmth toward fans who lionized him were memorable. In his pocket, he carries an ample supply of red plastic guitar picks with "B. B. King" inscribed on them. For blues pilgrims, these relics are proof of meeting "the King."

In 1979 I moved from Yale University to the University of Mississippi as the first director of the Center for the Study of Southern Culture. That fall the center hosted a historic concert by King that he later released as a two-record LP entitled *Live at Ole Miss*. King donated the proceeds from the sale of the album to the Red Cross to assist survivors of a flood that had devastated the Mississippi Delta earlier that year.

Shortly after his concert, King gave his massive record collection and other memorabilia to the University of Mississippi to help establish its Blues Archive. The B. B. King Blues Collection, the *Living Blues* Archive—amassed by Jim O'Neal and Amy van Singel—and the Kenneth Goldstein Folklife

Collection are unique resources for the study of blues and southern music. My own library of folklore records and books is also part of the Blues Archive. The archive continues to grow and to serve scholars and students interested in the blues. The University of Mississippi Center for the Study of Southern Culture also publishes *Living Blues* and hosts an annual blues symposium, both of which were inspired by King's gift to the Blues Archive.

In 1990 the center organized a *Delta Queen* "College on the Mississippi" that featured B. B. King, Alex Haley, Shelby Foote, and Eli Evans. During the trip I sat with King in his cabin as he spoke with Shelby Foote about the recently released Robert Johnson recordings. Shelby Foote grew up in Greenville, Mississippi, and he and King reminisced about their childhoods in the Delta and the importance of the blues for each of them.

One memorable evening at the W. C. Handy Blues Music Awards in Memphis, I sat backstage with King and Willie Nelson as they recalled their musical careers. At one point, Nelson turned to King and said, "B., I have to admit that I stole a few guitar licks from you over the years," to which King replied, "And I am proud to know you could use them."

Through my friendship with B. B. King, I met Sid Seidenberg, his manager for many years. Seidenberg was often present at concerts and events with King, and he played a key role in developing King's career.

In 1999, while I served as chairman of the National Endowment for the Humanities, the NEH gave King a humanities award. The award was presented in the Old Post Office, where King spoke to the staff and sang several of his best-known blues songs. My interview with King during the ceremony was published with a cover photo of King in the May–June 2000 issue of *Humanities Magazine.* It was the first time in the history of the NEH that a blues artist had been so honored, and the response to the issue was overwhelming. I also joined King when he spoke and performed in the White House while President Bill Clinton was in office.

In 2000 King and I appeared together at the Smithsonian Institution's tribute to King's life and music as part of its millennium celebration. When King learned that John Hope Franklin was in the hall celebrating his birthday, he and his guitar Lucille led the audience in singing a memorable "Happy Birthday" to Franklin.

Throughout his impressive career, King has honored his home state of Mississippi and his hometown of Indianola. Each year in June, he visits the state for two weeks, and he has given benefit concerts at Parchman Penitentiary, the Medgar Evers Homecoming Festival, and the B. B. King Blues Festival. The recently opened B. B. King Blues Museum in Indianola is a national treasure that honors King's home in the Mississippi Delta and his historic role in shaping the blues.

While many books, records, and films celebrate the amazing career of B. B. King, it is his music that speaks most eloquently to us. In "Why I Sing the Blues," he explains why the blues are so powerful, so enduring:

When I first got the blues, they brought me over on a ship.
Man was standing over me, and a lot more with a whip.
Now everybody want to know why I sing the blues.
Well I've been around a long time, I've really paid my dues.

# B. B. KING

I think the blues actually started during slavery. They didn't always think in terms of God freeing them because they were being sold and separated from their families. Many things of that sort were happening to them, and singing to God didn't seem to do much good. So they would sing about it, but not to a heavenly body. They were singing to the bodies down here on earth. A lot of the chanting and singing was to warn other people in the field that the boss was coming or something else was happening.

The earliest sound of the blues that I can remember was in the fields, where people would be picking or chopping cotton. Usually one guy would be plowing by himself or take his hoe and chop way out in front of everybody else. You would hear this guy sing most of the time—just a thing that would kind of begin, no special lyrics, just what he felt at the time. The song would be maybe something like this:

Oh, wake up in the morning, about the break
of day.

And you could hear it, just on and on, like that. Another early sound that I used to hear was my uncle Jack Bennett. Uncle Jack would go out early evenings, and on his way back home at night, you would hear him sing that same kind of thing. Let's see if I can remember one:

If I don't get home in the morning, things are
gonna be alright.

And you could hear it all over the bayous, all around the many little places. You could hear people say, "There goes Jack. He's going home."

These early sounds stay with me even today. When I sing and play now, I can hear those same sounds that I used to hear as a kid.

On Mondays and Wednesdays and Fridays, in our little neighborhood, there was nothing else hardly to do but sing. Usually we would go from house to house each week singing. Monday night, we would go to my house. And Wednesday night, we'd go to yours—and probably even Friday night because there wasn't much else to do. Singing kept us close together. That was another part of the blues that's sort of like church social workers. They keep you up on everything that's happening. And the feeling that you get from that, especially when the kids are growing up, is really togetherness.

It was a handed-down thing, a song you used to hear as a kid. Maybe you heard your grandmother or your mother sing it. When you grew up, some of these things you still would sing. Now if you go in and around where I came from, you would still hear a few of the older songs that I heard when I was a kid. For instance,

You go your way and I'll go mine.
We'll meet again . . . some old time.
But now she's gone, and I don't worry,
Cause I'm sitting on top of the world.

B. B. KING, LUCIFER'S CLUB, BOSTON, 1976

Now that's an old one that was made a long, long time ago. I don't know where it came from. I've heard it all my life. People still sing those kinds of things. We play them with my band. We take these songs and play them with the feeling of today. This has been handed down. You could trace those old songs way back. A lot of spirituals go way back. Each generation makes it sound a little different, but the roots are still right there. I got into the blues because that was practically the only kind of music that was played around where I lived.

We belonged to the Sanctified church. Now as far as I'm concerned, in the Sanctified church, the people can sing about as well as anybody you ever heard. The Baptist church was similar. But if you were in the Baptist church, they didn't want you to bring a guitar in. So I didn't really dig the Baptist church too much.

The Sanctified church, or Church of God in Christ, was very strict. Ladies were not supposed to wear rouge and lipstick or anything of that sort. At the Baptist church you could wear lipstick and most everything, but just

B. B. KING, LUCIFER'S CLUB, BOSTON, 1976

don't bring the guitar in. You can imagine what church I belonged to and enjoyed most—the Sanctified church, of course. They didn't care what instrument you played. If you were able to buy one and bring it in and play spirituals on it, it was okay.

My mother started me singing spirituals with her in church when I was about four years old. After she died, when I was nine, I continued to sing spirituals. We started a little quartet when I was about ten or eleven, and we would use the guitar to tune us up. But we could not go into the Baptist church when we were singing because of the guitar.

My uncle was married to a Sanctified preacher's sister. They had an old southern custom that the adults would have dinner first, and then the kids would eat. So this preacher would lay his guitar on the bed while they were eating. And as soon as they would close the kitchen door, right on the bed I would go. Finally, one day he caught me, but he didn't do what I thought he was gonna do. Instead of bawling me out about it, he taught me three chords. One of them was a C chord, the other one a F chord, and then a D chord. I still play those three chords. Everything I play, I use those three chords. I think it's like one's ABCs. You learn that first, and you still use it.

That's how I got started, and it seemed to me to sound so good. And to me, today, the Sanctified people are the singingest people in the world. I know that may sound weird. I think many people can sing, but to me they are the singingest.

I never thought that I would be into blues. After learning those three chords, we started another group. There was a group called the Golden Gate Quartet. When I was small, my teacher used to tell me that if I continued to play, one day I could be like the Golden Gate Quartet—singing spirituals. This Golden Gate Quartet was something like the Staple Singers are today. They sang spiritual songs—usually with a beat and with feeling—the way you want it to sound. So that's what I wanted to do.

I had one of those devilish little aunts. She was a teenager at the time I was about five or six, but I felt that I was as old as she was. She was more like a big sister to me. My aunt had all these records that I used to listen to—Blind Lemon Jefferson, Lonnie Johnson, Barbecue Bob, Leadbelly, and quite a few of the older blues singers. That was real blues to me. We couldn't just start a new thing all on our own and not be able to do some of the things that

they did. Nobody's ever been able to create the exact sound that those guys had—even though many of us tried.

It was later when I heard Sonny Boy Williamson, Peter Wheatstraw, and my cousin, Bukka White. In fact, I used to watch Bukka. I'd stand by his knee and watch him. He had one of those slides. There was something about the way they played them made me want to do what I'm doing today. I've been criticized a lot of times by a lot of people that don't care for this kind of music. But I laugh and say to myself, "If they could feel what I feel, they wouldn't criticize."

There were so many times when you played that people just gathered around you. They didn't have to give you money. If they gathered around you, you had a feeling of security. You had a feeling of being liked or loved. That was something I never did have quite enough of in my early years. My mother died when I was about nine, and my mother and father had separated. It was quite some time before I learned where my father was. I had relatives in the area, but I didn't have that closeness or that togetherness that I think one should have. That left me at a loss for love.

Whenever I would sing and have these people gather round me like they did, they seemed to me as a family—that family that one looks for, one tries to find. And that has followed me through the years. I still try to make everybody around me a part of my family. I feel close to anybody that takes an interest in me as a person. I seem to melt right off into saying that person's a friend. Whether they want to be or not, I accept them that way. I don't know whether it is heard through my music, but a lot of times it seems to me that I'm crying out to people, "Hey. I'm me. I would like to be with you. I would like to share whatever I have with you."

I think this is another reason the blues singer really goes on—the feeling of being wanted, the feeling of being needed, the feeling of wanting to tell somebody, "Let me bring you a glass of water. Let me help you push the car."

In other words, it isn't that you want something from the other person other than just a little bit of care, a little bit of love. This is another thing that has made the blues singer and the blues musician continue to go on—this is his way of crying out to people, trying to let them know not so much his needs, but the need of wanting to help others. It's the truth.

It's kind of hard to continuously open up, but you want to. Being a blues singer, I'm able to do it. I can sing and let people know that I've been hurt. I can sing and let people know that I've been happy. I can sing and let people know that there are many things that are going on that I don't like. I think all these little things help one sing the blues. You feel that you're communicating.

I believe that regardless of what race he is, if a kid grew up in Japan, he would speak Japanese. If he was in England, he would speak English as the English people do. He would speak fluently whatever tongue they spoke. Even if you take him away from that at an early age, the little things that happen he will remember for the rest of his life. He may not think of it constantly, but at some time some of it will come out.

Some of the things that happened to me as a kid, when I'm playing—and not looking for it or searching for it—some of it will come out. You just can't help it. And a lot of the time you welcome it. It's just like when one goes to school to learn something, you refer back to the things that you were taught when you run into a spot where you need it. You find it the same way musically. The same thing happens. I know a lot of nights when I play, sometimes something will happen to me, and I'll say, "Oh my God, where did I hear that before? When did I do that? Where did that come from?"

That is what I say to myself because I'm really amazed. How did I do that? Then when I come back to my room, I remember that it is a piece I heard a long time ago.

I would work all week to buy my groceries and then go to the nearest town and sit on the corner. I would play—not really like a blind man does. I would just sit and play. Somebody would come by and say, "Honey, would you sing me a song, please?"

I would ask them what they wanted to hear, and most of them would say, "Sing 'Christ Was Born,'" or something like that—some spiritual song.

Now this, mind you, was on a Saturday evening, after I had got off work. If anybody asked for a song, I would sing it. Because none of my church members was there, if I was asked to sing a spiritual or blues, it wouldn't make much difference. If this person asked me to sing a spiritual song, they usually would thank me very politely. "You sure can sing, son. Thank you."

B. B. KING, LUCIFER'S CLUB, BOSTON, 1976

But they didn't give nothing. It would always be some self-made manager that would come up and say, "Why don't somebody give this kid something?"

And all of a sudden, my heart would flutter a bit, saying, "God, I hope they will."

If a dude came by about half smashed, he would look at you and say, "Hey, how bout a song? Can you play that thing?"

I would look at him and bow my head, meaning yes. He would say, "Play me so and so"—whatever tune was popular at that time.

And if I knew it, I would sing it, using my same three chords. This guy might offer me a little taste out of his bottle, then maybe a quarter or half a dollar. He'd say, "Man, you know, you really wail."

That was the word at that time. I noticed that literally every guy that would pass and ask me to play a tune of that kind would usually give me a little tip. Well money don't mean nothing much, but it did to me then.

I started going to church with our group. We would sing, and they would pass the basket or the hat. People would say, "Bless you."

But if we would sing at a juke joint someplace

and play, they'd have some guy standing at the door: "You can't come in here unless you pay."

I liked that pretty well. So that's how I actually got started into the blues. Not that I was a real hypocrite, but I finally decided that if I was really going to sing blues, I'd just go on and get into it. And that's what I did.

We had these little juke joints, little taverns, and the people would sing there. In Indianola, after you had worked in the fields all week, you would go to town on Saturday evenings. Around six or seven, everybody was sitting around. We didn't have bars then. In Mississippi you could buy liquor illegally, but you could buy it. And usually you would buy your bottle and go to the nearest tavern. When you would get there, you would sit down and hide your bottle and call your friends. Everybody knew you were boozing up. We were getting together, and wine was plentiful at that time. Then you would start to sing.

You go to your favorite little bar, and the bartender was usually the owner of the place. He would sell you beer. You could buy beer, which also was illegal, but you still could get it. Then we would sing. Sometimes this would go on until curfew time, which was usually around twelve or one in the morning on Saturday. Around eight or nine, the whole town closed up, but on Saturday night you might stay out all night because there was usually some little place in the alley that stayed open all night. That was alright with the people downtown, and they would allow them to stay open. Usually that's where everybody would come after the town closed up.

During the day, there wasn't any place to go and make music because Indianola was a farming area and everybody was at work during the day. Radios wasn't very plentiful in that area at that time. Only the boss and a few of what we called "well-to-do" sharecroppers had radios because radios was very expensive at that time for us. Around our house they mostly sang spirituals. When I wanted to hear the blues, I would just go down to the store.

One of the first guys that I liked was Blind Lemon Jefferson. He was born in Texas, blind from birth, and the seventh kid in his family. From what I gathered, he must have been a very lonely fellow. I thought about him many times. Braille must have been hardly available to him at that time because his family was very poor.

But he had a sound that I wish I could do today. Of course, he only recorded for a short time—from the time I was born, 1925, until about 1930. They tell me that he froze to death in Chicago. Blind Lemon had an unusual rhythm pattern. His touch was very, very distinctive, and his notes were very clear. His singing seemed to really do something to me.

Later, there was a guy called Lonnie Johnson. I like to think of myself as Lonnie Johnson seemed to be, that link between the blues and jazz. There was a jazz guitarist called Charlie Christian who had altogether different kinds of chords.

If they played pop songs like "Stardust" or "Body and Soul" or one of those standards, they would use what we call diminished chords. That got me interested in jazz. Later on, I had a friend that went into the service. When he came back from France, he brought some records back by a jazz guitarist called Django Reinhardt. Each of these people sounds just a little bit different, but all of them have one thing in common. And that one thing was the way they phrased, which I think I stick with still. The last two that I mentioned, Charlie Christian and Django Reinhardt, were very fast. Their technique was good. The things they did with the guitar a lot of people are not able to do today.

But when I was listening to these people play guitar, along with many others like Elmore James, they seemed to have something that said you must listen. This is the way it is, right here. Listen. Just like somebody talking to you. They'd say, "Hey, do you understand what I'm saying? It's so and so. Do you get it?"

There were others I liked—Albert Ammons on piano and on saxophones, Charlie Parker and Louis Jordan.

One day in the early forties, during the war, I heard a song by a guy called T-Bone Walker. That was the first time that I had ever heard blues on an electric guitar. T-Bone Walker was singing "Stormy Monday." I felt that I would die if I didn't get an electric guitar after that. In 1946 I managed to get one. Of course, I owned a guitar before that, but not electric.

In '49, I was playing in a place called Twist, Arkansas. It's about forty-five miles northwest of Memphis, Tennessee. We had a good time there every Friday and Saturday night. In the wintertime, we had a big container—looked like a garbage pail—and we would sit it in the middle of the floor. They would fill it about half full with kerosene—down home they call it coal oil—and

they would light this fuel. This was all they had for heat. The people that was used to coming to this place would dance around this big container. You could get about seventy-five or eighty people in there at once, but some nights we would have two, three hundred people. We had what we called the "coming and going crowd." People would come in, get hot dancing, and walk out. Then others would come in.

This particular night, two guys started fighting, and one of them knocked the other one over on this container of kerosene. When he hit it, it spilled all over the floor. Everybody started trying to put it out, and that made it burn more. Everybody started making for the front door when they figured they couldn't put it out, including B. B. King. But when I got on the outside, I remembered that I'd left my guitar inside and I went back for it. Guys told me not to do it. The building started to collapse around me, and I almost lost my life trying to save my guitar. The next day we found that two men got trapped in rooms above the dance hall and burned to death. We also found that these same two men were fighting about a lady, and we learned that the lady's name was Lucille. I never did meet her, but I named my guitar Lucille to remind me never to do a silly thing like that again.

Instruments weren't very plentiful in the area where I grew up. We felt a need for music, so we would put up a broom wire. Usually we would nail it up on the back porch. In case you're not familiar, brooms had a kind of straight wire wrapped around the straw that would keep the broom together. We would find an old broom—

B. B. KING, YALE UNIVERSITY, 1977

or a new one, if we could get it without anybody catching us—and take that wire off of it. We would nail it on a board or on the back porch to one of those big, thick columns, put the wire around the two nails—one on this end and one on the other—and wrap it tight. Then we would take a couple of bricks and put one under one side and one under the other, and stretch the wire and make it tighter. We would keep pushing the brick—stretching the wire, making it tight—until it sounded like one string on a guitar. But it was only one. By putting your hand on it in different places, you actually could change

the sound of it. Some guys did it a little different than that. They would use a piece of steel like they do on a steel guitar with a bottleneck.

We used to take rubber strips from an inner tube that was inside your tire. This was very flexible rubber. We would cut it up in small strips and put them on a stick. You could tighten that, and we would take small pieces of rock or a piece of wood and put that on as a bridge—same thing we used those bricks for on the wire on the wall. Sometimes we would put two or three of these, or four or five, and sometimes six—like a guitar on a board—and then we would go and cut a stick. We would saw this like you would a violin. It made a very nice sound, and we would fret it with our hands as if it were a violin. If you put a little water on it and made it a little slick on the stick, you really could get a sound out of it. People did that.

There were other ways of making musical instruments. Guys would take a couple of spoons, and they would beat them together. We would also take a comb, a big heavy comb, and put thin paper against it. You could blow that. You made music that way also.

Usually, in the average home, there was an old guitar with strings broken, and in order to play this guitar we would make wooden clamps. We would put the wooden clamp on down below, where we had the string tied, and that would make the string sound good.

If you were living like I did, a harmonica was about all you could afford. There was a big company that you could order things from—Sears Roebuck. One fellow that had gotten rich was able to get him a guitar. When I say rich, he had been to the army and been mustered out and paid. Later on, he decided that he wanted to sell his guitar, and he was going to sell it for fifteen dollars. The family I was working for was pretty nice about paying me for farmwork, so I paid five dollars the first month, five dollars the second month, and five dollars the third. To me, it was the greatest thing that had ever been created because it was my guitar.

They often say you can take the boy out of the country, but you can't get the country out of the boy. When I first left Indianola, I was hitchhiking, and I ran across a guy with a truck. I asked him if he would let me ride with him to Memphis if I would help him unload his flour. I had walked about fifteen or twenty miles when I saw this guy. I helped him unload his flour, and then we got into Memphis at 3:30 in the morning. I didn't have any money, but this guy fed me. He had food with him in his truck.

When we got there, I said, "Where's the bus station?"

That's the only thing I could think of. He said, "I'll show you where the train station is. I don't know where the bus station is."

He took me to Union Station, and that's where I sat until the next morning because I didn't know any place to go. I had relatives there, but I didn't know how to get to them. The next day I started to look around and found where my cousin, Bukka White, lived. I went over to his house.

This was the very first time I had been to Memphis, and Memphis was to me then like New York City would be to the average person. I'd never seen a city as large as Memphis. Jackson, Mississippi, was as large as I'd ever seen. I was really like a kid in a candy store. I started looking at the big buildings and saw how the people lived there. I saw streetcars for the first time. I had a chance to get up close to trains. We had one that came through Indianola—it was called the Southern. But when I got to Memphis, I saw all of these big locomotives, and these were very long trains with people riding on them. All of this was new to me. They told me that at this station people could leave and go to Chicago, New York, or California—anyplace you wanted to go, even New Orleans. I was just like a kid that had been turned loose in a zoo, and all the animals were friends. It was really fun for me. I stayed in Memphis for about a year and a half, almost two years.

When Sonny Boy Williamson put me on the air, he called this lady at the place where he worked, the Sixteenth Street Grill, and he said, "Did you hear the boy who just sang?"

She said, "Yes, I heard him."

"How did you like him?"

"I liked him alright."

"Well I'm gonna let him work for you tonight."

So he looked at me, and Sonny Boy was a very big fellow, older, much older. You can imagine how I felt then at about nineteen or twenty years old. He said, "I want you to go down and play for Miss Anne at the Sixteenth Street Grill, and you better play."

I said, "Yes sir."

That was my first job, and she paid me twelve dollars. That was more money than I had ever made.

That's how I learned about this new radio station. She said they had just opened a new radio station. She said the kids liked it, and if I could get on the radio station like Sonny Boy, then she would give me a job paying twelve dollars a night with one night off and your room and board. I didn't think there was that much money in the world. So that's how I got started. That was my first professional job. The blues started from that radio station. Anybody who lived in and around Memphis at that time or had anything to do with any kind of music on Beale Street would come in the station to see

Mr. Handy, W. C. Handy, who wrote "Beale St. Blues."

I think young people like blues. They associate blues with truth. A lot of the lines we use are warnings to people about certain habits that one maybe wouldn't like. For instance, cheating—that's one. Not only habits that one wouldn't like, but habits that one would like, like love. Young people are for honesty, and they are for living. I think that's one of the reasons why they can relate to blues and to many other branches of the music. I like to think that rock and roll and soul music are sons of the blues.

One of the things we should do is to talk about the blues and discuss it so black kids wouldn't be ashamed to be identified with it. This is the thing that's different: white kids have never had to be ashamed of this kind of music, so when they get into it they either like it or don't like it. They don't have to think in terms of what I was taught. I was taught by my relatives that these were "reels." "Them reels," they'd say. "Bring these reels around here and you'll get a backhand slap."

They just didn't allow them around the house. And when we were kids, like the kids are today, we liked to get into our own thing. I could never listen to my favorite people around some of my relatives.

The reason why a lot of people weren't identifying themselves with my kind of music was because it was kind of like dirty clothes in the closet. A lot of people didn't want to touch it. And a lot of other people didn't have a chance to hear about it or know about it in the first place. Had they had a chance to hear about it and know about it, then they would listen and say, "Well I don't like it. It's not because of the artistic bit of it. It's just that I don't like that sound," instead of saying, "It's something to remind me of the years back, slavery or the segregated parts or whatever it may be."

When I was a teenager, if I heard Barbecue Bob or I heard Leadbelly, I would know one from the other. The reason why I didn't like them or did like them was a choice I made—not what somebody told me. The kids today don't have that choice because they do not have a chance to hear them. In '49 if somebody called me black, if he wasn't too big, I'd try to fight him because I figured he was trying to insult me. But if he said colored, well I'd go along with that. Today, it's just the opposite. I can laugh about it today and am not ashamed about it because I do think that people make mistakes. And there have been many mistakes made in the world, not only in this country. We can let people know that they can like the blues today, and nobody is going to laugh at them.

We still are not paid what a lot of other people are paid—especially the old blues singers. They're just trying to make a living. A lot of them are not so concerned about what or how much money they make as long as they get paid some money for their talents. And me, of course, I'm hoping that I can work.

I've had other jobs. I used to be a tractor driver. I used to weld. And I've done many other kinds of things. But I find—at least I believe—that I can play blues better than anything else I've tried to do. And it seems like to me that people enjoy my playing better than anything

else that I've done. I'm a pretty good driver, but I think people like my playing better than they do my driving. I also find happiness in what I'm doing. Many people have helped me to keep it going. I think that I am one of the leaders in the field and that I should fight for the blues because I believe in it.

I happen to be a blues musician that writes music. That's one of the big differences between King and older bluesmen. I carry a ten-piece orchestra, and they read music. All of them write and arrange. In my early years I didn't read music. Blues was an unwritten music for many, many people. Now we have fixed it where everybody can play.

People don't usually think that because one plays blues, one knows anything about music at all. Well that's a very big mistake. To play blues is just like playing any other kind of music. One should know as much as one can about his instrument, about the kind of music that's being played, so he can play with others. I don't think that one should just pick up an instrument—whether it's a guitar or harmonica—and think that he's the only person around that can play and not try to play with others.

I like to think that blues are just as important as any other kind of music. I like to think the reason it's been kept back so long is simply because people didn't listen to it like they did to other kinds of music—that is, with an open mind.

Young people, especially young musicians, have groundwork laid for them, or guidelines, shall we say. It would be just like if your father had a business and you take over the business.

Every person has a time, and the older ones have left something for you to build on. You use your own ideas, lay your own foundation on top of what has already been built. This makes you stand out in your generation. And then, when your father thinks you really are hip in the business, he starts to give you more leeway, meaning that he don't interfere with you as much because he figures that you know what you're doing.

I just was playing a tune that I recorded back in about '62. It says, "I got a boogie-woogie woman, and the way she boogies, it's alright."

There's another tune says, "I got a sweet little angel, and I like the way she spreads her wings."

The blues is like a tonic. When I went into radio, I used to advertise for a tonic called Pepticon. Pepticon was supposed to be good for whatever ails you, and that's the way I think of the blues. There's a blues for anything that bothers you. If you're happy, then you can sing "Sweet Little Angel" or the "Boogie-Woogie Woman."

I listen to soul music, I hear the same thing. I listen to pop music, I hear the same thing. I listen to gospel music, and, believe it or not, I hear the same thing. The only difference is these people are praying to God or Jesus Christ. The bluesmen would be saying, "Open the door. Don't keep me waiting. The gas station is closed. Let me in"—that kind of thing.

You're singing to somebody on earth. When I'm playing, I get the same feeling that I do if I went to church. If I went to church, I would get the same feeling when I'm playing—especially when everything is going well.

The blues are the three Ls, and that would be living, loving, and, hopefully, laughing—in other words, the regular old E formation on the guitar with the regular three changes. The blues are really life to me because all my friends, everything around me, the music that I hear, everything leads me back to the feeling of the blues, or the feeling that I get from playing or singing the blues or hearing others singing and playing. In fact, everything that I'm connected with—life itself—is the blues. If I had to try and play the way I feel about it, it would be something like this [plays guitar]. That tells my feeling. That's the blues.

# SACRED AND SECULAR WORLDS

*The church and the blues joint are pivotal worlds within the black community. Each weekend the preacher and the blues singer gather their followers together to celebrate with familiar rituals that have much in common. Both speak to black families with a deep knowledge of their needs and aspirations. Bluesmen perform at clubs and house parties on Friday and Saturday nights, and the preacher leads his church service on Sunday morning. This cycle of sacred and secular worlds has existed for more than a century and is a familiar part of the life of each speaker in this book. The blues cannot be understood apart from the church. Music, stories, and call and response define both the blues singer and the preacher as they reach out to the people of their community.*

# ROSE HILL CHURCH

The religious center of the farm where I grew up was Rose Hill Church, a classic whitewashed building that overlooks rolling fields from the crest of a tall hill. Its steeple rises above the front door, and the church bell stands beside it. The church has witnessed the revivals, weddings, and funerals of generations who passed through its doors.

During the sixties, the Rose Hill congregation gathered on the first Sunday of every month to hear Reverend Isaac Thomas preach his powerful sermons. The sound of its hymns drifting across graves on the hill always reminded me of the church's rich musical history. There were no hymnals in the church, and the congregation sang its Dr. Watts hymns—originally composed by Isaac Watts—from memory. In the familiar, chanted pattern known as "lining out," a lead singer spoke each line, and the congregation responded by singing it. This style of singing hymns originated in colonial America and is still used today in rural churches in Mississippi and other parts of the South. During each service at Rose Hill Church, Amanda Gordon, a tall, thin elder in her seventies, led the congregation as she lined out Dr. Watts hymns in her high-pitched voice. The sounds of slave music echoed in the hymns sung by Amanda Gordon.

When I was a child, our housekeeper, Mary Gordon, Amanda Gordon's stepdaughter, took me and my brother Grey to services at Rose Hill Church, where I learned to sing "Ring the Bell," a hymn that was sung as a member walked out of the water after being baptized. Mary Gordon brought a basket filled with fried chicken and biscuits that we ate after the service. The church was an intimate space for the black community, and whites rarely attended its services.

Rose Hill Church was originally built as a "brush arbor," a shelter made with tree limbs by worshippers who now lie buried in the hill around the church. For more than two hundred years, Rose Hill Church was the social and religious center for generations who worshipped there. Among the many visitors who admired the church were Cleanth Brooks, Alex Haley, Alice Walker, and Eudora Welty. After visiting the church, Alice Walker was inspired to write her poem "View from Rose Hill."

When I walk through the door of Rose Hill Church, I enter a sacred space whose walls have witnessed the religious history of a community. The church has sheltered generations of families whose lives reach from slavery to the present. Church services anchored its members from birth to baptism to marriage to death. Its floor—like the ocean floor—was a haven from storms that families endured in each generation.

In each generation, voices sang the familiar old Dr. Watts hymns, and the preacher delivered his sermon with the eloquent, emotionally charged power for which the black church is known. This tradition inspired the sermons and speeches of Martin Luther King Jr., and it is heard in Ralph Ellison's *Invisible Man* and in Richard Wright's *Black Boy*.

Years after I first entered Rose Hill Church as a child and learned to sing hymns like "Ring the Bell, I Done Got Over" and "The Lord Will Make a Way Somehow," I returned to film, photograph, and record the Rose Hill Church service. I tried to capture the familiar river of sound that moved me as a child. Reverend Isaac Thomas acknowledged my presence in his sermon when he said that the church doors would always "[swing] on the hinge of good welcome" for me. His words embraced me as part of the church community and reminded me that I was a guest in the church. He and his congregation granted me the privilege of entering their sacred space.

I recorded and filmed this service in 1968 using black-and-white Super 8 film. The sound recording and footage shot during that visit are included in

*Black Delta, Part 2*. I returned with a film crew in 1974 and filmed the Rose Hill service that is featured in *Two Black Churches*. Both of these films are included on the DVD that accompanies this book.

Today, Rose Hill Church is used only for burials and family gatherings. While some descendants of its families still live in the community, others have moved to Vicksburg, and still others have moved north to Aurora and Chicago, Illinois. At death, their bodies are returned for burial beside the church.

This Rose Hill service captures the voices of both young and old. From babies held in the arms of their mothers to church elders, as many as four generations in a single family often gathered to worship. Together, they transformed the church into a religious ship that tossed as their hymns, prayers, sermons, and cries moved the vessel toward a safe berth. It was a haven from their struggles in the outside world. It was that single space they possessed and empowered as their own through religious music and ceremony.

Reverend Isaac Thomas leads the service dressed in a dark suit. Behind him on the wall is a large color tapestry of Christ and his disciples at the Last Supper. This is the only image in the church. In summer the windows are all open to catch passing breezes. As electric fans blow inside, hand-held fans provided by local funeral homes move constantly during the service. One fan features two young girls praying, with the caption "Thank you, God." On the back, the fan advertises the services of Dillon Funeral Homes and Dillon Burial Association, with phone numbers for its homes in Leland, Greenville, Vicksburg, Indianola, and Cleveland. The fan reminds users that its offices are "completely air-conditioned for your comfort." In an experienced hand, this fan generously shares breezes with others who sit nearby. Without hymnals in the church pews, the congregation sings its hymns from memory in a slow pulsing rhythm.

Reverend Thomas's sermon begins deliberately with biblical quotes and stories. As the sermon develops, his voice grows more intense, and he begins to chant in short, staccato phrases. The congregation responds with hymns and calls of "Amen" and "Yes, Lord." Their voices blend together until the sermon reaches its emotional crescendo. At that point, the Holy Ghost enters the church, members are possessed with the spirit, and ushers lead them outside to cool off. During the sermon, Reverend Thomas moves from behind the pulpit and walks down several steps as he preaches in front of his congregation.

At the end of the sermon, a final hymn is sung, Reverend Thomas prays, and the congregation slowly walks outside the church. Members visit and hug each other, then get into their cars and wind down the hill on a gravel road to the main road. The church doors will remain locked, its walls silent, until the first Sunday of the next month.

This scene—the gathering of worshippers, the singing of hymns, and the preaching of the sermon—has been repeated in black communities throughout the South for generations. It is a key to memory in black history, and it is the foundation of all black music.

When I learned of Amanda Gordon's death in 1980, I wrote this poem for her.

 

For Amanda Gordon (1892–1980)
Who
*Killed*:  Possum with hoe,
        At night,
        Alone.

*Sewed*:  Colored worlds with
        Scraps

From cloth of white and black people,

Their shirts, sacks, curtains,

Frozen together.

From perch in Hamer Bayou—gold.

From evening sun—blood red.

From storm—purple.

Her vision of hours pieced together.

*Sang*:   Ring the bell, I done got over.

I done got over at last.

My knees been quainted with the morning dew.

Head been bent in the valley too.

Her song.

*Stood*:   Statue tall,

Eye fixed,

And rang sound and color together.

ROSE HILL CHURCH, 1975

# ROSE HILL CHURCH SERVICE

Ring the bell, I done got over.
I done got over at last.
Just watch that sun, how level she run,
Don't let her catch you with your work undone.
I done got over at last.

When I lay my burden down.
Burden down, Lord, burden down, Lord.
When I lay my burden down.
Burden down, Lord, burden down, Lord.

I'm going home to live with Jesus,
When I lay my burden down.
I'm going home to live with Jesus,
When I lay my burden down.

Glory, glory hallelujah,
When I lay my burden down.
Glory, glory hallelujah,
When I lay my burden down.

I'm gonner meet my loving mother,
When I lay my burden down.
I'm gonner meet my loving mother,
When I lay my burden down.

I'm gonner walk the streets of glory,
When I lay my burden down.
I'm gonner walk the streets of glory,
When I lay my burden down.

Talk about happy, I'll be happy,
When I lay my burden down.
Talk about happy, I'll be happy,
When I lay my burden down.

Glory, glory hallelujah,
When I lay my burden down.
Glory, glory hallelujah,
When I lay my burden down.

[Deacon James Burns chants prayer:]
So glad, our Heavenly Father, that you have
    mercy on us this evening.
Please sir, hear me this evening.
I'm calling on your holy name.
You know, Father, I'm calling on you this evening.
I'm so glad He heard me cry, and He caused me
    to get up this morning.
He said these words, "If you need me, call me."
I need Jesus when I'm in here.
I need Jesus when I'm walking up and down the
    road.
I'm so glad I can walk with you.
I'm so glad.
He say, "My word will set this world on fire."
I keep my arms around Him everywhere I go.
And don't let nothing come against Him.
And you need Jesus where you go.
He say, "I'll keep my own right at home until the
    sun rises."
And He shore will.
He'll shelter you.
And He told me His word, and I'm living on His
    word today.
And everybody that calls on His name is going
    in the kingdom.
He say, "It won't be nothing in the kingdom but
    the pure of heart."

Have mercy.
I thank you, Jesus, for calling on us name in
    Rose Hill here this evening.
And while your humble servant call on
    remission in your holy name,
Please don't leave me.
Don't leave me in a world of trouble.
Ain't nobody can help me in this world of
    trouble like you.
He take me by my hand and lead me.
Have mercy, Jesus.
Have mercy, Jesus.
Thank you, Jesus.

[Deacon:] We are thanking God for being here.
I think it's a fine thing to do unto others as they
do unto you. That's the key. That's the key to
happiness. I think the time has come for all of us
to unite. That's the only way to stand is together.
United we stand, divided we fall. There's a time
for all things. There's a time to give because our
life is too short to be selfish. And it's a time to
love and be loved. God loves those people who
love, and I don't think we can say we truly love
God and hate our neighbors.

[Reverend Isaac Thomas:] Thank you, brother.
I think we can thank God that all of us have a
chance to be assembled again in the house of
the Lord. Bless this meeting here. His mercies
have been bountiful and each of us should have
a mouthful of blessing for God for His blessings.
We are here and have much to thank the Lord
for. Amen. Much to thank the Lord for. The first
thing that I would like to do is, amen, to read
the Bible to open the service.

The poor you will have with you always, but
me you won't have. You have given to the poor,
now give to the Lord. The offering is coming
now. Let us give the poor people something.

[Congregation:]
Precious Lord, take my hand,
Lead me on, let me stand.
I am tired, I am weak, I'm alone.
Through the storm, through the rain,
Lead me on, let me stand.
Take my hand, precious Lord,
Lead me on.

[Reverend Thomas:] Now God bless you. We're
getting ready to move on to the next station. We
all appreciate seeing Miss Fanny. She was down
a while ago in bed. She wadn't able to do anything. Also Sister Gloria Lee was up in Chicago
to see about her children and was gone so long
we began to think about her. Amen. We're happy
to have her back on her porch. [Sister Gloria Lee
replies, "I'm glad to be back too."]

[Lined out by Reverend Thomas:]
Dark was the night and cold was the ground.
Dark was the night and cold was the ground.
On which the Lord was made to lay.
On which the Lord was made to lay.

[Reverend Thomas:] We want to welcome
Mr. Ferris to us today and tell him that the door
here swings on the hinge of good welcome at
all time. From the twenty-seventh chapter of
the book of Matthew, we have made note of this
fortieth verse, "If thou be a Son of God, come
down from above. If thou be a Son of God, come
down from above."

ROSE HILL CHURCH AND CONGREGATION, 1975

The theme today is "I can't come down. I just can't come down." The devil is extending this invitation to our Lord to come down and rebuild it in three days. You said, "You were a battle-ax in war. Now if you are the Son of God, come down. You told us that you was the Son of God, that you was sent direct from God. If that be so, you come down from the cross, and we will believe it. Until then, we just won't believe it, if you don't come down."

The theme is "I can't come down because I got to stay here to satisfy divine justice. If I come from the cross, heaven and earth will pass away because it's written in the word, 'Before my word shall fail, heaven and earth won't be no more.' Therefore I got to stay because my Father in heaven is depending on me. I got to stay."

Therefore the devil is extending an invitation to the church today to come down. We are on the wall doing progressive work, and Satan is extending you a invitation daily, telling you to come down. He's saying he has much pleasure for all of you, and he's extending you an invitation to come down. It's not but one thing to keep you from accepting this invitation, and that is to pray right because Satan's mighty. But God, he's

almighty. So he's here saying, "Come down from above."

We have so many young people in Warren County and elsewhere that are accepting the invitation from Satan. So I think the day and time is come when the church should wake up to the sense of duty, when the church should wake up and get on her feet. The church should wake up and do its job. We are neglecting our duty because there is so many young people in Warren County that are accepting the invitation from Satan. We don't have a program in the church for the young people. I think we should work out a program in our church so that the young people can be active in the church. If we fail to extend that invitation to them, there is another man over there telling them to come down to his program. "You come down to my program, and I'll have pleasure for you. I have many facilities that you can get pleasure from, if you come down to me."

Therefore Satan is begging today our young people to come down to his program. So many of our adult people is going down to accept the invitation of Satan to come down out of the field of religion, to come down off the post of progress and accept the lusters of the world. Therefore Satan is very busy in all these walks of life. He never be idle. He always is on his post because Satan, he is very cunning. Before he was cast out of heaven, he was called Lucifer, which mean beautiful. He was a beautiful angel up there in heaven, and he had the say-so round there. But one day he got lifted up in pride. But when he got lifted up in pride, the Lord let him know that he had all power to cast out the devil.

Satan was called the dragon. He was called the dragon because he drug a third part of the kingdom down with him. And he is still called the dragon because in America he's dragging so many people down to destruction.

He was called the devil because the word "devil" means "I'm busy. I stays on my porch. I stays on the job."

Not only that. He was called Satan because Satan means "meddlesome." He meddle everything that he see. He meddle with your hair. He meddle with your shoes. He meddle with your appearance. Therefore Satan is always on his porch.

Not only that, but he was called the demon. He was called the demon because he have so many disciples in his program. So here he is, extending a invitation to the Lord to come down from the cross. "You been round here thirty-three years. You been round here talking about that you are the Son of God, and now it's proving time. The proving time has come. And if you are the Son of God, come down from the cross."

Jesus, our theme is that "I can't come down because I got to stay here. If I come down, I can't be a poor man's friend. If I come down, I can't be bred in a starry land. I got to stay here."

And Jesus, the Lamb of God, came here for that purpose. He came here to suffer and die. He came here to pay the debt that we owe. There's nothing that he have did wrong. But we have voluntarily transgressioned. And we fell from the holy state. Now God sure gonner bring the voice of that holy choir. And Jesus came to take our place in death. And he had a few years to

◂ REVEREND ISAAC THOMAS, ROSE HILL CHURCH, 1975

accomplish his reign. And it taken him three years to get this organized. And he went through many ordeals of suffering. He went through many restless nights. And he came here for the purpose to overtake his brother and bring him back with God. So in these three years, he did a great job. And we too should do a great job, yes, in this field of religion.

Yes, we should work while it's day,
Yes, because night is coming,
Yes, when no man can work.
Yes, we should take a good chance while the
    good chance is around,
Yes, and Jesus is already on hand.
Yes, He is the bright morning star,
Yes, being a poor man's friend.
Yes, can we see the Lamb of God in the
    kingdom?
Yes, can we see the Lamb going down by Tiberia?
Yes, and going along the coast of Galilee,
Yes, getting His testament up in the hearts of
    men.
Yes, my challenge is here to save.
Yes, when Jesus, the Lamb, had worked, had
    done a good job,
Yeah, He had fed the hungry.
Yeah, He had helped the poor.
Yes, can you see Him, brethren, feeding the
    people?
Yes, the hungry.
And can we see today, brethren?
Yes, in the city of Washington,
Yeah, they tell me they have a poor people's
    march.
Yes, it was there in the poor people's march.

Yeah, and Jesus, He called a little boy,
Yeah, that had two little fish,
Yeah, and five little buns,
And He manifested.
Yeah, He magnified through His omnipotent
    power.
And He fed five thousand.
Yes, and He told them to gather up the
    fragments.
And it was twelve baskets of fragments that was
    left.
Yeah, He is a poor man's friend.
Yeah, and when He had stayed here,
Yeah, and about thirty-three years,
And it was time for Him to make a departure,
And go back to His Father.
And one Thursday, I say one Thursday,
Lord, He told His disciples to go in town,
And to find a man, he'll be dragging a pitcher of
    water.
Yeah, "You'll find that man.
And tell him that the master,"
Yes, "will have me for him,"
Yes, "in the upper room."
And Jesus, the Lamb, went on up in the winding
    stairs,
Yeah, while every round went higher and a little
    higher.
Yeah, around about the Christian's journey,
Yeah, every round we make,
Yeah, go higher and a little higher,
Yeah, to a perfection.
Yeah, we want to join,
Yeah, a perfection.
Yeah, they sat around a table,
And I heard the Lamb.

AMANDA GORDON, ROSE HILL CHURCH, 1968 ▶

And when He said,
Yeah, "I'm gonner eat this time with you,
And I won't eat no more."
Yeah, "I won't eat no more,"
Yeah, "until I am in my Father's kingdom."
Yeah, I heard the Lamb when He said,
Yeah, "My soul is exceedingly with sorrow,"
Yeah, "even until death."
And I heard Him say,
Yeah, "My enemy is setting by my side."
Yeah, "My enemy is eating with me."
Yeah, and He told him,
Yeah, "What you got to do, do it quick."
And Judas, he got up from the table,
Yeah, and joined himself to the other men,
Yeah, and told them, "What will you give me,"
Yeah, "if I put Him in your hand?"
Yeah, "I know Him,"
Yeah, "from John,"
Yeah, "because Him and John look something
    alike."
And "I know Him because I been with Him all
    along.
I say I know Him."

[Congregation sings.]

And He was betrayed.
And he led them to Him.
And he led, he led the mob.
Well he led the mob.
And he led them until they come to
    Gethsemane.
And Jesus was out there, He was praying to His
    Father.
Yeah, "Father, I want you to glorify me with the
    same glory,"

Yeah, "that I had with thee before the world
    was."
Yeah, "The same, the same, the same glory,"
Yeah, "the same glory in the wardrobe of
    eternity.
I'm getting ready to come home now.
I've done what you told me to do.
I've kept all you give me.
I said he was a devil,"
Yes, "from the beginning."
Oh yes, and Jesus, the Lamb of God.
Can't you see Him, brethren,
As He prayed His prayer to His Father,
And He went away the first, second, and third
    time,
And He prayed the same prayer.
And when the third prayer had been ended,
Yeah, I heard Him say, "Let us go."
Yeah, "He that betray me,"
Yeah, "is at hand."
And I saw, brethren,
Oh, 101 men coming down through the garden
    of Gethsemane.
Yeah, they had torches in their hand,
Yeah, because dark was the night,
And cold was the ground on which the Lord was
    laid.
Yeah, I looked at Judas,
And I heard him cry.
Yes, he was.
Yes, I saw Judas was even crying.
Yes, I heard him say,
Yeah, "That's Jesus of Nazarene,"
Yeah, "Jesus, the Lamb of God."
Yeah, can't you see him, brethren?
Oh, when He moved His magnetic power,

Oh, and they all fell like dead men,
Oh, and He gave them power to get up.
Oh, they tried Him five times.
Oh, I say they tried Him five times, yes they did,
Oh, before they condemned Him.
Oh, they took Him to the judgment hall,
Oh, stand Him in the judgment hall.
Oh, I heard Pilate tell Him,
Oh, "Are you the Son of God?"
Oh, that was in the scripture,
Oh, of Isaiah.
Oh, He laid,
Oh, like a sheep before the shearer,
Oh, and opened not his mouth.
Oh, I saw Pilate,
Oh, send Him to Herod.
Oh, Herod,
Oh, sent Him to Caesar.
Oh, and Caesar,
Oh, sent Him back to Pilate.
Oh, yeah.
Oh, tried Him.
Oh, tried Him.
Oh, and the church today,
Oh, is being tried,
Oh, yes,
Oh, with trials and tribulations.
Oh, you're being tried,
Oh, you're being tried today, brethren.
Oh, can you see?
Oh, Jesus,
Oh, that Lamb,
Oh, in Rome.
Oh, Jesus,
Oh, in Rome.
Oh, can you see Him,

Oh, running,
Oh, when He give up the struggle.
Oh, when they pulled off Him,
Oh, His royal garments.
Oh, put on Him,
Oh, a scandalous robe,
Oh, and led Him away.
Oh, led Him to the outskirts,
Oh, of Jerusalem,
Oh, to a little place,
Oh, called Calvary.
Oh, and they nailed Him,
Oh, nailed His hands,
Oh, to the rugged cross.
Oh, they nailed His feet,
Oh, to the rugged cross.
Oh, they made His tomb,
Oh, in the earth.
Oh, they laid Him down,
Oh, in a three-foot hole.
Oh, one foot represent faith,
Oh, the other foot charity,
Oh, and the other foot was hope.
Oh, they laid him down,
Oh, on the solid rock.
Oh, yeah, the rock,
Oh, a round rock,
Oh, a rock on a rock,
Oh, a rock over a rock,
Oh, a rock in a weary land.
Oh, yes, He stayed right there,
Oh, till the sixth to the ninth hour.
Oh, when the ninth hour come,
Oh, flames began,
Oh, to jump through the body.
Oh, Satan tried in the weakest hour,

Oh, he always make invasion in the weakest
    stage.
And he came up there,
Oh, and made his invitation.
Oh, said, "If thou be,"
Oh, "if thou be,"
Oh, "if thou be,"
Oh, "the Son of God,"
Oh, "come down,"
Oh, "from the cross."
Oh, I heard the invitation.
Oh, I heard Him,
Oh, reply with the answer.
Oh, yeah, "I can't come down."
Oh, yeah, "I got to stay here,"
Oh, "to satisfy,"
Oh, "the divine justice."
Oh, yeah, "I've got to stay here,"
Oh, "because heaven is depending on me."
Oh, yeah, "If I come down,"
Oh, "heaven and earth won't be no more."
Oh, "I've got to stay here,"
Oh, "because I'm making up,"
Oh, "a bed for my saints."
Oh, "And if I come down,"
Oh, "I can't be a dying bedmaker."
Oh, yeah, "I got to stay here,"
Oh, "to make up a dying bed."
Oh, "My saints,"
Oh, "gonner be hungry,"
Oh, "in about a week,"
Oh, "and if I come down,"
Oh, "I'm afraid,"
Oh, "they'll starve."
Yeah, "I've got to stay here,"
Yeah, "got to stay here,"

Yeah, "I can't come down."
Oh, "I've got to stay here.
"I've got to stay on the cross,
"Because I've got people coming through for me.
"Some coming by way of the cross,
"And I've got to stay here.
"And if I come down, I can't be Savior."
Yes, I know He's a savior.
Mmm, you know He's a savior.
I know He saved me.
You know He saved you.
Yeah, I'm gonner keep on running,
Until I make it home.
I got to keep on running,
Until I make it home.
Sometime we get fever.
Sometime we feel low-down in spirit.
Well just tell the world,
"I'm gonner keep on running,
"Till I make it home.
"Gonner keep on running,
"Till I make it home."
Are you all gonner run on?
I'm gonner run and see what the end will be.
I don't know what the end will be,
But John told me the other day,
Oooh, that the city was beautiful,
And that a river went down through the heart of
    town,
And that a tree was on the other side.
And when I get moving down here,
And when I been pointed at with the final stone,
And when my name gets on the highway,
Yeah, but one thing John consulates me.
And on the other side of the river is a tree over
    there,

And when you been moving by the way,
And when you been stumped around,
And when you been bumped around,
And you can go to the tree.
Yeah, I've got a right, I don't know about you,
Yeah, I've got a right to go to that tree.
Yeah, the leaves on that tree,
Yeah, they tell me that they good over there.
Yeah, I been wounded on the way,
Yeah, but I won't labor.
Yeah, they tell me one leaf is good for my
    wounds.
Yeah, it would heal, it would heal me.
Yeah, I say it would heal me.
Yeah, I'm gonner ride for the city, don't you
    want to go?
Yeah, I'm gonner ride for the city, don't you
    want to go?
Yeah, I'm gonner ride for the city.
Yeah, I been riding for the city,
Yeah, thirty-six years.
Yeah, I been rising, I been falling.
Yeah, I been losing, I been gaining.
Yeah, but one thing, I'm in route for the city.
Yeah, don't you want to go?
Yeah, I'm in route for the city.
Yeah, don't you want to go,

Yeah, in that city?
Yeah, in that city, I've got somebody waiting on
    me.
Yeah, in that city, they're looking on the bulletin
    board.
Yeah, in that city, they're waiting and they're
    watching.
Yeah, in that city, where it'll be always "Howdy."
Yeah, no more "Good-byes."
Yeah, every day will be Sunday.
Yeah, I'm gonner tell the world to go long, I'm in
    route for the city.
Yeah, don't you want to go?
Yeah, I'm in route for the city, don't you want
    to go?
I love the Lord, He heard my cry.
I love the Lord, He heard my cry.
Everybody oughta say that.
I lay unto His throne.
I lay unto His throne.
I got religion, and I'm satisfied.
It was late in the evening that I heard Him
    calling.

[The piano plays as the congregation sings, "One
day when I was lost, He died up on the cross." A
prayer follows, and the service ends.]

# CLARKSDALE

For over a century, house parties have nurtured blues musicians and dancers in the Mississippi Delta. Each Friday and Saturday night, an audience gathers to hear a bluesman play his guitar or piano and sing. The guitar player may be accompanied by a harmonica player, a drummer, and a musician who rubs a broom handle across the floor to provide rhythm. As the evening progresses, audience members sing along with their own verses and tell stories as part of the performance.

Food and drink are essential to the house party. Their sale provides the owner of the house with income to pay the musicians and to make a profit. Typical fare includes homemade corn whiskey and cold beer served with chitlins, sliced bologna, and fried catfish sandwiches on "light" (white) bread. Food and drink are carried from the kitchen to an adjacent room, where the musicians and dancers gather.

Stories, jokes, and music are all part of the blues performance at a house party. The small room fills with the smell of food, cigarette smoke, and alcohol as couples talk, dance the slow drag, and sing along with the performer. Dancers speak to the singer, who responds to them through his music. The blues singer "talks the blues" with his audience as he works the conversation into his blues verses. After he sings a verse, the musician may continue his instrumental accompaniment during a talk session. Then he sings another verse while audience members try to remember rhymes and jokes to share at the next verse break. As they force the singer to integrate their response with his song, audience members influence the length and structure of each blues song. Experienced bluesmen know that audience response is a measure of their musical skill, and a successful blues session is filled with remarks and jokes that are shared as the music is played. This "call and response" exchange between the blues performer and his audience is similar to the exchange that Reverend Isaac Thomas develops with his congregation in the Rose Hill Church service.

During a blues performance at a house party, there is constant verbal interplay between the singer and his audience. The role of performer shifts from the singer to the audience and back to the singer. After a joke is told by someone in the audience, the performer recaptures his audience by changing the musical beat or striking louder chords. While he allows the center of attention to shift to members of the audience, the performer maintains overall control through his music.

At this blues house party pianist Wallace "Pine Top" Johnson declares to Jasper Love, "I'm drifting."

Jasper Love replies, "He's trying to drift outta Mississippi. I know what he's trying to do."

Then Pine Top sings a verse:

You know I'm drifting and I'm drifting, just like a ship out on the sea.
Well I'm drifting and I'm drifting, like a ship out on the sea.
Well you know I ain't got nobody in this world to care for me.

Pine Top introduces "Drifting Blues" and integrates both storytelling and music into his performance. Throughout the house party, Pine Top and Jasper Love "talk" through the music. Pine Top sings a verse, and then he says, "That's what I'm talking about."

Later Jasper Love encourages Pine Top with the phrase, "Talk to them, Pine." The performer "talks" through his music.

At house parties the distinction between music and talk blurs as performer and audience respond to each other. Blues talk mixes with verses and at times is the focus of the performance. Blues talk is expressed in both short phrases and lengthy conversations. Jasper Love uses short phrases like "Play the blues." These phrases are reminiscent of how the blues disc jockey speaks over music when he plays a record. Rather than interrupt a blues verse, both the disc jockey and Jasper Love insert their phrases during instrumental breaks.

More lengthy blues talk draws the center of attention away from the verses. A long conversation between the singer and the audience is sometimes inserted like a verse within the song. Lengthy blues talk features obscene tales, toasts, and dozens that are performed with instrumental accompaniment.

Musicians may mention Delta towns in their verses. As he performs "Dust My Broom," Pine Top sings, "I'm gonner find me a Clarksdale woman, if she dumb and crippled and blind."

And later in "Santa Fe Blues," he sings:

I say Mobile on that Southern line, Jackson on that Santa Fe.
You know I got a woman in Tutwiler, I got a woman in Sumner too.

Mississippi is the central point on the musical compass at this house party. Pine Top tells Jasper Love, "I'm down in Mississippi, and I got to play the blues."

"Down in Mississippi" is both a geographical and an emotional location. Pine Top and Jasper Love declare their plans to move "up" to Chicago and escape the blues state. Imagining himself in Chicago, Love tells Pine Top, "I'm shore glad we up here on Seventy-ninth and Cottage Grove where we can be free . . . in Chicago, Illinois."

Love locates Mississippi on the "down" side of the blues map both literally and emotionally. He suggests that to leave Mississippi is to move up to a better life: "I'm a Mississippi boy, but I done skipped from it now."

When Pine Top sings the blues line, "Love, I've had my fun if I don't get well no more," Love associates Mississippi with sickness and death: "Long as you stay in Mississippi, you never will get well."

Later Pine Top sings that he is dying and plans to ship his body back home: "On the next train south, Love, look for my clothes back home."

To which Jasper Love comments that he would not even send a corpse back to the South: "You don't wanta go south. . . . Tell him to go west or north, but don't go south."

The arrival of Maudie Shirley and her friend Baby Sister energizes the house party with Shirley's strong female voice as she sings blues verses with Pine Top and adds her bawdy toasts to the session. When Pine Top sings that his woman is "running wild," Shirley replies, "Well you got your womens. Why can't I have my mens?"

At the end of the party, Shirley takes the group to her home, where she plays tapes of the house party to her children and then puts them to bed with a religious lullaby. As she mixes religious themes with the blues, she reminds us of how sacred and secular worlds are intimately entwined in black music.

I recorded and filmed this house party at the home of Floyd Thomas in Clarksdale in 1968 with Super 8 black-and-white film. The film is included on *Black Delta, Part 1*, which can be found on the DVD that accompanies this book. Throughout this transcription of the house party, blues talk is italicized and the singing is roman. Unless otherwise indicated, Pine Top does all the singing. The asterisks mean a break between songs.

# HOUSE PARTY

[Wallace "Pine Top" Johnson (P):] *I'm gonner play that "Pine Top Boogie-Woogie" first.*

Now look, let me tell you something about that "Pine Top Boogie-Woogie."

[Jasper Love (J):] *I wanta hear it.*

Now when I say stop, I mean stop.

[J:] *That means it's good to you.*

I say get it, I mean get it.
Do like I tell you.
I say hold it, I mean hold it.
That's what I'm talking about.
Now, Red [Jasper Love], hold yourself.
Don't move a peg.
Now get it.
Now boogie.

[J:] *Don't forget to break down that bass.*

Now look. You see that woman with her red dress on?

[J:] *I shore do, Pine.*

I want you to swing her right on back to me.

[J:] *No, I'm gonner keep her for myself.*

Don't forget it.

[J:] *Aw, naw.*

I say hold it, I mean hold it.
That's what I'm talking about.
Now boogie.

Now, Red, hold yourself again.
Don't move a peg.
Now get it, boogie.
Now shake it.[1]

\*   \*   \*

[P:] *I'm gonner try some more blues.*
[J:] *Play it like you was playing it when you was plowing them mules.*

Now tell me, little girl, where you stay last night.
It ain't none of your business, you know you ain't treating me right.
But that's alright.
I know you in love with another man, but that's alright.
Every now and then I wonder, who been loving you tonight.

Now look here, baby, see what you done done.
You done made me love you, now your man done come.
But that's alright.
I know you in love with another man, but that's alright.
Every now and then I wonder, who loving you tonight.

1. Clarence "Pine Top" Smith, "Pine Top's Boogie Woogie" (Vocalion 1245), recorded in Chicago, December 29, 1928. I am indebted to David Evans and Frank Scott for references to the recorded versions of blues songs performed in this session. For further information on recordings and singers, see Mike Leadbitter and Neil Slaven, *Blue Records, January 1943 to December 1966* (London: Hanover Books, 1968), and Robert M. W. Dixon, John Godrich, and Howard Rye, *Blues and Gospel Records, 1890–1943*, 4th ed. (Oxford: Clarendon Press, 1997).

WALLACE "PINE TOP" JOHNSON AND MAUDIE SHIRLEY, CLARKSDALE, 1968 ▶

I say tell me, little woman, where you stay last
    night.
It ain't none of your business, you ain't treating
    me right.
But that's alright.
I know you in love with another man, but that's
    alright.
Every now and then I wonder, who loving you
    tonight.

[J:] *I'm gonner go get me a pint of corn whiskey
    cause I'm thirsty.*

I got a great big woman, you know, got a little
    woman too.
Ain't gonner tell my big woman what my little
    woman do.
But that's alright.
I'm in love with another woman, but that's al-
    right.
Every now and then I wonder, who been loving
    you tonight.
Let's go. Shake it on out.[2]

*   *   *

Well now, I walked all night long, my forty-four
    in my hand.
Now I walked all night long, forty-four in my
    hand.
You know, I was looking for my other woman,
    been out with another man.
I done wore my forty-four so long, till it made
    my shoulder sore.

Now if I get you where I want you, baby, ain't
    gonner wear my forty-four no more.

It won't be the first time that forty-four blow.
Yeah, it won't be the first time that forty-four
    whistle blow.
You know it sound just like, baby, ain't gonner
    tell the truth no more.

[J:] *Tell me why you playing them blues like
    that.*

Say, I got a cabin, you know my room is number
    forty-four.
Love, I got a cabin, my room is number forty-
    four.
Now when I wake up every morning, baby, I de-
    clare the wolves steady knocking on my door.[3]

*   *   *

[P:] *This piano, she sticking on me, but I'm
    gonner try "This Country Shack."*

I'm setting here a thousand miles from nowhere
    in this one-room country shack.
I'm setting here a thousand miles from nowhere
    in this one-room country shack.

[J:] *I'm here with you.*

Ain't nothing for my company but that raggledy
    'leven-foot wall.
I wake up every night about midnight, Love, I
    just can't sleep.
I wake up every night about midnight, Love, I
    just can't sleep.

2. Jimmy Rogers and His Trio, "That's All Right" (Chess 1435), recorded in Chicago, 1950. See also Othum Brown with Little Walter (harmonica), "Ora Nelle Blues" ("That's Alright"), recorded in Chicago, 1947, and Little Junior Parker, "That's Al-right" (Duke 168), recorded in Houston, 1957–58.

3. A possible source is Roosevelt Sykes's "New 44 Blues" (BBB 5323, Sr. 3404), recorded in Chicago, 1933. Paul Oliver gives a history of this blues in *Screening the Blues* (New York: Da Capo Press, 1989), 90–127.

All the crickets keep me company, you know the wind howling round my feet.

[J:] *Don't worry, Pine. Our day is coming.*
[P:] *I'm gonner play the blues.*
[J:] *Play the blues.*

I'm gonner get up early in the morning, I believe I'll get outta my bed.
I'm gonner get up early in the morning, I believe I'll get outta my bed.
I'm gonner find me a Clarksdale woman, if she blind and crippled and lame.
That's it, people![4]

\*   \*   \*

[J:] *How you feeling this morning, Pine?*
[P:] *I'm feeling kind of down and out, man.*
[J:] *I know how it is. I hope we can get lucky, Pine.*
[P:] *Yeah. We gonner get lucky. My baby woke up early this morning, and you know what she told me?*
[J:] *What'd she tell you?*
[P:] *She told me she wanted to rock one time.*
[J:] *Well alright.*

Rock me, baby, rock me all night long.
Rock me, baby, rock me all night long.
I want you to rock me like my back don't have no bone.

Roll me, baby, roll your wagon wheel.
Roll me, baby, roll your wagon wheel.
I want you to roll me, Love, you don't know how it make me feel.

[P:] *Well, Love, I'm down in Mississippi, and I got to play the blues.*
[J:] *I know what you mean, Pine. But soon as we get lucky, we'll cut out from here.*
[P:] *I'm telling you the truth, boy. I ain't gonner plow. I ain't gonner plow no mule no more.*
[J:] *What you think about going out in California?*
[P:] *Yeah.*
[J:] *We gonner get lucky. Play the blues for me now.*

Rock me, baby, rock your baby child.
Rock me, baby, like I'm your baby child.
I want you to rock me like my back don't have no bone.

Looka here, Love.
See me coming, baby, go get your rocking chair.
See me coming, baby, go get your rocking chair.
You know I ain't no stranger cause I been living round with you.
Play it one more time.[5]

[J:] *Play it good, Pine.*
[P:] *Well alright.*

\*   \*   \*

[J:] *What's on your mind this morning, Pine?*
[P:] *Boy, I'm telling you, I'm thinking about the hard work.*
[J:] *Hard work?*
[P:] *Yeah.*

4. Mercy Dee Walton, "One Room Country Shack" (Specialty 458), recorded in Los Angeles, 1953–54.

5. Muddy Waters, "All Night Long" (Chess 1509), recorded in Chicago, 1952; Muddy Waters, "Rock Me" (Chess 1652), recorded in Chicago, 1957. See also Arthur "Big Boy" Crudup, "Rock Me Momma" (Victor 20-29-78), recorded in Chicago, December 15, 1944, and Lil' Son Jackson, "Rockin' and Rollin'" (Imperial LP 9142), recorded in Los Angeles, December 16, 1950.

MAUDIE SHIRLEY AND WALLACE "PINE TOP" JOHNSON, CLARKSDALE, 1968

Love, I'm setting here a thousand miles from
    nowhere in this one-room country shack.
Yeah, now I'm setting here a thousand miles
    from nowhere in this one-room country
    shack.

[J:] *Why you so lonesome, Pine?*
[P:] *I got the blues.*
[J:] *How come?*
[P:] *My woman done quit me.*

You know the only thing I can confess, that old
    'leven-foot raggledy cotton shack.

You know I wake up every night about mid-
    night, Love, I just can't sleep.
I wake up every night about midnight, you know
    I just can't sleep.
You know all the crickets and frogs keep me
    company, you know the wind howling round
    my bed.

\*  \*  \*

[P:] *I'm out on Mr. Jamison's place.*
[J:] *Driving that tractor for three dollars a day?*
[P:] *That's right. I'm gonner play the blues now,*
    *boy.*

[J:] *While you playing the blues, I want to ask you a question. You talk about Mr. Jamison. That's a big man. You mean he don't pay but three dollars a day?*

[P:] *Two and a half.*

[J:] *For his best tractor driver?*

[P:] *The best one.*

[J:] *But when you was plowing that mule, you was doing that for nothing?*

[P:] *Dollar and a quarter.*

[J:] *That's the reason why you playing them blues today?*

[P:] *Yeah. I left there walking.*

[J:] *I'm trying to go to California.*

I'm gonner get up early in the morning, I believe I'll get outta my bed.
I'm gonner get up early in the morning, I believe I'll get outta my bed.
I'm gonner find me a Clarksdale woman, if she dumb and crippled and blind.

[J:] *Play the blues now and bring me a bottle of snuff.*

[P:] *One more time, and I gotta go.*

\* \* \*

[P:] *I'm gonner leave here, boy.*

[J:] *Yeah, let's go down to Vicksburg. I was down a little bit below here, coming toward Louisiana, and I looked up the road, and I see a stick I thought was across the road, but it was a black snake.*

[P:] *Black snake?*

[J:] *Yeah, and I run up there, and I went to kill the snake. And you know what the snake did? He threwed up both hands and told me don't hurt him, cause he was trying to get outta Mississippi too.*

[P:] [Laughs.] *I hear you.*

I got the blues for Vicksburg, baby, sing em everywhere I go.
Now I got the blues for Vicksburg, sing em everywhere I go.
Now the reason I sing them blues, you know my woman don't love me no more.

I say Vicksburg's on a high hill, Louisiana just below.
I say Vicksburg's on a high hill, Louisiana just below.

[P:] *What you say, Love?*

[J:] *I hope we can make some money Saturday night.*

[P:] *Look here, Love.*

[J:] *Tell me about it.*

I say if you don't love me, little woman, why don't you tell me so?
You know I got more women, baby, than a freight train can haul.

[P:] *Love, I'm gonner play the blues cause I'm moving on.*

[J:] *Tell me how they did you down in Vicksburg.*

[P:] *I'm going away.*

I say there ain't nothing I can do, ain't no more I can say.
There ain't nothing I can do, ain't nothing I can say.
I do all I can, baby, you know, just to get along with you.

Good-bye, baby.[6]

*   *   *

[J:] *What you want to do for me now?*

[P:] *I wanta dust my broom.*

[J:] *By meaning you gonner "dust that broom,"*
*is you gonner cut out or you gonner stick*
*around, Pine?*

[P:] *I'm gonner put my old lady to sweeping.*

[J:] *What's gonner happen to you?*

I'm gonner get up in the morning, believe I'll
dust my broom.

I'm gonner get up in the morning, I believe I'll
dust my broom.

My best woman quit me, and my friends can
have my room.

I'm gonner write a letter, telephone every town
I know.

I'm gonner write a letter, telephone every town
I know.

I gotta find my woman, if she be in Ethiopia, I
know.

[J:] *Why you gonner dust your broom?*

[P:] *My woman left me.*

[J:] *Why did she leave you?*

[P:] *I didn't treat her right.*

[J:] *Why don't you just tell it like it is. You didn't*
*have the money to give her. You couldn't afford*
*the money.*

I don't want no woman want every downtown
man she meets.

I don't want no woman want every downtown
man she meets.

She's a no-good doney, they shouldn't allow her
on the street.

[J:] *Well I ain't worried about a thing. If I get in*
*trouble, I know my boss gonner get me out.*

I'm gonner go home. I believe, I believe my time
ain't long.

I believe, I believe my time ain't long.

I believe, I believe my time ain't long.

I gotta call Mr. Harris, tell him please send my
sow back home.[7]

*   *   *

[J:] *What about my boss, J. P. Davis? He's a good*
*man.*

[P:] *What you say, man?*

[J:] *Mr. Harris is a good man.*

[P:] *But he don't put out no money.*

[J:] *Well Davis ain't putting out none neither.*

[P:] *He'll loan you some, though.*

[J:] *Say, Pine, what happened in your child*
*days?*

[P:] *Well, boy. I was plowing a mule and cutting*
*stalks with a kaiser blade. Fifty cents a day.*
*My daddy told me, "Son you can't feed your-*
*self."*

*I say, "Okay, Poppa. One day I'll be a man."*
*I left. Left the mule in the field and told*
*him good-bye.*

[J:] *Told the mule good-bye?*

6. Eurreal "Little Brother" Montgomery, "Vicksburg Blues" (Paramount 13006), recorded in Grafton, Wisconsin, ca. September 1930. See also Oliver, *Screening the Blues*, 90–127.

7. Robert Johnson, "I Believe I'll Dust My Broom" (Vocalion 03475, Conqueror 8871), recorded in San Antonio, November 23, 1936. A later, more popular version by Elmore James, "Dust My Broom" (Trumpet 146), recorded in Jackson, Mississippi, 1952, was reissued several times by James.

[P:] *"Good-bye. Good-bye. I don't never want to see you no more."*

> *But that mule got his pension before I got mine. He on welfare, and I ain't.*

[J:] *You still fooling with the mule?*

[P:] *No, I'm through with the mule.*

[J:] *In other words, you wouldn't tell the mule to "Get up" if he was setting in your lap.*

[P:] *If he was setting on my neck.*

[J:] *What would you tell him, "Move?"*

[P:] *"Set on down."*

[J:] *Well if he was running off with the world, what would you tell him?*

[P:] *"Save my part. I'll be there direckly."*

\* \* \*

[Pine Top begins playing the tune of "After Hours."]

[J:] *On this here right now, this "After Hours." We got a curfew. I want you to talk to me and play it and tell me about it. Other words, since the last time I seen you, I have moved up, and I come back to find out what was happening. I been to California, and I'm doing pretty good. They tell me you "after hours" or something down here.*

[P:] *Yeah. I'm running late. They don't 'low me to stay up in Clarksdale after twelve o'clock. I'm gonner give the police a little bit of this "After Hours," you know, by Erskine Hawkins.*

[J:] *You mean that's why you playing that, because they don't allow you to stay up after hours? Look here, man. It ain't but ten o'clock now. What time you have to go to bed?*

[P:] *I have to go to bed at twelve o'clock.*

[J:] *You mean you got to go to bed, and you can't be up?*

[P:] *I got to.*

[Floyd Thomas (F):] *Wait a minute, man. Let's correct that. This town is open now.*

[P:] *I know it is now, but it didn't used to be.*

[J:] *You say this town's open now?*

[F:] *Yes sir. All night long.*

[J:] *But where you going, though? You can't find a drink.*

[P:] *Boy, you better hush talking so loud. Mr. Billy's gonner hear you. It's eleven o'clock. I'm going to Nashville where I can get with the wee wee hours. Let me play it one time.*

[J:] *Pine, you got a chance to go head on out to California with me if you want to.*

[P:] *I'm going. Put the light out.*

[J:] *You playing the blues, Pine, but you ain't telling me nothing about it.*

[P:] *I'm fixing to go now.*

[J:] *You mess with my woman, I'll make my butcher knife eat you up.*

[F:] *Whip out some sound, Pine.*

[J:] *Is I got a soul brother in the house?*

[F:] *Aw yeah, man. Aw yeah.*

Big Boss, don't you hear me when I call?
Big Boss, don't you hear me when I call?
Yes, you ain't all that tall, you just big, that's all.

You long-legged, you just make a fuss.
You just fucking round, trying to be someone.
Big Boss Man, don't you hear me when I call?
Yes, you long and tall, you ain't getting nowhere.

[J:] *Saturday night!*

Now you try to take my woman, you ain't doing no good.

Running round here talking, trying to be someone.
Now, Big Boss Man, don't you hear me when I
call?
Now you ain't that strong, you just big, that's
all.[8]

\* \* \*

[J:] *I been gone away from here two years, and
now I own a Cadillac. Play the old road blues
now.*
[P:] *Shore nuff?*
[J:] *Yes sir. Find that snuff-dipping key.*
[P:] *Let's leave that on that Santa Fe.*

I say Mobile on that Southern Line, Jackson on
that Santa Fe.
I say Mobile on that Southern Line, Jackson on
that Santa Fe.
You know I got a woman in Tutwiler, I got a
woman in Sumner too.
I say, Lord have mercy, please get me way from
here.
I say, Lord have mercy, please get me way from
here.
I done got tired of working for Mr. Harris, working for five dollars a day.

[J:] *Talk to me now.*

Early in the morning, that Santa Fe gonner run.
I say early in the morning, you know that Santa
Fe gonner run.
If I don't carry my woman, Love, you know I'm
gonner carry my little Juicy Fruit.

8.  Jimmy Reed, "Big Boss Man" (VJ 380), recorded in Chicago, March 29, 1960.

I say the engineer blowed the whistle, you know
the fireman, he rung too.
That must of been my baby, Love, she was getting off that old seventy-two.

My baby got a thirty-eight, and she got a thirty-
two-twenty too.
My baby got a thirty-eight, and she got a thirty-
two-twenty too.
Say if she put me in the graveyard, I declare she
won't have to go to jail.

I say early in the morning, they tell me that
Santa Fe shore gonner run.
I say early in the morning, that Santa Fe shore
gonner run.
I say it took my woman, come back and got my
used-to-be.

[J:] *You make me think of when I used to walk
through ice and snow. But I done got lucky. I
don't have to do it no more.*
[P:] *What say, Love?*
[J:] *I know what make you play em like that.*
[P:] *I got the blues.*
[J:] *Man drive up to your door soon in the morn-
ing telling you to go to work. Then he come all
up in the house, sitting there where you and
your wife at.*
[P:] *I'm telling you.*
[J:] *That was Ole Boss.*
[P:] *I'm gonner tell about that.*

You know my woman done got funny, she don't
want me to have my pussy.
My woman done got funny, Love, she don't want
me to have my pussy.

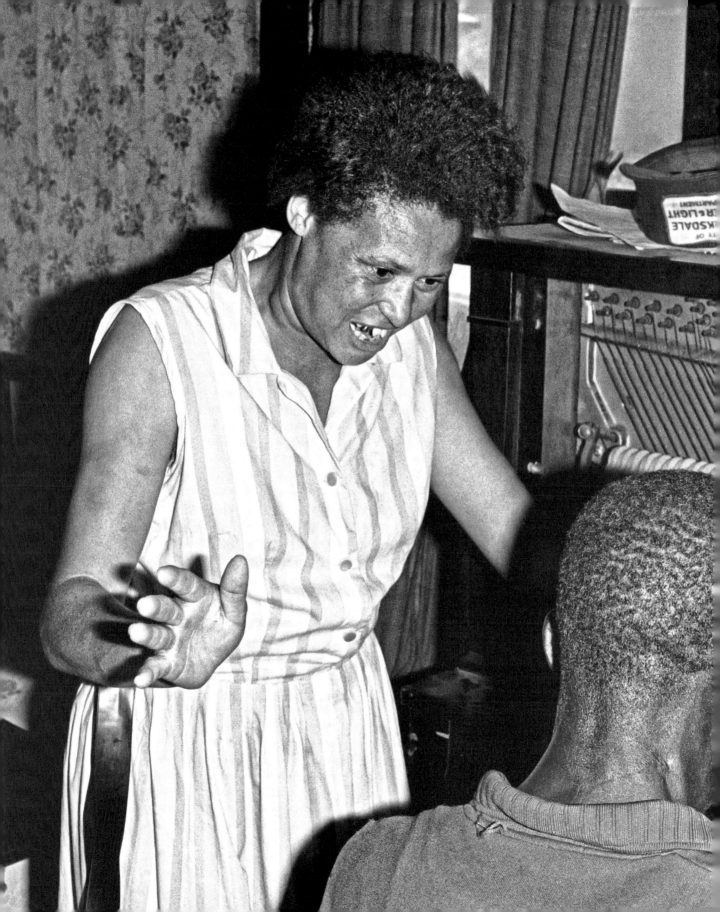

She cook cornbread for her husband, she cook
    biscuits for her man.

You should of been down here in nineteen and
    thirty-five.
You should of been down here in nineteen and
    thirty-five.

[J:] *What happened?*

The womens was quitting the mens and didn't
    have no place to hide.
Merry Christmas, see what Santa Claus gonner
    bring.
I say Merry Christmas, see what Santa Claus
    gonner bring.
He may bring you an apple, baby, and he might
    not bring you a doggone thing.[9]

[P:] *Tell her to come back, Love.*
[J:] *You been disappointed a'many a Christmas
    by Santa Claus, haven't you?*
[P:] *My stocking had ashes in it.*
[J:] *Come on and go with me, and you can get it
    filled up.*
[P:] *Where we going?*
[J:] *We're going where they open the door and let
    all them Christians out.*
[P:] *What?*
[J:] *With them angels. I don't do nothing now*

9. Eurreal "Little Brother" Montgomery, "Santa Fe" (BB
B681), recorded in New Orleans, July 1936. See also Thunder
Smith, "Santa Fe Blues" (Gold Star 644, Arhoolie 2006). Karl Gert
zur Heide includes a complete text of the version by Little Brother
Montgomery in *Deep South Piano: The Story of Little Brother
Montgomery* (London: Studio Vista, 1970), 99. Oliver shows how
blues singers use Santa Claus in their music in *Screening the
Blues*, 26–43.

*but ride a Cadillac. I'm a Mississippi boy, but
    I done skipped from it now.*

Well I got my ticket, and my suitcase all ready
    to go.
You know I got my ticket, and my suitcase all
    ready to go.
I'm gonner catch my baby, we gonner ride that
    Santa Fe.
Alright, Love.

[J:] *You remember what happened in '35, Pine?
    That's when the panic was on. You couldn't
    get a can of Prince Albert tobacco. Fifty cents
    a day on the levee. The women was leaving the
    mens and couldn't get nowhere. No bus run-
    ning.*
[F:] *That must of been in President Hoover's
    time?*
[P:] *It was in Hoover's time.*
[J:] *That was the time of that NRA or something
    like that.*
[P:] *Yeah. Womens couldn't wear dresses. They
    had to wear cotton sacks, them sacks they used
    to pick cotton in.*
[J:] *You mean that rough material?*
[P:] *Cotton sacks. That's right.*

* * *

You used to be the sweetest girl I ever known.
Looked to me, you want to be left on your own.
Now you gone away and left me, you make me
    go through black night.

Used to be, I could call you on the phone.
Me and you, our work was almost done.
Now you gone away and left me, you wanta be
    on your own, black night.

Play the blues, Love.

[J:] *I'm shore glad we up here on Seventy-ninth and Cottage Grove where we can be free. I believe I'll take you to* WVON. *That's down on Cicero in Chicago, Illinois.*

Used to be, I could call you my own.
Looked to me, your love is almost gone.
Now you gone away and left me, you wanta be by yourself, black night.

[J:] *Boy, you playing that just like my brother, Willie. Why you play "Black Night" like that, Pine?*
[P:] *Done got too late now. We going with the blues.*

Used to be, I could call you mine alone.
Looked to me, you was mine all alone.
Now you a mess, baby, you make me go through black night.[10]

\*    \*    \*

Love, I've had my fun if I don't get well no more.

[J:] *Long as you stay in Mississippi, you never will get well.*

I've had my fun if I don't get well no more.
You know my head is killing me, and I'm going down slow.

I want you to write my mother, tell her the shape I'm in.
Want you to write my mother, tell her the shape I'm in.

10.  Lowell Fulson, "Black Night" (Kent 431), recorded in Los Angeles, 1965.

Tell her to pray for me, Love, forgive me for all my sins.

[J:] *Man, you must be broke and hungry, raggledy and dirty too.*
[P:] *I'm in bad shape.*

Tell her don't send me no doctor, doctor can't do no good.
Tell her don't send me no doctor, doctor can't do no good.
You know it's all my fault, I didn't do the things I should.

[J:] *What about this Old Granddaddy Eighty-six whiskey? Will that help you any?*
[P:] *Yeah, boy. I know one thing. I may not get well, but I am gonner try to get well.*
[J:] *You can have a good feeling.*
[P:] *I'm trying to tell you.*

Now on the next train south, Love, look for my clothes back home.

[J:] *You don't wanta go south.*

On the next train south, look for my clothes back home.
If you don't see my body, Floyd, you can view my bones.

[J:] *Tell him to go west or north, but don't go south.*

Now, Mother, don't you worry, this is all over now.
Mother, don't you worry, this is all over now.
You know your son is lost out in this world somewhere.

[P:] *That's all, Love.*

[J:] *Play it and talk to me a little bit. Man, you must be worried to play the blues like that.*

[P:] *I'm is, boy. You know one thing?*

[J:] *What?*

[P:] *The doctor said I wadn't gonner live long. So I'm trying to tell you.*

On the next train south, look for my clothes
 back home.
On the next train south, look for my clothes
 back home.
If you don't see my body, you can view my
 bones.
Good-bye![11]

\* \* \*

Well I don't want a lot. I just want a little bit.

[J:] *Little bit of what?*

Well I don't want a lot. I just want a little bit.
I just want a little bit, just a teenie-weenie bit,
 teenie-weenie bit of your love.

Turn your lamp down low, it's getting late at
 night.
I love you, baby, don't you hear my prayers?
Just a teenie-weenie bit, teenie-weenie bit of
 your love.

[F:] *Work out.*

[J:] *Go head, soul brother.*

I love you, baby, and I'm sick at night.
I love you, baby, and I'm sick at night.

Just a teenie-weenie bit, teenie-weenie bit of
 your love.

Well I don't want it all, just want a teenie-
 weenie bit.
I don't want it all, just want a little bit.
Just a teenie-weenie bit, teenie-weenie bit of
 your love.[12]

\* \* \*

[P:] *Say, Floyd.*

[F:] *Yeah, man.*

[P:] *You know one thing, boy?*

[F:] *What's that?*

[P:] *I'm drifting.*

[F:] *You must be going somewhere.*

[J:] *He's trying to drift outta Mississippi. I know what he's trying to do.*

You know I'm drifting and I'm drifting, just like
 a ship out on the sea.
Well I'm drifting and I'm drifting, like a ship out
 on the sea.
Well you know I ain't got nobody in this world
 to care for me.

[J:] *Tell me, Pine.*

If my baby only take me back again. (She done
 quit me, Floyd.)
If my baby only take me back again.
Well she say I ain't no good, I haven't got no
 friend.

[J:] *You mean you working all day but ain't making no money?*

---

11. "St. Louis" Jimmy Oden, "Going Down Slow" (Bluebird B-8889, RCA Victor 20-2598), recorded in Chicago, November 11, 1941.

12. Roscoe Gordon, "Just a Little Bit" (VeeJay 332), recorded in Chicago, 1959.

I give her all my money, tell me what more can
    I do?
I give her all my money, tell me what more can
    I do?
Now you a good woman, baby, but you just
    won't be true.

[J:] *You can't do no more, man. You can't do no
    more.*

I say bye, bye, baby. Bye, bye, bye.
Bye, bye, baby. Tell you bye, bye, bye.
Now it gonner be too late, and I'll be so far
    away.[13]

[J:] *Play it. I don't care what happens. Play the
    blues all night long.*
[P:] *Bye, baby.*
\* \* \*
[P:] *I'm gonner try this old blues now.*

Let me tell you, baby, tell what I will do.
Rob, steal, and kill somebody, just to get home
    to you.
Ain't that loving you, baby?
Ain't that loving you, baby?
Ain't that loving you, baby, and you don't even
    know my name.

They may kill me, baby, do me like they used
    to do.
My body might rise and swim to the ocean and
    come back home to you.

Ain't that loving you, baby?
Ain't that loving you, baby?
Ain't that loving you, baby, and you don't even
    know my name.[14]

[J:] *Aw yeah. That's loving alright.*
[F:] *Work out, Pine.*
[J:] *Love her in your own way.*
[P:] *I'm gonner play it one more time.*
\* \* \*
[J:] *Have a Saturday night ball.*
[P:] *What's that, Love?*
[J:] *Sunday night you gotta go to sleep cause you
    gotta get up and go to work on Monday morn-
    ing.*

You know the war is over, I'm going down that
    sunny road.

[J:] *Done got tired of soldiering now.*
[F:] *Wait a minute, man. They still fighting in
    Vietnam.*

I say the war is over, I'm going down that sunny
    road.
I done got tired of Clarksdale, working for my
    room and board.

[J:] *I know what you mean, man.*

I say when I was making good money, you treat
    me like I was a king.

[J:] *She lied to you then.*

When I was making good money, darling, you
    treat me like I was a king.

13. Johnny Moore and His Three Blazers (Charles Brown, vocalist), "Drifting Blues" (Aladdin 112), recorded in Los Angeles, September 14, 1945; James "Beale Street" Clarke, "Drifting" (Victor 20-1887, Bluebird 34-0748), recorded in Chicago, February 22, 1946.

14. Jimmy Reed, "Ain't That Loving You Baby?" (VJ 168), recorded in Chicago, November 9, 1955.

[J:] *Then what happened?*

Now you know all my money gone, and your
   love don't mean a thing.

Hey, baby, bring me my hat and coat.
I can feel the green grass growing under your
   doorstep.
You know this time tomorrow I'll be way down
   that sunny road.

Well I done did all, I did all I could afford.
You know I done did all, I did all I could afford.
You know this time tomorrow, baby, I'll be down
   that sunny road.

[J:] *Work that bass again for me, Pine.*
[P:] *What you say, Love?*
[J:] *I hear you now. I see you buying a ticket,
   man. Where you fixing to go?*
[P:] *I'm going to Chicago.*
[J:] *The West Side or the South Side?*
[P:] *I'm going to the South.*

Bye, bye, baby, I did all I could for you.
Bye, bye, baby, I did all I could for you.
You's a bad-headed woman, and I don't want
   you no more.[15]

[J:] *If you going to the South Side, you must be
   going over to Stoney Island where it's happening at.*
[P:] *Yeah, boy, I got my ticket.*
[F:] *Man, you better go on the North Side. They
   raising hell on the South Side.*

[J:] *Detroit is on fire, and Chicago is burning
   down.*
*   *   *
[P:] *Let me see what I wanta do.*
[J:] *What's fixing to happen, Pine?*
[P:] *How about "Juicy Fruit"?*
[J:] *Go ahead. You's a free man. You ain't got
   nothing to worry about.*
[F:] *Your way or the highway.*
[P:] *Here I go.*
[J:] *Work that bass way down.*

Hello, Juicy Fruit, how do you do?
Hello, Juicy Fruit, how do you do?
You remember me? I remember you.

Hello, Juicy Fruit, how do you do?
Hello, Juicy Fruit, how do you do?
Do you remember me? I remember you.
I used to carry you by here, by the railroad too.[16]
*   *   *
I wants to know how much longer, baby, have I
   got to wait on you.
I wants to know how much longer, baby, have I
   got to wait on you.
How long, how long, how much more long?

I lay down last night, I saw you in my sleep.
I lay down last night, I saw you in my sleep.
I began to wondering what do you want
   with me.

How long, how much more long?
How long, how much more long?
How long, now, you want your rolling done?

15. Roosevelt Sykes, "Sunny Road" (RCA Victor 20-1906),
recorded in Chicago, February 18, 1946.

16. Fats Domino, "My Girl Josephine" (Imperial 5704), recorded in New Orleans, 1960.

[J:] *If you should die before your time, what would happen?*

[P:] *What you say, Love?*

[J:] *If you die before your time, remember she'd be ever on your mind.*

If I should die, die before my time.

[J:] *Well alright.*

If I should die, die before my time.
I want you to know what will become of me.

I lay down last night, I missed you in my arms.
I lay down last night, I missed you in my arms.
I began to wonder what do you think of me.

[J:] *Push way back and gimme some of that low bass now.*

How long, how much more long, how long?
How long, how much more long, how long?
How long, how long you want your loving done?

I wants to know how much more longer, baby, have I got to wait on you.
I wants to know how much more longer, baby, have I got to wait on you.
How long, now, baby, you want your loving done?[17]

[P:] *What you say, Floyd?*

[F:] *I hear you, Pine. Work out.*

[P:] *How long!*

[J:] *Don't stop now. Gimme one of them good road blues.*

[P:] *Good road blues coming up. I wants to know why my baby always play around.*

I wonder, baby, why you don't settle down.
I wants to know.
I wants to know.
I just got to know.

Look like you got me flunking, if I'm wrong, please tell me so.
I know I was wrong, but some day I will realize.
I wants to know.
I wants to know.
I just got to know.

I used to believe what you'd tell me.
I used to believe every word you say.
But look like from your way, I believe you gonner put me down.
I wants to know.
I wants to know.
I just got to know.
Now I wants to know, Floyd.[18]

\* \* \*

[P:] *Remember that, Love? Remember that, buddy? Let me get another good blues now. I'm gonner play the blues one more time.*

[J:] *Let me hear you, Pine Top.*

[F:] *Work out. Work out, Pine. Let your hair down now.*

Yes, my baby love to boogie, and I love to boogie too.
Yes, my baby love to boogie, and I love to boogie too.

17. J. B. Lenoir, "How Much More" (JOB 1008), recorded in Chicago, 1952. Another version, "How Long—How Long Blues" (Vocalion 1191), was recorded by Leroy Carr in Indianapolis in 1928.

18. Possibly from Cecil Gant, "I Wonder" (Gilt Edge 501, Bronze 117, Star 1159, Sound 601, Decca 30320), recorded in Los Angeles, 1944–46.

I'm gonner boogie this time, and I ain't gonner
boogie no more.

[J:] *Well alright.*

You know she do that boogie and shout it down
through the street.
She does that boogie and shout it down through
the street.
She howls so loud, they run up and down the
street.
Boogie one time.

Don't the sun look lonesome, shining down
through the tree.
Don't the sun look lonesome, shining down
through the tree.
Don't your hair look lovely when you put it back
up for me.

[Maudie Shirley (M) and Baby Sister (BS) enter
the room.]
[J:] *Well alright. Look who just come in. Work
out, Pine.*
[F:] *Look like we got to shore nuff boogie now.*

I love my baby and I tell the world I do.

[M:] *Do you really, darling?*

I love my baby and I tell the world I do.

[M:] *I wanta marry you.*

Well I hope she'll come to love me too.

[M:] *I already do.*
* * *
Next time I see you, things won't be the same.
Next time I see you, things won't be the same.

If it hurts you, darling, you only have yourself to
blame.

[M:]
You know you lied, cheated, oh so long.
You know you lied, cheated, oh so long.
You just a no-good man, you only have yourself
to blame.

Next time you see me, things won't be the same.
Next time you see me, things won't be the same.
If it hurts you, my darling, you only have your-
self to blame.

[M and P:]
Well you lied, you cheated, oh so long.
Well you lied, you cheated, oh for so long.
You just no-good, you only have yourself to
blame.

[M:] *Work out, baby.*

[P:]
You drink your whiskey, I'll drink my wine.
You tend to your business, baby, I'll tend to
mine.
Next time you see me, things won't be the same.

[J:] *What you got against the girl?*
[P:] *She's a heartbreaker.*

[M:]
Yes, next time you see me, things won't be the
same.
If it hurt you, my darling, you only have yourself
to blame.[19]

19. Junior Parker, "Next Time You See Me" (Duke 164), recorded in Houston, 1956.

* * *
[P:]
I say God made a elephant, he made him big
   and stout.
Wadn't satisfied till he made his snout.
He made his snout, made it long and round.
Wadn't satisfied till he made his tail.
He made his tail, made it to fan the fly.
Wadn't satisfied till he made his eye.
He made his eye, made it to look on the grass.
Wadn't satisfied till he made his ass.
He made his ass so he could stick in his dick.
Wadn't satisfied till he made his prick.
He made his prick, made it hard as a rock.
His nuts would crack when he coughed a lot.
He's a dirty little man.
He's a dirty little man.
Dirty little man.[20]

Children round that house having a fit.
Your mother in the house making jam outta shit.
She's a nasty little woman.
She's a nasty little woman.
As dirty a little woman as you'll find.

I want all you women, want you to fall in line.
I want you to shake it like I shake mine.
Shake it quick, baby, shake it fast.

20.  Oliver calls this the "elephant stanza" and discusses its
history in *Screening the Blues*, 242–43. See Eddie "One-String"
Jones, "The Dozens" (Takoma B 1023), recorded in Los Angeles, February 1, March 1, 1960. Newman Ivey White includes an
expurgated version that H. C. Abbot recorded in Florida in 1915
in *American Negro Folk Songs* (Hatboro, Pa.: Folklore Associates, 1965), 136. See also Rufus "Speckled Red" Perryman, "Dirty
Dozens" (Delmark DL 601), recorded in St. Louis, September 2,
1956.

If you can't shake it quick, shake your little black
   ass.
You a dirty little woman.
Dirty little woman to me.

I had your momma, your sister too.
I throwed a brick at your old man too.
He's a running old man.
He's a running old man.
He's a running old man, running old man.

I want all you women, want you to fall in line.
I want you to shake like I shake mine.
Shake it quick, baby, shake it fast.
If you can't shake it quick, shake your little black
   ass.
Shake your little ass.
You a shaking little woman, shaking little
   woman.

Sit round the house and tote that brick.
Your momma in the kitchen making jam outta
   shit.
She's a nasty little woman.
She's a nasty little woman.
She's a nasty little woman, nasty little woman
   to me.

[P:] *I'm fixing to put "Running Wild" on there.*
[M:] *Aw, baby. I got words for you. You gonner
   run wild?*
[P:] *Running wild.*
[M:] *I know you ain't gonner run wild all your
   life. I'll slow you down one of these days.*

Listen here, woman, where'd you stay last night?
It ain't none of your business.

You know you ain't treating me right.

Aw, woman, baby, you steady running wild.

Now the baby I'm loving, she don't treat me right.

[M:] *You got the nerve to tell me I'm running wild?*

[P:] *What you say?*

[M:]

When I stay at home every day, trying to treat you right,

You come home late at night, jump on me and there's a fight.

Baby, you know, you know that ain't right.

[P:] *What say, baby?*

[M:] *You heard me.*

[P:]

Say, I work hard every day, bring home my pay.

You tell me, baby, I got nowhere to stay.

Now looka here, baby, you know you running wild.

You just running round, baby, baby, you ain't no good.

[M:] *Yeah, baby. I know just what you mean. You must think I'm a fool, don't you?*

[P:] *Naw, I don't.*

[M:] *Yeah, I know you think I'm a fool.*

[P:] *I love you, baby.*

[M:] *I don't love you, darling.*

[P:] *Why, baby?*

[M:] *Because you always doing me wrong.*

[P:] *Ha ha!*

Now tell me, woman, what you got on your mind.

Tell me, woman, what you got on your mind.

[M:] *Nothing but love, baby.*

That way you treat me, you just running wild.

[J:] *Better see me, then.*

[M:]

Well I'll tell you this one thing, baby.

If you love me, darling, I'll do anything you say.

If you love me, darling, I'll do anything you say.

But as long as you messing up, baby, I don't have no say.

I'm gonner tell you now, baby, ain't gonner tell you no more.

I'm gonner tell you now, baby, ain't gonner tell you no more.

Well you running wild, baby, you just got to go.

[P:] *What you say about that, baby?*

[M:] *Well you got your womens. Why can't I have my mens?*

[P:] *I don't like that.*

[M:] *Neither do I.*

[P:] *You ought not to do that. I'm gonner finish up.*

[J:] *That's just like a woman.*

[M:] *Let me tell you one thing.*

[P:] *What you say, honey?*

[M:] *Baby, you know I love you.*

[P:] *I love you too, honey.*

[M:] *Don't worry, darling. We'll make it.*

[P:] *Good-bye, baby.*

[M:] *See you later, sugar.*

\*   \*   \*

[P:]

Rock me, baby, rock me all night long.

Rock me, baby, rock me all night long.
I want you to rock me like my back don't have
   no bone.

Roll me, baby, roll your wagon wheel.
Roll me, baby, roll your wagon wheel.
I want you to roll me, you don't know how it
   makes me feel.
Play it, Baby Sister.

[J:] *Work out, Pine.*

See me coming, better get your rocking chair.
See me coming, better get your rocking chair.
Baby, you know I ain't no stranger cause I'm
   used to living here.
Play it, Baby Sister.

[F:] *Go head on, Pine.*

Rock me, baby, rock me all night long.
Rock me, baby, rock me all night long.
I want you to rock me like my back don't have
   no bone.

Roll me, baby, roll your wagon wheel.
Roll me, baby, roll your wagon wheel.
I want you to roll me, you don't know how it
   makes me feel.
Play it, Baby Sister, one more time.
Aw, rock me, baby.[21]

\*   \*   \*

[M:]
Yeah, see, See See Rider,
Yeah, see what you done done.
Yeah, yeah, yeah, see, See See Rider,
See what you have done.
Well you made me love you,
Now your man has come.

Yes, I'm going away, baby, and I won't be back
   till fall.
Yeah, yeah, yeah, going away, baby, and I won't
   be back till fall.
If I find me a good boy, I won't be back at all.

Yeah, see, See See Rider,
Yeah, see what you have done.
Yeah, yeah, yeah, See See Rider,
See what you have done.[22]

\*   \*   \*

[P:] *Alright now. We going with some Louis Jordan.*
[M:] *"Ain't That Just Like a Woman." I know what it is. I know everything he sing.*

[P:]
There was Eve and Adam happy as can be.
Eve got up under that apple tree.
Ain't that just like a woman.
Ain't that just like a woman.
Ain't that just like a woman, they'll do it every
   time.
Now play a little bit!

All them young ones with their mammy at the
   gate.

21. Muddy Waters, "All Night Long" (Chess 1509), recorded in Chicago, 1952; Muddy Waters, "Rock Me" (Chess 1652), recorded in Chicago, 1957. See also Arthur "Big Boy" Crudup, "Rock Me Momma" (Victor 20-29-78), recorded in Chicago, December 15, 1944, and Lil' Son Jackson, "Rockin' and Rollin'" (Imperial LP 9142), recorded in Los Angeles, December 16, 1950.

22. Ma Rainey, "See See Rider Blues—1" (Pm 12252), recorded in New York, 1924. A later version by Muriel "Wee Bea Booze" Nicholls is "See See Rider Blues" (Decca 8633, 48055), recorded in New York, March 26, 1942.

They was down there crying for bread.
Said Elijah come to the door and said let them
    children get something to eat.
Ain't that just like a woman.
Ain't that just like a woman.
Ain't that just like a woman, they'll do it every
    time.
That's just like a woman.

[F:] *Do it every time!*

* * *

[P:] *Well I'm going.*

Let me tell you, tell you what I will do.
Rob, steal, and kill somebody just to go back
    home to you.
Ain't that loving you, baby?
Ain't that loving you, baby?
Ain't that loving you, baby, and you don't even
    know my name.

They may kill me, baby, baby, like they used
    to do.
My body might rise and swim to the ocean and
    come on home to you.
Now ain't that loving you, baby?
Ain't that loving you, baby?
Ain't that loving you, and you don't even know
    my name.

[M:]
Let me tell you, baby, what I'm gonner do.
Swim the ocean, baby, to get back home to you.
Ain't that loving you, baby?
Ain't that loving you, baby?
Ain't that loving you, baby, and you don't even
    know my name.

[P:] *Play the blues.*
[F:] *Play it, Pine.*

[P:]
Let me tell you, baby, tell you what I will do.
Rob, steal, and kill somebody, just to go back
    home to you.
Ain't that loving you, baby?
Ain't that loving you, baby, and you don't even
    know my name.
That's all![23]

* * *

[M:]
Early one morning, the skies was blue.
Down through the alley the shitwagon flew.
Wadn't a sound heard.
Pine got hit by a flying turd.
Baby that's alright.
He told me that was alright.
Well we was down on Funky Broadway one day.
They was having a good dinner down there.
Do y'all know what they was having?
They was having some french-fried potatoes,
Some inner-tube sausage,
Bow-wow spaghetti,
Blowed-out beans,
That's down on Funky Broadway.
Yeah, baby, you going down there too?
They have a good dessert.
They having wind pie,
Shitty gum smothered down in doo-doo soup.
If you like that, baby,
Go down on the four round corners.

23. Jimmy Reed, "Ain't That Lovin' You Baby?" (VeeJay 168), recorded in Chicago, December 5, 1955.

Listen, I'm gonner tell you what the preacher
   told us yesterday.
He got up in church and said these words.
He said, "Ladies and Gentlemules,
"I stand before you, as I stand behind you,
"To tell you of something I know nothing about.
"Next Thursday is Good Friday.
"They having fathers' meeting for mothers only.
"If you can come, please stay at home.
"Wear your best, if you don't have any.
"Admission free, pay at the door.
"Come in, have a seat, set your damn ass on the
   floor.
"That's at four round corners, baby."
Work out, sugar [to Pine Top].

[P:]
Up she run and down she fell.
Her legs flew open like a mussel shell.
Cause she a dirty little woman.
She a dirty little woman.[24]

[M:] *Let me tell you this, man.*
[P:] *What?*
[M:] *Let me tell you what happened.*

[M:]
Momma kilt a chicken, she thought it was a
   duck.
Put that thing on the table with his leg sticking up.

You got to bottle up and go.
Yeah, you got to bottle up and go.
Cause when momma kilt that chicken, she had
   to bottle up and go.[25]

[P:] *Why was that?*
[M:] *She was full of booze.*

\*   \*   \*

[P:]
Let me tell you, ladies, what I must do.
Everybody tell me in your neighborhood,
That you got good business.
That you got good business.
You got good business, think I'm gonner trade
   with you.

If you do business, but you can't do it right,
I won't hang around in your arms all night.
Cause you got good business.
Cause you got good business.
You got good business, I wants to trade with
   you.

[J:] *I hear you.*

Looka here, baby, what you trying to do?
Make me love you and I don't want to.
Cause you got good business.
Cause you got good business.
You got good business, I wants to trade with
   you.

\*   \*   \*

[P:] *This is the old blues I'm coming with now.*
   *Y'all don't know nothing about this.*

24. Commercial recordings of toasts performed with music are on *Snatch and the Poontangs* (Kent KST 557x). A series of Rudy Ray Moore albums includes *Eat Out More Often* (Comedians COMS 1104), *Merry Christmas, Baby* (Comedians COMS 1108), *The Second Rudy Ray Moore Album* (Comedians COMS 1105), and *Jody the Grinder* (Comedians COMS 1110).

25. Tommy McClennan, "Bottle 'Em Up and Go" (Bluebird B 8373), recorded in Chicago, November 22, 1939.

How long, baby, how long,
Has that evening train been gone?
How long, how long?

I woke this morning, I sat and mourned.
Thought about the good times I have known.
How long, how long, how long?

[F:] *Work out, Pine.*

I can see the green grass growing up on the hill.
Ain't none of the green grass for a dollar bill.
How long, how long, baby, how long?

I'm going up on the mountain, like a mountain
  jack.
I'm gonner call my baby back.
How long, how long, baby, how long?

How long, baby, how long,
Has that evening train been gone?
How long, how long?

Worked all the summer and all the fall,
I had to take up my old guitar.
How long, how long?[26]

*   *   *

Now the war is over, I'm going down that sunny
  road.
I say the war is over, I'm going down that sunny
  road.
You know I ain't making nothing in Clarksdale,
Baby, but my room and board.

Now when I was making good, you treated me
  like I was a king.
When I was making good, you treated me like I
  was a king.
Now you know I ain't got no war-plant job,
My love don't mean a thing.

[P:] *Play the blues, Maudie, we going to Louisiana, ain't we?*
[F:] *I'm going to get me a mojo hand.*

Now, baby, I'm gone, you can cry your blues
  away.
Baby, I'm gone, you can cry your blues away.
I'll find some other, darling, gonner let you have
  your way.

Bring me my hat and coat.

[M:] *Don't forget your shoes.*

I can feel the green grass growing under your
  doorstep.
You know this time tomorrow I'll be way down.

Well I done did all, I did all I could do.

[M:] *Don't tell that lie.*

Well I done did all, I did all I could do.
You know this time tomorrow, I'll be down
  where I want to.

[BS:] *He told me he'd give me fifty dollars.*
[M:] *I don't know how. He told you the same
  thing he told me.*
[BS:] *What you talking about?*
[M:] *That's a thing he got going on.*
[BS:] *Who you want, Pine, me or her?*

---

26. See J. B. Lenoir, "How Much More" (JOB 1008), recorded
in Chicago, 1952. Another version, "How Long—How Long Blues"
(Vocalion 1191), was recorded by Leroy Carr in Indianapolis in
1928. This may be based on one of Carr's later versions.

[P:] *I want you.*

[BS:] *Alright then.*

[M:] *You mean to tell me you don't want me now?*

[J:] *Somebody ain't doing their bed work right here.*

[M:] *He's cutting me off with that damn music.*

[J:] *If Pine can't take care of y'all, you come to my home.*

[BS:] *We don't wanta come to your home. We like Pine's home.*

[J:] *I do some mighty good things. I'll hold your legs up and ride you all night long.*

Bye bye, baby, I did all I could afford.

[M:] *Oh, darling, don't leave me.*

Bye bye, baby, I did all I could afford.

[M:] *Darling, please don't leave me.*

You know this time tomorrow, I'll be down that sunny road.[27]

\* \* \*

[P:] *Let's have some toasts. Who gonner say the first? You go.*

[M:]

*It was early one morning when the sky was blue.*
*It was dark in Clarksdale when among the flying herd,*
*Bill got hit by a flying turd.*
*Up jumped the monkey from the coconut tree.*
*He had keen-toed shoes and a spinach coat.*

---

27. Roosevelt Sykes, "Sunny Road" (RCA Victor 20-1906), recorded in Chicago, February 18, 1946.

*He was a sharp-looking monkey and that wadn't no joke.*

\* \* \*

[M:] *There was two ladies setting out on the damn bank one day. They was fishing. One said to the other old lady, "It's time to go home."*

*"No, I'm gonner stay till a little later."*

*The other lady went home. Her friend was sitting out there, and you know how those old-timey ladies wore long dresses with no drawers. She had both feet cocked up on the bank fishing. It was two bullfrogs out in the middle of the lake. It was getting late over in the evening. One bullfrog said to the other one, "Hey, man. It's getting pretty late. Let's find a hole to go in."*

*The other bullfrog say, "Hey, man."*

*"Hey, man, what?"*

*"I see two holes setting over there. You go in one and I go in the other'n."*

*"Where about, man?"*

*"Right up under that curtain over there."*

*So sure enough, one bullfrog jumped in her pussy, and the other one jumped in her asshole. The lady went home, and along about two o'clock in the morning, her husband decided he would have intercourse with her.*

[J:] *What is intercourse?*

[M:] *They fucked. Put it that way.*

[J:] *Alright.*

[M:] *About four o'clock that morning, the frogs decided they would hop out back down to the lake. They hopped on back down to the lake. The big frog said to the little frog, "Hey, man."*

"What's that?"

"How did you sleep last night?"

"Man, let me tell you something. I didn't sleep worth a damn."

"Me either."

"What happened to you?"

"Let me tell you something. Long about two o'clock, a son of a bitch come in there and tried to root me out of there. I tried to get out, but it was two sacks over the damn hole and I couldn't get out, and I had to stay there until this morning."

"Aw, man. You ain't been in no hell yet. Let me tell you something. Along about that same time that son of a bitch tried to root you out, they tried to root me out too. I pushed and I shoved, and I pushed again, and I shoved again trying to get out, and I hauled off and bit the motherfucker. And do you know what he did to me?"

"Naw, man. What?"

"That son of a bitch hauled off and puked in my face."

*　*　*

[F:]

I wadn't invited, but I'm down here.

I ain't dressed so fine, but I'm around here.

I'm so happy, look like I could shout and shit.

And ain't a son of a bitch in here can put me out.

*　*　*

I know an old lady, she lived on a hill.

Shitted in a stocking, and she carried it to the mill.

Told the old man to don't take no toll,

Cause it may come a double-asshole.

*　*　*

[M:]

Let me tell all y'all something.

I hate to talk about your mammy.

She's a good old soul.

Got a grass pussy and a bull asshole.

I remember your momma didn't have no stove.

Cooked flapjacks on her pussy hole.

I remember your momma fucked a dick of bologna.

Had ninety-nine cows and one Shetland pony.[28]

[J:] Don't talk about my momma. My daddy loves her.

*　*　*

[F:]

I am a fucking pee eye.

I wear my fucking clothes.

Once I went uptown one day, the police caught me fucking.

I say, "Police, what is my fine?"

He said, "Ninety-nine dollars and one fucking dime."

I say, "Look, police, you take this ninety-nine dollars and one fucking dime,

"Cause you may catch this poor child fucking most any time."

Go on!

*　*　*

[J:] Play the blues.

Baby, please don't go.

Baby, please don't go.

Baby, please don't go back to New Orleans.

28. Roger Abrahams discusses the dozens and their texts in *Deep Down in the Jungle: Negro Narrative Folklore from the Streets of Philadelphia* (Chicago: Aldine, 1970). Oliver explains their role in blues in *Screening the Blues*, 235–46.

You got me way down here.
You got me way down here.
You got me way down here, just treat me like a
    dog.

[J:] *Sing out, Pine.*

Turn your lamp down low.
Turn your lamp down low.
I beg you all night long,
Baby, please don't go.

Before I be your dog.
Before I be your dog.
Before I be your dog, I make you walk the log.
Baby, please don't go.[29]

[F:] *Go head on, Pine.*

\* \* \*

I say, the gypsy woman told my mammy, fore I
    was born,
"You got a boy-child coming, for a son of a gun.
"He gonner make all young women call him by
    the name.
"The world gonner know what it's all about."
You know everybody knows I'm here.
I'm your hoochie koochie man, Baby Sister,
    everybody knows I'm here.

[J:] *Work out, Pine.*

I got a black cat bone.
Got a mojo too.
Got a John the Conquerer root.
I'm gonner mess with you.

I'm gonner make you women take me by the
    hand.
Everybody hollering, I'm the hoochie koochie
    man.
Yeah, everybody knows I'm the man.

I'm your hoochie koochie man.
Everybody knows I am.
Play it. Play it, Muddy Waters.

On the seventh hour.
On the seventh day,
On the seventh month,
Seven doctors say,
"He was born with good luck, that you see."
I got seven hundred dollars, and you don't fuck
    with me.
Yeah, I'm here.
Everybody knows I'm here.
I'm your hoochie koochie man, Baby Sister,
    everybody knows I'm here.
You want me to play it, Baby Sister?[30]

[M:] *Go head on, Pine. Go on, baby. Work out.*
[J:] *Yeah. What the hell is going on here?*
[P:] *One more time, Baby Sister.*
[BS:] *I don't need it now.*
[P:] *What's that, baby?*
[BS:] *Be sweet, angel, because I love you.*
[P:] *Is that so?*
[BS:] *Sugar supposed to be sweet, but ain't noth-
    ing sweeter than you.*
[P:] *Everybody know I'm here!*

\* \* \*

29. Big Joe Williams, "Baby Please Don't Go" (Bluebird B 8969), recorded in Chicago, 1941; reissued in 1947 (Columbia 37945) and in 1958 (Delmark DL 602).

30. Muddy Waters, "Hoochie Koochie Man" (Chess LP 1427), recorded in Chicago, January 7, 1964.

[P:] *Now listen, buddies. My woman done messed me up.*

You got bad blood, baby, I believe you needs a shot.
You got bad blood, I believe you needs a shot.
I said turn around here, baby, let me see what else you got.

Love your way of loving, baby, and your skin is nice and soft.
Love your way of loving, baby, and your skin is nice and soft.
If you don't quit that jumping, baby, you're gonner break my needle off.

[F:] *Work out, Pine.*
[J:] *Go head and play it.*

My needle's in you, baby, and you seem to feel alright.
My needle's in you, baby, and you seem to feel alright.
Now when your medicine go to coming down, Baby Sister, I want you to hug me tight.
Bad blues![31]

[F:] *Play the blues, Pine.*
[P:] *That come from Walter Davis.*

*    *    *

[J:] *It's old blues, but it feels good.*
[F:] *Work out, Pine.*

I wants to know, I wants to know, I just got to know.

31. Walter Davis, "Think You Need a Shot (The Needle)" (Bluebird B 6498), recorded in Chicago, April 3, 1936. Oliver discusses this version and others by Jimmy Gordon, Brownie Mc-Ghee, and Champion Jack Dupree in *Screening the Blues*, 189–90.

[F:] *What you want to know?*

Why you always play around.
I wonder if you got that same feeling for me.
Baby Sister, why don't you settle down?

[J:] *You ain't treating her right at night.*

I wants to know, I wants to know, I just got to know.
Looks like you got me fucking.
If I'm wrong, please tell me why.

[M:] *You ain't wrong.*

I knows I'm out in the dark alone.
I wants to know, I wants to know, I just got to know.
Play the blues.

You used to prove that you loved me.
You used to prove every word you say.
But looks like from your ways, I believe you gonner put me down.
I wants to know, I wants to know, I just got to know.

Look like you got me fucking.
If I'm wrong, please tell me.

[J:] *The girls will use you now.*

I know I been in trouble, but some day I will see the light.
I wants to know, I wants to know, I just got to know.
One more time!

*    *    *

[P:] *That's the blues, boys. Baby Sister, is you Caldonia?*

[BS:] *Hell yes, I'm Caldonia.*

I'm going with my baby, she got great big feet.
She long-legged and tall, and ain't had a bite to
    eat.
But she's my woman, and I love her just the
    same.
I'm crazy bout you, Caldonia is your name.

Say, Love. You know what my momma told me?
She said, "You know that woman called 'Caldo-
    nia'?
"I want you to leave that woman alone."
I said, "Look here, Momma.
"You don't know what Caldonia putting down.
"I'm going down to her house and I'm gonner
    talk with her one more time."

I believe I'll call her up.
"Caldonia, what makes your head so big and
    hard?
"Caldonia, Caldonia.
"I'm crazy bout you, Caldonia is your name."
Gonner wrap it up now.
Good-bye.[32]

\*   \*   \*

[Maudie suggests that we all go over to her
    house and play our recordings for her chil-
    dren. Pine Top, Floyd, Jasper, Baby Sister,
    and I follow Maudie to her home. Her two

boys—ten and twelve years old—are still
awake. As they listen to the tape, they recite
the dozens and toasts their mother recorded
and sing the blues lyrics with her. Then she
puts them to bed and sings this prayer.]

Now I lay me down to sleep.
I pray the Lord my soul to keep.
If I should die before I wake,
I pray the Lord my soul to take.
And I say, Jesus, hold me.
Please hold me in thy loving arms.
But that's alright, boys.

You saw me crying in the chapel.
The tears I shed was tears of joy.
I know the meaning of contentment.
Now I'm happy with my Lord.

Just a plain and simple chapel,
Where the people go to pray.
I pray the Lord that I grow stronger,
As I live from day to day.[33]

[P:] *Good night, boys.*
[M:] *Good night, boys. See you later. That's a
    song I made up for my kids. I sings it for them
    and nobody else. When they go to bed, I sing
    it to them. Just like a lot of people say, "Now I
    lay me down to sleep. I pray the Lord my soul
    to keep." I don't say it. I sing it to them.*

32. Joe Pollum, "Black Gal What Makes Your Head So Hard?"
(Bluebird B 5459), recorded in San Antonio, April 3, 1934; later
issued by Louis Jordan as "Caldonia Boogie" (Decca 8670), recorded in New York, ca. 1945.

33. Elvis Presley, "Crying in the Chapel" (RCA Victor 0643),
recorded in Los Angeles, 1965.

# EPILOGUE

Looking back on my visits with each of these speakers, their voices remind me of how surely, how ruthlessly race defined each of their lives, as well as my own. Whether in Rose Hill Church, in Parchman Penitentiary, or in Poppa Jazz's home, race was always on their minds and on mine. It shaped their music, their tales, their very consciousness, and my own.

From slavery to the present in the United States, race has defined the core of our being as blacks and as whites. These voices part the veil of black worlds and reveal the beauty, the fear, the violence that the burden of race has placed on the shoulders of each generation.

Music clearly was a powerful, effective shelter from racism both in slavery and in segregated worlds. It offered a safe haven through both sacred and secular song. Whether black people were working in the fields, dancing in juke joints, or worshipping in church, music provided an escape from the hostile, violent white world.

Gender also shapes the speakers in important ways. Mary Gordon, Martha Dunbar, and Fannie Bell Chapman bring forceful female voices to these narratives, as Gordon and Chapman describe their spiritual journeys and Dunbar recalls how she worked alongside men doing hard manual labor.

Sacred and secular worlds constantly intersect in each speaker's stories. Lee Kizart's description of preachers in Chicago who drink whiskey in the church basement and then preach their sermons upstairs and Poppa Jazz's tale of the brothers Heaven and Hell touch a theme that is familiar among bluesmen. Reverend Isaac Thomas recalls a parrot who tells the preacher that the "same gang" who go to the blues joint on Saturday night attend church on Sunday morning. And Mary Gordon parodies a hymn about a preacher who tries to seduce her.

The colorful personality and language of each speaker come through their voices. From the gentle religious narrative of Mary Gordon, to the comic tales of Scott Dunbar, to the angry voice of Gussie Tobe, each speaker establishes his or her tone. And each has deep roots in the place where he or she lives.

Place is the stage on which the drama of each life plays out. From isolated rural communities like Rose Hill, Lake Mary, Gravel Springs, and Parchman Penitentiary, to Delta towns like Leland and Clarksdale, to cities like Jackson and Memphis, each narrative is shaped by the place where the speaker lives. While my interviews with Willie Dixon and B. B. King were recorded at Yale University in New Haven, both Dixon and King anchor their stories with memories of their childhoods in Vicksburg and Indianola. As celebrities whose music is known and loved throughout the world, Dixon and King remain deeply attached to and defined by the places where they grew up.

Like a chorus, these voices frame the black experience and the music associated with its world.

They take our hand, introduce us to their people and places, and teach us to endure and survive in the face of adversity.

When my first book, *Blues from the Delta*, appeared in 1970, I sent copies to all of the blues artists featured in it. They wrote me back with news of their family and friends. By that time, Jasper Love had moved to Memphis, and he wrote:

Hi Dr. Ferris,

How's life treating you and family? Fine I truly hope. I enjoyed the copy that you sent, although I haven't had a chance to read it, because my family hasn't given me a chance, everytime I wants it some of them has it. Dr. Ferris send me some of that 100 proof up here so that I can get rid of these pains. I like to not have known who you was in those overalls and pipe stuck in your mouth [refers to his photo] (smile). I'm working harder here than I was in Mississippi. My wife is getting fat and ugly and my kids are going to school everyday hollering give me a dollar (smile). I'll close for now but hope to hear and see you in the future.

A friend

Jasper Love

James Thomas dictated a letter to his daughter Earlier Mae "Ninnie" Thomas that included news from Gussie Tobe and Poppa Jazz:

Someone called Tobe and [told] him that he had to have $3,000[.]

About 3 o'clock he went to the police station to get a gun. The police asked him did he have one. Tobe said that he might have one that would shoot. Jazz is doing fine and also Little Son.

Looking back on this work which was done in the sixties, I am struck by how the blues world has changed during the past forty years. Today the blues are a respected part of American music, and educational, museum, and performance venues now exist in many of the places featured in this book, a change that neither I nor the artists whom I recorded could have imagined at the time. Whereas few if any whites ventured into rural Mississippi in search of musicians in the sixties, today busloads of white tourists regularly visit the state to hear the blues.

These changes are symbolized by the impressive B. B. King Museum, which opened in 2008 in King's hometown of Indianola. King began his musical career playing for change on the streets of Indianola, and today a $13 million facility at 400 Second Street showcases his life and the history of black music in the Mississippi Delta for thousands of visitors who come there from throughout the world. One of my former students, John Hubbell, helped develop the museum's resources, and some of the photos and text in this book are featured in its exhibits.

In nearby Clarksdale, Shelley Ritter, another former student of mine, directs the Delta Blues Museum. Founded in 1979, the museum has long been an anchor for educational programs on the blues in the Delta. The museum's activities are enhanced by Morgan Freeman's music club Ground Zero and his restaurant Madidi, which are also in Clarksdale.

Clarksdale's hip-hop music scene is the subject of Ali Neff's fine book, *Let the World Listen Right: Freestyle Hip-Hop at the Contemporary Crossroads of the Mississippi Delta*. Drawn from San Francisco to Clarksdale after reading *Blues from the Delta*, Ali immersed herself in hip-hop music and then moved to the University of North Carolina, where she completed her M.A. in the Curriculum in Folklore and wrote her thesis on Clarksdale hip-hop music. As my teaching assistant, Ali invited hip-hop artist Jerome "TopNotch the Villain" Williams to travel from Clarksdale to speak and perform for students in my southern music class. The program reminded me of when my old friend James "Son Ford" Thomas visited my classes over the years at Jackson State University, Yale University, and the University of Mississippi. The circle is clearly unbroken.

Memphis asserts its claim as "the home of the blues" through important blues programs. At the Center for Southern Folklore, Judy Peiser produces concerts, exhibits, and cultural events that feature blues artists. At the University of Memphis, David Evans's music courses and his High Water Record Company showcase blues artists in important ways. Beale Street now features twenty-five clubs and shops, including Wet Willies, Blues City Café, and B. B. King's Blues Club. Sun Records and Graceland feature the iconic figures of Elvis Presley, Jerry Lee Lewis, Carl Perkins, and Johnny Cash, all of whom were influenced by the blues. The Stax Museum of American Soul Music offers exciting programs on musicians like Otis Redding and Carla Thomas who are associated with the Stax label. For over thirty years, the Blues Foundation in Memphis

has awarded its Annual Blues Music Awards. And Memphis filmmaker Craig Brewer's latest film, *Black Snake Moan*, celebrates the blues and features documentary footage of Son House.

The Blues Archive and *Living Blues* magazine at the University of Mississippi, the Delta Center for Culture and Learning at Delta State University, and the B. B. King Recording Studio at Mississippi Valley State University offer exciting academic resources for students interested in the blues. The Mississippi Arts Commission, Mississippi Humanities Council, and Mississippi Public Broadcasting (MPB) support important blues projects, including MPB's weekly public radio blues program, *Highway 61*, which I hosted for ten years as the "Blues Doctor." While playing my favorite blues records, I loved to say, "If you got the headache, the heartache, or you're just plain lonely, stay tuned, because I've got a blues cure for you, right here on *Highway 61*."

The Mississippi Blues Commission and the Mississippi Blues Foundation have done significant work to celebrate the state's blues legacy. Official markers now recognize homes, clubs, and grave sites associated with blues artists. And the *Festivals and Events* website (<http://www.msbluestrail.org/festivals.html>) maintained by the Mississippi Blues Commission lists hundreds of festivals, clubs, restaurants, and concerts held in the state throughout the year.

Jackson is home to Malaco Records, which for over thirty years has issued classic recordings of soul, rhythm-and-blues, and gospel artists under the leadership of Dave Clark, Tommy Couch (father and son), and Wolf Stephenson. Artists it has recorded include Bobby Blue Bland, Tyrone

Davis, Z. Z. Hill, Benny Latimore, Little Milton, Dorothy Moore, Denise LaSalle, and Johnnie Taylor. Jackson also hosts an annual blues festival. And Willie Dixon's hometown of Vicksburg boasts the Vicksburg Blues Society, several casinos, and L. D.'s Blues Club, all of which regularly feature blues artists.

In Leland Pat Thomas continues the legacy of his father James "Son Ford" Thomas by playing the blues and molding clay sculpture. He works with the Highway 61 Museum in Leland and has his own website at <http://www.myspace.com/patcathead>.

Instead of letters, I now get emails from the grandchildren of the musicians with whom I worked in the sixties. In 2008 James Thomas's grandson, Johnny Thomas Jr., emailed me that he saw his grandfather in one of my films on the Folkstreams website: "I seen a video of my Grandad on your post and I was wondering do you have any more films of him. This is my first time seeing this one and it brought tears to my eyes. His name was James Sonny Ford Thomas. I can see my aunts and uncles in the back ground as kids."

James Thomas's nephew, Nathaniel "Al" Allen, is an artist who grew up in Flint, Michigan, where his mother, Velma Thomas Allen, was president and CEO of the Mott Children's Health Center. Inspired by his uncle's clay sculptures, Allen did his M.A. in studio art at the University of Mississippi and now teaches at Andrew College in Eufala, Alabama. Allen is also an accomplished musician who plays with the LGs and has a website at <http://www.thelgs.com/bio.php>.

The blues have clearly come a long way since the sixties. The music that for so long was more appreciated in England than in the United States has come of age. It is especially heartening to see the music recognized in the places that produced its amazing artists. I only wish the speakers in this book could have lived to see President Barack Obama in the White House and to visit the B. B. King Museum in Indianola. Both would have lifted their spirits in a special way, as they do mine.

Blues are the key to the cultural and intellectual history of the black, the southern, and the American experience. They affirm our spirit through love, protest, spirituality, humor, pathos, and celebration. They are a way of life, forged in the shadow of racism and violence, that teaches us how to endure and survive in the face of adversity.

# SELECTED BIBLIOGRAPHY, DISCOGRAPHY, FILMOGRAPHY, AND WEBSITES

When I began to study the blues in the late sixties, I found few books on the subject. With the exception of Howard Odum and Guy Johnson's *The Negro and His Songs* (1925) and *Negro Workaday Songs* (1926) and W. C. Handy's *A Treasury of the Blues* (1949) and *Father of the Blues* (1941), the pioneering studies of the blues were published in the sixties in England by Paul Oliver, Mike Leadbitter, and Neil Slaven and in the United States by William "Big Bill" Broonzy, Samuel Charters, Charles Keil, Harry Oster, and Frederick Ramsey Jr. In 1970 my book *Blues from the Delta* appeared in a series of blues studies edited by Paul Oliver and Tony Russell and published in England by Studio Vista.

Since that time, the number of books published on the blues in the United States has grown dramatically. Blues scholar David Evans has edited over seventy-three volumes—many of which deal with the blues—in his American Made Music Series at the University Press of Mississippi. Today the rich array of books listed below treat topics as varied as fife and drum music, work songs, the blues and jazz, regional blues styles, blues artists, black radio, the blues as literature, and the blues, rock and roll, and soul.

The number of sound recordings has undergone a similar explosion since the sixties. At that time, the Library of Congress and labels like Arhoolie, Atlantic, Belzona, Delmark, Folkways, Origin Jazz Label, Takoma, Testament, and Yazoo provided the only access to traditional blues recordings. Today

major anthologies of field recordings done in Mississippi by David Evans, Alan and John Lomax, and George Mitchell are available. There are also many fine commercial recordings by blues artists like Willie Dixon and B. B. King.

In the sixties, virtually no films were available on blues. Since that time, numerous films on the subject have been produced. These range from documentaries by Les Blank and Alan Lomax to commercial productions like Walter Hill's *Crossroads* (1986) and Martin Scorsese's blues series, *The Blues: A Musical Journey* (2003). Many of these films are available for viewing on the Folkstreams website.

Websites that feature the blues are a dramatic new resource for the music. With over 219 million hits on the internet for the word "blues," there is virtually no limit to the information, musical recordings, and films that are now accessible. The websites listed below are important resources for the study of the blues and its artists, and they include the sites of archival collections at the Columbia College Center for Black Music Research, the Center for Southern Folklore, the Delta Blues Museum, the Library of Congress, *Living Blues* magazine, the Smithsonian Institution, the University of Mississippi Blues Archive, and the University of North Carolina Documenting the American South project.

Suffice it to say, when the recordings, photographs, and films in this book were made, neither the

speakers nor I could have imagined that so much attention would one day focus on their music and culture. What follows is a selection of the print sources, sound recordings, films, and internet resources that help frame this work.

Aaron Smithers provided invaluable assistance in compiling these resources.

## SELECTED BIBLIOGRAPHY

### BLUES AND JAZZ

Abbott, Lynn, and Doug Seroff. *Out of Sight: The Rise of African American Popular Music, 1889–1895*. Jackson: University Press of Mississippi, 2002.

Buerkle, Jack V., and Danny Barker. *Bourbon Street Black*. New York: Oxford University Press, 1973.

Hentoff, Nat. *Jazz Country*. New York: Dell, 1967.

Hodier, Andre. *Jazz: Its Evolution and Its Essence*. New York: Grove Press, 1956.

Jones, Le Roi. *Black Music*. New York: William Morrow, 1968.

———. *Blues People*. New York: William Morrow, 1963.

Lomax, Alan. *Mister Jelly Roll*. New York: Grosset & Dunlap, 1950.

Mezzrow, Mezz, and Bernard Wolfe. *Really the Blues*. Garden City, N.Y.: Doubleday, 1972.

Sargeant, Winthrop. *Jazz, Hot and Hybrid*. New York: Da Capo Press, 1975.

Schuller, Gunther. *Early Jazz*. New York: Oxford University Press, 1969.

Shapiro, Nat, and Nat Hentoff, eds. *Hear Me Talkin' to Ya*. New York: Dover, 1966.

Stearns, Marshall. *The Story of Jazz*. New York: New American Library, 1958.

Stearns, Marshall, and Jean Stearns. *Jazz Dance: The Story of American Vernacular Dance*. New York: Schirmer, 1964.

Wilmer, Valerie. *Jazz People*. London: Allison & Busby, 1970.

## BLUES AND WHITE MUSIC

Baraka, Imamu Amiri. *Blues People: Negro Music in White America*. New York: William Morrow, 1999.

Groom, Bob. *The Blues Revival*. London: Studio Vista, 1971.

Malone, Bill C. *Country Music, U.S.A.* Rev. ed. Austin: University of Texas Press, 2002.

Malone, Bill, and Judith McCulloh. *Stars of Country Music*. Chicago: University of Illinois Press, 1975.

McIrney, Jay. "White Man at the Door: One Man's Mission to Record the 'Dirty Blues'—Before Everyone Dies." *New Yorker*, February 4, 2002, 54–63.

Otto, John Solomon, and Augustus M. Burns. "The Use of Race and Hillbilly Recordings as Sources for Historical Research: The Problem of Color Hierarchy among Afro Americans in the Early Twentieth Century." *Journal of American Folklore* 85 (October–December 1972): 344–55.

Russell, Tony. *Blacks, Whites, and Blues*. New York: Stein & Day, 1970.

Walton, Ortiz M. *Music: Black, White, and Blue*. New York: William Morrow, 1972.

## BLUES AND WOMEN

Albee, Edward. *The Death of Bessie Smith*. New York: Coward-McCann, 1960.

Albertson, Chris. *Bessie*. New York: Stein & Day, 1972.

Bourgeois, Anna Stong. *Blueswomen: Profiles of 37 Early Performers, with an Anthology of Lyrics, 1920–1945*. Jefferson, N.C.: McFarland, 1996.

Davis, Angela Y. *Blues Legacies and Black Feminism: Gertrude "Ma" Rainey, Bessie Smith, and Billie Holiday*. New York: Pantheon Books, 1998.

Freeland, David. *Ladies of Soul*. American Made Music Series. Jackson: University Press of Mississippi, 2001.

Harrison, Daphne Duval. *Black Pearls: Blues Queens of the 1920s*. New Brunswick, N.J.: Rutgers University Press, 1988.

Jackson, Buzzy. *A Bad Woman Feeling Good: Blues and the Women Who Sing Them*. New York: W. W. Norton, 2005.

Lieb, Sandra R. *Mother of the Blues: A Study of Ma Rainey*. Amherst: University of Massachusetts Press, 1981.

Moore, Carman. *Somebody's Angel Child: The Story of Bessie Smith*. New York: T. Y. Crowell, 1969.

Stewart-Baxter, Derrick. *Ma Rainey and the Classic Blues Singers*. New York: Stein & Day, 1970.

## BLUES ARTISTS

Broonzy, William (as written to Yannick Bruyoghe). *Big Bill Blues: William Broonzy's Story*. New York: Macmillan, 1955.

Calt, Stephen, and Gayle Wardlow. *King of the Delta Blues: The Life and Music of Charley Patton*. Newton, N.J.: Rock Chapel Press, 1988.

Charters, Samuel. *The Bluesmen: The Story and Music of the Men Who Made the Blues*. New York: Oak Publications, 1967.

———. *The Legacy of the Blues: Art and Lives of Twelve Great Bluesmen*. New York: Da Capo Press, 1977.

———. *Sweet As the Showers of Rain*. New York: Oak Publications, 1977.

Cohn, Lawrence. *Nothing but the Blues: The Music and the Musicians*. New York: Abbeville Press, 1993.

Congress, Richard. *Blues Mandolin Man: The Life and Music of Yank Rachell*. Jackson: University Press of Mississippi, 2001.

Danchin, Stephen. *Earl Hooker: Blues Master*. Jackson: University Press of Mississippi, 2001.

Evans, David. *Tommy Johnson*. London: Studio Vista, 1971.

Fahey, John. *Charley Patton*. London: Studio Vista, 1970.

Garon, Paul. *The Devil's Son-in-Law: The Story of Peetie Wheatstraw and His Songs*. London: Studio Vista, 1971.

Gordon, Robert. *Can't Be Satisfied: The Life and Times of Muddy Waters*. Boston: Little, Brown, 2002.

Handy, W. C. *Father of the Blues: An Autobiography*. 1941. Reprint, New York: Da Capo Press, 1985.

Mann, Woody. *Six Black Blues Guitarists*. New York: Oak Publications, 1973.

Murray, Charles Shaar. *Boogie Man: The Adventures of John Lee Hooker in the American Twentieth Century*. New York: St. Martin's, 2000.

Myers, Sam, and Jeff Horton. *Sam*

*Myers: The Blues Is My Story*. Jackson: University Press of Mississippi, 2006.

Obrecht, Jas. *Rollin' and Tumblin': The Postwar Blues Guitarists*. San Francisco: Miller Freeman Books, 2000.

Rooney, Jones. *Bossmen: Bill Monroe and Muddy Waters*. New York: Dial Press, 1971.

Tipaldi, Art. *Children of the Blues: 49 Musicians Shaping a New Blues Tradition*. San Francisco: Backbeat Books, 2002.

Wald, Elijah. *Escaping the Delta: Robert Johnson and the Invention of the Blues*. New York: Amistad, 2004.

Wilson, Al. *Son House*. Collectors Classics. Bexhill-on-Sea, East Sussex, England: Blues Unlimited, 1966.

Wolfe, Charles K., and Kip Lornell. *The Life and Legend of Leadbelly*. New York: HarperCollins Publishers, 1992.

*Willie Dixon*

Dixon, Willie. *The Master Blues Composer, 1915–1992*. Milwaukee: Hal Leonard, 1992.

Dixon, Willie, and Don Snowden. *I Am the Blues: The Willie Dixon Story*. New York: Da Capo Press, 1989.

*B. B. King*

Danchin, Sebastian. *Blues Boy: The Life and Music of B. B. King*. Jackson: University Press of Mississippi, 1998.

Ferris, William R. "The Blues—Past and Future: An Interview with B. B. King." In *Reflections on American Music: The Twentieth Century and the New Millennium*, edited by James R. Heintze and Michael Saffle, 243–57. New York: Pendragon Press, 2000.

———. "'Everything Leads Me Back to the Feeling of the Blues': B. B. King, 1974." *Southern Cultures* 12, no. 4 (Winter 2006): 5–28.

King, B. B., and David Ritz. *Blues All Around Me: The Autobiography of B. B. King*. New York: Avon Books, 1996.

King, B. B., and Dick Waterman. *The B. B. King Treasures: Photos, Mementos, and Music from B. B. King's Collection*. New York: Bulfinch Press, 2005.

Kostelanetz, Richard, and Jesse Reiswig. *The B. B. King Reader: 6 Decades of Commentary*. Milwaukee: Hal Leonard, 2005.

McGee, David. *B. B. King: There Is Always One More Time*. San Francisco: Backbeat Books, 2005.

Sawyer, Charles. *The Arrival of B. B. King: The Authorized Biography*. New York: Doubleday, 1984.

Shirley, David. *Every Day I Sing the Blues: The Story of B. B. King*. New York: Franklin Watts, 1995.

BLUES AS LITERATURE

Brown, Sterling A., Arthur P. Davis, and Ulysses Lee, eds. *The Negro Caravan*. New York: Dryden Press, 1941.

Charters, Samuel. *The Poetry of the Blues*. New York: Oak Publications, 1963.

Ellison, Ralph. *Shadow and Act*. New York: Vintage Books, 1972.

Garon, Paul. *Blues and the Poetic Spirit*. London: Edison Press, 1975.

Handy, W. C., ed. *Blues: An Anthology*. New York: Collier Books, 1972.

Hughes, Langston. *The Weary Blues*. New York: Knopf, 1947.

Murray, Albert. *The Hero and the Blues*. Columbia: University of Missouri Press, 1973.

———. *The Omni-Americans*. New York: Avon Books, 1970.

———. *Stomping the Blues*. New York: McGraw-Hill, 1976.

Plumpp, Sterling. *Blues Narratives*. Chicago: Tia Chuca, 1999.

Prahlad, Anand. *African-American Proverbs in Context*. Jackson: University Press of Mississippi, 1996.

Sackheim, Eric. *The Blues Line: A Collection of Blues Lyrics*. New York: Schirmer Books, 1975.

Springer, Robert, ed. *Nobody Knows Where the Blues Come From: Lyrics and History*. Jackson: University Press of Mississippi, 2006.

Taft, Michael. *The Blues Lyric Formula*. New York: Routledge, 2006.

———. *Blues Lyric Poetry: A Concordance*. 3 vols. New York: Garland, 1984.

———. *Blues Lyric Poetry: An Anthology*. New York: Garland, 1983.

———. *Talkin' to Myself: Blues Lyrics, 1921–1942*. New York: Routledge, 2005.

Titon, Jeff. *Downhome Blues Lyrics: An Anthology from the Post–World War II Era*. Urbana: University of Illinois Press, 1990.

Tracy, Steven C. *Write Me a Few of Your Lines: A Blues Reader*. Amherst: University of Massachusetts Press, 1999.

BLUES INTERVIEWS

Leadbitter, Mike. *Nothing but the Blues*. London: Hanover Books, 1971.

*Living Blues: A Journal of the African American Blues Tradition.* University: Center for the Study of Southern Culture, University of Mississippi.

Mitchell, George. *Blow My Blues Away.* Baton Rouge: Louisiana State University Press, 1971.

Oliver, Paul. *Conversation with the Blues.* New York: Horizon Press, 1965.

O'Neal, Jim, and Amy van Singel. *The Voice of the Blues: Classic Interviews from Living Blues Magazine.* New York: Routledge, 2002.

Oster, Harry. *Living Country Blues.* Detroit: Folklore Associates, 1969.

BLUES PIANO

Gert zur Heide, Karl. *Deep South Piano: The Story of Little Brother Montgomery.* London: Studio Vista, 1970.

Govenar, Alan B., and Lavada Durst. *The Blues and Jives of Dr. Hepcat.* Racine, Wis.: Arcadian Press, 1994.

Kriss, Eric. *Six Blues-Roots Pianists.* New York: Oak Publications, 1973.

Page, Christopher I. *Boogie Woogie Stomp: Albert Ammons and His Music.* Cleveland: Northeast Ohio Jazz Society, 1997.

BLUES REFERENCE VOLUMES

Bogdanov, Vladimir, Chris Woodstra, and Stephen Thomas Erlewine. *All Music Guide to the Blues: The Definitive Guide to the Blues.* San Francisco: Backbeat Books, 2003.

Dixon, Robert M. W., and John Godrich. *Recording the Blues.* New York: Stein & Day, 1970.

Dixon, Robert M. W., John Godrich, and Howard Rye. *Blues and Gospel Records, 1890–1943.* 4th ed. Oxford: Clarendon Press, 1997.

Erlewine, Michael. *All Music Guide to the Blues: The Experts' Guide to the Best Blues Recordings.* San Francisco: Miller Freeman Books, 1996.

Ford, Robert. *A Blues Bibliography: The International Literature of an Afro-American Music Genre.* Bromley, U.K.: Paul Pelletier, 1999.

Hart, Mary L., Brenda M. Eagles, and Lisa N. Howorth. *The Blues: A Bibliographical Guide.* New York: Garland, 1989.

Herzhaft, Gerard. *Encyclopedia of the Blues.* Fayetteville: University of Arkansas Press, 1992.

Komara, Edward M. *Encyclopedia of the Blues.* New York: Routledge, 2006.

Leadbitter, Mike, and Neil Slaven. *Blues Records, January 1943 to December 1966.* London: Hanover Books, 1968.

Maloney, Don. *The Columbia 13/14000 D Series.* Stanhope, N.J.: Walter C. Allen, 1966.

Moore, Allan F., ed. *The Cambridge Companion to Blues and Gospel Music.* Cambridge: Cambridge University Press, 2002.

Oliver, Paul, ed. *The Blackwell Guide to Blues Records.* Oxford: Blackwell Reference, 1989.

Scott, Frank, et al. *The Down Home Guide to the Blues.* Pennington, N.J.: A Cappella Books, 1991.

Vreede, Max E. *Paramount 12000/13000 Series.* London: Storyville, 1971.

BLUES REGIONAL STUDIES

Bastin, Bruce. *Crying for the Carolines.* London: Studio Vista, 1971.

Bearden, William. *Memphis Blues: Birthplace of a Music Tradition.* Memphis: Arcadia Publishing, 2006.

Broven, John. *Walking to New Orleans: The Story of New Orleans Rhythm and Blues.* Bexhill-on-Sea, East Sussex, England: Blues Unlimited, 1974.

Charters, Samuel. *The Country Blues.* New York: Holt, Rinehart, 1959.

Cheseborough, Steve. *Blues Traveling: The Holy Sites of Delta Blues.* Jackson: University Press of Mississippi, 2008.

Ferris, William R. *Blues from the Delta.* London: Studio Vista, 1970. Rev. ed., New York: Da Capo Press, 1988.

Gioia, Ted. *Delta Blues: The Life and Times of the Mississippi Masters Who Revolutionized American Music.* New York: W. W. Norton, 2008.

Keil, Charles. *Urban Blues.* Chicago: University of Chicago Press, 1967.

Komara, Edward. *The Road to Robert Johnson: The Genesis and Evolution of Blues in the Delta from the Late 1800s through 1938.* Emeryville, Calif.: Hal Leonard, 2007.

Lomax, Alan. *The Land Where the Blues Began.* New York: New Press, 1993.

Lornell, Kip, and Tracey E. W. Laird, eds. *Shreveport Sounds in Black and White.* Jackson: University Press of Mississippi, 2008.

Olson, Bengt. *Memphis Blues.* London: Studio Vista, 1970.

Palmer, Robert. *Deep Blues.* New York: Penguin Books, 1981.

Rowe, Mike. *Chicago Breakdown.* London: Eddison Press, 1973.

Sacré, Robert, ed. *The Voice of the Delta: Charley Patton and the Mississippi*

*Blues—Traditions, Influences, and Comparisons.* Liege, Belgium: Presses Universitaires Liege, 1987.

Work, John, Lewis Wade Jones, and Samuel C. Adams Jr. *Lost Delta Found: Rediscovering the Fisk University–Library of Congress Coahoma County Study, 1941–1942.* Edited by Robert Gordon and Bruce Nemerov. Nashville: Vanderbilt University Press, 2005.

BLUES, ROCK AND ROLL, AND SOUL

Christian, Robert. *Any Old Way You Choose It: Rock and Other Pop Music, 1967–1973.* Baltimore: Penguin Books, 1973.

Cohen, Rich. *Machers and Rockers: Chess Records and the Business of Rock and Roll.* New York: Atlas Books, 2004.

Cohn, Nick. *Rock.* New York: Pocket Books, 1970.

Covach, John. *What's That Sound: An Introduction to Rock and Its History.* New York: W. W. Norton, 2006.

Friedlander, Paul. *Rock and Roll: A Social History.* Boulder, Colo.: Westview Press, 1996.

Garland, Phyl. *The Sound of Soul.* New York: Pocket Books, 1971.

Gillett, Charlie. *The Sound of the City: The Rise of Rock and Roll.* New York: Duterbridge & Dienstfrey, 1970.

Gordon, Robert. *It Came from Memphis.* New York: Pocket Books, 1995.

Guralnick, Peter. *Feel Like Going Home.* New York: Duterbridge & Dienstfrey, 1971.

———. *Sweet Soul Music: Rhythm and Blues and the Southern Dream of Freedom.* New York: HarperPerennial, 1994.

Haralambos, Michael. *Right On: From Blues to Soul in Black America.* London: Eddison Press, 1974.

Morse, David. *Grandfather Rock.* New York: Delacorte Press, 1972.

———. *Motown and the Arrival of Black Music.* New York: Macmillan, 1971.

Nicholas, A. X. *The Poetry of Soul.* New York: Bantam Books, 1971.

Palmer, Robert. *Rock and Roll: An Unruly History.* New York: Harmony Books, 1995.

Ripani, Richard J. *The New Blue Music: Changes in Rhythm and Blues, 1950–1999.* Jackson: University Press of Mississippi, 2006.

Shaw, Arnold. *Honkers and Shouters: The Golden Years of Rhythm and Blues.* New York: Collier Books, 1978.

———. *The World of Soul.* New York: Paperback Library, 1971.

Whitcomb, Ian. *After the Ball: Pop Music from Rag to Rock.* Baltimore: Penguin Books, 1974.

Williams, Paul. *Dalton Blues: A Book of Rock Music.* New York: E. P. Dutton, 1969.

BLUES SURVEYS

Charters, Ann, and Samuel Barclay Charters. *Blues Faces: A Portrait of the Blues.* Jaffrey, N.H.: David R. Godine, 2000.

Cohn, Lawrence, ed. *Nothing but the Blues: The Music and the Musicians.* New York: Abbeville Press, 1999.

Cohodas, Nadine. *Spinning Blues into Gold: The Chess Brothers and the Legendary Chess Records.* New York: St. Martin's, 2000.

Collis, John. *The Story of Chess Records.* New York: Bloomsbury, 1998.

Cook, Bruce. *Listen to the Blues.* New York: Charles Scribner's Sons, 1973.

Duffy, Timothy. *Music Makers: Portraits and Songs from the Roots of America.* Foreword by B. B. King. Athens, Ga.: Hill Street Press, 2002.

Evans, David. *Big Road Blues: Tradition and Creativity in the Folk Blues.* New York: Da Capo Press, 1987.

———, ed. *The NPR Curious Listener's Guide to Blues.* New York: Perigee Trade, 2005.

———, ed. *Ramblin' on My Mind: New Perspectives on the Blues.* Urbana: University of Illinois Press, 2008.

Guralnick, Peter, and Martin Scorsese. *Martin Scorsese Presents the Blues: A Musical Journey.* New York: Amistad, 2003.

Gussow, Adam. *Journeyman's Road: Modern Blues Lives from Faulkner's Mississippi to Post-9/11 New York.* Knoxville: University of Tennessee Press, 2007.

———. *Mister Satan's Apprentice: A Blues Memoir.* New York: Pantheon Books, 2007.

———. *Seems Like Murder Here: Southern Violence and the Blues Tradition.* Knoxville: University of Tennessee Press, 2002.

Hamilton, Marybeth. *In Search of the Blues.* New York: Basic Books, 2008.

Jackson, Bruce. *Wake Up Dead Man: Hard Labor and Blues.* Athens: University of Georgia Press, 1999.

Neff, Robert, and Anthony Conner. *Blues.* Boston: David R. Godine, 1975.

Oakley, Giles. *The Devil's Music: A History of the Blues.* London: British Broadcasting Corporation, 1976.

Oliver, Paul. *The Meaning of the Blues.* New York: Collier Books, 1966.

———. *Screening the Blues.* New York: Da Capo Press, 1989.

———. *The Story of the Blues.* New York: Chilton, 1969.

Oliver, Paul, Tony Russell, and Robert M. W. Dixon. *Yonder Come the Blues: The Evolution of a Genre.* Cambridge: Cambridge University Press, 2001.

Ramsey, Frederic, Jr. *Been Here and Gone.* New Brunswick, N.J.: Rutgers University Press, 1969.

Ryan, Marc W. *Trumpet Records: Diamonds on Farish Street.* Jackson: University Press of Mississippi, 2004.

Titon, Jeff. *Early Downhome Blues: A Musical and Cultural Analysis.* Urbana: University of Illinois Press, 1977.

Urban, Michael, and Andrei Evdokimov. *Russia Gets the Blues: Music, Culture, and Community in Unsettled Times.* Ithaca, N.Y.: Cornell University Press, 2004.

Van Rijn, Guido. *Kennedy's Blues: African-American Blues and Gospel Songs on JFK.* Jackson: University Press of Mississippi, 2007.

———. *Roosevelt's Blues: African-American Blues and Gospel Songs on FDR.* Jackson: University Press of Mississippi, 1997.

———. *The Truman and Eisenhower Blues: African-American Blues and Gospel Songs, 1945–1960.* New York: Continuum, 2004.

Wardlow, Gayle. *Chasin' That Devil Music: Searching for the Blues.* San Francisco: Backbeat Books, 1998.

Welding, Pete, and Toby Byron. *Bluesland: Portraits of Twelve Major American Blues Masters.* New York: Dutton, 1991.

Woods, Clyde Adrian. *Development Arrested: The Blues and Plantation Power in the Mississippi Delta.* London: Verso, 1998.

Work, John W., Lewis Wade Jones, and Samuel C. Adams Jr. *Lost Delta Found: Rediscovering the Fisk University–Library of Congress Coahoma County Study, 1941–1942.* Edited by Robert Gordon and Bruce Nemerov. Nashville: Vanderbilt University Press, 2005.

AFRICAN AMERICAN FOLKLORE

Abrahams, Roger, and John F. Szwed, eds. *An Annotated Bibliography of Afro-American Folk Culture.* Philadelphia: American Folklore Society Bibliographical and Special Series, 1978.

Courlander, Harold. *A Treasury of Afro-American Folklore.* New York: Crown Publishers, 1976.

Dundes, Alan, ed. *Mother Wit from the Laughing Barrel: Readings in the Interpretation of Afro-American Folklore.* Jackson: University Press of Mississippi, 1990.

Ferris, William R. *Afro-American Folk Art and Crafts.* Jackson: University Press of Mississippi, 1986.

———. *Local Color: A Sense of Place in Folk Art.* Edited by Brenda McCallum. New York: Anchor Books, 1992.

Ferris, William R., and Mary L. Hart. *Folk Music and Modern Sound.* Jackson: University Press of Mississippi, 1982.

Ferris, William R., Judy Peiser, and Carolyn Lipson, eds. *American Folklore Films and Videotapes: An Index.* Memphis: Center for Southern Folklore, 1976.

Herskovits, Melville. *The Myth of the Negro Past.* Boston: Beacon Press, 1958.

Levine, Lawrence W. *Black Culture and Black Consciousness: Afro-American Folk Thought from Slavery to Freedom.* New York: Oxford University Press, 1977.

Mullen, Patrick B. *The Man Who Adores the Negro.* Urbana: University of Illinois Press, 2008.

Neff, Ali Colleen. *Let the World Listen Right: Freestyle Hip-Hop at the Contemporary Crossroads of the Mississippi Delta.* Jackson: University Press of Mississippi, 2009.

Rublowsky, John. *Black Music in America.* New York: Basic Books, 1971.

Southern, Eileen. *The Music of Black Americans: A History.* New York: W. W. Norton, 1971.

———, ed. *Readings in Black American Music.* New York: W. W. Norton, 1971.

Southern, Eileen, and Norman E. Whitten Jr., eds. *Afro-American Anthropology.* New York: Free Press, 1970.

Szwed, John F., ed. *Black America.* New York: Basic Books, 1970.

Thompson, Robert Farris. *African Art in Motion.* Berkeley: University of California Press, 1974.

———. *Flash of the Spirit: African and Afro-American Art and Philosophy.* New York: Vintage Books, 1984.

Vansina, Jan. *Oral Tradition.* London: Routledge & Kegan Paul, 1965.

Wilson, Charles Reagan, and William Ferris, eds. *Encyclopedia of Southern Culture.* Chapel Hill: University of North Carolina Press, 1989.

## BANJO AND FIDDLE MUSIC

Abrahams, Roger D. *Singing the Master: The Emergence of African American Culture in the Plantation South.* New York: Pantheon Books, 1992.

Barkley, Elizabeth F. *Crossroads: The Multicultural Roots of America's Popular Music.* Upper Saddle River, N.J.: Pearson Prentice Hall, 2007.

*Black Banjo Then and Now Gathering, April 7–10, 2005, Appalachian State University, Boone, NC: Let the Banjo Ring!* Boone, N.C.: Appalachian State University, 2005.

Carlin, Bob. *The Birth of the Banjo: Joel Walker Sweeney and Early Minstrelsy.* Jefferson, N.C.: McFarland, 2007.

Conway, Cecelia. *African Banjo Echoes in Appalachia: A Study of Folk Traditions.* Knoxville: University of Tennessee Press, 1995.

Epstein, Dena J. Polacheck. *The Folk Banjo: A Documentary History.* Los Angeles: John Edwards Memorial Foundation at the Folklore & Mythology Center, University of California, 1975.

Manifold, J. S. *The Violin, the Banjo, and the Bones: An Essay on the Instruments of Bush Music.* The Black Bull Chapbooks, no. 6. Ferntree Gully, Australia: Rams Skull Press, 1957.

Wolfe, Charles K. *The Devil's Box: Masters of Southern Fiddling.* Nashville: Country Music Foundation Press, 1997.

## BLACK RADIO

Barlow, William. *Voice Over: The Making of Black Radio.* Philadelphia: Temple University Press, 1999.

Cantor, Louis. *Wheelin' on Beale: How WDIA-Memphis Became the Nation's First All-Black Radio Station and Created the Sound That Changed America.* New York: Pharos Books, 1992.

Hayes, Bernie. *The Death of Black Radio: The Story of America's Black Radio Personalities: A Personal Perspective.* New York: iUniverse, 2005.

Hiss, George L. *The Joe Bostic Story: First Black American Radio Announcer.* Bloomington: AuthorHouse, 2006.

Newman, Mark. *Entrepreneurs of Profit and Pride: From Black-Appeal to Radio Soul.* Media and Society Series. New York: Praeger, 1988.

Sampson, Henry T. *Swingin' on the Ether Waves: A Chronological History of African Americans in Radio and Television Broadcasting, 1925–1955.* Lanham, Md.: Scarecrow Press, 2005.

Ward, Brian. *Radio and the Struggle for Civil Rights in the South.* Gainesville: University Press of Florida, 2004.

Webb, Jacqueline Gales, Lex Gillespie, Sonja Williams, and Lou Rawls. *Black Radio.* Washington, D.C.: Smithsonian Institution Press, 1996.

Williams, Gilbert Anthony. *Legendary Pioneers of Black Radio.* Westport, Conn.: Praeger, 1998.

Zook, Kristal Brent. *I See Black People: The Rise and Fall of African American–Owned Television and Radio.* New York: Nation Books, 2008.

## FAITH HEALING AND FOLK BELIEF

Baer, Hans A., and Merrill Singer. *African American Religion: Varieties of Protest and Accommodation.* Knoxville: University of Tennessee Press, 2002.

Gevitz, Norman. *Other Healers: Unorthodox Medicine in America.* Baltimore: Johns Hopkins University Press, 1988.

Hurston, Nora Zeale. *Mules and Men.* New York: Harper & Row, 1970.

Hyatt, Harry Middleton. *Hoodoo-Conjuration-Witchcraft-Rootworks.* 4 vols. Washington, D.C.: American University Bookstore, 1970.

Mitchem, Stephanie Y. *African American Folk Healing.* New York: New York University Press, 2007.

Mitchem, Stephanie Y., and Emilie Maureen Townes. *Faith, Health, and Healing in African American Life.* Westport, Conn.: Praeger, 2008.

Puckett, Newbell Niles. *The Magic and Folk Beliefs of the Southern Negro.* New York: Dover, 1969.

Tyson, Ruel W., Jr., James L. Peacock, and Daniel W. Paterson, eds. *Diversities of Gifts: Field Studies in Southern Religion.* Chicago: University of Chicago Press, 1988.

## FIFE AND DRUM MUSIC

Courlander, Harold. *The Drum and the Hoe.* Berkeley: University of California Press, 1960.

Evans, David. "African Elements in Twentieth-Century United States Black Folk Music." *Jazzforschung* 10 (1978): 85–110.

———. "Black Fife and Drum Music in Mississippi." *Mississippi Folklore Register* 6, no. 3 (Fall 1972): 94–107.

———. "The Origins of Blues and Its Relationship to African Music." In *Images de L'africaine de l'antiquite au XXe siecle*, edited by Daniel

Droixhe and Klaus H. Kiefer, 129–
41. Frankfurt: Peter Lang, 1987.

Ferris, William R. "Othar Turner,
Cane Fife Maker." In *Local Color:
A Sense of Place in Folk Art*, edited
by William R. Ferris and Brenda
McCallum, 157–74. New York:
Anchor Books, 1992.

Oliver, Paul. *Savannah Syncopators*.
New York: Stein & Day, 1970.

Vlach, John. *The Afro-American
Tradition in Decorative Arts*.
Cleveland: Cleveland Museum of
Art, 1978.

FOLK MUSIC

Asch, Moses, and Alan Lomax. *The
Leadbelly Songbooks*. New York:
Oak Publications, 1962.

Courlander, Harold. *Negro Folk
Music, U.S.A.* New York: Columbia
University Press, 1966.

Garvin, Richard M., and Edmond G.
Addeo. *The Midnight Special*. New
York: Bernard Geis Associates, 1971.

Lomax, Alan. *The Folk Songs of
North America*. Garden City, N.Y.:
Doubleday, 1960.

Lomax, John, and Alan Lomax. *The
Leadbelly Legend*. New York:
Folkways Publishers, 1965.

———. *Negro Folk Songs as Sung by
Leadbelly*. New York, 1936.

———. *Rainbow Round My Shoulder:
The Blue Trail of Black Ulysses*.
1928. Reprint, New York: Krause,
1972.

Odum, Howard W., and Guy B.
Johnson. *The Negro and His Songs:
A Study of Typical Negro Songs in
the South*. 1925. Reprint, New York:
New America Library, 1969.

———. *Negro Workaday Songs*. 1926.
Reprint, Mansfield Centre, Conn.:
Martino Publishing, 2002.

Oliver, Paul. *Songster and Saints:
Vocal Traditions on Race Records*.
Cambridge: Cambridge University
Press, 1984.

Ramsey, Frederick, Jr. *Been Here and
Gone*. New Brunswick, N.J.: Rutgers
University Press, 1969.

Scarborough, Dorothy. *On the Trail
of Negro Folk Songs*. Hatboro, Pa.:
Folklore Associates, 1965.

Thomas, Velma Maia. *No Man Can
Hinder Me: The Journey from
Slavery to Emancipation through
Song*. New York: Crown, 2001.

White, Newman Ivey. *American Negro
Folksongs*. Hatboro, Pa.: Folklore
Associates, 1965.

GOSPEL MUSIC

Boyer, Horace Clarence. *The Golden
Age of Gospel*. Urbana: University of
Illinois Press, 2000.

Harris, Michael W. *The Rise of Gospel
Blues: The Music of Thomas Andrew
Dorsey in the Urban Church*. New
York: Oxford University Press, 1992.

Heilbut, Tony. *The Gospel Sound*. New
York: Simon & Schuster, 1971.

Hinson, Glenn. *Fire in My Bones:
Transcendence and the Holy Spirit
in African American Gospel*.
Philadelphia: University of
Pennsylvania Press, 1999.

Jackson, Irene V. *Afro-American
Religious Music: A Bibliography
and a Catalogue of Gospel Music*.
Westport, Conn.: Greenwood Press,
1979.

Jackson, Jerma A. *Singing in My Soul:
Black Gospel Music in a Secular Age*.
Chapel Hill: University of North
Carolina Press, 2004.

Johnson, Clifton H., ed. *God Struck Me
Dead*. Boston: Pilgrim Press, 1969.

Lornell, Kip. *Happy in the Service of

the Lord: Afro-American Gospel
Quartets in Memphis*. Urbana:
University of Illinois Press, 1988.

Reagon, Bernice Johnson. *If You Don't
Go, Don't Hinder Me: The African
American Sacred Song Tradition*.
Lincoln: University of Nebraska
Press, 2001.

———. *We'll Understand It Better
By and By: Pioneering African
American Gospel Composers*.
Washington, D.C.: Smithsonian
Institution Press, 1992.

———. *We Who Believe in Freedom:
Sweet Honey in the Rock—Still on
the Journey*. New York: Anchor
Books, 1993.

Ward, Andrew. *Dark Midnight When
I Rise: The Story of the Jubilee
Singers, Who Introduced the World
to the Music of Black America*. New
York: Farrar, Straus, and Giroux,
2000.

Warren, Gwendolin Sims. *Ev'ry
Time I Feel the Spirit: 101 Best-
Loved Psalms, Gospel Hymns, and
Spiritual Songs of the African-
American Church*. New York: Henry
Holt, 1997.

Young, Alan. *The Pilgrim Jubilees*.
Jackson: University Press of
Mississippi, 2001.

———. *Woke Me Up This Morning:
Black Gospel Singers and the Gospel
Life*. Jackson: University Press of
Mississippi, 1997.

Zolten, J. Jerome. *Great God A'mighty!
The Dixie Hummingbirds:
Celebrating the Rise of Soul Gospel
Music*. Oxford: Oxford University
Press, 2003.

MISSISSIPPI HISTORY

Cobb, James. *The Most Southern Place
on Earth: The Mississippi Delta

and the Roots of Regional Identity. New York: Oxford University Press, 1992.

Cohn, David L. Where I Was Born and Raised. Boston: Houghton Mifflin, 1948.

Daniel, Pete. Deep'n As It Come: The 1927 Mississippi River Flood. New York: Oxford University Press, 1977.

———. The Shadow of Slavery: Peonage in the South, 1901–1960. Urbana: University of Illinois Press, 1990.

Davis, Allison, Burleigh B. Gardner, and Mary R. Gardner. Deep South: A Social Anthropological Study of Caste and Class. Chicago: University of Chicago Press, 1941.

Dollard, John. Caste and Class in a Southern Town. New Haven, Conn.: Yale University Press, 1937.

Ferris, William R. "Black Folklore from the Mississippi Delta." Ph.D. diss., University of Pennsylvania, 1969.

———. Mississippi Black Folklore: A Research Bibliography and Discography. Jackson: University Press of Mississippi, 1971.

Hudson, Arthur Palmer. Specimens of Mississippi Folk-Lore. Ann Arbor, Mich.: Edwards Brothers, 1928.

Jones, Lewis W. "The Mississippi Delta." Unpublished monograph, Fisk University Social Science Institute, Nashville, 1941.

Loewen, James W. Mississippi: Conflict and Change. New York: Pantheon, 1974.

Norris, Randall, Jean-Philippe Cypres, and Morgan Freeman. Highway 61: Heart of the Delta. Knoxville: University of Tennessee Press, 2008.

Powdermaker, Hortense. After Freedom: A Cultural Study in the Deep South. New York: ACLS Humanities E-Book, 2008.

Rogers, Kim Lacy. Life and Death in the Delta: African American Narratives of Violence, Resilience, and Social Change. New York: Palgrave Macmillan, 2006.

Wharton, Vernon Lane. The Negro in Mississippi. New York: Harper & Row, 1965.

Wirt, Frederick M. Politics of Southern Equality: Law and Social Change in a Mississippi County. Chicago: Aldine, 1970.

Woofter, T. J., Jr. Landlord and Tenant on the Cotton Plantation. New York: Negro Universities Press, 1969.

NARRATIVE TRADITIONS

Abrahams, Roger. Deep Down in the Jungle: Negro Narrative Folklore from the Streets of Philadelphia. Chicago: Aldine, 1970.

Brownderville, Greg Alan. Deep Down in the Delta: Folktales and Poems. Cotton Plant, Ark.: Doodlum Brothers Press, 2005.

Dorson, Richard. American Negro Folktales. New York: Fawcett, 1967.

Dundes, Alan, ed. Mother Wit from the Laughing Barrel. Englewood Cliffs, N.J.: Prentice Hall, 1973.

Ferris, William R. Black Prose Narrative from the Mississippi Delta. Graz, Austria: Jazzforschung, 1974/75.

Jackson, Bruce. Get Your Ass in the Water and Swim Like Me. Cambridge: Harvard University Press, 1974.

Roberts, John W. From Trickster to Badman: The Black Folk Hero in Slavery and Freedom. Philadelphia: University of Pennsylvania Press, 1989.

Rosengarten, Theodore. All God's Dangers: The Life of Nate Shaw.

Chicago: University of Chicago Press, 2000.

PHOTOGRAPHY

Burdine, Jane Rule. Delta Deep Down. Jackson: University Press of Mississippi, 2008.

Charters, Ann, and Samuel Charters. Blues Faces: A Portrait of the Blues. Boston: David R. Godine, 2000.

Clay, Maudie Schuyler. Delta Land. Jackson: University Press of Mississippi, 1999.

Dain, Martin. Faulkner's County: Yoknapatawpha. New York: Random House, 1964.

———. Faulkner's World: The Photographs of Martin Dain. Edited by Tom Rankin. Jackson: University Press of Mississippi, 1997.

Eggleston, William (photographs), and Willie Morris (text). Faulkner's Mississippi. Birmingham: Oxmoor House, 1990.

———. William Eggleston: Democratic Camera, Photographs, and Video, 1961–2008. New Haven: Yale University Press, 2008.

———. William Eggleston's Guide. Cambridge: MIT Press, 1976.

Freeman, Roland. A Communion of the Spirits: African-American Quilters, Preservers, and Their Stories. Nashville: Thomas Nelson, 1996.

———. Southern Roads/City Pavements: Photographs of Black Americans. New York: International Center of Photography, 1981.

Light, Ken. Delta Time: Mississippi Photographs by Ken Light. Washington, D.C.: Smithsonian Institution Press, 1995.

Mauskopf, Norman. A Time Not Here: The Mississippi Delta. Santa Fe: Twin Palms, 1997.

McDaris, Wendy, ed. *Visualizing the Blues*. Memphis: Dixon Gallery and Gardens, 2000.

Ramsey, Frederic, Jr. *Been Here and Gone*. New Brunswick, N.J.: Rutgers University Press, 1960.

Rankin, Tom. *Sacred Space: Photographs from the Mississippi Delta*. Jackson: University Press of Mississippi, 1993.

Walker, James Perry. *The Reverend*. Jackson: University Press of Mississippi, 2006.

Waterman, Dick. *Between Midnight and Day: The Last Unpublished Blues Archive*. New York: Thunder's Mouth Press, 2003.

Welty, Eudora. *Eudora Welty Photographs*. Jackson: University Press of Mississippi, 1989.

RELIGION

Lincoln, Charles E., and Lawrence H. Mamiya. *The Black Church in the African American Experience*. Durham, N.C.: Duke University Press, 1991.

Matthews, Donald Henry. *Honoring the Ancestors: An African Cultural Interpretation of Black Religion and Literature*. New York: Oxford University Press, 1998.

Spencer, Jon Michael. *Black Hymnody: A Hymnological History of the African-American Church*. Knoxville: University of Tennessee Press, 1992.

SERMONS

Brewer, John Mason. *The Word on the Brazos: Negro Preacher Tales from the Brazos Bottoms of Texas*. Austin: University of Texas Press, 1953.

Crawford, Evans E., and Thomas H. Troeger. *The Hum: Call and Response in African American Preaching*. Nashville: Abingdon Press, 1995.

Davis, Gerald L. *I Got the Word in Me and I Can Sing It, You Know: A Study of the Performed African-American Sermon*. Philadelphia: University of Pennsylvania Press, 1985.

Mitchell, Henry H. *Black Preaching*. New York: J. B. Lippincott, 1970.

Pipes, William H. *Say Amen, Brother! Old-Time Negro Preaching: A Study in American Frustration*. Westport, Conn.: Negro Universities Press, 1970.

Rosenberg, Bruce A. *Can These Bones Live?: The Art of the American Folk Preacher*. Urbana: University of Illinois Press, 1988.

Spencer, Jon Michael. *Sacred Symphony: The Chanted Sermon of the Black Preacher*. New York: Greenwood Press, 1988.

SLAVERY

Abrahams, Roger D. *Singing the Master: The Emergence of African-American Culture in the Plantation South*. New York: Penguin Books, 1992.

Armstrong, Orland Kay. *Old Massa's People: The Old Slaves Tell Their Story*. Indianapolis: Bobbs-Merrill, 1931.

Blassingame, John W. *The Slave Community*. New York: Oxford University Press, 1972.

———. *Slave Testimony: Two Centuries of Letters, Speeches, Interviews, and Autobiographies*. Baton Rouge: Louisiana State University Press, 1977.

Botkin, B. A., ed. *Lay My Burden Down: A Folk History of Slavery*. Chicago: University of Chicago Press, 1965.

Joyner, Charles. *Down by the Riverside: A South Carolina Slave Community*. Urbana: University of Illinois Press, 1986.

Parrish, Lydia. *Slave Songs of the Georgia Sea Islands*. Hatboro, Pa.: Folklore Associates, 1965.

White, Shane, and Graham White. *The Sounds of Slavery: Discovering African American History through Songs, Sermons, and Speech*. Boston: Beacon Press, 2006.

SPIRITUALS

Chase, Gilbert. *America's Music, from the Pilgrims to the Present*. Urbana: University of Illinois Press, 1987.

Cone, James H. *The Spirituals and the Blues: An Interpretation*. New York: Seabury Press, 1972.

Cooper, Michael L. *Slave Spirituals and the Jubilee Singers*. New York: Clarion Books, 2001.

Epstein, Dena J. Polacheck. *Sinful Tunes and Spirituals: Black Folk Music to the Civil War*. Urbana: University of Illinois Press, 2003.

Jackson, George Pullen. *White and Negro Spirituals, Their Life Span and Kinship: Tracing 200 Years of Untrammeled Song Making and Singing among Our Country Folk, with 116 Songs As Sung by Both Races*. New York: Da Capo Press, 1975.

Jackson, Judge. *The Colored Sacred Harp, for Singing Class, Singing School, Convention, and General Use in Christian Work and Worship*. Montgomery, Ala.: Brown Printing, 1992.

Jones, Arthur, and Ingrid Hansen Thomson. *Wade in the Water*

*Spirituals*. Maryknoll, N.Y.: Orbis Books, 1993.

Kirk-Duggan, Cheryl A. *Exorcizing Evil: A Womanist Perspective on the Spirituals*. Maryknoll, N.Y.: Orbis Books, 1997.

Lehmann, Theo. *Negro Spirituals*. Berlin: Eckart-Verlag, 1965.

Lomax, Alan. *The Rainbow Sign*. New York: Duell, Sloan & Pearce, 1959.

Lovell, John. *Black Song—The Forge and the Flame: The Story of How the Afro-American Spiritual Was Hammered Out*. New York: Schirmer Books, 1980.

Newman, Richard. *Go Down Moses: A Celebration of the African-American Spiritual*. New York: Clarkson Potter, 1998.

Peters, Erskine. *Lyrics of the Afro-American Spiritual: A Documentary Collection*. Westport, Conn.: Greenwood Press, 1993.

Spencer, Jon Michael. *Black Sacred Music*. Durham, N.C.: Duke University Press, 1993.

———. *Sing a New Song: Liberating Black Hymnody*. Minneapolis: Fortress Press, 1995.

Thurman, Howard. *Deep River and The Negro Spiritual Speaks of Life and Death*. Richmond, Ind.: Friends United Press, 1996.

Work, John W. *American Negro Songs and Spirituals: A Comprehensive Collection of 230 Folk Songs, Religious and Secular*. Whitefish, Mont.: Kessinger Publishing, 2007.

STREET LANGUAGE AND DRESS STYLE

Abrahams, Roger. *Positively Black*. Englewood Cliffs, N.J.: Prentice Hall, 1970.

Caponi-Tabery, Gena. *Signifyin(g),*

*Sanctifyin' and Slam Dunking: A Reader in African American Expressive Culture*. Amherst: University of Massachusetts Press, 1999.

Foster, Herbert L. *Ribbin', Jivin', and Playin' the Dozens*. Cambridge: Ballinger Press, 1974.

Kochman, Thomas, comp. *Rappin' and Stylin' Out: Communication in Urban Black America*. Urbana: University of Illinois Press, 1972.

Labov, William. *Language in the Inner City*. Philadelphia: University of Pennsylvania Press, 1972.

McCollom, Michael. *The Way We Wore: Black Style Then*. New York: Glitterati Incorporated, 2006.

White, Shane, and Graham J. White. *Stylin': African American Expressive Culture from Its Beginnings to the Zoot Suit*. Ithaca, N.Y.: Cornell University Press, 1998.

## SELECTED DISCOGRAPHY

ANTHOLOGIES

*American Roots Music*. CD (4 discs). New York: Palm, 2001. (Soundtrack to the documentary television series of the same name.)

*Anthology of the Blues: Mississippi Blues*. LP. Los Angeles: Kent, 1970s. (Recorded in Clarksdale, Miss., 1952. With Boyd Gilmore, Houston Boines, and Charlie Booker.)

*Before the Blues—The Early American Black Music Scene: Classic Recordings from the 1920s and 30s*. Vols. 1–3. CD (3 discs). Newton, N.J.: Yazoo, 1996.

*Blues Masters*. Vol. 8, *Mississippi Delta Blues*. CD. Los Angeles: Rhino, 1993. (With Tommy Johnson, Charley Patton, Willie Brown, Son

House, Robert Johnson, Robert Petway, and Muddy Waters.)

*Blues 1920's–40's*. Disc 2. LP. Tokyo: RCA, 1975. (With Daddy Stovepipe, Mississippi Sarah, Tommy McClennan, Big Joe Williams, Robert Petway, and Robert Lockwood Jr.)

*Blues Roots: Mississippi*. CD. Custom Compact Disc Series. Washington, D.C.: Smithsonian Folkways, 2000. (Originally released on RBF, 1966. Compiled by Samuel Charters. With Tommy Johnson, Big Joe Williams, Bo Carter, Robert Johnson, Charlie McCoy, Tommy McClennan, Robert Petway, and Sonny Boy Williamson.)

*Blues Scene U.S.A.: Mississippi Blues*. Vol. 4. LP. Hamburg, Germany: Storyville, 1970s.

*Blues Southside Chicago*. LP. Bexhill-on-Sea, East Sussex, England: Flyright, 1976. (Recorded in 1965. With Shakey Horton, Johnny Young, Sunnyland Slim, and Robert Nighthawk.)

*The Blues Tradition, 1927–1932*. LP. New York: Milestone, 1971. (With Big Bill Broonzy, King Solomon Hill, Bumble Bee Slim, Willie Brown, Roosevelt Graves, Blind Lemon Jefferson, Bobby Grant, and Walter Hawkins.)

*Catfish Blues: Mississippi Blues*. Vol. 3, *1936–1942*. CD. Whithorn, Newton Stewart, U.K.: Document, 2002. (With Robert Petway, Mississippi Matilda, and Sonny Boy Nelson.)

*Drop Down Mama*. CD. Chicago: Chess, 1990. (With Johnny Shines, Little Walter, Robert Nighthawk, Honeyboy Edwards, Floyd Jones, Big Boy Spires, and Blue Smitty.)

*Folk Festival of the Blues*. CD. Los Angeles: Chess, 1989. (Recorded in

1963. With Muddy Waters, Willie Dixon, Buddy Guy, Sonny Boy Williamson, and Howlin' Wolf.)

*From Where I Stand: The Black Experience in Country Music.* CD. Burbank, Calif.: Warner Bros., 1998.

*Genesis: The Beginnings of Rock.* Vols. 1–3. LP. London: Chess, 1972. (With Sunnyland Slim, Muddy Waters, Memphis Minnie, Washboard Sam, Leroy Foster, Forest City Joe, Robert Nighthawk, Little Johnny Jones, Big Bill Broonzy, and Jimmy Rogers.)

*Great Bluesmen at Newport.* CD. New York: Vanguard, 1976. (Recorded in 1959–65. With John Lee Hooker, Son House, Mississippi John Hurt, Skip James, and Fred McDowell.)

*The Griots.* CD. Compiled and edited by Samuel Charters. Custom Compact Disc Series. Washington, D.C.: Smithsonian Folkways, 2001.

*High Water Blues.* LP. Bexhill-on-Sea, East Sussex, England: Flyright, 1974. (With Isaiah Chattman, L. V. Conerly, Bubba Brown, Melvin Brown, Fiddlin' Joe Martin, Woodrow Adams, Ditty Mason, et al.)

*I Have to Paint My Face: Mississippi Blues, 1960.* CD. Compiled and edited by Chris Strachwitz. El Cerrito, Calif.: Arhoolie, 1995. (With Sam Chatman, Butch Cage, Willie Thomas, Jasper Love, Kathryn Pitman, Wade Walton, Robert Curtis Smith, and Columbus Jones.)

*Jackson Blues, 1928–1938.* CD. New York: Yazoo, 1991.

*Jook Joint Blues: Good Time Rhythm and Blues.* CD (4 discs). London: JSP, 2007. (With Lightfoot, Papa George, Lightnin' Slim, Little Al, Joe Hill Louis, Frankie Lee Sims, Little Sam Davis, Jesse Thomas, et al.)

*Let's Get Loose: Folk and Popular Blues Styles from the Beginnings to the Early 1940's.* CD. New York: DRAM, 2007. (Originally released on New World, 1978. With Yank Rachell, Pillie Bolling, Hattie Hudson, Willie Tyson, Clara Smith, George O'Connor, Rufus Quillian, et al.)

*Living Chicago Blues.* Vols. 1–4. CD. Chicago: Alligator ALCD 7701–7704, 1978.

*Living Legends.* LP. New York: Verve Folkways, 1966. (With Son House, Skip James, Bukka White, and Big Joe Williams.)

*Lonesome Road Blues: 15 Years in the Mississippi Delta, 1926–1941.* CD. New York: Yazoo, 1997. (With Big Joe Williams, Arthur Petties, Mississippi Bracy, Sonny Boy Nelson, Sam Collins, Robert Petway, and Freddie Spruell.)

*Martin Scorsese Presents the Blues: A Musical Journey.* CD. Santa Monica, Calif.: Hip-O, 2003.

*Masters of the Delta Blues: The Friends of Charley Patton.* CD. Notes by Don Kent. Newton, N.J.: Yazoo, 2002. (With Son House, Tommy Johnson, Willie Brown, Kid Bailey, Bertha Lee, Ishmon Bracey, Louise Johnson, and Bukka White.)

*Memphis and the Delta.* LP. Berkeley, Calif.: Blues Classics, 1968. (With Houston Boines, Luther Huff, Junior Brooks, Frank Floyd, Sunnyland Slim, Forest City Joe, and Model T Slim.)

*Memphis Blues Festival.* LP. New York: Sire, 1969. (With Nathan Beauregard, Bukka White, Furry Lewis, Robert Wilkins, and Joe Callicott.)

*Memphis Swamp Jam: Memphis Blues Festival.* LP. Beverly Hills, Calif.:

Blue Thumb, 1969. (With Fred McDowell, Johnny Woods, Bukka White, Nathan Beauregard, Furry Lewis, Sleepy John Estes, John Williams, R. L. Watson, Josiah Jones, and Napoleon Strickland.)

*Mississippi Blues, 1927–1941.* LP. New York: Yazoo, 1968.

*The Mississippi Blues,* no. 1. LP. Santa Monica, Calif.: Origin Jazz, 1966. (With Son House, Bukka White, Willie Brown, Kid Bailey, Robert Wilkins, Mississippi John Hurt, William Harris, and Skip James.)

*The Mississippi Blues,* no. 2. LP. Santa Monica, Calif.: Origin Jazz, 1966. (With Son House, Louise Johnson, Charley Patton, J. D. Short, Blind Joe Reynolds, Robert Wilkins, Henry Brown, Joe Callicott, and Garfield Akers.)

*Mississippi Blues: Library of Congress Recordings, 1940–1942.* CD. Notes by Ray Templeton. N.p.: Travelin' Man, 1991. (Originally released on Interstate Music Ltd., 1973.)

*The Mississippi Blues: Transition, 1926–1937,* no. 3. LP. Santa Monica, Calif.: Origin Jazz, 1968. (With Mississippi Bracy, Hambone Willie Newbern, Robert Johnson, Johnny Temple, Blind Joe Amos, Skip James, and Bo Weavil Jackson.)

*Mississippi Bottom Blues.* LP. New York: Mamlish, 1970s. (Recorded in 1926–35. With Freddie Spruell, Papa Harvey Hull, Long Cleve Reed, Tommie Bradley, Otto Virgial, and Charley Patton.)

*Really Chicago's Blues.* CD. Silver Spring, Md.: Adelphi, 1970. (With Johnny Shines, Honeyboy Edwards, Sunnyland Slim, John Lee Ganderson, Big Joe Williams, Walter Horton, and Backwards Sam Firk.)

*Sic 'em Dogs on Me.* LP. Glen Cove, N.Y.: Herwin, 1972. (With Elizabeth Johnson, Mae Glover, Bukka White, Ishman Bracey, Rosie Mae Moore, DeFord Bailey, D. H. Bilbro, Furry Lewis, and Charley Patton.)

*Sound of the Delta.* CD. Oakland, Calif.: Testament, 1994. (Recorded in 1963–65 of Mississippi bluesmen living in St. Louis.)

*They Sang the Blues.* LP. Jersey City, N.J.: Historical Recordings, 1968. (With Jelly Roll Anderson, Robert Wilkins, Skip James, Big Boy Cleveland, Willie Jones, Furry Lewis, and Josh White.)

*Violin, Sing the Blues for Me: African-American Fiddlers, 1926–1949.* CD. Raleigh, N.C.: Old Hat, 1999.

FIELD RECORDINGS

Conway, Cecelia. *Black Banjo Songsters.* CD. Washington, D.C.: Smithsonian Folkways, 1998. (With Scott Odell, John Snipes, Dink Roberts, Joe Thompson, Odell Thompson, James Roberts, Etta Baker, Cora Phillips, John Jackson, John Homer Walker, Irvin Cook, Leonard Bowles, Lewis Hairston, John Tyree, and Rufus Kasey.)

Danielou, Alain. *Anthology of World Music: The Ba-Benzele Pygmies.* CD. Somerville, Mass.: Rounder RDR5107, 1998. (Sounds similar to bottle-blowing style of Louis Dotson.)

Evans, David. *Goin' up the Country.* LP. Somerville, Mass.: Rounder 2012, 1975. (With Roosevelt Holts, Isaiah Chattman, Arzo Youngblood, L. V. Conerly, and Jack Owens.)

———. *The Legacy of Tommy Johnson.* LP. Bristol, England: Saydisc Specialized Recordings SDM224, 1972. (With Isaac Youngblood, Herb Quinn, Mager Johnson, Arzo Youngblood, Bubba Brown, Houston Stackhouse, Ditty Mason, et al.)

———. *Sorrow, Come Pass Me Around.* LP. Manhattan Beach, Calif.: Advent 2805, 1975. (With Norma Jean, Ephram Carter, Willard Burrell, Babe Stovall, Annie Lee, Oscar Crawford, and Annie Mae Jones.)

———. *South Mississippi Blues.* LP. Somerville, Mass.: Rounder 2009, 1973. (With Babe Stovall, Herb Quinn, Roosevelt Holts, O. D. Jones, Dink Brister, Eli Owens, Esau Weary, Myrt Holmes, and Isaac Youngblood.)

———. *Traveling through the Jungle: Fife and Drum Band Music from the Deep South.* CD. Oakland, Calif.: Testament 5017, 1995.

Ferris, William R. *The Blues Are Alive and Well.* LP. London: Transatlantic, XTRA 1105, 1970. (With James "Son" Thomas, Lee Kizart, and Lovey Williams.)

———. *Blues from the Delta.* LP. Bristol, England: Saydisc Specialized Recordings SDM226, 1976. (With James "Son" Thomas, Lee Kizart, Lovey Williams, and Scott Dunbar.)

———. *Mississippi Folk Voices.* LP. Memphis: Southern Folklore Records 101, 1983. (Features Parchman prison work chants and blues by James "Son" Thomas.)

Lomax, Alan. *Afro-American Folk Music from Tate and Panola Counties, Mississippi.* CD. Cambridge, Mass.: Rounder 1515, 2000. (Recordings by Alan Lomax, 1942. Recordings by David Evans, 1969–71.)

———. *Blues in the Mississippi Night.* CD. The Alan Lomax Collection. Cambridge, Mass.: Rounder Select 18602, 2003. (Recorded in 1947. Original LP 1959. With Big Bill Broonzy, Memphis Slim, Sonny Boy Williamson.)

———. *The Blues Roll On.* LP. New York: Atlantic SD 1352, 1967. (Recorded in the field by Alan Lomax, assisted by Shirley Collins. With Forest City Joe, Boy Blue, Fred McDowell, Lonnie Young, and Rosalie Hill.)

———. *Deep South—Sacred and Sinful.* LP. Southern Journey, no. 5. Bergenfield, N.J.: Prestige PR-INT 25006, 1961.

———. *Negro Church Music.* LP. Southern Folk Heritage Series. New York: Atlantic SD 1351, 1961.

———. *Negro Prison Songs from the Mississippi State Penitentiary.* LP. New York: Tradition TR 1020, 1950.

———. *Roots of the Blues.* CD. Southern Folk Heritage Series. New York: Atlantic SD 1348, 1961.

———. *Sounds of the South: A Musical Journey from the Georgia Sea Islands to the Mississippi Delta.* CD (4 discs). New York: Atlantic 82496, 1993. (Original LP 1961.)

———. *Yazoo Delta Blues and Spirituals.* LP. Bergenfield, N.J.: Prestige International PR-INT 25010, 1961. (With Fred McDowell, Ed Young, Miles Pratcher, Mattie Gardner, Ida Mae Towns, Jessie Pratcher, and Sid Hemphill.)

Lomax, Alan, and John Avery Lomax. *Afro-American Spirituals, Work Songs, and Ballads.* CD. Library of Congress Archive of Folk Culture. Cambridge, Mass.: Rounder, 1998.

Lomax, John Avery, Ruby Pickens Tartt, Alan Lomax, and Ruby T.

Lomax. *Afro-American Blues and Game Songs.* CD. Cambridge, Mass.: Rounder Select, 1999.

———. *Mississippi River Blues.* LP. Flyright-Matchbox Library of Congress Series, vol. 1. Bexhill-on-Sea, East Sussex, England: Flyright, 1973. (Recorded in Natchez, Miss., on October 19, 1940. With Lucious Curtis, Willie Ford, and George Boldwin.)

Mitchell, George. *The George Mitchell Collection.* CD. Oxford, Miss.: Fat Possum, 2007. (Recorded in the 1960s and 1970s. With Fred McDowell, R. L. Burnside, Rosa Lee Hill, Teddy Williams, William "Do-Boy" Diamond, Jesse Mae Hemphill, et al.)

———. *Mississippi Delta Blues: Blow My Blues Away.* Vols. 1 and 2. CD. El Cerrito, Calif.: Arhoolie, 1994. (Recorded in the late 1960s.)

Oliver, Paul. *Conversation with the Blues: A Documentary of Field Recordings.* CD. Cambridge, U.K.: Cambridge University Press, 1997. (Original Decca LP 1965.)

Ramsey, Frederic. *Music from the South: Been Here and Gone.* Vol. 10. LP. Music from the South. New York: Folkways, 1960. (Includes performance by Scott Dunbar in the early 1950s.)

Stearns, Marshall Winslow. *Negro Blues and Hollers.* CD. Cambridge, Mass.: Rounder, 1997. (Recordings of Son House in 1942 by Alan Lomax, Lewis Jones, and John W. Work.)

INDIVIDUAL ARTISTS

Bell, Carey. *Blues Harp.* LP. Roots of Jazz Series. Chicago: Delmark, 1969.

———. *Harpslinger.* CD. London: JSP, 1988.

———. *Last Night.* LP. Los Angeles: Bluesway, 1973.

Bracey, Ishman. *The Famous Tommy Johnson–Ishman Bracey Session.* LP. Bristol, England: Roots, 1970s. (With Tommy Johnson and Charlie McCoy.)

———. *Ishman Bracey and Charley Taylor: Complete Recorded Works in Chronological Order, 1928–1929.* CD. Vienna: Document, 1991. (With Charley Taylor.)

Brewer, Jim. *Jim Brewer.* LP. North Ferrisburg, Vt.: Philo, 1974.

Broonzy, Big Bill. *The Best of Big Bill Broonzy: Big Bill Blues.* CD. N.p.: Blues Forever, 2001.

———. *Big Bill Broonzy.* CD. Kings of the Blues. London: Sanctuary, 2004.

———. *Big Bill Broonzy.* LP. Los Angeles: Archive of Folk Music, 1967.

———. *Big Bill Broonzy: Complete Recorded Works in Chronological Order.* Vols. 1–12. CD (12 discs). Vienna: Document, 1991. (Original recordings from 1934–47.)

———. *Big Bill Broonzy: The War and Post War Years, 1940–1951.* Vol. 3. CD. London: JSP, 2007.

———. *Big Bill Broonzy Sings Country Blues.* LP. New York: Folkways, 1957.

———. *Big Bill Broonzy Sings Folk Songs.* CD. Washington, D.C.: Smithsonian Folkways, 1989.

———. *An Evening with Big Bill Broonzy.* CD. Denmark: Storyville, 1991.

———. *Good Time Tonight.* CD. Roots 'n' Blues. New York: Columbia, 1990.

———. *Remembering Big Bill.* LP. Chicago: Mercury, 1964.

Broonzy, Big Bill, and Pete Seeger. *Trouble in Mind.* CD. Washington, D.C.: Smithsonian Folkways, 2000.

Broonzy, Big Bill, and Studs Terkel. *Big Bill Broonzy Interviewed by Studs Terkel.* CD. Custom Compact Disc Series. Washington, D.C.: Smithsonian Folkways, 2000.

Burns, Eddie. *Bottle Up and Go.* LP. London: Action, 1972.

Burnside, R. L. *Mississippi Hill Country Blues.* CD. Oxford, Miss.: Fat Possum, 2001.

Burnside, R. L., Rosa Lee Hill, and Joe Callicott. *Mississippi Delta Blues.* Vol. 2. LP. Berkeley, Calif.: Arhoolie, 1969.

Callicott, Mississippi Joe. *Ain't Gonna Lie to You.* CD. Oxford, Miss.: Fat Possum, 2003. (Original recordings by George Mitchell, 1967–68.)

———. *Deal Gone Down.* LP. London: Revival, 1967.

———. *North Mississippi Blues.* CD. New Orleans: Southland, 2004.

———. *Presenting the Country Blues.* LP. London: Blue Horizon, 1969.

Carter, Bo. *Bo Carter: Complete Recorded Works in Chronological Order.* CD. Vienna: Document, 1991.

———. *Bo Carter: Greatest Hits, 1930–1940.* LP. New York: Yazoo, 1968.

———. *Twist It Babe, 1931–1940.* CD. New York: Yazoo, 2002.

Cat Iron. *Cat Iron.* LP. London: Xtra, 1969.

———. *Cat-Iron Sings Blues and Hymns.* LP. New York: Folkways, 1958.

Chatmon, Sam. *The Mississippi Sheik.* LP. New York: Blue Goose, 1972.

———. *Mississippi Sheiks: Complete Recorded Works in Chronological Order.* Vol. 4, *26 March 1934 to 19 January 1935.* CD. Vienna: Document, 1991.

———. *The New Mississippi Sheiks.* LP. Somerville, Mass.: Rounder, 1972.

———. *Sam Chatmon, 1970–1974.* CD. Bexhill-on-Sea, East Sussex, England: Flyright, 1999.

Collins, Sam. *Jailhouse Blues.* CD. Newton, N.J.: Yazoo, 1990.

———. *Sam Collins: Complete Recorded Works in Chronological Order, 1927–1931.* CD. Vienna: Document, 1990s.

Cooke, Sam. *Ain't That Good News.* CD. New York: ABKCO Music, 2003. (Original LP 1969.)

———. *At the Copa.* CD. New York: ABKCO Music, 2003. (Original LP 1978.)

———. *The Best of Sam Cooke.* CD. New York: RCA/Legacy, 2005. (Original LP 1962.)

———. *Hits of the '50s.* LP. New York: RCA Victor, 1960.

———. *Night Beat.* CD. New York: RCA Victor, 2005. (Original LP 1963.)

———. *One Night Stand!: Sam Cooke Live at the Harlem Square Club, 1963.* CD. New York: RCA/Legacy, 2005. (Original LP 1985.)

———. *Try a Little Love.* LP. New York: RCA Victor, 1965.

———. *The Unforgettable Sam Cooke.* CD. New York: RCA, 1993. (Original LP 1966.)

Cooke, Sam, René Hall, and Horace Ott. *Mr. Soul.* LP. New York: RCA Victor, 1963.

Cooke, Sam, René Hall, and Torrie Zito. *Shake.* LP. New York: RCA Victor, 1965.

Cotton, James. *Cut You Loose!* CD. Santa Monica, Calif.: Vanguard, 1988. (Original LP 1968.)

———. *James Cotton.* CD. Vanguard Visionaries. Santa Monica, Calif.: Vanguard, 2007.

———. *100% Cotton.* CD. New York: Universe, 2004. (Original LP Buddah 1974.)

———. *Pure Cotton.* CD. St. Petersburg, Russia: Lilith, 2007. (Original LP Verve 1968.)

———. *Taking Care of Business.* LP. Hollywood, Calif.: Captol, 1971.

Crudup, Arthur. *Arthur "Big Boy" Crudup: Complete Recorded Works, 1941–1954, in Chronological Order.* Vols. 1–4. CD (4 discs). Vienna: Document, 1993.

———. *Arthur "Big Boy" Crudup: The Father of Rock and Roll.* LP. New York: RCA Victor, 1971.

———. *Crudup's Mood.* LP. Roots of Jazz Series. Chicago: Delmark, 1969.

———. *Look on Yonder's Wall.* CD. Chicago: Delmark, 1997. (Original LP 1968.)

———. *Mean Ol' Frisco.* CD. Narberth, Pa.: Collectables, 1994. (Original 1960s Fire sessions.)

———. *Roebuck Man.* CD. London: Sequel, 1992. (Original United Artists LP 1970.)

———. *That's Alright Mama.* CD. New York: Bluebird, 1992. (Original 1941–54 Bluebird recordings.)

Crudup, Arthur, Jerry McCain, and Frank Frost. *Harpin' on It.* LP. England: Carnival Gold Standard, 1972.

Davis, Jimmy. *Maxwell Street: Jimmy Davis.* LP. New York: Elektra, 1965.

Davis, Walter. *Think You Need a Shot.* LP. London: RCA International, 1970.

Davis, Walter, and Cripple Clarence Lofton. *Cripple Clarence Lofton and Walter Davis.* LP. New York: Yazoo, 1971.

Diddley, Bo. *Another Dimension.* New York: Chess, 1971.

———. *Bo Diddley.* CD. Original Chess Masters. Universal City, Calif.: MCA/Chess, 1986. (Originally issued on 2 LP recordings: Chess 1341 [1957] and Checker 1436 [1958].)

———. *Bo Diddley and Company.* LP. Chicago: Checker, 1955.

———. *Bo Diddley Is a Gunslinger.* CD. Santa Monica, Calif.: Geffen/Chess, 2004. (Original LP 1954.)

———. *Bo Diddley Is a Lover.* LP. Chicago: Checker, 1955.

———. *Bo Diddley's a Twister.* LP. Chicago: Checker, 1962.

———. *Bo Diddley's Beach Party.* LP. Chicago: Checker, 1963.

———. *500% More Man.* LP. Beverly Hills, Calif.: Telstar, 1988. (Original Checker LP 1965.)

———. *Go Bo Diddley.* CD. Original Chess Masters. Universal City, Calif.: Chess, 1986.

———. *Hey! Bo Diddley.* CD. London: Instant, 1990.

———. *Hey, Good Lookin'!* LP. Chicago: Checker, 1965.

———. *In the Spotlight.* CD. Original Chess Masters. Universal City, Calif.: Chess, 1987. (Original LP 1961.)

———. *The Super, Super Blues Band.* CD. Universal City, Calif.: Chess, 1992. (Original LP 1967. With Muddy Waters and Howlin' Wolf.)

———. *Surfin' with Bo Diddley.* LP. Chicago: Checker, 1963.

Dixon, Willie. *Boss of the Chicago Blues.* CD. Los Angeles: Fuel, 2005.

———. *The Chess Box.* CD. Chicago: Chess, 1988.

———. *Giant of the Blues.* CD. Vilvoorde, Belgium: Blues Boulevard Records, 2008.

———. *I Am the Blues.* CD. Chicago: Sony/Bmg Custom Marketing Group, 2008.

———. *The Original Wang Dang Doodle: The Chess Recordings and More*. CD. Universal City, Calif.: MCA, 1995.

———. *The Songs of Willie Dixon*. CD. Cleveland: Telarc Blues, 1999.

———. *A Tribute to Willie Dixon, 1915–1992*. CD. London: Charly Records, 1992.

———. *Willie Dixon*. CD. New York: Columbia, 1990.

———. *Willie Dixon: Poet of the Blues*. CD. Los Angeles: Columbia, 1998.

———. *The Willie Dixon Songbook*. CD. Holland: Zillion Records, Stemra, 1992.

Dixon, Willie, and Diana Haig. *The Cobra Records Story: Chicago Rock and Blues, 1956–1958*. CD. Nashville: Capricorn, 1993.

Dixon, Willie, Johnny Winter, Lafayette Leake, Lee Jackson, Big Walter Horton, and Clifton James. CD. *Spoonful of Blues*. Vilvoorde, Belgium: Music Avenue, 2006.

Douglas, K. C. *Big Road Blues*. CD. Original Blues Classics. Berkeley, Calif.: Prestige/Bluesville, 1994. (Original LP 1961.)

———. *K. C. Douglas: A Dead-Beat Guitar and the Mississippi Blues*. CD. Custom Compact Disc Series. Washington, D.C.: Smithsonian Folkways, 2001. (Original Cook Laboratories LP 1955.)

———. *K. C.'s Blues*. CD. Original Blues Classics. Berkeley, Calif.: Prestige/Bluesville, 1990. (Original LP 1961.)

Dunbar, Scott. *From Lake Mary*. CD. Oxford, Miss.: Fat Possum, 2000. (Original Ahura Mazda LP 1970.)

Edwards, Dave "Honeyboy." *Blues, Blues: December 10, 1975*. CD. Vienna: Document, 2005.

———. *Crawling Kingsnake*. CD.

Los Angeles: Testament, 1997. (Original recordings by Pete Welding, 1967.)

———. *Old Friends: Sunnyland Slim, Honeyboy Edwards, Kansas City Red, Big Walter Horton, Floyd Jones*. CD. Chicago: Earwig, 1993.

Fuller, Johnny. *Fuller's Blues*. LP. Australia: Bluesmaker, 1973.

Griffith, Shirley. *Mississippi Blues*. LP. New York: Blue Goose, 1973.

———. *Saturday Blues*. LP. Bergenfield, N.J.: Prestige/Bluesville, 1961.

Griffith, Shirley, and J. T. Adams. *Indiana Avenue Blues*. LP. Bergenfield, N.J.: Prestige, 1962.

Guitar Slim. *Eddie "Guitar Slim" Jones: The Things That I Used to Do*. CD. Los Angeles: Varase Sarabandas, 1994. (Original Specialty LP 1970.)

———. *Sufferin' Mind*. CD. Berkeley, Calif.: Specialty, 1991.

Guitar Slim and Jelly Belly. *Guitar Slim and Jelly Belly*. LP. Berkeley, Calif.: Arhoolie, 1964.

Holts, Roosevelt. *Presenting the Country Blues*. LP. New York: Blue Horizon, 1968.

———. *Roosevelt Holts and His Friends*. LP. Berkeley, Calif.: Arhoolie, 1972.

Hooker, John Lee. *. . . And Seven Nights*. LP. New York: Verve Folkways, 1977.

———. *Big Red Blues*. LP. New York: Buddah, 1969.

———. *The Big Soul of John Lee Hooker*. CD. Narberth, Pa.: Collectables, 2000. (Original Vee-Jay LP 1963.)

———. *The Blues Man*. LP. San Francisco: Battle, 1960.

———. *The Boogie Man*. CD (4 discs). London: Proper, 2006.

———. *Boogie with the Hook/Never Get Out of These Blues Alive*. 45 rpm. New York: ABC, 1972.

———. *Burnin'*. CD. Narberth, Pa.: Collectables, 2000. (Original Vee-Jay LP 1962.)

———. *Coast to Coast Blues Band: Anywhere, Anytime, Anyplace*. CD. Bury St. Edmunds, Suffolk, England: BGO, 1997. (Originally recorded in Detroit, 1946–52.)

———. *The Country Blues of John Lee Hooker*. CD. Original Blues Classics. Berkeley, Calif.: Riverside, 1991.

———. *Detroit Special*. CD. Blues Originals, vol. 5. New York: Atlantic, 1992. (Original LP 1972.)

———. *Don't Go Baby; Moaning and Stompin' Blues*. 45 rpm. Cincinnati: King, 1949.

———. *Don't Turn Me from Your Door*. CD. Atlantic & Atco Remasters Series. New York: Atco, 1992. (Original LP 1962.)

———. *Endless Boogie*. CD. Universal City, Calif.: MCA, 1991. (Original ABC LP 1971.)

———. *Folk Blues*. LP. Culver City, Calif.: Crown, 1959.

———. *The Folklore of John Lee Hooker*. CD. Chicago: Vee-Jay, 1991. (Original LP 1971.)

———. *Goin' Down Highway 51*. CD. Hollywood, Calif.: Specialty, 1994. (Original LP 1971.)

———. *The Great John Lee Hooker*. LP. Culver City, Calif.: Crown, 1950.

———. *House of the Blues*. CD. Original Chess Masters. Universal City, Calif.: MCA/Chess, 1987. (Original LP 1960.)

———. *How Long Blues*. LP. Battle Records Blues Series. New York: Battle, 1960s.

———. *I Feel Good*. CD. New York:

Great American Music Company, 2007. (Original Jewel LP 1972.)

———. *I'm John Lee Hooker*. CD. Los Angeles: Shout! Factory, 2007.

———. *In Person*. CD. Narberth, Pa.: Collectables, 2001. (Original Vee Jay LP 1974.)

———. *It Serves You Right to Suffer*. CD. Los Angeles: MCA, 1999. (Original Impulse! LP 1965.)

———. *John Lee Hooker*. LP. Century City, Calif.: Everest Record Group, 1968.

———. *John Lee Hooker Concert at Newport*. CD. Narberth, Pa.: Collectables, 2000. (Original Vee-Jay LP 1964.)

———. *John Lee Hooker on Campus*. CD. Narberth, Pa.: Collectables, 2001. (Original Vee-Jay LP 1964.)

———. *John Lee Hooker Presents His House Rent Boogie*. CD. London: Ace, 2001. (Original recordings from the 1940s and 1950s.)

———. *John Lee Hooker Sings Blues*. CD. Cincinnati: King, 1988. (Original LP 1961.)

———. *John Lee Hooker Sings the Blues: That's My Story*. CD. Original Blues Classics. Berkeley, Calif.: Riverside, 1991. (Original Crown LPs 1960s.)

———. *The Legendary Modern Recordings, 1948–54*. CD. London: Ace, 1993.

———. *Live at Sugar Hill*. Vols. 1 and 2. CD. London: Ace, 1990. (Original Galaxy LP 1968.)

———. *Live at the Café Au Go-Go (and Soledad Prison)*. CD. Universal City, Calif.: MCA, 1996. (Original 2 ABC/ Bluesway LPs 1966.)

———. *No Friend Around*. CD. Diss, Norfolk, England: Red Lightnin', 1992. (Original LP 1972.)

———. *Original Folk Blues—Plus*. CD. London: Ace, 1994. (Original Kent LP 1967.)

———. *The Real Blues*. LP. Los Angeles: Tradition/Everest, 1969.

———. *Simply the Truth*. CD. Orange, Calif.: Hep Cat, 2006. (Original Bluesway LP 1968.)

———. *That's Where It's At!* CD. Berkeley, Calif.: Stax, 2001. (Original LP 1969.)

———. *Travelin'*. CD. Narbert, Pa.: Collectables, 2000. (Original Vee-Jay LP 1960.)

———. *Whiskey and Wimmen*. CD. St. Laurent, Quebec: Retro Music, 1994.

Hooker, John Lee, and Big Maceo Merriweather. *John Lee Hooker and Big Maceo Merriweather*. LP. Detroit: Fortune, 1963.

Hooker, John Lee, Phil Upchurch, Eddie Taylor, and Al Duncan. *Urban Blues*. CD. Universal City, Calif.: MCA, 1993. (Original Bluesway LP 1967.)

Horton, Big Walter. *The Soul of Blues Harmonica*. LP. Universal City, Calif.: Chess, 1987. (Original Argo LP 1964.)

Horton, Big Walter, and Carey Bell. *Big Walter Horton with Carey Bell*. CD. Chicago: Alligator, 1989. (Original LP 1972.)

Horton, Big Walter, and Paul Butterfield. *An Offer You Can't Refuse*. CD. Englewood, N.J.: M.I.L. Multimedia, 1999. (Original Red Lightning LP 1972.)

House, Son. *Complete Recorded Works of Son House and the Great Delta Blues Singers*. CD. Vienna: Document, 2005. (Original recordings from 1930.)

———. *Delta Blues*. CD. Los Angeles: Biograph, 2003. (Includes 1941 and 1942 Library of Congress recordings and 1930 Paramount recordings.)

———. *Father of Folk Blues*. CD. New York: Sony Music, 2004. (Original Columbia LP 1965.)

———. *Son House: The Complete Library of Congress Sessions, 1941–1942*. CD. Crawley, West Sussex, England: Travelin' Man, 1990. (Original 1942 recordings by Alan Lomax.)

———. *Son House "At Home": The Legendary 1969 Rochester Sessions, Complete*. CD. Vienna: Document, 1992.

House, Son, Willie Brown, Leroy Williams, Willie Blackwell, Joe Martin, Honeyboy Edwards, and Alan Lomax. *Walking Blues*. LP. Bexhill-on-Sea, East Sussex, England: Flyright, 1979.

House, Son, Skip James, Bukka White, and Big Joe Williams. *Living Legends*. LP. New York: Verve Folkways, 1966.

House, Son, and J. D. Short. *Blues from the Mississippi Delta*. CD. Custom Compact Disc Series. Washington, D.C.: Smithsonian Folkways, 2003. (House's performances were originally recorded for the Library of Congress in 1942; Short's performances were recorded by Samuel Charters in 1960.)

House, Son, Leroy Williams, Willie Brown, Fiddlin' Joe Martin, and Alan Wilson. *Son House*. CD. New York: Columbia Legacy, 2003.

House, Son, and Robert Pete Williams. *Son House and Robert Pete Williams Live!* LP. Berlin: Roots, 1966.

Howlin' Wolf. *Ain't Gonna Be Your Dog*. CD (2 discs). Universal City, Calif.: MCA, 1994. (Rare and previously unissued recordings from the 1950s and 1960s.)

———. *The Back Door Wolf*. CD. Original Chess Masters. Santa Monica, Calif.: Chess/MCA, Distributed by Universal Music & Video, 2003.

———. *Change My Way*. CD. Original Chess Masters. Universal City, Calif.: Chess/MCA, 1990. (Original LP 1975.)

———. *Going Back Home*. LP. Norfolk, England: Syndicate Chapter, 1971.

———. *His Best*. CD. Chess 50th Anniversary Collection. Universal City, Calif.: Chess/MCA, 1997.

———. *Howlin' Wolf/ Moanin' in the Moonlight*. CD. Universal City, Calif.: Chess, 1986. (Original 2 LPs 1962 and 1959.)

———. *Live and Cookin' at Alice's Revisited*. CD. Chicago: Msi Music Corporation, 2004. (Original Chess LP 1972.)

———. *The London Howlin' Wolf Sessions*. CD. Universal City, Calif.: Chess, 2003. (Original LP 1971. With Eric Clapton, Charlie Watts, Bill Wyman, Steve Winwood, and Hubert Sumlin.)

———. *The Real Folk Blues/More Real Folk Blues*. CD. Blues Classics, Remastered and Revisited. Santa Monica, Calif.: MCA/Chess, 2002. (Original 2 LPs 1966 and 1967.)

Howlin' Wolf and Muddy Waters. *London Revisited*. LP. Chicago: Chess, 1974.

Hurt, Mississippi John. *The Best of Mississippi John Hurt*. LP. Santa Monica, Calif.: Vanguard, 1986. (Original LP 1970.)

———. *The Complete Studio Recordings*. CD. Santa Monica, Calif.: Vanguard, 2000.

———. *Frankie and Albert*. CD. New York: Tomato, 2002.

———. *Mississippi John Hurt: 1928 Sessions*. CD. Newton, N.J.: Yazoo, 1990.

———. *Worried Blues*. CD. Cambridge, Mass.: Rounder, 1991. (Original Piedmont LP 1960.)

James, Elmore. *Anthology of the Blues: The Legend of Elmore James*. LP. Los Angeles: Kent, 1969.

———. *Blues after Hours*. CD. London: Ace, 2005. (Original Ember LP 1968.)

———. *The Blues in My Heart, the Rhythm in My Soul*. LP. Los Angeles: United/Superior, 1969.

———. *Cotton Patch Hot Foot*. LP. London: Polydor, 1973. (With Big Walter Horton.)

———. *Elmore James*. CD. Blues King Pins. New York: Virgin, 2003.

———. *The Great Elmore James*. LP. Linden, N.J.: Up Front, 1970.

———. *The Resurrection of Elmore James*. LP. Original Folk Blues. Los Angeles: Kent, 1960.

———. *The Sky Is Crying: The History of Elmore James*. CD. Los Angeles: Rhino, 1993.

———. *To Know a Man*. Vols. 1 and 2. LP. London: Blue Horizon, 1962.

———. *The Very Best of Elmore James*. CD. Los Angeles: Rhino, 2000.

———. *Whose Muddy Shoes*. CD. Original Chess Jazz Masters. Universal City, Calif.: Chess, 1991. (Original LP 1969.)

James, Elmore, and John Brim. *Tough*. LP. London: Blue Horizon, 1960.

James, Skip. *King of the Delta Blues Singers, 1928–1964*. LP. Canaan, N.Y.: Biograph, 1971.

———. *Skip James*. CD. Vanguard

Visionaries. Santa Monica, Calif.: Vanguard, 2007.

———. *Skip James: Complete 1931 Recordings in Chronological Order*. CD. Vienna: Document, 1990.

———. *Skip James: Greatest of the Delta Blues Singers*. CD. Canaan, N.Y.: Biograph, 1992.

———. *Skip James: The Complete Bloomington, Indiana, Concert, March 30, 1968*. Vols. 1 and 2. CD. Vienna: Document, 1999.

———. *Today!* CD. Santa Monica, Calif.: Vanguard, 1988. (Original LP 1966.)

Jefferson, Blind Lemon. *King of the Country Blues*. CD. Newton, N.J.: Yazoo, 1990.

Jefferson, Blind Lemon, and Son House. *Son House—Blind Lemon Jefferson*. LP. Canaan, N.Y.: Biograph, 1972.

Johnson, Robert. *Robert Johnson: The Complete Recordings*. Roots 'n' Blues. CD (2 discs). New York: Columbia/Legacy, 1996. (Includes every recording Johnson ever made.)

———. *Robert Johnson, King of the Delta Blues Singers*. Vols. 1 and 2. CD. New York: Columbia/Legacy, 2004.

Johnson, Tommy. *Tommy Johnson (1928–1929): Complete Recorded Works in Chronological Order*. CD. Vienna: Document, 2000.

———. *Tommy Johnson and Associates*. CD. Blue Cats Collection. Guildford, Surrey, England: Catfish, 1999.

Johnson, Tommy, Ishman Bracey, and Charlie McCoy. *The Famous 1928 Tommy Johnson–Ishman Bracey Session*. LP. Bristol, England: Roots, 1970s.

King, Albert. *Albert King*. CD. Stax Profiles. Berkeley, Calif.: Stax, 2006.

———. *The Best of Albert King*. CD. Berkeley, Calif.: Stax, 1986.

———. *The Big Blues*. CD. Cincinnati: King, 1987.

———. *The Complete King and Bobbin Recordings*. CD. Nashville: King, 2004.

———. *Door to Door*. CD. Original Chess Masters. Universal City, Calif.: Chess/MCA, 1990. (Original LP 1969. With Otis Rush.)

———. *King Does the King's Things*. LP. Memphis: Stax, 1969. (Songs of Elvis Presley.)

———. *King of the Blues Guitar*. CD. New York: Atlantic, 1989. (Original LP 1969.)

———. *Live Wire, Blues Power*. LP. Berkeley, Calif.: Stax, 1999.

———. *Lovejoy*. CD. Berkeley, Calif.: Stax, 1990. (Original LP 1971.)

———. *More Big Blues*. CD. London: Ace, 2001.

———. *Travelin' to California*. LP. Cincinnati: King, 1969.

———. *Truckload of Lovin'*. CD. New York: Tomato, 1989. (Original Utopia LP 1976.)

———. *Years Gone By*. CD. Berkeley, Calif.: Stax, 1983.

King, B. B. *Anthology of the Blues: B. B. King, 1949–1950*. LP. Los Angeles: Kent, 1968.

———. *Back in the Alley*. CD. Universal City, Calif.: MCA, 1988. (Original LP 1970.)

———. *B. B. King and Friends*. CD (2 discs). Los Angeles: Stardust, 2007. (With Sonny Boy Williamson, Bobo Thomas, Luther Huff, Kansas Joe, Fred McDowell, and Willie Love.)

———. *B. B. King in London*. CD. University City, Calif.: MCA, 1993. (Original ABC LP 1971.)

———. *B. B. King Live at the Regal and B. B. King Live in Cook County Jail*. CD. Universal City, Calif.: MCA, 1987. (Original 2 LPs 1972.)

———. *The Best of the Kent Singles, 1958–1971*. CD. London: Ace, 2000.

———. *Better than Ever*. LP. Nashville: Kent, 1984.

———. *Blues in My Heart*. LP. London: Ace, 2004. (Original Crown LP 1962.)

———. *Blues Is King*. CD. Universal City, Calif.: MCA, 1987. (Original ABC LP 1967.)

———. *Blues on the Bayou*. CD. Los Angeles: MCA, 1998.

———. *Boss of the Blues*. LP. Los Angeles: Kent, 1965.

———. *A Christmas Celebration of Hope*. CD. New York: MCA, 2001.

———. *Completely Well*. CD. Universal City, Calif.: MCA, 1995. (Original Bluesway LP 1969.)

———. *Confessin' the Blues*. CD. Bury St. Edmunds, Suffolk, England: BGO, 2005. (Original ABC LP 1965.)

———. *Doing My Thing, Lord*. LP. Los Angeles: Kent, 1988.

———. *Easy Listening Blues*. CD. London: Ace, 2004. (Original Crown LP 1962.)

———. *The Electric B. B. King: His Best*. CD. Universal City, Calif.: MCA, 1998. (Original LP 1968.)

———. *Friends*. LP. New York: ABC, 1974. (With Wade Marcus.)

———. *From the Beginning*. LP. Los Angeles: Kent, 1970.

———. *The Great B. B. King*. CD. London: Crown/Ace, 2005. (Original Crown LP 1963.)

———. *Guess Who; Better Lovin' Man*. 45 rpm. New York: ABC, 1972.

———. *A Heart Full of Blues*. LP. Los Angeles: United/Superior, 1962.

———. *His Best*. CD. Bury St. Edmunds, Suffolk, England: BGO, 1990. (Original Bluesway LP 1969.)

———. *The Incredible Soul of B. B. King*. LP. Los Angeles: Kent, 1970.

———. *Indianola, Mississippi, Seeds*. CD. Universal City, Calif.: MCA, 1989. (Original ABC LP 1970.)

———. *The Jungle*. CD. London: Ace, 2007. (Original Kent LP 1967.)

———. *King of the Blues*. CD (4 discs). Universal City, Calif.: MCA, 1992. (Original recordings from 1945–91.)

———. *King Size*. LP. Los Angeles: ABC, 1977.

———. *L.A. Midnight*. LP. New York: ABC, 1972.

———. *Let Me Love You*. LP. Los Angeles: Kent, 1960.

———. *Let the Good Times Roll: The Music of Louis Jordon*. CD. Hollywood: MCA, 1999.

———. *Live! B. B. King on Stage*. LP. Los Angeles: United, 1965.

———. *Live and Well*. CD. Universal City, Calif.: MCA, 1983. (Original Bluesway LP 1969.)

———. *Lucille*. CD. Universal City, Calif.: MCA, 1983. (Original Bluesway LP 1968.)

———. *Lucille Talks Back*. CD. Universal City, Calif.: MCA, 1990. (Original ABC LP 1975.)

———. *Makin' Love Is Good for You*. CD. Hollywood: MCA, 2000.

———. *Mr. Blues*. CD. New York: Hip-O-Select, 2006. (Original ABC LP 1963.)

———. *One Kind Favor*. CD. Los Angeles: Gellen Records, 2008.

———. *Reflections*. CD. Sherman Oaks, Calif.: MCA, 2003.

———. *Riding with the King*. CD. Los Angeles: Reprise, 2000.

———. *Singin' the Blues*. CD. London: Ace, 2005. (Original Crown LP 1956.)

———. *The Soul of B. B. King*. CD. London: Ace, 2003. (Original Crown LP 1963.)

———. *Sweet Sixteen*. LP. Los Angeles: United, 1970.

King, Little Freddy. *Freddy King Sings*. CD. Pearl River, N.Y.: Modern Blues Recordings, 1989. (Original King LP 1961.)

———. *Ultimate Collection*. CD. Santa Monica, Calif.: Hip-O, 2001.

———. *The Very Best of Freddy King*. Vols 1–3. CD (3 discs). Memphis: King/Collectables, 2002. (Original 2002 King recordings.)

Lenoir, J. B. *Natural Man*. CD. Universal City, Calif.: Chess, 1990. (Original LP 1969.)

———. *One of These Mornings*. CD. London: JSP, 2003.

———. *Vietnam Blues: The Complete L+R Recordings*. CD. Conshohocken, Pa.: Evidence, 1995. (Rerelease of *Alabama Blues*, 1969, and *Down in Mississippi*, 1980, featuring recordings from 1967.)

Lewis, Furry. *At Home with Friends*. LP. Seattle: ASP, 1968. (With Bukka White.)

———. *Back on My Feet Again*. LP. Bergenfield, N.J.: Prestige/ Bluesville, 1961.

———. *Blues Magician*. CD. Cambridge, Mass.: Lucky Seven, 1999.

———. *Done Changed My Mind*. LP. Bergenfield, N.J.: Prestige/ Bluesville, 1961.

———. *Fourth and Beale*. CD. Memphis: Universal Music, 2004. (Original Barclay LP 1975.)

———. *Furry Lewis*. CD. Custom Compact Disc Series. Washington, D.C.: Smithsonian Folkways, 2003. (Original LP recorded by Samuel Charters, 1959.)

———. *Furry Lewis: Original 1927–1929 Recordings—The Early Years*. LP. London: Spokane, 1971.

———. *Furry Lewis in His Prime, 1927–1928*. CD. Newton, N.J.: Yazoo, 1991. (Original LP 1975.)

———. *Good Morning Judge*. CD. Oxford, Miss.: Fat Possum, 2003. (Original recordings by George Mitchell, 1961.)

———. *Live at the Gaslight*. LP. New York: Ampex, 1971.

———. *Shake 'em on Down*. CD. Berkeley, Calif.: Fantasy, 1992. (Original LP 1972.)

Littlejohn, Johnny. *Chicago Blues Stars*. LP. El Cerrito, Calif.: Arhoolie, 1991. (With Monroe Jones, Alvin Nichols, Robert Pulliam, Willie Young, Sidgrave Booker, and John Funchess.)

———. *Funky from Chicago*. LP. Los Angeles: Bluesway, 1973. (With Dave Myers, Eddie Taylor, and Freddie Below.)

———. *Slidin' Home*. CD. El Cerrito, Calif.: Arhoolie, 2001. (With Monroe Jones, Alvin Nichols, Robert Pulliam, Willie Young, and Sidgrave Booker.)

———. *When Your Best Friend Turns Their Back on You*. CD. London: JSP, 1999.

Little Milton. *The Complete Checker Hit Singles*. CD. London: Connoisseur Collection, 2001.

———. *Friend of Mine*. LP. Hialeah, Fla.: Glades, 1976.

———. *Grits Ain't Groceries*. CD. Berkeley, Calif.: Stax, 1984. (Original Checker LP 1969.)

———. *If Walls Could Talk*. CD. Original Chess Masters. Chicago: Chess, 1989. (Original Checker LP 1970.)

———. *Raise a Little Sand*. LP. Ilford, Essex, England: Red Lightnin', 1975.

———. *The Very Best of Little Milton*. CD. Berkeley, Calif.: Stax, 2007. (Original 1971–75 Stax recordings.)

———. *Waiting for Little Milton*. CD. Berkeley, Calif.: Stax, 1987. (Original LP 1972.)

———. *We're Gonna Make It: Little Milton Sings Big Blues*. CD. Universal City, Calif.: Chess, 1986. (Original Checker LP 1965.)

Macon, John Wesley "Shortstuff." *Hell Bound and Heaven Sent*. CD. Custom Compact Disc Series. Washington, D.C.: Smithsonian Folkways, 2004. (Original LP 1968. With Big Joe Williams.)

———. *Mr. Shortstuff*. LP. Brooklyn, N.Y.: Spivey, 1964. (With Big Joe Williams.)

Maghett, Samuel "Magic Sam." *Black Magic*. CD. Chicago: Delmark, 1994. (Original LP 1968.)

———. *The Essential Magic Sam: The Cobra and Chief Recordings, 1957–1961*. CD. Chicago: Fuel, 2006.

———. *Magic Sam, 1937–1969*. LP. Chicago: Blue Horizon, 1969.

———. *West Side Soul*. CD. Chicago: Delmark, 1993. (Original LP 1967.)

McClennan, Tommy. *Tommy McClennan*. Vol. 1, *1939–1940, Whiskey Head Woman*. CD. Whithorn, Newton Stewart, U.K.: Document, 2002.

———. *Tommy McClennan*. Vol. 2, *1940-1942, Cross Cut Saw*. CD. Whithorn, Newton Stewart, U.K.: Document, 2002.

———. *Tommy McClennan: The Bluebird Recordings, 1939-1942*. CD. Bluebird Blues and Heritage Series. New York: RCA, 1997. (With Robert Petway and Ransom Knowling.)

McDowell, Fred. *Amazing Grace: Mississippi Delta Spirituals by Hunter's Chapel Singers of Como, MS*. CD. Oakland, Calif.: Testament, 1994. (Original LP 1966.)

———. *The Blues of Fred McDowell: Long Way from Home*. CD. Berkeley, Calif.: Milestone, 1990. (Original LP 1966.)

———. *Eight Years Ramblin'*. CD. London: Revival, 1970.

———. *Fred McDowell: The First Recordings*. CD. Alan Lomax Collection. Cambridge, Mass.: Rounder, 1997. (Recorded by Alan Lomax in 1959. With Fannie Davis, Miles Pratcher, Sidney Carter, Rose Hemphill, Annie Mae McDowell, and James Shorty.)

———. *Fred McDowell and His Blues Boys*. LP. Berkeley, Calif.: Arhoolie, 1970. (With Mike Russo, John Kahn, and Bob Jones.)

———. *Good Morning Little School Girl*. CD. El Cerrito, Calif.: Arhoolie, 1994. (Original LP 1964.)

———. *I Do Not Play No Rock 'n' Roll*. CD (2 discs). Capitol Blues Collection, no. 12. Hollywood, Calif.: Capitol, 1995. (Original LP 1970.)

———. *Keep Your Lamp Trimmed*. LP. El Cerrito, Calif.: Arhoolie, 1981.

———. *Levee Camp Blues*. CD. Oakland, Calif.: Testament, 1998. (Original recordings from 1968.)

———. *Mama Says I'm Crazy*. CD. Oxford, Miss.: Fat Possum, 2002. (Original recordings by George Mitchell, 1967. With Johnny Woods.)

———. *Mississippi Delta Blues*. CD. El Cerrito, Calif.: Arhoolie, 1989. (Original LP 1964.)

———. *Mississippi Fred McDowell*. CD. Cambridge, Mass.: Rounder, 1995. (Original LP 1962.)

———. *Mississippi Fred McDowell: Live in New York*. LP. New York: Oblivion, 1971.

———. *Mississippi Fred McDowell in London*. Vols. 1 and 2. LP. London: Transatlantic, 1969.

———. *My Home Is in the Delta: Blues and Spirituals*. CD. Oakland, Calif.: Testament, 1995. (Original LP 1965. With Annie Mae McDowell.)

———. *Somebody Keeps Callin' Me*. LP. Los Angeles: Antilles, 1973.

———. *Steakbone Slide Guitar*. CD. Salem, Mass.: Tradition, 1996. (Originally released as *In London*, vol. 2, 1969.)

———. *You Gotta Move*. CD. El Cerrito, Calif.: Arhoolie, 1994. (Original LP 1964.)

Memphis Slim and Willie Dixon. *Memphis Slim and Willie Dixon at the Village Gate*. CD. Washington, D.C.: Smithsonian Folkways, 2003.

———. *Memphis Slim, Willie Dixon aux Trois Mailletz*. France: Gitanes Jazz Productions, 2000.

———. *Songs of Memphis Slim and Willie Dixon*. CD. Custom Compact Disc Series. Washington, D.C.: Smithsonian Folkways, 1990s.

Mississippi Sheiks. *Honey Babe, Let the Deal Go Down: The Best of Mississippi Sheiks*. CD. Roots 'n' Blues. New York: Columbia/Legacy, 2004.

———. *Stop and Listen*. CD. Newton, N.J.: Yazoo, 1992.

Nighthawk, Robert. *Black Angel Blues*. CD. London: Charly, 1991. (With Forest City Joe.)

———. *Live on Maxwell Street*. CD. Cambridge, Mass.: Rounder, 1990. (Original LP 1964. Field recordings, including Johnny Young and Carey Bell.)

———. *Prowling with the Nighthawk*. CD. N.p.: Document, 2004.

———. *Robert Lee McCoy (Robert Nighthawk): Complete Recorded Works in Chronological Order, 1937-1940*. CD. Vienna: Wolf, 1990. (With Big Joe Williams, Sonny Boy Williamson, and Speckled Red.)

———. *Robert Nighthawk with Johnny Young, John Wrencher; Houston Stackhouse with Robert Nighthawk, Peck Curtis*. CD. Masters of Modern Blues. Oakland, Calif.: Testament, 1994. (Original LP 1969.)

Owens, Jack, and Bud Spires. *It Must Have Been the Devil: Mississippi Country Blues*. CD. Oakland, Calif.: Testament, 1995. (Original LP 1971.)

Patton, Charley. *Founder of the Delta Blues, 1929-1934*. CD. Newton, N.J.: Yazoo, 1995.

———. *Screamin' and Hollerin' the Blues*. CD (7 discs). Austin, Tex.: Revenant, 2001. (With notes by John Fahey, David Evans, Dick Spottswood, Paul Mitchell, and Edward Komara. Original recordings from 1929-34.)

Pryor, Snooky. *Do It If You Want To*. LP. Los Angeles: Bluesway, 1973.

———. *An Introduction to Snooky Pryor*. CD. Hollywood, Calif.: Fuel 2000, 2006.

———. *Snooky Pryor*. LP. Bexhill-on-Sea, East Sussex, England: Flyright,

1973. (Original 1949–59 JOB recordings.)

———. *Snooky Pryor and the Country Blues*. LP. New York: Today, 1973. (With Fred Below, Mighty Joe Young, Dave Myers, and Homesick James.)

Reed, Jimmy. *Big Boss Man/Down in Virginia*. CD. Maidenhead, Berkshire, England: See for Miles, 1997. (Original 2 Bluesway LPs 1974.)

———. *Blues Is My Business*. LP. Los Angeles: Rhino, 2000. (Original Vee-Jay LP 1974.)

———. *Found Love*. CD. Narberth, Pa.: Collectables, 2000. (Original Vee-Jay LP 1959.)

———. *The History of Jimmy Reed*. Vols. 1 and 2. LP. Linden, N.J.: Trip, 1972.

———. *I Ain't from Chicago*. LP. Los Angeles: Bluesway, 1973.

———. *Jimmy Reed at Carnegie Hall*. CD. Los Angeles: Shout! Factory, 2007. (Original Suite Beat LP 1961.)

———. *Jimmy Reed at Soul City*. CD. Narberth, Pa.: Collectables, 2000. (Original Vee-Jay LP 1964.)

———. *Jimmy Reed, The Essential Boss Man: The Very Best of the Vee-Jay Years, 1953–1966*. CD (3 discs). London: Vee Jay/Charly, 2004.

———. *The Legend, the Man*. CD. Narberth, Pa.: Collectables, 2000. (Original Vee-Jay LP 1964. Includes interviews by Calvin Carter.)

———. *The New Jimmy Reed Album: Soulin'*. CD. Maidenhead, Berkshire, England: See for Miles, 1997. (Original 2 Bluesway LPs 1967.)

———. *The Very Best of Jimmy Reed*. CD. Blues Masters. Los Angeles: Rhino, 2000. (Original Bhudda LP 1974.)

———. *Wailin' the Blues*. LP. Los Angeles: Tradition/Everest, 1969.

Robinson, Fenton. *Somebody Loan Me a Dime*. CD. Chicago: Alligator, 1994. (Original LP 1974.)

Rogers, Jimmy. *Chicago Bound*. CD. Universal City, Calif.: Chess, 1990. (Original LP 1976. With Little Walter and Muddy Waters.)

———. *The Complete Chess Recordings*. CD. Chess 50th Anniversary Collection. Universal City, Calif.: MCA/Chess, 1997.

———. *Complete Shelter Recordings: Chicago Masters*. Vol. 2. CD. Los Angeles: Capitol, 1995. (Original Shelter LP, *Gold Tailed Bird*, 1972.)

Ross, Isaiah "Doctor." *Boogie Disease*. CD. El Cerrito, Calif.: Arhoolie, 1992.

———. *Call the Doctor: Breakdowns and Blues by Mississippi One-Man Band Dr. Isaiah Ross*. CD. Los Angeles: Testament, 1994. (Original LP 1965.)

———. *Dr. Ross: His First Recordings*. LP. El Cerrito, Calif.: Arhoolie, 1972. (Original 1950s Sun recordings.)

———. *The Harmonica Boss*. LP. Detroit: Fortune, 1971. (Original 1958 Fortune and Hi-Q recordings.)

———. *Live at Montreux*. LP. New York: Atlantic, 1973. (Original recordings from 1972.)

Rush, Otis. *All Your Love, I Miss Loving: Live at the Wise Fools Pub, Chicago*. CD. Chicago: Delmark, 2005. (Original recordings from 1976.)

———. *Door to Door*. CD. Original Chess Masters. Universal City, Calif.: Chess/MCA, 1990. (With Albert King. Original LP 1970.)

———. *The Essential Otis Rush: The Classic Cobra Recordings, 1956–*

1958. CD. Universal City, Calif.: Fuel 2000/Varèse Sarabande, 2000.

———. *Mourning in the Morning*. CD. Atlantic & Atco Remasters Series. New York: Cotillion, 2005. (Original LP 1969.)

———. *Right Place, Wrong Time*. CD. Alameda, Calif.: Hightone, 1985. (Original LP 1976. Original recordings from 1971.)

———. *Troubles Troubles: The Sonet Blues Story*. CD. New York: Verve, 2006. (Original Sonet LP 1978.)

Short, J. D. *The Sonet Blues Story: J. D. Short*. CD. New York: Verve, 2005. (Original Sonet LP 1962. Recorded by Samuel Charters.)

———. *Stavin' Chain Blues*. CD. Chicago: Delmark, 1991. (Original LP 1965.)

Smith, Robert Curtis. *Clarksdale Blues*. LP. Bergenfield, N.J.: Prestige Bluesville, 1962.

Spann, Otis. *Best of the Vanguard Years*. CD. Santa Monica, Calif.: Vanguard, 1999.

———. *The Biggest Thing since Colossus*. CD. New York: Sony International, 1999. (Original Bluesville LP 1969. With Fleetwood Mac.)

———. *The Blues Is Where It's At*. CD. Bury St. Edmunds, Suffolk, England: BGO, 1994. (Original Bluesway LP 1967.)

———. *The Blues Never Die!* CD. Berkeley, Calif.: Prestige, 1990. (Original LP 1965.)

———. *The Blues of Otis Spann: Cracked Spanner Head*. CD. Bury St. Edmunds, Suffolk, England: BGO, 2005. (Original Decca/Deram LPs 1964/1969.)

———. *The Complete Blue Horizon*

*Sessions*. CD. London: Sony BMG, 2006.

———. *Cryin' Time*. CD. Santa Monica, Calif.: Vanguard, 1989. (Original LP 1969. With Lonnie Taylor, Jos Davidson, Barry Melton, Luther Johnson, and Lucille Spann.)

———. *Down to Earth: The Bluesway Recordings*. CD. Universal City, Calif.: MCA, 1995. (Includes LPs *The Blues Is Where It's At*, 1967, and *Bottom of the Blues*, 1968.)

———. *Live the Life*. CD. Oakland, Calif.: Testament, 1997. (Original recordings from 1964–69.)

———. *Otis Spann Is the Blues*. CD. American Jazz Classics. London: Candid, 1999. (Original Barnaby LP 1960.)

———. *Sweet Giant of the Blues*. LP. New York: Flying Dutchman Bluestime, 1969.

———. *Walking the Blues*. CD. London: Candid, 1999. (Original Barnaby LP 1960. With Robert Lockwood Jr. and St. Louis Jimmy Oden.)

Stackhouse, Houston. *Cryin' Won't Help You*. CD. Blues Vault Series. Silver Spring, Md.: GENES, 1994.

———. *Houston Stackhouse, 1910–1980*. CD. Vienna: Wolf, 1999. (Original LP 1983.)

———. *Robert Nighthawk with Johnny Young, John Wrencher; Houston Stackhouse with Robert Nighthawk, Peck Curtis*. CD. Masters of Modern Blues. Oakland, Calif.: Testament, 1994. (Original LP 1969.)

Stovall, Babe. *Babe Stovall*. CD. Bexhill-on-Sea, East Sussex, England: Flyright, 1999. (Original Verve LP 1964.)

———. *The Old Ace*. CD. Seattle: Arcola, 2003. (Original recordings from 1968.)

Sunnyland Slim. *Chicago Blues Sessions*. CD. New Orleans: Southland, 1998. (Original "77" Records LP 1994. With Little Brother Montgomery.)

———. *Chicago Piano, 1951–1958: From Cobra and Job*. CD. Bexhill-on-Sea, East Sussex, England: Flyright, 1990. (With Memphis Slim and Eddie Boyd.)

———. *Complete Blue Horizon Sessions*. CD. Irvine, Calif.: Super D/ Phantom Sound & Visi, 2008. (With Johnny Shines.)

———. *Highway 61*. CD. Fuel 2000 Blues Essentials. N.p.: Fuel 2000, 2004. (Original 1950s Solo recordings.)

———. *House Rent Party*. CD. Chicago: Delmark, 1992. (Original 1949 Apollo recordings. With St. Louis Jimmy, Willie Mabon, Jimmy Rogers, Sam Casimir, and Andrew Harris.)

———. *Midnight Jump*. CD. Bury St. Edmunds, Suffolk, England: BGO, 1999. (Original Blue Horizon LP 1969. With Big Walter Horton, Johnny Shines, Willie Dixon, and Clifton James.)

———. *Sad and Lonesome*. CD. Shreveport, La.: Jewel, 1997. (Original LP 1972.)

———. *Slim's Got His Thing Goin' On*. LP. Los Angeles: World Pacific, 1969.

———. *Slim's Shout*. CD. Berkeley, Calif.: Prestige/Bluesville, 1993. (Original LP 1969. With King Curtis, Robert Banks, Leonard Gaskin, and Belton Evans.)

———. *Sunnyland Slim: The Sonet Blues Story—One of the Chicago Pioneers Plays Some Southside Piano Blues*. CD. New York: Verve, 2005. (Original Sonet LP 1974.)

———. *Sunnyland Slim and His Pals: The Classic Sides, 1947–1955*. CD (4 discs). London: JSP, 2006.

———. *Sunnyland Slim Plays the Ragtime Blues*. LP. Los Angeles: Bluesway, 1973. (With Freddie Below, Dave Myers, and Louis Myers.)

Taylor, Eddie. *Bad Boy*. CD. London: Charly R&B, 1993. (Original 1950s Vee-Jay recordings.)

———. *I Feel So Bad: The Blues of Eddie Taylor*. CD. Oakland, Calif.: HighTone, 1991. (Original Advent LP 1972.)

———. *Masters of Modern Blues*. Vol. 3. CD. Santa Monica, Calif.: Testament, 1994.

———. *Ready for Eddie . . . Plus*. CD. London: Sanctuary, 2003. (Original Big Bear LP 1972.)

———. *Ride 'em on Down*. CD. London: Charly R&B, 1989. (Alternate Vee-Jay recordings. With Jimmy Reed.)

———. *Street Talkin'*. CD. New York: Muse, 1989. (Original LP 1976. With Elmore James.)

Taylor, Hound Dog. *Beware of the Dog*. CD. Chicago: Alligator, 1989. (Original LP 1975.)

———. *Hound Dog Taylor and the HouseRockers*. CD. Chicago: Alligator, 1989. (Original LP 1971.)

———. *Live at Joe's Place*. CD. Paris: New Rose/Fan Club, 1992. (Recorded in Boston in 1972.)

———. *Natural Boogie*. CD. Chicago: Alligator, 1989. (Original LP 1974.)

Townsend, Henry. *The Blues in St.*

*Louis.* Vol. 3, *Henry Townsend.*
CD. Custom Compact Disc Series.
Washington, D.C.: Smithsonian
Folkways, 2001. (With Tommy
Bankhead.)

———. *Cairo Blues.* CD. Blues Vault
Series. Silver Spring, Md.: Adelphi/
GENES, 1999. (Original LP 1969.
With Backwards Sam Firk, Henry
Brown, Vernell Townsend, and
Andrew Cauthen.)

———. *Henry's Worry Blues.* CD.
Guildford, Surrey, England: Catfish,
2000. (With J. D. Short, Roosevelt
Sykes, Robert Nighthawk, and
Sonny Boy Williamson.)

———. *Henry Townsend and Henry
Spaulding (1929-37): Complete
Recordings in Chronological Order.*
LP. Vienna: Wolf, 1986.

———. *Music Man.* LP. Silver
Spring, Md.: Adelphi, 1974. (With
Backwards Sam Firk, Henry Brown,
and Vernell Townsend.)

———. *Tired of Being Mistreated.*
LP. Bergenfield, N.J.: Prestige
Bluesville, 1962.

Turner, Ike. *A Black Man's Soul.* CD.
New York: Pompeii, 2008. (Original
LP 1969.)

———. *Bold Soul Sister: The Best of
the Blue Thumb Recordings.* CD.
Universal City, Calif.: Universal
Music Special Markets, 1997.
(Includes 1969 LPs *Out of Season*
and *The Hunter.* With Tina Turner.)

———. *Cussin', Cryin', and Carryin'
On.* LP. New York: Pompeii, 1969.

———. *His Woman, Her Man.* CD.
New York: Funky Delicacies, 2004.
(Original recordings from 1970-73.)

———. *Ike and Tina Turner Revue
Live.* CD. Los Angeles: Kent, 1994.
(Original LP 1964.)

———. *The Ike and Tina Turner Story,
1960-1975.* CD (3 discs). Legends of
American Music. New York: Time
Life, 2004. (Includes 1969 LP *In
Person.*)

———. *Ike Turner, 1958-1959.* CD.
Shreveport, La.: Paula, 1991.
(Original 1992 Cobra recordings.
With Otis Rush and Willie Dixon.)

———. *The Kent Years.* CD. Los
Angeles: Kent, distributed by
Ace, 2000. (Original 1960s Kent
recordings. With Tina Turner.)

———. *River Deep, Mountain High.*
CD. Enfield, England: Prism
Leisure, 1999. (Original recordings
by Phil Specter, 1966. With Tina
Turner.)

———. *The Sun Sessions.* CD. Studio
City, Calif.: Varèse Sarabande, 2001.
(Original recordings from 1950-58.
With Johnny O'Neal, Billy Emerson,
Raymond Hill, and Bonnie Turner.)

———. *Trailblazer.* CD. London: King
Masters, 1998. (Original recordings
from 1956-57.)

Waters, Muddy. *The Anthology, 1947-
1972.* CD (2 discs). Universal City,
Calif.: Chess, 2001. (Original LP
1975.)

———. *The Best of Muddy Waters.* CD.
Original Chess Masters. Universal
City, Calif.: Chess, 1990. (Original
LP 1975.)

———. *Can't Get No Grindin'.* CD.
Original Chess Masters. Universal
City, Calif.: Chess, 1990. (Original
LP 1973.)

———. *The Chess Box.* CD (3 discs).
Universal City, Calif.: Chess,
distributed by MCA/Warner Bros.,
1994. (Original recordings from
1957-72.)

———. *The Complete Plantation
Recordings: The Historic 1941-
42 Library of Congress Field
Recordings.* CD. Universal City,
Calif.: Chess/MCA, 1993. (Recorded
by John W. Work and Alan Lomax.
Includes interviews by Alan Lomax.)

———. *Down on Stovall's Plantation.*
CD. Los Angeles: Universe, 2004.
(Original Testament LP 1966.
Recorded by Alan Lomax in 1941-
42.)

———. *Electric Mud.* CD. Original
Chess Masters. Universal City, Calif.:
Chess, 1990. (Original LP 1968.)

———. *Hard Again.* CD. New York:
Blue Sky, 1990. (Original LP 1977.
With Johnny Winter.)

———. *The London Muddy Waters
Sessions.* CD. Original Chess
Masters. Universal City, Calif.:
Chess/MCA, 1989. (Original LP
1972.)

———. *McKinley Morganfield: A.K.A.
Muddy Waters.* LP. Chicago: Chess,
1971.

———. *Muddy, Brass, and the Blues.*
CD. Original Chess Masters.
Universal City, Calif.: Chess, 1989.
(Original LP 1967.)

———. *Muddy Waters, 1941-1947.*
CD. Blues and Rhythm Series. N.p.:
Classics, 2001.

———. *Muddy Waters at Newport,
1960.* CD. Blues Classics,
Remastered and Revisited. Santa
Monica, Calif.: MCA/Chess, 2001.
(Original LP 1960. With James
Cotton, Otis Spann, and Pat Hare.)

———. *Muddy Waters, Folk Singer.*
CD. Universal City, Calif.: Chess,
1999. (Original LP 1964. With
Buddy Guy, Willie Dixon, and
Clifton James.)

———. *Muddy Waters, Rare and
Unissued.* CD. Universal City, Calif.:
Chess, 1991. (Original 1947-54
Chess recordings.)

———. *Muddy Waters Sings Big Bill Broonzy*. CD. Original Chess Masters. Universal City, Calif.: Chess, 1986. (Original LP 1960.)

———. *The Muddy Waters Woodstock Album*. CD. Original Chess Masters. Universal City, Calif.: Chess/MCA, 1995. (Original LP 1975.)

———. *The Real Folk Blues/More Real Folk Blues*. CD. Santa Monica, Calif.: MCA/Chess, 2002. (Original 2 Chess LPs 1965, 1967.)

———. *Sail On*. CD. Vienna: Wolf, 1999. (Original LP 1969.)

———. *They Call Me Muddy Waters*. CD. Universal City, Calif.: Chess/MCA, 1990. (Original LP 1971.)

———. *"Unk" in Funk*. CD. Santa Monica, Calif.: Hip-O Select, 2006. (Original LP 1977.)

White, Bukka. *Baton Rouge: Mosby Street*. CD. Munich: Blues Beacon, 1992. (Original LP 1972.)

———. *Big Daddy*. CD. Los Angeles: Shout! Factory, 2004. (Original Biograph LP 1974.)

———. *The Complete Bukka White*. CD. Roots 'n' Blues. New York: Columbia/Legacy, 1994. (With Washboard Sam.)

———. *The Complete Sessions, 1930–1940*. CD. Crawley, West Sussex, England: Travelin' Man, 1996.

———. *Memphis Hot Shots*. CD. Columbia Rewind. New York: Columbia/Legacy, 1995. (Original Blue Horizon LP 1968.)

———. *Sky Songs*. CD. El Cerrito, Calif.: Arhoolie, 1990. (Includes 2 1965 LPs.)

———. *The Sonet Blues Story: Bukka White*. CD. New York: Verve, 2005. (Original recordings by John Fahey, 1963. Previously released 1963 on Takoma.)

Wilkins, Robert. *Memphis Blues, 1928–1935*. CD. Bladnoch, Newton Stewart, England: Document, 2000.

———. *The Original Rolling Stone*. CD. Newton, N.J.: Yazoo, 1989. (Original recordings from 1928–35.)

———. *Rev. Robert Wilkins*. LP. Arlington, Va.: Piedmont, 1964.

Williams, Big Joe. *Back to the Country*. CD. Los Angeles: Testament 5013, 1995. (Original LP 1964.)

———. *Big Joe Williams: Complete Recorded Works in Chronological Order*. Vol. 1, *1935–1941, Break 'em on Down*. CD. Whithorn, Newton Stewart, U.K.: Document DOCD6003, 1991.

———. *Big Joe Williams: Complete Recorded Works in Chronological Order*. Vol. 2, *1945–1949, Somebody's Been Worryin'*. CD. Whithorn, Newton Stewart, U.K.: Document DOCD6004, 1991.

———. *Big Joe Williams and Sonny Boy Williamson*. LP. El Cerrito, Calif.: Arhoolie Blues Classics BC21, 1969. (Original recordings from 1937–47.)

———. *Blues on Highway 49*. CD. Chicago: Delmark DS604, 1997. (Original LP 1962.)

———. *Classic Delta Blues*. CD. Original Blues Classics. Berkeley, Calif.: Milestone OBCCD545-2, 1991. (Original LP 1964.)

———. *Crawlin' King Snake*. CD. London: Catfish 128, 1999. (Original RCA International LP 1970.)

———. *Hand Me Down My Walking Stick*. CD. London: Sequel 504, 1992. (Original LP 1968.)

———. *Malvina, My Sweet Woman*. CD. Amsterdam: Oldie Blues 7004, 1997. (Original LP 1974.)

———. *Mississippi's Big Joe Williams and His Nine-String Guitar*. CD. Washington, D.C.: Smithsonian Folkways 40052, 1995. (Original LP 1962.)

———. *Nine-String Guitar Blues*. CD. Chicago: Delmark DS627, 1997.

———. *Piney Woods Blues*. CD. Chicago: Delmark DS602, 1997. (Original LP 1958.)

———. *Shake Your Boogie*. CD. El Cerrito, Calif.: Arhoolie CD315, 1989. (Original 2 LPs, *Tough Times*, 1960, and *Thinking of What They Did*, 1969.)

———. *Shake Your Boogie Live*. CD. Vienna: Wolf 120916, 2007. (Recorded on November 22, 1974.)

———. *The Sonet Blues Story: Big Joe Williams*. CD. Universal City, Calif.: Verve 628802, 2005. (Original Sonet LP 1962.)

———. *Stavin' Chain Blues*. CD. Chicago: Delmark DS609, 1991. (Original LP 1965.)

———. *Walking Blues*. CD. Berkeley, Calif.: Fantasy F24724, 1992. (Original 2 1961 Bluesville LPs, *Studio Blues* and *Blues for 9 Strings*.)

Williamson, Sonny Boy. *Bummer Road*. CD. Universal City, Calif.: Chess/MCA CHD9324, 1990. (Original LP 1969.)

———. *Down and Out Blues*. CD. Universal City, Calif.: Chess/MCA CHD31272, 1990. (Original LP 1959.)

———. *The Essential Sonny Boy Williamson*. CD. Universal City, Calif.: Chess/MCA CHD9343, 1993.

———. *King Biscuit Time*. CD. El Cerrito, Calif.: Arhoolie CD310, 1989. (Original 1951 Trumpet recordings.)

———. *One Way Out*. CD. Universal

City, Calif.: Chess/MCA CHD9116, 1990. (Original LP 1959.)

———. *Sonny Boy Williamson: Blues Masters*. Vol. 12. CD. Copenhagen: Storyville 8012, 1990.

———. *Sonny Boy Williamson: More Real Folk Blues*. CD. Universal City, Calif.: Chess/MCA CHD9277, 1990. (Original LP 1966.)

———. *Sonny Boy Williamson: The Real Folk Blues*. CD. Universal City, Calif.: Chess/MCA CHD9272, 1987. (Original LP 1965.)

Young, Johnny. *Chicago Blues*. CD. El Cerrito, Calif.: Arhoolie CD325, 1993. (Original LP 1968. Includes *Johnny Young and His Chicago Blues Band*, 1966. With Otis Spann, Big Walter Horton, and James Cotton.)

———. *Johnny Young: The Complete Blue Horizon Sessions*. CD. London: Sony BMG 88697079152, 2007. (Original 2 LPs, *Fat Mandolin*, 1970, and *Blues Master, No. 9*, 1972.)

———. *Johnny Young and His Friends*. CD. Los Angeles: Testament 5003, 1994. (Original LP 1966. With Otis Spann, Robert Nighthawk, Little Walter, and Big Walter Horton.)

## SELECTED FILMOGRAPHY

Note: Many of these films are available for viewing on the Folkstreams website(<www.folkstreams.net>.)

*Afro-American Work Songs in a Texas Prison*. 16mm film. Produced by Pete Seeger, Daniel Adams Seeger, Toshi Seeger, Bruce Jackson, and W. D. Alexander. Weatogue, Conn.: Stefan Grossman's Guitar Workshop and Vestapol Videos, 1966.

*All Day and All Night: Memories from Beale Street Musicians*.
VHS. Featuring B. B. King, Rufus Thomas, and Evelyn Young. Directed by Robert Gordon and Louis Guida. Produced by Judy Peiser. Memphis: Center for Southern Folklore, 1990.

*American Roots Music*. DVD (4 discs). Directed by Jim Brown. A Ginger Group production. New York: Palm Pictures, 2001.

*Beale Street*. VHS. Produced by Alexis Krasilovsky, Ann H. Rickey, and Walter Baldwin. New York: Canyon Cinema Co-op, 1978.

*Bessie Smith*. 16mm film and ½-inch video. Produced by Charles Levine. San Francisco: Film-Makers' Cooperative, Canyon Cinema Co-op, 1968.

*Black Delta Religion*. DVD. Produced by Judy Peiser and William Ferris. Memphis: Center for Southern Folklore, 1974.

*The Blues: A Musical Journey*. DVD (7 discs). Presented by Martin Scorsese. Directed by Martin Scorsese, Clint Eastwood, Richard Pearce, Charles Burnett, Marc Levin, Mike Figgis, Paul G. Allen, Jody Patton, Ulrich Felsberg, and Wim Wenders. Produced by Alex Gibney. New York: Sony Music Entertainment, 2003.

*The Blues accordin' to Lightnin' Hopkins: The Sun's Gonna Shine*. DVD. Featuring Skip Gerson, Lightnin' Hopkins, Billy Bizor, Mance Lipscomb, and Ruth Ames. Produced by Les Blank. El Cerrito, Calif.: Flower Films, 2004. (Original 16mm films 1969.)

*Blues Houseparty*. DVD. Directed by Jackson Frost. Produced by the Folklore Society of Greater Washington and Eleanor Ellis.
Berlin, Vt.: Multicultural Media; New York: Lyrichord Discs, 2006. (Original video 1989.)

*Blues Like Showers of Rain: Lightnin' Hopkins*. VHS. Directed by John Jeremy. New York: Rhapsody Films, 1986.

*Blues Maker*. VHS. Featuring Fred McDowell. Directed by Christian Garrison. Produced by the Department of Educational Film Production, University Extension, University of Mississippi. University, Miss.: Center for the Study of Southern Culture, 1980. (Original motion picture 1969.)

*Blues Summit Concert*. DVD. Featuring B. B. King. Directed by Steve Purcell. Produced by Anthony Payne. Santa Monica, Calif.: MCA, 2000.

*Born for Hard Luck: Peg Leg Sam Jackson*. VHS. Produced by Tom Davenport. Delaplane, Va.: Davenport Films, 1976.

*Bottle Up and Go*. VHS. Produced by Judy Peiser and William Ferris. Memphis: Center for Southern Folklore, 1980.

*Buckdancer*. VHS. Featuring Ed Young. Produced by Bess Lomax Hawes, Alan Lomax, and Edmund Carpenter. Berkeley: University of California Extension Media Center, 1980. (Original 16mm film 1965.)

*Chicago Blues, Featuring Muddy Waters, Johnnie Lewis, Buddy Guy, Junior Wells, J. B. Hutto*. DVD. Produced by Harley Cokliss. Cambridge, Mass.: Vestapol Productions, 2004. (Original film 1972.)

*Crossroads*. DVD. Featuring Ralph Maccio, Joe Seneca, Jami Gertz, Joe Morton, and Robert Judd. Directed by Walter Hill. Produced by Sony Pictures. Hollywood, 2004.

*Deep Blues: A Musical Pilgrimage to the Crossroads*. DVD. Featuring Booker T. Loury and R. L. Burnside. Directed by Robert Mugge, with Robert Palmer and David Stewart. Los Angeles: Shout! Factory, 1991.

*Delta Blues Festival 1985: Bring'n Home the Blues*. VHS. Southern Culture Video. Produced by the University of Mississippi Telecommunications Resource Center. University, Miss.: Center for the Study of Southern Culture, 1985.

*Delta Blues Singer: James "Sonny Ford" Thomas*. VHS. Produced by William R. Ferris and Josette Ferris. Memphis: Center for Southern Folklore, 1986. (Original 16mm film 1970.)

*Fannie Bell Chapman, Gospel Singer*. DVD. Produced by William R. Ferris, Judy Peiser, and Bobby Taylor. Memphis: Center for Southern Folklore, 2004. (Original 16mm film 1975.)

*Faulkner's Mississippi: Land into Legend*. VHS. Directed by Robert Oesterling. Produced by the University of Mississippi Department of Educational Film Production. University, Miss.: Center for the Study of Southern Culture, 1980. (Original 16mm film 1965.)

*Four Women Artists*. VHS. Featuring Ethel Wright Mohamed, Eudora Welty, Pecolia Warner, and Theora Hamblett. Directed by William R. Ferris. Produced by Judy Peiser. Memphis: Center for Southern Folklore, 1980. (Original 16mm film 1977.)

*Fred McDowell and Big Joe Williams:*

*Masters of the Country Blues*. VHS. Produced by John S. Ullman. Seattle: Seattle Folklore Society, Yazoo Video, 2002. (Original video 1992.)

*Gandy Dancers*. VHS. Produced by Barry Dornfeld and Maggie Holtzberg-Call. New York: Cinema Guild, 1994. (Original 16mm film 1994.)

*The Georgia Sea Island Singers*. DVD. Produced by Edmund Carpenter, Bess Lomax Hawes, and Alan Lomax. Berkeley: University of California Extension Media Center, 1963.

*Give My Poor Heart Ease: Mississippi Delta Bluesmen*. VHS. Featuring B. B. King, James "Son" Thomas, Shelby "Poppa Jazz" Brown, James "Blood" Shelby, Cleveland "Broom Man" Jones, and inmates from Parchman Penitentiary. Produced by William R. Ferris for the Yale University Media Design Studio in cooperation with the Center for Southern Folklore. New Haven, Conn., 1975. University of North Carolina Southern Folklife Collection. (Original 16mm film 1975.)

*Good Morning Blues*. VHS. Produced by the Mississippi Authority for Educational Television and PBS Video. Washington, D.C.: Distributed by PBS Video, 1988.

*Gospel*. DVD. Featuring Shirley Caesar, Walter Hawkins, James Cleveland, David Leivick, and Frederick Ritzenberg. Golden Door Productions. Thousand Oaks, Calif.: Monterey Media, 2002. (Original video 1982.)

*Gravel Springs Fife and Drum*. VHS. Featuring Otha Turner. Produced

by William Ferris, Judy Peiser, and David Evans. Memphis: Center for Southern Folklore, 1980. (Original motion picture 1972.)

*Hellhounds on My Trail: The Afterlife of Robert Johnson*. DVD. Featuring Robert Johnson, Robert Mugge, and Robert Santelli. New York: WinStar Productions, 1999.

*Home of the Double Headed Eagle*. DVD. Produced by Ali Colleen Neff and Brian Graves. Chapel Hill, N.C.: DarSan Productions, 2006.

*Hush, Hoggies, Hush: Tom Johnson's Praying Pigs*. DVD. Produced by William Ferris, Judy Peiser, and Bobby Taylor. Memphis: Center for Southern Folklore, 1978. (Original motion picture 1978.)

*I Ain't Lyin': Folktales from Mississippi*. VHS. Produced by William Ferris and Yale University Media Design Studio in association with the Center for Southern Folklore and Howard Sayre Weaver. New Haven, Conn., 1975. University of North Carolina Southern Folklife Collection. (Original 16mm film 1975.)

*James "Son" Thomas, Leland, MS, Dec. 1986*. VHS. Directed by Judith McWillie. University, Miss.: Center for the Study of Southern Culture, 1986.

*The Land Where the Blues Began*. DVD. Featuring Jack Owens, Sam Chatman, and Otha Turner. Directed by Alan Lomax, John M. Bishop, and Worth W. Long. Produced by Alan Lomax and Mississippi Authority for Educational Television. Distributed by Media Generation. Jackson, Miss., 1990. (Original video 1981.)

*Legends of the Delta Blues*. DVD.

Featuring Son House, Johnny Shines, John Lee Hooker, and Bukka White. Vestapol Productions. Cambridge, Mass.: Distributed by Rounder, 2003.

*Let the World Listen Right.* DVD. Produced by Brian Graves, Ali Colleen Neff, and Jerome Williams. Chapel Hill, N.C.: DarSan Productions, 2006.

*Made in Mississippi: Black Folk Art and Crafts.* VHS. Produced by William R. Ferris and the Yale University Media Design Studio with the Center for Southern Folklore. New Haven, Conn., 1975. University of North Carolina Southern Folklife Collection. (Original 16mm film 1975.)

*Masters of the Country Blues.* DVD. Featuring Son House, Bukka White, Gary Davis, Sonny Terry, Mance Lipscomb, Lightnin' Hopkins, George Sempepos, Stefan Grossman, and Taj Mahal. Newton, N.J.: Yazoo Video, a division of Shanachie, 2000. (Original video 1991.)

*Mississippi Blues.* VHS. Directed by Bertrand Tavernier and Robert Parrish. Paris: MPI Home Video, 1988. (Original motion picture 1984.)

*Mississippi Catfish, Blues Musician.* DVD. Produced by Kimberly Fisher and Dean Armstrong. Princeton, N.J.: Films for the Humanities & Sciences, 2002.

*Mississippi Delta Blues.* VHS. Produced by William Ferris and Judy Peiser. Memphis: Center for Southern Folklore, 1974. (Original motion picture 1974.)

*Mississippi Delta Blues with Son*

*Thomas and Friends.* VHS. Produced by Anthony Herrera. New York: ICAP, 1984.

*Painting in the South: Artists and Regional Heritage.* VHS. Narrated by James Earl Jones. Directed by William Ferris. Oxford, Miss.: Phillip Morris, 1983.

*The Parchman Trials.* DVD. Directed by Les Anderson. Written by Edward Cohen and Robert Earl Jones. Produced by Michael M. Seymour. Jackson: Mississippi Educational Television, 1980.

*Ray Lum: Mule Trader.* DVD. Produced by William Ferris and Judy Peiser. Memphis: Center for Southern Folklore, 1973. (Original motion picture film.)

*Remembering Son Thomas.* VHS. Featuring Son Thomas, Raymond Thomas, and William R. Ferris. Directed by Kevin Hudson. Louisville, Miss.: Dark Horse, 1993.

*Return to the River: A Television Voyage.* VHS. Produced by Jody Jaeger. Jackson: Mississippi Educational Network, 1998.

*Roots of American Music: Country and Urban Music.* Parts 1, 2, and 3. DVD. Featuring Son House, Fred McDowell, Mance Lipscomb, and the Georgia Sea Island Singers. Seattle: University of Washington School of Music, distributed by University of Washington Archives of Ethnic Music and Dance, 1971.

*Say Amen, Somebody.* DVD. Featuring George T. Nierenberg, Karen Nierenberg, Willie Mae Ford Smith, Thomas Andrew Dorsey, and Delois Barrett Campbell. New York: Ryko Filmworks, 2007.

*A Singing Stream: A Black Family*

*Chronicle.* VHS. Produced by Tom Davenport of Davenport Films, Dan Patterson, and Allen Tullos of the University of North Carolina at Chapel Hill Curriculum in Folklore. Delaplane, Va.: Davenport Films, 1989. (Original video 1987.)

*Sonny Terry: Shoutin' the Blues.* VHS. Southern Culture Video. Produced by Aginsky Films. Mendocino, Calif.: Lawren Productions, 1979.

*They Sing of a Heaven.* VHS. Directed by Jerry Stimpfle. University: Mississippi Arts Commission and Motion Picture Production of the University of Mississippi, 1980. (Original motion picture 1972.)

*Three Songs by Leadbelly.* DVD. Produced by Blanding Sloan and Wah Mong Chong. Edited by Pete Seeger. Distributed by American Folklife Center, Library of Congress, 1945. (Original 16mm film.)

*To Hear Your Banjo Play: Stations of the Elevated.* VHS. Featuring Irving Lerner, Willard Van Dyke, Alan Lomax, Manfred Kirchheimer, Pete Seeger, Woody Guthrie, Sonny Terry, Brownie McGhee, and Charles Mingus. Produced by Alan Lomax and Creative Age Films. New York: Museum of Modern Art, 1997. (Original film 1947.)

*A Well Spent Life.* DVD. Featuring Les Blank, Skip Gerson, and Mance Lipscomb. Produced by Les Blank. El Cerrito, Calif.: Flower Films, 2003. (Original film 1971.)

*Wild Women Don't Have the Blues.* DVD. Featuring Christine Dall, Carol Doyle Van Valkenburgh, and Vinie Burrows. San Francisco: California Newsreel, 1989.

*You See Me Laughin': The Last of the*

*Hill Country Bluesmen*. DVD. Featuring R. L. Burnside, Junior Kimbrough, Cedell Davis, T-Model Ford, and Asie Paton. Directed by Mandy Stein. Oxford, Miss.: Fat Possum, 2005.

## SELECTED WEBSITES

African American Odyssey
<http://lcweb2.loc.gov/ammem/ aaohtml/aohome.html>
> This website from the Library of Congress National Digital Library program includes a wide array of important and rare books, government documents, manuscripts, maps, musical scores, plays, films, and recordings from the library's vast African American collections.

African American Religion, Parts 1 and 2
<http://nationalhumanitiescenter.org/ tserve/nineteen/nkeyinfo/aareligion .htm>
> This online educational guide written by Laurie Maffly-Kipp for the National Humanities Center explores the history of African American religion.

African American Visual Art
<http://www.liu.edu/cwis/cwp/library/ aavawww.htm>
> This resource guide of internet sources was compiled by the B. David Schwartz Memorial Library at Long Island University.

American Folklife Center at the Library of Congress
<http://www.loc.gov/folklife/>
> This website provides news about programs and activities, online presentations of multiformat collections, and other resources to facilitate folklife projects and study.

American Memory at the Library of Congress
<http://memory.loc.gov/ammem/index .html>
> This website features archival collections of the Library of Congress on African American music in the American South.

American Roots Music
<http://www.pbs.org/ americanrootsmusic/>
> This website provides information about the history and culture of American musical styles explored in the four-part PBS documentary of the same name.

American Routes
<http://www.amroutes.com>
> This weekly two-hour public radio show based in New Orleans and programmed by folklorist Nick Spitzer explores the shared musical and cultural history of American music.

Archives of African American Music and Culture
<http://www.indiana.edu/%7Eaaamc/>
> This website is a repository of materials on various musical idioms and cultural expressions from the post–World War II era.

Arhoolie Records and Foundation
<http://arhoolie.com/>
> This foundation was created in 1995 to document, present, and disseminate authentic traditional and regional vernacular music.

Association for Cultural Equity
<http://www.culturalequity.org/index .html>
> Founded by Alan Lomax, the Association for Cultural Equity acts as a center for the exploration and preservation of the world's expressive traditions.

B. B. King Museum and Delta Interpretive Center
<http://www.bbkingmuseum.org/>
> Opened in 2008 in Indianola, Mississippi, the B. B. King Museum presents the legacy of B. B. King and the rich musical heritage of the Mississippi Delta.

Blues Archive
<http://dm.olemiss.edu/archives/blues/ index.html>
> The Blues Archive at the University of Mississippi acquires and conserves blues and blues-related materials in a variety of formats for scholars of the blues, African American studies, and southern culture.

Blues Foundation
<http://www.blues.org/>
> This organization promotes and preserves blues music around the globe.

Blues Net
<http://bluesnet.hub.org/>
> This website is a blues bibliographic database.

Center for Black Music Research
<http://www.colum.edu/cbmr/>
> A research unit of Columbia College Chicago, the Center for Black Music Research is devoted to research, preservation, and dissemination of information about the history of black music on a global scale.

Center for the Study of Southern Culture
<http://www.olemiss.edu/depts/south/ index.html>
> Based at the University of Mississippi at Oxford, the Center

for the Study of Southern Culture provides education and research in all areas of culture in the American South.

Center for the Study of the American South

<http://www.unc.edu/depts/csas/>
    Based at the University of North Carolina at Chapel Hill, the Center for the Study of the American South is committed to exploring the history, culture, and contemporary experience of the American South.

The Church in the Southern Black Community

<http://docsouth.unc.edu/church/>
    This collection of Documenting the American South includes autobiographies, biographies, church documents, sermons, histories, encyclopedias, and other published materials that present a collected history of the way southern African Americans experienced and transformed Protestant Christianity into the central institution of community life.

Crossroads of the Heart: Creativity and Tradition in Mississippi

<http://www.arts.state.ms.us/crossroads/main.html>
    This project of the Mississippi Arts Council is dedicated to educating visitors about Mississippi expressive culture. Topics include music, oral traditions, material culture, and maritime traditions.

Delta Blues Museum

<http://www.deltabluesmuseum.org/>
    Located in Clarksdale, Mississippi, the Delta Blues Museum collects, preserves, and makes accessible to the public information, programs, and related services concerning

the history and significance of the blues.

Delta Center for Culture and Learning

<http://www.blueshighway.org/>
    A project of Delta State University, the Delta Center for Culture and Learning promotes the understanding of the history and culture of the Mississippi Delta and its significance to the rest of the world.

Documenting the American South

<http://docsouth.unc.edu/>
    A digital publishing initiative sponsored by the University Library at the University of North Carolina at Chapel Hill, DocSouth provides access to digitized primary materials that offer southern perspectives on American history and culture.

Folkstreams

<http://www.folkstreams.net/>
    This National Preserve of Documentary Films about American Roots Cultures includes essays about traditions and filmmaking.

*Living Blues* Magazine

<http://www.livingblues.com/>
    This long-lasting magazine covers all facets of blues music.

Memphis Rock and Soul Museum

<http://memphisrocknsoul.org/home.htm>
    The Memphis Rock and Soul Museum presents the rich history of Memphis musical culture.

Mississippi Blues Commission

<http://www.msbluestrail.org/>
    Curators of the Mississippi Blues Trail, the Mississippi Blues Commission seeks to foster an appreciation of the blues and the culture that created it.

Mississippi, the Birthplace of American Music

<http://birthplaceofamericanmusic.blogspot.com/>
    This website features both history and contemporary events related to Mississippi music.

Music Maker Relief Foundation

<http://www.musicmaker.org/>
    The Music Maker Relief Foundation is dedicated to helping the pioneers and forgotten heroes of southern music.

Smithsonian Center for Folklife and Cultural Heritage

<http://www.folklife.si.edu/index.html>
    A research and educational unit of the Smithsonian Institution, the Center for Folklife and Cultural Heritage promotes the understanding and continuity of diverse, contemporary grassroots cultures in the United States and around the world.

Smithsonian Folkways Recordings

<http://www.folkways.si.edu/index.aspx>
    As the nonprofit record label of the Smithsonian Institution, Smithsonian Folkways is dedicated to supporting cultural diversity and increased understanding among peoples through the documentation, preservation, and dissemination of sound.

Southern Folklife Collection at the University of North Carolina at Chapel Hill

<http://www.lib.unc.edu/mss/sfc1/>
    The Southern Folklife Collection ranks as one of the nation's foremost archival resources for the study of American folk music and popular

culture. SFC holdings extensively document all forms of southern musical and oral traditions across the entire spectrum of individual and community expressive arts, as well as mainstream media production. Includes the William R. Ferris Collection: <http://www.lib .unc.edu/mss/inv/f/Ferris,William_ R.html>

Southern Mosaic: The John and Ruby Lomax 1939 Southern States Recording Trip <http://memory.loc.gov/ammem/ lohtml/lohome.html>

This multiformat collection from the American Folklife Center includes 700 sound recordings, as well as field notes, dust jackets, and other manuscripts documenting a three-month, 6,502-mile trip through the southern United States.

# INDEX

# H. EUGENE AND LILLIAN YOUNGS LEHMAN SERIES

Lamar Cecil, *Wilhelm II: Prince and Emperor, 1859–1900* (1989).

Carolyn Merchant, *Ecological Revolutions: Nature, Gender, and Science in New England* (1989).

Gladys Engel Lang and Kurt Lang, *Etched in Memory: The Building and Survival of Artistic Reputation* (1990).

Howard Jones, *Union in Peril: The Crisis over British Intervention in the Civil War* (1992).

Robert L. Dorman, *Revolt of the Provinces: The Regionalist Movement in America* (1993).

Peter N. Stearns, *Meaning Over Memory: Recasting the Teaching of Culture and History* (1993).

Thomas Wolfe, *The Good Child's River*, edited with an introduction by Suzanne Stutman (1994).

Warren A. Nord, *Religion and American Education: Rethinking a National Dilemma* (1995).

David E. Whisnant, *Rascally Signs in Sacred Places: The Politics of Culture in Nicaragua* (1995).

Lamar Cecil, *Wilhelm II: Emperor and Exile, 1900–1941* (1996).

Jonathan Hartlyn, *The Struggle for Democratic Politics in the Dominican Republic* (1998).

Louis A. Pérez Jr., *On Becoming Cuban: Identity, Nationality, and Culture* (1999).

Yaakov Ariel, *Evangelizing the Chosen People: Missions to the Jews in America, 1880–2000* (2000).

Philip F. Gura, *C. F. Martin and His Guitars, 1796–1873* (2003).

Louis A. Pérez Jr., *To Die in Cuba: Suicide and Society* (2005).

Peter Filene, *The Joy of Teaching: A Practical Guide for New College Instructors* (2005).

John Charles Boger and Gary Orfield, eds., *School Resegregation: Must the South Turn Back?* (2005).

Jock Lauterer, *Community Journalism: Relentlessly Local* (2006).

Michael H. Hunt, *The American Ascendancy: How the United States Gained and Wielded Global Dominance* (2007).

Michael Lienesch, *In the Beginning: Fundamentalism, the Scopes Trial, and the Making of the Antievolution Movement* (2007).

Eric L. Muller, *American Inquisition: The Hunt for Japanese American Disloyalty in World War II* (2007).

John McGowan, *American Liberalism: An Interpretation for Our Time* (2007).

Nortin M. Hadler, M.D., *Worried Sick: A Prescription for Health in an Overtreated America* (2008).

William Ferris, *Give My Poor Heart Ease: Voices of the Mississippi Blues* (2009).

# CD AND DVD NOTES

*The following is a list of the original music and film that can be found on the CD and DVD that accompany this book.*

## CD

### ROOTS OF THE MISSISSIPPI BLUES

1. Joe "Poppa Rock" Louis, "Why B. B. King Sings the Blues," 0:35*
   Recorded by William R. Ferris at WOKJ, Jackson, June 28, 1974
2. Sonny Boy Williams, "Going Down to the Station," 3:09
   Recorded by William R. Ferris in Leland, July 1968
3. Lovey Williams, "Going Away Blues," 2:38
   Recorded by William R. Ferris in Morning Star, December 1963
4. The Chapman Family led by Fannie Bell Chapman, "So Glad to Be Here," 3:58
   Recorded by William R. Ferris in Jackson, June 16, 1972
5. The Chapman Family led by Velma Chapman, "He's My Rock, My Sword, My Shield," 3:46
   Recorded by William R. Ferris in Jackson, June 16, 1972
6. Inmates at Camp B, Parchman Penitentiary, "Lazarus," 2:46
   Recorded by William R. Ferris at Parchman Penitentiary in Lambert, July 15, 1968
7. Anonymous, "Hidden Violence," 1:02
   Recorded by William R. Ferris in Clarksdale, August 1968
8. Inmates at Camp B, Parchman Penitentiary, "Oh Rosie," 2:58
   Recorded by William R. Ferris at Parchman Penitentiary in Lambert, July 15, 1968
9. Southland Hummingbirds, "There Are Days," 2:57

(Robert Ballinger, Songs of Universal Inc., BMI)
   Recorded by William R. Ferris in Lula, July 3, 1968
10. Mary Gordon, "You Shall Be Free," 1:26*
    Recorded by William R. Ferris in Vicksburg, June 29, 1974
11. James "Son Ford" Thomas, "You Can't Carry Blues and Go to Church," 0:53
    Recorded by William R. Ferris in Leland, July 1968
12. Lee Kizart, "I Got the World in a Jug and the Stopper in My Hand," 2:35
    Recorded by William R. Ferris in Tutwiler, July 28, 1967
13. Jasper Love, "It Gives Me Ease," 1:05
    Recorded by William R. Ferris in Clarksdale, August 1968
14. James "Son Ford" Thomas, "Highway 61 Blues," 2:51*
    Recorded by William R. Ferris in New Haven, February 27, 1974
15. Scott Dunbar, "It's So Cold Up North," 3:41
    Recorded by William R. Ferris in Woodville, Summer 1968
16. Arthur Lee Williams, "Blues Is Round You Every Day," 0:34
    Recorded by William R. Ferris in Birdie, July 1968
17. Lovey Williams, "Mystery Train (Train I Ride)," 2:21
    (Herman Parker Jr.–Sam C. Phillips, Unichappell Music Inc./Hi-Lo Music Inc., BMI)
    Recorded by William R. Ferris in Morning Star, Summer 1968
18. Napoleon Strickland (vocal and fife),

with Bernice Turner (bass drum) and Otha Turner (snare drum), "Somebody Knocking On My Door," 2:16
    Recorded by William R. Ferris in Jackson, March 1972
19. Scott Dunbar, "Jaybird," 8:51
    Recorded by William R. Ferris in Woodville, Summer 1968
20. Lovey Williams, "Boogie Chillun," 1:49*
    (John Lee Hooker–Bernard Bessman, Universal Music–Careers, BMI)
    Recorded by William R. Ferris in Morning Star, January 2, 1967
21. Reverend Isaac Thomas, "One Drop," 2:20*
    Recorded by William R. Ferris at Rose Hill Church in Vicksburg, June 30, 1974
22. James "Son Ford" Thomas, "Cairo Blues," 4:28
    (Melvin Jackson, Tradition Music Co., BMI)
    Recorded by William R. Ferris in Leland, Summer 1968

*Tracks 1, 10, 14, 20, and 21 were previously unreleased.

All tracks were remastered from the original ¼ open-reel field tapes except tracks 15, 17, 19, and 22, which were mastered from vinyl.

Original compositions and arrangements published by Drop Top Music (BMI). Other tracks traditional/public domain except as noted.

Engineers: Gerald J. Schoenherr and John Loy, with help from Elizabeth McLeod and Jamie Vermillion (Southern Folklife Collection, Wilson Library, University of North Carolina at Chapel Hill)

Licensing and song research: Jim O'Neal, BluEsoterica Archives & Productions, and Dr. David Evans

Producer: Joshua Guthman

## DVD

### FILMS OF WILLIAM FERRIS

1. *Black Delta, Part 1*. Featuring Louis Dotson (Lorman); Cleveland "Broom Man" Jones, James "Son Ford" Thomas, and "Little Son" Jefferson (Leland); and Wade Walton, Jasper Love, Maudie Shirley, and Wallace "Pine Top" Johnson (Clarksdale). 1968.

2. *Black Delta, Part 2*. Featuring Rose Hill Church service and Reverend Isaac Thomas (Rose Hill, Vicksburg); baptism in Mississippi Delta; and Church of God in Christ service (Clarksdale). 1968.

3. *Parchman Penitentiary*. Featuring work chants sung while chopping wood, sermon in mess hall, and gospel singing at Camp B, Parchman Penitentiary, Lambert. 1968.

4. *Give My Poor Heart Ease: Mississippi Delta Bluesmen*. Featuring Joe "Big Daddy" Louis (WOKJ, Jackson); B. B. King (Yale University); Wade Walton (Clarksdale); Ben Gooch and James "Blood" Shelby (Camp B, Parchman Penitentiary, Lambert); James "Son Ford" Thomas, Shelby "Poppa Jazz" Brown, Joe Cooper, and Cleveland "Broom Man" Jones (Leland); and Robert Shaw (Lansky's, Memphis). 1975.

5. *I Ain't Lyin': Folktales from Mississippi*. Featuring James "Son Ford" Thomas, Shelby "Poppa Jazz" Brown, Joe Cooper, Cleveland "Broom Man" Jones, and Joe "Skeet" Skillet (Leland); and Mary Gordon, Amanda Gordon, and Reverend Isaac Thomas (Rose Hill, Vicksburg). 1975.

6. *Made in Mississippi: Black Folk Art and Crafts*. Featuring Richard Foster (Hickory Flat); Leon "Peck" Clark (Sharon); Mary Gordon and Amanda Gordon (Rose Hill, Vicksburg); Louise Williams and Esther Kriss (Leland); Otha Turner (Gravel Springs); Luster Willis (Crystal Springs); and James "Son Ford" Thomas and Shelby "Poppa Jazz" Brown (Leland). 1975.

7. *Two Black Churches*. Featuring Reverend Isaac Thomas, Amanda Gordon, Mary Gordon, and the McGowan Family Singers (Rose Hill Church, Vicksburg); and Bishop A. Coward, Willie Ransome, Mae Gibson Brown, and Gloria Kuror (St. James Church, New Haven). 1975.

Original rights and clearances for performances on these films by Yale University Media Design Studio.

Producer: Brian Graves